HODGE AND HIS MASTERS

Hodge and his Masters

Richard Jefferies

QUARTET BOOKS
LONDON MELBOURNE NEW YORK

This edition first published by Quartet Books Limited 1979
A member of the Namara Group
27 Goodge Street, London W1P 1FD

First published by Smith, Elder & Co. in 1880

Introduction copyright © 1979 by Andrew Rossabi

ISBN 0 7043 3259 0

Frontispiece reproduced by courtesy of
The Mansell Collection

Printed in Great Britain at The Anchor Press Ltd
and bound by Wm Brendon & Son Ltd
both of Tiptree, Essex

CONTENTS

INTRODUCTION

RICHARD Jefferies wrote the series of agricultural studies which make up *Hodge and his Masters* when he was thirty. They first appeared as articles in *The Standard*, a London Tory newspaper, and were later collected by the author and published in book form, in two volumes, by Smith, Elder & Co. in 1880. Nowadays first editions of Jefferies' books are scarce and command high prices, and it is an ironical comment on the struggling, poverty-stricken life of the author that this should be so—poor Jefferies who when he was ill and dying of tuberculosis, and too weak to hold a pen, refused to seek a grant from the Royal Literary Fund on the grounds that the fund was maintained by dukes and marquises, rather than by authors and publishers and journalists. He abhorred the idea of charity for himself as he abominated the workhouse for the agricultural poor. "The idea of literature being patronised in these days is too utterly nauseous," he wrote to Mr C. P. Scott. Yet the first edition covers of *Hodge* have a deeper significance than their commercial value; they show, embossed in gold, two pictures: one of a horse-drawn plough at work, symbol of the old order of the English countryside, the other of a steam-drawn plough, symbol of the new.

The theme of change is central to *Hodge and his Masters*—change not only in the methods of agricultural production through the spread of mechanization, but also in the relation of the labourer to his employer through his agitation for better pay and conditions. It is announced in the opening chapter with the dogmatic professor preaching the panacea of scientific farming as the remedy for the ills of the depression years of the 1870s (caused by a succession of bad harvests, falling prices and increased foreign competition, the arrival of cheap food from abroad, grain from America and Russia, meat from Australasia). The professor's discourse, which falls on the politely attentive but mistrustful ears of the assembled farmers, is preceded by the timeless sound of the church bells ringing forth over the busy market-square outside; it is concluded against a background of thunder, lightning and rain. The

vi

farmers think of their crops and wonder what science would do against a thunderstorm. The chapter closes with a cut to Hodge, who has eschewed the meeting, seeking shelter as best he can in the open fields. It is all very simply done, the points are made artfully yet without fuss, but the storm continues to rumble and mutter through the rest of the book. It was an apt metaphor for the uneasy state of agriculture at that time. "There has grown up," writes Jefferies, "a general feeling in the villages and agricultural districts that the landed estates around them are no longer stable and enduring. A feeling of uncertainty is abroad, and no one is surprised to hear that some place, or person, is going." The second chapter, in fact, is titled "Leaving His Farm".

Jefferies, of course, knew the difficulties facing the farmer at first hand. His father was a smallholder of some forty acres in the hamlet of Coate near Swindon in North Wiltshire. The farm got into debt and Jefferies' father sold up and ended his days as an odd-job gardener in Bath. Two miles down the road from Coate at Swindon was the Great Western Railway workshop and repair centre, the subject of a graphic article Jefferies wrote for *Fraser's Magazine* in 1875 called "The Story of Swindon" (reprinted in *The Hills and the Vale*, 1909). The railways not only helped to break down the isolation and parochialism of the old village communities: they also offered alternative employment to those who would move away from the land, of whom there were a growing number, attracted by the higher wages paid by the manufacturing industries in the towns and cities. And on the conditions and life of the Wiltshire labourer Jefferies considered himself something of an authority, as shown by his three letters on the subject, published in *The Times* in November 1872.

The letters were written at a time of increasing militancy on the part of the farm labourers, who had at last found what they had always lacked, a spokesman and leader. For decades the agricultural labourer, despite the often appalling conditions in which he lived and worked, especially in the low-paid southern counties, had remained politically largely apathetic. He preferred to grumble in the sanctuary of his local ale-house rather than risk concerted action. And who can blame him? The last labourers' "revolt" in the south in 1830 had ended in widespread hangings and transportations. Four years later, at Tolpuddle in Dorset (not far from Hardy's birthplace) six men who tried to form a trade-union branch were arrested, tried, found guilty as "evil disposed persons" under a statute of 1797 intended for the suppression of seditious societies, and sentenced to seven years' transportation—a sentence later revoked as a result of public outcry. But for the next thirty years the labourers remained on the whole quiescent: besides the deterrent effect of the authorities' actions, the labourers' isolation from the mainstream of working-class life in the towns and cities, their dispersal in small scattered groups under the eyes of their employers, have been given as causes. By the late 1860s, however, attempts at union formation began again in the underpaid south. The railways, newspapers, the penny post and the activities of the emigration agents gradually helped break down the isolation and ignorance of the rural labourer and brought him more into the current of contemporary life. Perhaps the renewed ferment also had something to do with the publicity surrounding the passage of the 1871 Trade Union Act, which confirmed the legal status of trade unions and gave protection to their funds. Sporadic union activity broke out in Kent, Buckinghamshire, Hertfordshire, Herefordshire and Lincolnshire. But it was in 1872, in Warwickshire, that the movement gathered real strength.

On 14 February of that year Joseph Arch, a stocky forty-five-year-old hedgecutter and lay Methodist preacher, mounted his pig-stool under a chestnut-tree at Wellesbourne, and addressed a crowd of Warwickshire farm labourers, many hundreds of whom had gathered from miles around, drawn entirely by word of mouth. It was a chill February evening and the night, as Arch wrote later in his *Life* (1898), one of the great documents of labour history,

> had fallen pitch dark; but the men had got bean poles and hung lanterns on them, and we could see well enough. It was an extraordinary sight, and I shall never forget it, not to my dying day. I mounted an old pig-stool and in the flickering light of the lanterns I saw the earnest upturned faces of these poor brothers of mine—faces gaunt with hunger and pinched with want—all looking towards me and ready to listen to the words that would fall from my lips.

The men were at the end of their tether: "Oppression, and hunger, and misery, made them desperate, and desperation was the mother of Union." Night after night during the spring of 1872 Arch tramped from village to village addressing meetings, in the belief that a beacon had been lit "which would prove a rallying point for the agricultural labourers throughout the country".

And so it proved. Early in March the Warwickshire men put forward demands for an increase in their wages to two shillings and eightpence a day and a reduction in their hours of work, so that they started at 6 A.M. and ended at 5 P.M. on weekdays "and to close to three on Saturday". These proposals were incorporated in a circular letter sent out to local farmers in the Wellesbourne area. The farmers ignored the letter, believing the new organization would prove too weak for effective industrial action. On 11 March the men came out on strike. Press publicity followed: the strikers were helped by favourable reports of their case not only in the local press but also in the national newspapers like the liberal *Daily News* and the *Daily Telegraph*. The strikers won their increase, and the dispute was finally settled in mid-April. Meanwhile on 29 March, at a large demonstration at Leamington, all existing union organizations were formally merged into one body, known as the Warwickshire Agricultural Labourers' Union, under Joseph Arch.

Arch's fame had now spread beyond his own county. Thomas Hardy wrote in "The Dorsetshire Labourer" (*Longman's Magazine*, 1883) that "nobody who saw and heard Mr Arch . . . ever forgot him and the influence his presence exercised over the crowds he drew". But though a stirring speaker, Arch was also a realistic and reasonable one, as Hardy again noted:

. . . there was a remarkable moderation in his tone, and an exhortation to contentment with a reasonable amelioration, which, to an impartial auditor, went a long way in the argument. His views showed him to be rather the social evolutionist—what M. Émile de Laveleye would call a "Possibilist"—than the anarchic irreconcilable. The picture he drew of a comfortable cottage life as it should be, was so cosy, so well within the grasp of his listeners' imagination, that an old labourer in the crowd held up a coin between his finger and thumb exclaiming "Here's zixpence towards that, please God!" "Towards what?" said a bystander. "Faith, I don't know that I can spak the name o't, but I know 'tis a good thing," he replied.

Arch spoke in favour of gradual improvement, limited objectives—in terms of better wages, cottage improvement, access to land. Land indeed was the issue which could be counted on to arouse the labourers. In the ale-houses they enlarged on the evil of land which had been allowed to fall out of cultivation or locked up uselessly in the landowners' parks. They had a vague notion that once the land had belonged to all and had been appropriated in the distant past, with the enclosure of the commons for instance, which still rankled in village memory, by the wealthy classes. "What was the land sent for, if it wasn't for the poor to live off?" they asked.

A mushrooming of local combinations of labourers continued throughout many of the low-wage counties of southern and central England—in Kent, Oxfordshire, Dorset, Norfolk. Against this background of unrest the Warwickshire men organized a further conference at Leamington to establish a national union of agricultural labourers. This was held, with much press publicity, on 29 May 1872, and Arch was unanimously elected president of the new National Agricultural Labourers' Union (NALU). In the months that followed, the workers' pressure for higher wages continued and it was against the background of agitation that a letter signed Richard Jefferies, Coate Farm, Swindon, appeared in the columns of *The Times* on 14 November 1872.

The letter claimed that the Wiltshire labourer was an average specimen of his class, both in wages and general intelligence. He was strong, but slow, and his gait graceless and disjointed— a lumbering style of walk "caused by following the plough in early childhood, when the weak limbs find it a hard labour to pull the heavy nailed boots from the thick clay soil". He ate chiefly bread and cheese, with cheap bacon twice or thrice a week, and vegetables cooked "in detestable style", saturated in potato juice. Jefferies compared his cuisine unfavourably with that of the French peasantry, who knew how to prepare savoury potages. There was, the correspondent went on, scarcely any limit to his capacity for absorbing beer, a gallon was not beyond his means when he was at work in the fields, poor thin beer it was true. He was better clothed than formerly, with often "really good clothes" on Sundays. But "his unfortunate walk betrays him, dress how he will". As for the cottages, they were "infinitely" better than they were, and the new ones had scarcely room for improvement. The cottages had sufficient gardens, and the allotment system had been extended. On what Jefferies admitted was the "difficult" question of wages he held that there had been no strikes in Wiltshire and few meetings "for the simple reason that the agitators can gain no hold upon a county where, as a mass, the labourers are well paid". Indeed the only thing wrong with the labourers was their own base ingratitude: "I can confidently say that there is no class of persons in England who receive so many attentions and benefits from their superiors as the agricultural labourers." "No term," he went on, "is too strong in condemnation for those persons who endeavour to arouse an agitation among a class of people so short-sighted and so ready to turn against their own benefactors and their own interests." Those who blamed the farmers should remember that they worked largely on borrowed capital, and ran great risks. The wonder was that they had done what they had for the labourer "finding him with better cottages, better wages, better education, and affording him better opportunities for rising in the social scale".

The letter sparked off a lively correspondence, much of it hostile: support came from Lord Shaftesbury, while "The Son of a Wiltshire Labourer" was quick to reply to Jefferies' accusations. Jefferies retaliated with two more letters. The first, dated 23 November, answered the remarks of "The Son of a Wiltshire Labourer" concerning conditions in the cottages —remarks which Jefferies said he felt "bound to resent on the part of the farmers of this county". Jefferies asserted that it was the labourers themselves who would not rise —who claimed that they could not afford to pay threepence a week in school fees. In his other letter, Jefferies praised "the noble clergy of the Church of England" for their work with allotments, and the way they had been "silently labouring for the good of the people committed to their care for years before the agitators bestowed one thought on the agricultural poor".

All this was grossly misleading and a distortion of the truth which Jefferies knew, and told elsewhere, in other articles he wrote at this time, such as "A True Tale of the Wiltshire Labourer" and many of the other pieces later collected under the title *The Toilers of the Field*. In fact the agitators did make some impact on Wiltshire, where they forced up wages by about a shilling a week, and this was long overdue. Throughout the nineteenth century Wiltshire competed with Dorset and some eastern counties for the honour of having the worst-paid labourers in all England. "The story of Hodge in nineteenth-century Wiltshire," writes a modern commentator, "is not a happy one. Ireland was not the only place in the British Isles where the potato prevented a population from starving." Alexander Somerville, who during the 1840s was commissioned by the Anti-Corn Law League to travel round England and write articles on what he saw, later collected under the title of *The Whistler at the Plough*, the most comprehensive and biting survey of rural England since Cobbett's *Rural Rides*, found some of his worst cases of destitution among the Wiltshire labourers.

Quite what were Jefferies' motives in writing the letters can now only be guessed at. Perhaps he wrote them out of loyalty to his father, or to please the Conservative readership of *The Times* and make a name for himself by giving them what they wanted to hear. Certainly, as a result of the attention the letters attracted, Jefferies afterwards found no difficulty in placing his articles and papers on rural themes. But even the address he put on the letters was a gloss on the truth, as his father recalled in later years: "How he could think of describing Coate as such a pleasant place and deceive so I could not imagine, in fact nothing scarcely he mentions is in Coate proper only the proper one was not a pleasant one Snodshill was the name on my Waggon and Cart, he styled it Coate Farm it was not worthy of the name of Farm it was not Forty Acres of Land."

The same vein of lower middle-class snobbery—condescending towards the labourers, and fawning towards his social superiors—mars many of the pages of *Hodge and his Masters*. For all his reputation as a lanky dreamer, Jefferies had an alert eye for the realities of wealth and power; there are more than traces of sycophancy and flattery in the narrative, as in his complacent regard for the advantages of a benevolent despotism, the kindly feudalism such as he describes in the chapter on "Fleeceborough" (Marlborough or Cirencester). "An entire absence of state and ceremony marks this almost unseen but powerful sway. The cycle of the seasons brings round times of trial here as over the entire world, but the conditions under which the trial is sustained could scarcely in our day, and under our complicated social and political system, be much more favourable." At moments like these his tone is reminiscent of one of the old Roman poets, Vergil or Horace flattering Augustus. Poor envious, romantic Jefferies ogling from the sidelines, admiring the rich ladies in their fine carriages! "For till and counter gauge long descent and heraldic quarterings and ancestral crusades far below the chink of ready money, that synonym for all the virtues."

Jefferies, in short, was writing out of sympathy with the class of small farmers to which he belonged by birth and who had been hard hit by the depression years. His built-in partisan bias gives the lie to his claim to have written the book in "a fair and impartial spirit". Consciously or not he regarded the labourers from a middle-class point of view, and the very title *Hodge* betrayed his prejudice. Hodge was the popular nickname for the whole body of agricultural labourers in England, and was a synonym for all that was slow, solid, sure and stupid; a concept which was criticized by Hardy in *Tess of the D'Ubervilles*—"the pitiable dummy known as Hodge"—because he felt it lumped together many thousands of individual human beings who were in reality very different. Jefferies himself seemed half aware of this when he wrote in the preface that there was no class of the community less uniform than the agricultural, where individuality of character was "most marked"—but he was thinking of the farmers more than the labourers. The title, anyway, was a misnomer as the book tells us much more about the "masters" than about Hodge. In the first two-thirds of the book at least he remains an abstraction, the rural equivalent of the lumpen proletariat, dragged in towards the end of a chapter as a more or less somnolent extra, to add a nice dramatic touch. Yet, this said, Jefferies leaves the reader in no doubt that it is Hodge who sustains this world by his labours, albeit the point is usually made ironically. Just when he is most forgotten, slipped back into his place, the background, Hodge will put in an unexpected appearance, as when the reapers divide rank at the approach of young know-all Master Phillip on his bicycle, the young gentleman farmer up to his eyebrows in theory, diplomas, and the-right-way-to-do-it. Master Phillip is a character observed with all Jefferies' considerable and lethal powers of irony, as when at the end of his dinner-table lecture on the proper way to run a farm he reaches for his glass of claret and "thus incidentally exhibited his own hand, which was as white as a lady's". The reapers, meanwhile,

. . . had been at work all day in the uplands among the corn, cutting away with their hooks low down the yellow straw. They began in the early morning, and had first to walk two miles or more up to the harvest field. Stooping, as they worked, to strike low enough, the hot sun poured his fierce rays upon their shoulders and the backs of their necks. The sinews of the right arm had to drive the steel through straw and tough weeds entangled in the wheat. There was no shadow to sit under for luncheon, save that at the side of the shocks, where the sheaves radiated heat and interrupted the light air, so that the shadow was warmer than the sunshine. Coarse cold bacon and bread, cheese, and a jar of small beer, or a tin can of weak cold tea, were all they had to supply them with fresh strength for further labour.

At last the evening came, the jackets so long thrown aside were resumed, and the walk home began. After so many hours of wearisome labour it was hardly strange that their natural senses were dulled—that they did not look about them, nor converse gaily.

And towards the end of the book Hodge comes more and more to the forefront of the stage. Nothing could be finer, for example, than the description of the labourer rising early on a winter's morning, with the pale beams of the waning moon still casting a shadow on his cottage; while in the closing chapter, again, where we are shown poor old Hodge dragged off from home against his will to end his days in the workhouse, Jefferies the novelist, a man of warm and tender sympathies, takes over, and we have a restrained but deeply moving picture of the last days of the old man, that is written straight from the heart. The old man is miserable in the workhouse: he is looked after, adequately clothed and fed, better than he would be at home, but he misses the old familiar trees, the hedges where he has worked so many years, the meadows where he has walked so often. Now

The end came very slowly; he ceased to exist by imperceptible degrees, like an oak tree. He remained for days in a semi-conscious state, neither moving nor speaking. It happened at last. In the grey of the winter dawn, as the stars paled and the whitened grass was stiff with hoar-frost, and the rime coated every branch of the tall elms, as the milker came down from the pen and the young ploughboy whistled down the road to his work, the spirit of the aged man departed.

What amount of production did that old man's life of labour represent? What value must be put upon the service of the son that fought in India; of the son that worked in Australia; of the daughter in New Zealand, whose children will help to build up a new nation? These things surely have their value. Hodge died, and the very grave-digger grumbled as he delved through the earth hard-bound in the iron frost, for it jarred his hand and might break his spade. The low mound will soon be level, and the place of his burial shall not be known.

Such passages, and they are by no means isolated, redeem the book and make one readier to forgive Jefferies for condoning the low rate of farm wages and white-washing the cruel manner in which men were laid off in winter, his airy dismissal of the Cottage Charter and general reluctance to concede Hodge his right to better himself. And to be fair to Jefferies, who was caught in the ambiguities of his own social position, uprooted, like Hardy and Lawrence after him, by his intelligence from his class, *Hodge and his Masters* by no means contains Jefferies' last thoughts on the Labour Question, a subject which occupied him all his life and which he never wearied of discussing. As the years went by, and Jefferies' own life became stained with suffering, his line became harder. The same man who had praised "the noble clergy of the Church of England" later compared the Church to a Huge Octopus, and saw the clergy as hand-in-glove with the land-owning aristocracy for the suppression of the poor. If we want to know the views of the mature Jefferies—not the rather callow young journalist—not only on the Labour Question but on the whole structure of rural society, we should, as Raymond Williams recommends in his excellent introduction to the Fitzroy edition of *Hodge* (MacGibbon & Kee, 1966), go on to read not only the essays in *The Toilers of the Field* (1892) but also "The Wiltshire Labourer", "Unequal Agriculture", "Village Organisation" and "After the County Franchise" (in *The Hills and the Vale*, 1909), "One of the New Voters"—the story of a day in the life of a reaper, one of the most powerful pieces Jefferies ever wrote, with its stark epigrammatic conclusion "The wheat is beautiful, but human life is labour"—(in *The Open Air*, 1885, and reprinted in *The Pageant of Summer*, Quartet Books, 1979), "The Field Play" (in *The Life of the Fields*, 1884), and the radical essays of Jefferies' last years—the remarkable "Primrose Gold in Our Village" (1887) which describes the organization of a Conservative caucus at grass-roots, and shows how small tradesmen who conformed, went to church and voted Tory were patronized by the local élite, while those who did not were left out in the cold: "This is not boycotting, it is Primrosing." "If you are pliant and flexible and don't mind being petted you have nice things put in your way . . . If you are not pliant, you are not harrowed, but you are not watered, and it is best to get out of the local village." And "Thoughts on the Labour Question" and "The Divine Right of Capital" (in *Field and Farm*, edited by Samuel J. Looker, 1957) are an amazing denunciation, never printed in Jefferies' life time, of the class-system in Victorian England, contrasting the wealthy capitalists with the workers who keep them in luxury, and reveal Jefferies gravitating towards a virtually Marxist conception of history. How far are passages like these from the letters he wrote to *The Times*:

The history of the last hundred years, not the mere base chronicle of the movements of kings and queens, of armies, but the cause of the heavings and throbbings of nations, has been written in blood by the workman's tool. The future, growing as inevitably out of the present as the

tree from the acorn, will be shaped by the voices sounding
from the bench, the mine and the plough.

*

But politics aside, what a marvellously fresh, intelligent, lively
and informative book *Hodge* is! Through a succession of rapid,
incisive, yet full-bodied and richly detailed tableaux Jefferies
builds up a magnificent panoramic picture of the men and
women who formed the basis of the farming community a
hundred years ago—they are all here, a complete gallery of
rural types: squires, good and bad, farmers of all hues, shades
and colours, the showy and brash, the stick-in-the-mud, the
progressive and adventurous, the prudent and cautious, the ill-
starred, the reckless, the muddler, as well as those other pillars
of the farming community, the bank-manager, the solicitor, the
newspaper editor, the curate, the parson's wife, and not least
Hodge himself in all his guises, carter, hedger, fogger, cowman,
reaper, drover and humble cottager. They are presented as types
but each preserves just that degree of uniqueness and individuality that makes them come alive as people, they never fade into
caricature or become composite creations. And as individuals
they possess just that amount of universality that makes them
representatives of a class and speak for more than themselves.
There are many memorable portraits: the ruthless Squire
Filbard, equally ruthlessly observed by Jefferies, with his neck
"perhaps a little thick and apoplectic-looking, but burnt to a
healthy brick-red colour by exposure to the sun", and his sharp,
scratchy fingernail pointing to each of the names in turn on the
Round Robin he receives one morning from his tenant farmers.
There is the tale of the country curate, which begins with a
sample of Jefferies' best and most agreeable vein of humour—
the curate baulking at the deep puddle which bars his way along
the lane, all the while secretly watched by two women hidden
behind a hedge, a projecting bough quietly lifting his hat off,
then bravely tucking up his trousers and wading in, and the
cruel tragedy of its conclusion. There is the saga of the farmer
going downhill, an Aeschylean tragedy in miniature, the fatal
mistake (the farmer only repays £500 of the £1000 he owes to
the bank, although he could quite as easily have repaid it all)

being visited by a remorseless fate—leading to failure, humilia-
tion and final destruction—a terrifying conspiracy of events, a
gaunt Hardy-like little tale, with its web of coincidence, the
accumulation of circumstances, that reminds us that Jefferies
felt his own life was hounded by just such an evil destiny, his
illness a punishment for intellectual hubris. There is little
Arcadian peace in this world, no sense of rural calm, only "the
weariness, the fever, and the fret", as experienced by the
harassed newspaper editor, bespectacled before his time by
incessant reading, who seeks solace in his garden, in the
meadows, in the sight of green sward and leaf. Perhaps, in this
frenetic world of anxiety, nervous strain and constant mental
activity, Hodge has the last laugh after all. For "Hodge sleeps
sound and sees the days go by with calm complacency. The
man who holds that solid earth, as it were, in japanned boxes
finds a nervous feeling growing upon him despite his strength
of will. Presently nature will have her way: and, weary and
hungry for fresh air, he rushes off for a while to distant trout-
stream, moor, or stubble." There is much unhappiness and
failure in the book, a black sun seems to hang over the destinies
of many of the characters, whose fortunes are recounted with a
grim, often sardonic and rather spiteful relish—there was a
cruel streak in Jefferies, curiously akin to that in Hardy,
another writer who seemed to enjoy his characters' hapless
destinies, torturing them like flies for his sport. Much of the
book does not leave a pleasant taste in the mouth, it must be
admitted; there is a cold, almost schizoid feel to the way
Jefferies himself haunts the pages, a cold clinical eye divorced
from the body. Hence perhaps the almost cinematic realism of
many of the scenes, the astonishing modernity of the style with
its dramatic cuts and visual emphasis, as in the extraordinary
picture of the deserted railway station, empty, waiting in the
August sun, like a de Chirico canvas, charged with an eerie
stimmung, an indefinable sense of foreboding, and the sudden
shift to the same scene at night, when the station is a bustle of
activity, full of lowing cattle and bleating lambs as they are driven
into the trucks, flashing lights, and shunting engines. There is a
Kafkaesque feel to the scene in the solicitor's waiting-room, the
whispering clerks, the brass rail, the ticking clock, the scratching
pen, the endless waiting, the close-ordered hierarchy, the

oppressive atmosphere. These scenes are all superbly done, the observation and telling detail quite masterly, and how astonishingly fresh it reads, as fresh today as when the book was written, over one hundred years ago, glistening like a canvas still wet upon the easel, catching the light. That is the hallmark of a great book—one that grows up to modernity.

There is a sense of urgency, a force and pace in the narrative, too, as if Jefferies were writing against time, aware that this world was fading before his eyes, or at least that the light was changing, the tones of the landscape shifting. In this connection it is worth recalling that Jefferies, later in his life, expressed regret that White of Selborne had not left a natural history of the men and women of his day:

> If the great observer had put down what he saw of the people of his day just as he has put down his notes of animals and birds, there would have been a book composed of extraordinary interest. Walking about among the cottages, he saw and heard all their curious ways, and must have been familiar with their superstitions . . . He knew the farmers and the squires: he had access everywhere, and he had the quickest of eyes. It must ever be regretted that he did not leave a natural history of the people of his day. We should then have a picture of England just before the beginning of our present era, and a wonderful difference it would have shown.

It is just such a picture that Jefferies attempted in *Hodge*, a canvas on a broad and ambitious scale, yet there was no one better equipped to tackle it. Much of the material for *Hodge* must have been gathered in the course of Jefferies' daily round of work as a provincial journalist, both on the *North Wilts Herald* and the *Wiltshire and Gloucestershire Standard*, and to it must be added Jefferies' already rich store of country knowledge, his familiarity with the ways of farmers and labourers, his love of the past, of tradition, strange legends and old crafts. No one better understood the innate conservatism of the agricultural mind, that slowness and refusal to hurry—or be hurried—so valuable and moving in what was already a railroad age of progress and innovation. Jefferies looks back with nostalgia—everywhere he finds the old ways dying out, everything is touched by the machine: milk tins, he complains, are no longer of wood, "the old country material for almost every purpose". The traditional virtues, too, are in decline—the country girls are unwilling to work in the dairy, to soil their hands, now that they have acquired education. They no longer notice the rich tones of the wheat when they come home from school, they rather despise the farm and everything to do with it, look down upon the rough manners and accents of their parents, stay closeted in their rooms reading novels. Yet Jefferies does not condemn them. He realizes that education is the light of the future, that there is no turning back the clock, the world must go on:

> You cannot blame these girls . . . for thinking of something higher, more refined and elevating than the cheese-tub or the kitchen. It is natural, and it is right, that they should wish to rise above that old, dull, dead level in which their mothers and grandmothers worked from youth to age. The world has gone on since then—it is a world of education, books and wider sympathies. In all this they must and ought to share.

His hope is with the future. Education, he foresaw, would be the cause of a great awakening among the labouring class, he anticipates the growth of a whole generation like Jude the Obscure: "Here, in the agricultural labourer class, are many hundred thousand young men . . . educating themselves in moral, social and political opinion." Yet Jefferies was a complex and in many ways divided character. His head—his adventurous intelligence, that spirit of exploration already apparent in the young Bevis, looked one way, his heart another. He notes the arrival of the newspaper vendor in the village with a wince of disgust at the discordant note of his trumpet—"he is a product of modern days, almost the latest"—and then goes on to describe, lovingly and in elaborate detail, the age-old art of willow-work. He lingers, too, on the farmer's weather eye:

> He leans on his prong, facing to windward, and gazing straight into the teeth of the light breeze, as he has done these forty and odd summers past. Like the captain of a sailing ship, the eye of the master haymaker must be always watching the horizon to windward. He depends on the

sky, like the mariner, and spreads his canvas and shapes his course by the clouds. He must note their varying form and drift; the height and thickness and hue; whether there is a dew in the evenings; whether the distant hills are clearly defined or misty; and what the sunset portends. From the signs of the sunset he learns, like the antique Roman husbandman—

> When the south projects a stormy day,
> And when the clearing north will puff the clouds away.

According as the interpretation of the signs be favourable, adverse, or doubtful, so he gives his orders.

But I must stop quoting and let you read the book for yourselves. I have said nothing about the many descriptions of natural beauty in *Hodge*—the changing colours of the wheat, or the sweep of the seasons majestically chronicled in "Hodge's Fields" where Jefferies is on home ground as it were—the rapture with which he details the first spikes of green, the catkins, the unfolding of leaf, the March wind, the star between the clouds in the sky, the first chaffinch song, and so on. The background of the seasons plays a dramatic part in the story: November's troops of fluttering leaves harrying the ankles of the declining farmer; Harry Hodson, prudent and thoughtful, basking in the October sunshine; the glare of the August sun reflected from the white dust of the road, "the intense heat that caused a flickering motion like that which may be seen over a flue". We are always reminded that this is a pleasant land withal—a land of hill and vale, of wood and copse—an ancient land that still echoes to the sound of the horn. Nor have I mentioned the mouth-watering meal in the Fleeceborough chapter, worthy of Iden's feasts in *Amaryllis at the Fair*. But as usual with Jefferies his writing can be left safely to speak for itself.

ANDREW ROSSABI

SELECT BIBLIOGRAPHY

Arch, Joseph. *Joseph Arch: the Story of his Life. Told by Himself.* Ed. Countess of Warwick, Hutchinson, London 1898

Ashby, M. K. *Joseph Ashby of Tysoe 1859–1919: a Study of English Village Life.* Cambridge University Press, 1961

Caird, James. *English Agriculture in 1850–51.* Cass, London 1852, new ed. 1968

Cobbett, William. *Rural Rides*, London 1830

Dunbabin, J. P. D. *Rural Discontent in Ninteenth Century Britain.* Faber & Faber, London 1974

Engels, Friedrich. *Conditions of the Working Class in England in 1844*, London 1892

Graham, P. Anderson. *The Rural Exodus: the Problem of the Village and the Town.* Methuen, London 1892

Haggard, H. Rider. *Rural England.* 2nd ed., Longmans, London 1906

Hardy, Thomas. "The Dorsetshire Labourer", *Longman's Magazine*, July 1883

Hasbach, Wilhelm. *History of the English Agricultural Labourer.* London 1908

Horn, Pamela. *Labouring Life in the Victorian Countryside.* Gill and Macmillan Ltd, Dublin 1976

Jefferies, Richard. *The Toilers of the Field.* Longman, 1892

Jefferies, Richard. *The Hills and the Vale*, ed. Edward Thomas. Duckworth, London 1909

Jefferies, Richard. *Field and Farm*, ed. Samuel J. Looker, Phoenix House, London 1957

Keith, W. J. *Richard Jefferies: A Critical Study.* University of Toronto Press; Oxford University Press, 1965

Keith, W. J. *The Rural Tradition: William Cobbett, Gilbert White, and other non-fiction prose writers of the English Countryside.* Harvester Press, 1975

Marx, Karl. *Capital.* London 1887. II 23, section E, "The British Agricultural Proletariat"

SELECT BIBLIOGRAPHY

Mingay, G. E. *Rural Life in Victorian England*. Heinemann, London 1977

Samuel, Raphael. *Village Life and Labour*. Routledge, London 1975

Street, A. G. *Farmer's Glory*. Faber & Faber, London 1932

Warren, C. Henry. Introduction to *Hodge and his Masters* by Richard Jefferies. Uniform edition, Eyre and Spottiswoode, London 1949

Williams, Merryn. *Thomas Hardy and Rural England*. Macmillan 1972

Williams, Raymond. Preface to the Fitzroy edition of *Hodge and his Masters* by Richard Jefferies, Vols. I & II. MacGibbon & Kee, 1966

Williams, Raymond. "Literature and Rural Society", *The Listener*, 16 November 1967

Victoria County History of Wiltshire. London 1959

PREFACE
TO THE ORIGINAL EDITION

THE papers of which these volumes are composed originally appeared in *The Standard*, and are now republished by permission of the Editor.

In manners, mode of thought, and way of life, there is perhaps no class of the community less uniform than the agricultural. The diversities are so great as to amount to contradictions. Individuality of character is most marked, and, varying an old saw, it might be said, so many farmers so many minds.

Next to the tenants the landowners have felt the depression, to such a degree, in fact, that they should perhaps take the first place, having no one to allow them in turn a 20 per cent. reduction of their liabilities. It must be remembered that the landowner will not receive the fruits of returning prosperity when it comes for some time after they have reached the farmer. Two good seasons will be needed before the landowner begins to recoup.

Country towns are now so closely connected with agriculture that a description of the one would be incomplete without some mention of the other. The aggregate capital employed by the business men of these small towns must amount to an immense sum, and the depreciation of their investments is of more than local concern.

Although the labourer at the present moment is a little in the background, and has the best of the bargain, since wages have not much fallen, if at all; yet he will doubtless come to the front again. For as agriculture revives, and the sun shines, the organisations by which he is represented will naturally display fresh vigour.

But the rapid progress of education in the villages and outlying districts is the element which is most worthy of thoughtful consideration. On the one hand, it may perhaps cause a powerful demand for corresponding privileges; and on the other, counteract the tendency to unreasonable expectations. In any case, it is a fact that cannot be ignored. Meantime, all I claim for the following sketches is that they are written in a fair and impartial spirit.

RICHARD JEFFERIES

CHAPTER I

THE FARMERS' PARLIAMENT

THE doorway of the Jason Inn at Woolbury had nothing particular to distinguish it from the other doorways of the same extremely narrow street. There was no porch, nor could there possibly be one, for an ordinary porch would reach half across the roadway. There were no steps to go up, there was no entrance hall, no space specially provided for crowds of visitors; simply nothing but an ordinary street-door opening directly on the street, and very little, if any, broader or higher than those of the private houses adjacent. There was not even the usual covered way or archway leading into the courtyard behind, so often found at old country inns; the approach to the stables and coach-houses was through a separate and even more narrow and winding street, necessitating a detour of some quarter of a mile. The dead, dull wall was worn smooth in places by the involuntary rubbings it had received from the shoulders of foot-passengers thrust rudely against it as the market-people came pouring in or out, or both together.

Had the spot been in the most crowded district of the busiest part of the metropolis, where every inch of ground is worth an enormous sum, the buildings could not have been more jammed together, nor the inconvenience greater. Yet the little town was in the very midst of one of the most purely agricultural counties, where land, to all appearance, was plentiful, and where there was ample room and "verge enough" to build fifty such places. The pavement in front of the inn was barely eighteen inches wide; two persons could not pass each other on it, nor walk abreast. If a cart came along the roadway, and a trap had to go by it, the foot-passengers had to squeeze up against the wall, lest the box of the wheel projecting over the kerb should push them down. If a great waggon came loaded with wool, the chances were whether a carriage could pass it or not; as for a waggon-load of straw that projected from the sides, nothing could get by, but all must wait—coroneted panel or plain four-wheel—till the huge mass had rumbled and jolted into the more open market-place.

But hard, indeed, must have been the flag-stones to with-

15

stand the wear and tear of the endless iron-shod shoes that tramped to and fro these mere ribbons of pavements. For, besides the through traffic out from the market-place to the broad macadamised road that had taken the place and the route of an ancient Roman road, there were the customers to the shops that lined each side of the street. Into some of these you stepped from the pavement down, as it were, into a cave, the level of the shop being eight or ten inches below the street, while the first floor projected over the pavement quite to the edge of the kerb. To enter these shops it was necessary to stoop, and when you were inside there was barely room to turn round. Other shops were, indeed, level with the street; but you had to be careful, because the threshold was not flush with the pavement, but rose a couple of inches and then fell again, a very trap to the toe of the unwary. Many had no glass at all, but were open, like a butcher's or fishmonger's. Those that had glass were so restricted for space that, rich as they might be within in the good things of the earth, they could make no "display." All the genius of a West-end shopman could not have made an artistic arrangement in that narrow space and in that bad light; for, though so small below, the houses rose high, and the street being so narrow the sunshine rarely penetrated into it.

But mean as a metropolitan shopman might have thought the spot, the business done there was large, and, more than that, it was genuine. The trade of a country market-town, especially when that market-town, like Woolbury, dates from the earliest days of English history, is hereditary. It flows to the same store and to the same shop year after year, generation after generation, century after century. The farmer who walks into the saddler's here goes in because his father went there before him. His father went in because his father dealt there, and so on farther back than memory can trace. It might almost be said that whole villages go to particular shops. You may see the agricultural labourers' wives, for instance, on a Saturday leave the village in a bevy of ten or a dozen, and all march in to the same tradesman. Of course in these latter days speculative men and "co-operative" prices, industriously placarded, have sapped and undermined this old-fashioned system. Yet even now it retains sufficient hold to be a marked feature of country life. To the through traffic, therefore, had to be added the steady flow of customers to the shops.

On a market-day like this there is, of course, the incessant entry and exit of carts, waggons, traps, gigs, four-wheels, and a large number of private carriages. The number of private carriages is, indeed, very remarkable, as also the succession of gentlemen on thoroughbred horses—a proof of the number of resident gentry in the neighbourhood, and of its general prosperity. Cart-horses furbished up for sale, with straw-bound tails and glistening skins; "baaing" flocks of sheep; squeaking pigs; bullocks with their heads held ominously low, some going, some returning, from the auction yard; shouting drovers; lads rushing hither and thither; dogs barking; everything and everybody crushing, jostling, pushing through the narrow street. An old shepherd, who has done his master's business, comes along the pavement, trudging thoughtful and slow, with ashen staff. One hand is in his pocket, the elbow of the arm projecting; he is feeling a fourpenny-piece, and deliberating at which "tap" he shall spend it. He fills up the entire pavement, and stolidly plods on, turning ladies and all into the roadway; not from intentional rudeness, but from sheer inability to perceive that he is causing inconvenience.

Unless you know the exact spot it is difficult in all this crowd and pushing, with a nervous dread of being gored from behind by a bull, or thrown off your feet by a sudden charge of sheep, to discover the door of the Jason Inn. That door has been open every legitimate and lawful hour this hundred years; but you will very likely be carried past it and have to struggle back. Then it is not easy to enter, for half a dozen stalwart farmers and farmers' sons are coming out; while two young fellows stand just inside, close to the sliding bar-window, blocking up the passage, to exchange occasional nods and smiles with the barmaid. However, by degrees you shuffle along the sanded passage, and past the door of the bar, which is full of farmers as thick as they can stand, or sit. The rattle of glasses, the chink of spoons, the hum of voices, the stamping of feet, the calls and orders, and sounds of laughter, mingle in confusion. Cigar-smoke and the steam from the glasses fill the room—all too small—with a thick white mist, through which rubicund faces dimly shine like the red sun through a fog.

Some at the table are struggling to write cheques, with continual jogs at the elbow, with ink that will not flow, pens that scratch and splutter, blotting-paper that smudges and blots. Some are examining cards of an auction, and discussing the prices which they have marked in the margin in pencil. The good-humoured uproar is beyond description, and is increased by more farmers forcing their way in from the rear, where are their horses or traps—by farmers eagerly inquiring for dealers or friends, and by messengers from the shops loaded with parcels to place in the customer's vehicle.

At last you get beyond the bar-room door and reach the end of the passage, where is a wide staircase, and at the foot a tall eight-day clock. A maid-servant comes tripping down, and in answer to inquiry replies that that is the way up, and the room is ready, but she adds with a smile that there is no one there yet. It is three-quarters of an hour after the time fixed for the reading of a most important paper before a meeting specially convened, before the assembled Parliament of Hodge's masters, and you thought you would be too late. A glance at the staircase proves the truth of the maid's story. It has no carpet, but it is white as well-scrubbed wood could well be. There is no stain, no dust, no foot-mark on it; no heavy shoe that has been tramping about in the mud has been up there. But it is necessary to go on or go back, and of the two the first is the lesser evil.

The staircase is guarded by carved bannisters, and after going up two flights you enter a large and vacant apartment prepared for the meeting of the farmers' club. At the farther end is a small mahogany table, with an armchair for the president, paper, pens, ink, blotting-paper, and a wax candle and matches, in case he should want a light. Two less dignified chairs are for the secretary (whose box, containing the club records, books of reference, etc., is on the table), and for the secretary's clerk. Rows of plain chairs stretch across the room, rank after rank; these are for the audience. And last of all are two long forms as if for Hodge, if Hodge chooses to come.

A gleam of the afternoon sun—as the clouds part awhile—attracts one naturally to the window. The thickness of the wall in which it is placed must be some two or three feet, so that there is a recess on which to put your arms, if you do not mind the dust, and look out. The window is half open, and the sounds of the street come up, "baaing" and bellowing and squeaking, the roll of wheels, the tramp of feet, and, more distant, the shouting of an auctioneer in the market place, whose stentorian tones come round the corner as he puts up rickcloths for sale. Noise of man and animal below; above, here in the chamber of science, vacancy and silence. Looking upward, a narrow streak of blue sky can be seen above the ancient house across the way.

After awhile there comes the mellow sound of bells from the church which is near by, though out of sight; bells with a soft, old-world tone; bells that chime slowly and succeed each other without haste, ringing forth a holy melody composed centuries ago. It is as well to pause a minute and listen to their voice, even in this railroad age of hurry. Over the busy market-place the notes go forth, and presently the hum comes back and dwells in the recess of the window. It is a full hour after the time fixed, and now at last, as the carillon finishes, there are sounds of heavy boots upon the staircase. Three or four farmers gather on the landing; they converse together just outside. The secretary's clerk comes, and walks to the table; more farmers, who, now they have company, boldly enter and take seats; still more farmers; the secretary arrives; finally the president appears, and with him the lecturer. There is a hum of greeting; the minutes are read; the president introduces the professor, and the latter stands forth to read his paper—"Science, the Remedy for Agricultural Depression."

Farmers, he pointed out, had themselves only to blame for the present period of distress. For many years past science had been like the voice crying in the wilderness, and few, a very few only, had listened. Men had, indeed, come to the clubs; but they had gone away home again, and, as the swine of the proverb, returned to their wallowing in the mire. One blade of grass still grew where two or even three might be grown; he questioned whether farmers had any real desire to grow the extra blades. If they did, they had merely to employ the means provided for them. Everything had been literally put into their hands; but what was the result? Why, nothing—in point of fact, nothing. The country at large was still undrained. The very A B C of progress had been neglected. He should be afraid to say what proportion of the land was yet undrained, for he should be contradicted, called ill names, and cried down. But if they would look around them they could see for themselves. They would see meadows full of rank, coarse grass in the furrows, which neither horse nor cattle would touch. They would see in the wheat-fields patches of the crop sickly, weak, feeble, and altogether poor; that was where the water had stood and destroyed the natural power of the seed. The same cause gave origin to that mass of weeds which was the standing disgrace of arable districts.

19

But men shut their eyes wilfully to these plain facts, and cried out that the rain had ruined them. It was not the rain—it was their own intense dislike of making any improvement. The *vis inertiae* of the agricultural class was beyond the limit of language to describe. Why, if the land had been drained the rain would have done comparatively little damage, and thus they would have been independent of the seasons. Look, again, at the hay crop; how many thousand tons of hay had been wasted because men would not believe that anything would answer which had not been done by their forefathers! The hay might have been saved by three distinct methods. The grass might have been piled against hurdles or light framework and so dried by the wind; it might have been pitted in the earth and preserved still green; or it might have been dried by machinery and the hot blast. A gentleman had invented a machine, the utility of which had been demonstrated beyond all doubt. But no; farmers folded their hands and watched their hay rotting.

As for the wheat crop, how could they expect a wheat crop? They had not cleaned the soil—there were horse-hoes, and every species of contrivances for the purpose; but they would not use them. They had not ploughed deeply: they had merely scratched the surface as if with a pin. How could the thin upper crust of the earth—the mere rind three inches thick—be expected to yield crop after crop for a hundred years? Deep ploughing could only be done by steam: now how many farmers possessed or used steam-ploughs? Why, there were whole districts where such a thing was unknown. They had neglected to manure the soil; to restore to it the chemical constituents of the crops. But to speak upon artificial manure was enough to drive any man who had the power of thought into temporary insanity. It was so utterly dispiriting to see men positively turning away from the means of obtaining good crops, and then crying out that they were ruined. With drains, steam-ploughs, and artificial manure, a farmer might defy the weather.

Of course, continued the professor, it was assumed that the farmer had good substantial buildings and sufficient capital. The first he could get if he chose; and without the second, without capital, he had no business to be farming at all. He was simply stopping the road of a better man, and the sooner he was driven out of the way the better. The neglect of machinery was most disheartening. A farmer bought one machine, perhaps a reaping-machine, and then because that solitary article did not immediately make his fortune he declared that machinery was useless. Could the force of folly farther go? With machinery they could do just as they liked. They could compel the earth to yield, and smile at the most tropical rain, or the most continuous drought. If only the voice of science had been listened to, there would have been no depression at all. Even now it was not too late.

Those who were wise would at once set to work to drain, to purchase artificial manure, and set up steam power, and thereby to provide themselves with the means of stemming the tide of depression. By these means they could maintain a head of stock that would be more than double what was now kept upon equal acreage. He knew full well one of the objections that would be made against these statements. It would be said that certain individuals had done all this, had deep ploughed, had manured, had kept a great head of valuable stock, had used every resource, and yet had suffered. This was true. He deeply regretted to say it was true.

But why had they suffered? Not because of the steam, the machinery, the artificial manure, the improvements they had set on foot; but because of the folly of their neighbours, of the agricultural class generally. The great mass of farmers had made no improvements; and, when the time of distress came, they were beaten down at every point. It was through these men and their failures that the price of stock and of produce fell, and that so much stress was put upon the said individuals through no fault of their own. He would go further, and he would say that had it not been for the noble efforts of such individuals—the pioneers of agriculture and its main props and stays—the condition of farming would have been simply fifty times worse than it was. They, and they alone, had enabled it to bear up so long against calamity. They had resources; the agricultural class, as a rule, had none. Those resources were the manure they had put into the soil, the deep ploughing they had accomplished, the great head of stock they had got together, and so on. These enabled them to weather the storm.

The cry for a reduction of rent was an irresistible proof of what he had put forth—that it was the farmers themselves who were to blame. This cry was a confession of their own incompetency. If you analysed it—if you traced the general cry home to particular people—you always found that those

21

people were incapables. The fact was, farming, as a rule, was conducted on the hand-to-mouth principle, and the least stress or strain caused an outcry. He must be forgiven if he seemed to speak with unusual acerbity. He intended no offence. But it was his duty. In such a condition of things it would be folly to mince matters, to speak softly while everything was going to pieces. He repeated, once for all, it was their own fault. Science could supply the remedy, and science alone; if they would not call in the aid of science they must suffer, and their privations must be upon their own heads. Science said, Drain, use artificial manure, plough deeply, keep the best breed of stock, put capital into the soil. Call science to their aid, and they might defy the seasons.

The professor sat down and thrust his hand through his hair. The president invited discussion. For some few minutes no one rose; presently, after a whispered conversation with his friend, an elderly farmer stood up from the forms at the very back of the room. He made no pretence to rounded periods, but spoke much better than might have been expected; he had a small piece of paper in his hand, on which he had made notes as the lecture proceeded.

He said that the lecturer had made out a very good case. He had proved to demonstration, in the most logical manner, that farmers were fools. Well, no doubt, all the world agreed with him, for everybody thought he could teach the farmer. The chemist, the grocer, the baker, the banker, the wine merchant, the lawyer, the doctor, the clerk, the mechanic, the merchant, the editor, the printer, the stockbroker, the colliery owner, the ironmaster, the clergyman, and the Methodist preacher, the very cabmen and railway porters, policemen, and no doubt the crossing-sweepers—to use an expressive Americanism, all the whole "jing-bang"—could teach the ignorant jackass of a farmer.

Some few years ago he went into a draper's shop to bring home a parcel for his wife, and happened to enter into conversation with the draper himself. The draper said he was just going to sell off the business and go into dairy farming, which was the most paying thing out. That was just when there came over from America a patent machine for milking cows. The draper's idea was to milk all his cows by one of these articles, and so dispense with labour. He saw no more of him for a long time, but had heard that morning that he went into a dairy farm, got rid of all his money, and was now tramping the country as a pedlar with a pack at his back. Everybody thought he could teach the farmer till he tried farming himself, and then he found his mistake.

One remark of the lecturer, if he might venture to say so, seemed to him, a poor ignorant farmer of sixty years' standing, not only uncalled-for and priggish, but downright brutal. It was that the man with little capital ought to be driven out of farming, and the sooner he went to the wall the better. Now, how would all the grocers and other tradesmen whom he had just enumerated like to be told that if they had not got £10,000 each they ought to go at once to the workhouse! That would be a fine remedy for the depression of trade.

He always thought it was considered rather meritorious if a man with small capital, by hard work, honest dealing, and self-denial, managed to raise himself and get up in the world. But, oh no; nothing of the kind; the small man was the greatest sinner, and must be eradicated. Well, he did not hesitate to say that he had been a small man himself, and began in a very small way. Perhaps the lecturer would think him a small man still, as he was not a millionaire; but he could pay his way, which went for something in the eyes of old-fashioned people, and perhaps he had a pound or two over. He should say but one word more, for he was aware that there was a thunderstorm rapidly coming up, and he supposed science would not prevent him from getting a wet jacket. He should like to ask the lecturer if he could give the name of one single scientific farmer who had prospered?

Having said this much, the old gentleman put on his overcoat and bustled out of the room, and several others followed him, for the rain was already splashing against the windowpanes. Others looked at their watches, and, seeing it was late, rose one by one and slipped off. The president asked if any one would continue the discussion, and, as no one rose, invited the professor to reply.

The professor gathered his papers and stood up. Then there came a heavy rolling sound—the unmistakable boom of distant thunder. He said that the gentleman who had left so abruptly had quite misconstrued the tenour of his paper. So far from intending to describe farmers as lacking in intelligence, all he wished to show was that they did not use their natural abilities, from a certain traditionary bowing to custom. They did not like their neighbours to think that they were doing anything novel. No one respected the feelings that had grown up and strengthened from childhood, no one respected the habits of our ancestors, more than he did; no one knew better the solid virtues that adorned the homes of agriculturists. Far, indeed, be it from him to say aught—[Boom! and the rattling of rain against the window]—aught that could—but he saw that gentlemen were anxious to get home, and would conclude.

A vote of thanks was hurriedly got over, and the assembly broke up and hastened down the staircase. They found the passage below so blocked with farmers who had crowded in out of the storm that movement was impossible. The place was darkened by the overhanging clouds, the atmosphere thick and close with the smoke and the crush. Flashes of brilliant lightning seemed to sweep down the narrow street, which ran like a brook with the storm-water; the thunder seemed to descend and shake the solid walls. "It's rather hard on the professor," said one farmer to another. "What would science do in a thunderstorm!" He had hardly spoken when the hail suddenly came down, and the round white globules, rebounding from the pavement, rolled in at the open door. Each paused as he lifted his glass and thought of the harvest. As for Hodge, who was reaping, he had to take shelter how he might in the open fields. Boom! flash! boom!—splash and hiss, as the hail rushed along the narrow street.

CHAPTER II

LEAVING HIS FARM

A LARGE white poster, fresh and glaring, is pasted on the wall of a barn that stands beside a narrow country lane. So plain an advertisement, without any colour or attempt at "display," would be passed unnoticed among the endless devices on a town hoarding. There nothing can be hoped to be looked at unless novel and strange, or even incomprehensible. But here the oblong piece of black and white contrasts sufficiently in itself with red brick and dull brown wooden framing, with tall shadowy elms, and the glint of sunshine on the streamlet that flows with a ceaseless murmur across the hollow of the lane. Every man that comes along stays to read it.

The dealer in his trap—his name painted in white letters on the shaft—pulls up his quick pony, and sits askew on his seat to read. He has probably seen it before in the bar of the wayside inn, roughly hung on a nail, and swaying to and fro with the draught along the passage. He may have seen it, too, on the handing-post at the lonely cross-roads, stuck on in such a manner that, in order to peruse it, it is necessary to walk round the post. The same formal announcement appears also in the local weekly papers—there are at least two now in the smallest place—and he has read it there. Yet he pauses to glance at it again, for the country mind requires reiteration before it can thoroughly grasp and realise the simplest fact. The poster must be read and re-read, and the printer's name observed and commented on, or, if handled, the thickness of the paper felt between thumb and finger. After a month or two of this process people at last begin to accept it as a reality, like cattle or trees—something substantial, and not mere words.

The carter, with his waggon, if he be an elderly man, cries "Whoa!" and, standing close to the wall, points to each letter with the top of his whip—where it bends—and so spells out "Sale by Auction." If he be a young man he looks up at it as the heavy waggon rumbles by, turns his back, and goes on with utter indifference.

The old men, working so many years on a single farm, and whose minds were formed in days when a change of tenancy happened once in half a century, have so identified themselves with the order of things in the parish that it seems to personally affect them when a farmer leaves his place. But young Hodge cares nothing about his master, or his fellow's master. Whether they go or stay, prosperous or decaying, it matters nothing to him. He takes good wages, and can jingle some small silver in his pocket when he comes to the tavern a mile or so ahead; so "gee-up" and let us get there as rapidly as possible.

An hour later a farmer passes on horseback; his horse all too broad for his short legs that stick out at the side and show some inches of stocking between the bottom of his trousers and his boots. A sturdy, thick-set man, with a wide face, brickdust colour, fringed with close-cut red whiskers, and a chest so broad—he seems compelled to wear his coat unbuttoned. He pulls off his hat and wipes his partly bald head with a coloured handkerchief, stares at the poster a few minutes, and walks his horse away, evidently in deep thought. Two boys—cottagers' children—come home from school; they look round to see that no one observes, and then throw flints at the paper till the sound of footsteps alarms them.

Towards the evening a gentleman and lady, the first middle-aged, the latter very young—father and daughter—approach, their horses seeming to linger as they walk through the shallow stream, and the cool water splashes above their fetlocks. The shooting season is near at hand, Parliament has risen, and the landlords have returned home. Instead of the Row, papa must take his darling a ride through the lanes, a little dusty as the autumn comes on, and pauses to read the notice on the wall. It is his neighbour's tenant, not his, but it comes home to him here. It is the real thing—the fact—not the mere seeing it in the papers, or the warning hints in the letters of his own steward. "Papa" is rather quiet for the rest of the ride. Ever since he was a lad—how many years ago is that?—he has shot with his neighbour's party over this farm, and recollects the tenant well, and with that friendly feeling that grows up towards what we see year after year. In a day or two the clergyman drives by with his low four-wheel and fat pony, notes the poster as the pony slackens at the descent to the water, and tells himself to remember and get the tithe. Some few Sundays, and Farmer Smith will appear in church no more.

Farmer Smith this beautiful morning is looking at the wheat, which is, and is not, his. It would have been cut in an ordinary season, but the rains have delayed the ripening. He wonders how the crop ever came up at all through the mass of weeds that choked it, the spurrey that filled the spaces between the stalks below, the bindweed that climbed up them, the wild camomile flowering and flourishing at the edge, the tall thistles lifting their heads above it in bunches, and the great docks whose red seeds showed at a distance. He sent in some men, as much to give them something to do as for any real good, one day, who in a few hours pulled up enough docks to fill a cart. They came across a number of snakes, and decapitated the reptiles with their hoes, and afterwards hung them all up—tied together by the tail—to a bough. The bunch of headless snakes hangs there still, swinging to and fro as the wind plays through the oak. Vermin, too, revel in weeds, which encourage the mice and rats, and are, perhaps, quite as much a cause of their increase as any acts of the game-keeper.

Farmer Smith a few years since was very anxious for the renewal of his lease, just as those about to enter on tenancies desired leases above everything. All the agricultural world agreed that a lease was the best thing possible—the clubs discussed it, the papers preached it. It was a safeguard; it allowed the tenant to develop his energies, and to put his capital into the soil without fear. He had no dread of being turned out before he could get it back. Nothing like a lease—the certain preventative of all agricultural ills. There was, to appearance, a great deal of truth in these arguments, which in their day made much impression, and caused a movement in that direction. Who could foresee that in a few short years men would be eager to get rid of their leases on any terms? Yet such was the fact. The very men who had longed so eagerly for the blessing of security of tenure found it the worst thing possible for their interest.

Mr. Smith got his lease, and paid for it tolerably stiffly, for at that period all agricultural prices were inflated—from the price of a lease to that of a calf. He covenanted to pay a certain fixed rental for so many acres of arable and a small proportion of grass for a fixed time. He covenanted to cultivate the soil by a fixed rotation; not to sow this nor that, nor to be guided by the change of the markets, or the character of the seasons, or the appearance of powerful foreign competitors. There was the parchment prepared with all the niceties of wording that so many generations of lawyers had polished to the highest pitch; not a loophole, not so much as a *t* left uncrossed, or a doubtful interlineation. But although the parchment did not alter a jot, the times and seasons did. Wheat fell in price, vast shipments came even from India, cattle and sheep from America, wool from Australia, horses from France; tinned provisions and meats poured in by the ton, and cheese, and butter, and bacon by the thousand tons. Labour at the same time rose. His expenditure increased, his income decreased; his rent remained the same, and rent audit came round with the utmost regularity.

Mr. Smith began to think about his lease, and question whether it was such an unmixed blessing. There was no getting out of it, that was certain. The seasons grew worse and worse. Smith asked for a reduction of rent. He got, like others, ten per cent. returned, which, he said, looked very liberal to those who knew nothing of farming, and was in reality about as useful as a dry biscuit flung at a man who has eaten nothing for a week. Besides which, it was only a gracious condescension, and might not be repeated next year, unless he kept on his good behaviour, and paid court to the clergyman and the steward. Unable to get at what he wanted in a direct way, Smith tried an indirect one. He went at game, and insisted on its being reduced in number. This he could do according to the usual terms of agreement; but when it came to the point he found that the person called in to assess the damage put it at a much lower figure than he had himself; and who was to decide what was or was not a reasonable head of game? This attack of his on the game did him no good whatever, and was not unnaturally borne in mind—let us not say resented.

He next tried to get permission to sell straw—a permission that he saw granted to others in moderation. But he was then reminded of a speech he had made at a club, when, in a moment of temper (and sherry), he had let out a piece of his mind, which piece of his mind was duly published in the local papers, and caused a sensation. Somebody called the landlord's attention to it, and he did not like it. Nor can he be blamed; we none of us like to be abused in public, the more especially when, looking at precedents, we do not deserve it. Smith next went to the assessment committee to get his taxes reduced, on the ground of a loss of revenue. The committee sympathised with him, but found that they must assess him according to his rent. At least so they were then advised, and only did their duty.

By this time the local bankers had scented a time of trouble approaching in the commercial and agricultural world; they began to draw in their more doubtful advances, or to refuse to renew them. As a matter of fact, Smith was a perfectly sound man, but he had so persistently complained that people began to suspect there really was something wrong with his finances. He endeavoured to explain, but was met with the tale that he had himself started. He then honestly produced his books, and laid his position bare to the last penny.

The banker believed him, and renewed part of the advance for a short period; but he began to cogitate in this wise: "Here is a farmer of long experience, born of a farming family, and a hardworking fellow, and, more than that, honest. If this man, who has hitherto had the command of a fair amount of capital, cannot make his books balance better than this, what must be the case with some of our customers? There are many who ride about on hunters, and have a bin of decent wine. How much of all this is genuine? We must be careful; these are hard times." In short, Smith, without meaning it, did his neighbours an immense deal of harm. His very honesty injured them. By slow degrees the bank got "tighter" with its customers. It leaked out—all things leak out—that Smith had said too much, and he became unpopular, which did not increase his contentment.

Finally he gave notice that unless the rent was reduced he should not apply to renew the lease, which would soon expire. He had not the least intention in his secret mind of leaving the farm; he never dreamed that his notice would be accepted. He and his had dwelt there for a hundred years, and were as much part and parcel of the place as the elm-trees in the hedges. So many farms were in the market going a begging for tenants, it was not probable a landlord would let a good man go for the sake of a few shillings an acre. But the months went by and the landlord's agents gave no sign, and at last Smith realised that he was really going to leave.

Though he had so long talked of going, it came upon him like a thunderbolt. It was like an attack of some violent fever that shakes a strong man and leaves him as weak as a child. The farmer, whose meals had been so hearty, could not relish his food. His breakfast dwindled to a pretence; his lunch fell off; his dinner grew less; his supper faded; his spirits and water, the old familiar "nightcap," did him no good. His jolly ringing laugh was heard no more; from a thorough gossip he became taciturn, and barely opened his lips. His clothes began to hang about him, instead of fitting him all too tight; his complexion lost the red colour and became sallow; his eyes had a furtive look in them, so different to the old straight-forward glance.

Some said he would take to his bed and die; some said he would jump into the pond one night, to be known no more in this world. But he neither jumped into the pond nor took to his bed. He went round his fields just the same as before—perhaps a little more mechanically; but still the old routine of daily work was gone through. Leases, though for a short period, do not expire in a day; after a while time began to produce its usual effect. The sharpness of the pain wore off, and he set to work to make the best of matters. He understood the capacity of each field as well as others understand the

yielding power of a little garden. His former study had been
to preserve something like a balance between what he put in
and what he took out of the soil. Now it became the subject of
consideration how to get the most out without putting anything in. Artificial manures were reduced to the lowest quantity and of the cheapest quality, such as was used being, in
fact, nothing but to throw dust, literally, in the eyes of other
people. Times were so bad that he could not be expected,
under the most favourable circumstances, to consume much
cake in the stalls or make much manure in that way.

One by one extra expenditures were cut off. Gates, instead
of being repaired, were propped up by running a pole across.
Labour was eschewed in every possible way. Hedges were left
uncut; ditches were left uncleaned. The team of horses was
reduced, and the ploughing done next to nothing. Cleaning
and weeding were gradually abandoned. Several fields were
allowed to become overrun with grass, not the least attention
being paid to them; the weeds sprang up, and the grass ran
over from the hedges. The wheat crop was kept to the smallest
area. Wheat requires more previous labour and care as to
soil than any other crop. Labour and preparation cost money,
and he was determined not to spend a shilling more than he
was absolutely compelled. He contrived to escape the sowing
of wheat altogether on some part of the farm, leaving it out
of the rotation. That was a direct infringement of the letter of
the agreement; but who was to prove that he had evaded it?
The steward could not recollect the crops in several hundred
acres; the neighbouring tenants, of course, knew very well;
but although Smith had become unpopular, they were not
going to tell tales of him. He sold everything he dared off the
farm, and many things that he did not dare. He took everything out of the soil that it was possible to take out. The last
Michaelmas was approaching, and he walked round in the
warm August sunshine to look at the wheat.

He sat down on an old roller that lay in the corner of the
field, and thought over the position of things. He calculated
that it would cost the incoming tenant an expenditure of from
one thousand two hundred pounds to one thousand five
hundred pounds to put the farm, which was a large one, into
proper condition. It could not be got into such condition
under three years of labour. The new tenant must therefore
be prepared to lay out a heavy sum of money, to wait while
the improvement went on, must live how he could meanwhile,

and look forward some three years for the commencement of his profit. To such a state had the farm been brought in a brief time. And how would the landlord come off? The new tenant would certainly make his bargain in accordance with the state of the land. For the first year the rent paid would be nominal; for the second, perhaps a third or half the usual sum; not till the third year could the landlord hope to get his full rental.That full rental, too, would be lower than previously, because the general depression had sent down arable rents everywhere, and no one would pay on the old scale.

Smith thought very hard things of the landlord, and felt that he should have his revenge. On the other hand, the landlord thought very hard things of Smith, and not without reason. That an old tenant, the descendant of one of the oldest tenant-farmer families, should exhaust the soil in this way seemed the blackest return for the good feeling that had existed for several generations. There was great irritation on both sides.

Smith had, however, to face one difficulty. He must either take another farm at once, or live on his capital. The interest of his capital—if invested temporarily in Government securities—would hardly suffice to maintain the comfortable style of living he and his rather large family of grown-up sons and daughters had been accustomed to. He sometimes heard a faint, far off "still small voice," that seemed to say it would have been wiser to stay on, and wait till the reaction took place and farming recovered. The loss he would have sustained by staying on would, perhaps, not have been larger than the loss he must now sustain by living on capital till such time as he saw something to suit him. And had he been altogether wise in omitting all endeavours to gain his end by conciliatory means? Might not gentle persuasion and courteous language have ultimately produced an impression? Might not terms have been arranged had he not been so vehement? The new tenant, notwithstanding that he would have to contend with the shocking state of the farm, had such favourable terms that if he only stayed long enough to let the soil recover, Smith knew he must make a good thing of it.

But as he sat on the wooden roller under the shade of a tree and thought these things, listening to the rustle of the golden wheat as it moved in the breeze, he pulled a newspaper out of his pocket, and glanced down a long, long list of farms to let. Then he remembered that his pass-book at the bank

31

showed a very respectable row of figures, buttoned up his coat, and strolled homeward with a smile on his features.

The date fixed for the sale, as announced by the poster on the barn, came round, and a crowd gathered to see the last of the old tenant. Old Hodge viewed the scene from a distance, resting against a gate, with his chin on his hand. He was thinking of the days when he first went to plough, years ago, under Smith's father. If Smith had been about to enter on another farm old Hodge would have girded up his loins, packed his worldly goods in a waggon, and followed his master's fortunes thither. But Smith was going to live on his capital awhile; and old Hodge had already had notice to quit his cottage. In his latter days he must work for a new master. Down at the sale young Hodge was lounging round, hands in pocket, whistling—for there was some beer going about. The excitement of the day was a pleasurable sensation, and as for his master he might go to Kansas or Hong-Kong.

CHAPTER III

A MAN OF PROGRESS

THE sweet sound of rustling leaves, as soothing as the rush of falling water, made a gentle music over a group of three persons sitting at the extremity of a lawn. Upon their right was a plantation or belt of trees, which sheltered them from the noonday sun; on the left the green sward reached to the house; from the open window came the rippling notes of a piano, and now and again the soft accents of the Italian tongue. The walls of the garden shut out the world and the wind—the blue sky stretched above from one tree-top to another, and in those tree-tops the cool breeze, grateful to the reapers in the fields, played with bough and leaf. In the centre of the group was a small table, and on it some tall glasses of antique make, and a flask of wine. By the lady lay a Japanese parasol, carelessly dropped on the grass. She was handsome, and elegantly dressed; her long, drooping eye-lashes fringed eyes that were almost closed in luxurious enjoyment; her slender hand beat time to the distant song. Of the two gentlemen one was her brother—the other, a farmer, her husband. The brother wore a pith helmet, and his bronzed cheek told of service under tropical suns. The husband was scarcely less brown; still young, and very active-looking, you might guess his age at forty; but his bare forehead (he had thrown his hat on the ground) was marked with the line caused by involuntary contraction of the muscles when thinking. There was an air of anxiety, of restless feverish energy, about him. But just for the moment he was calm and happy, turning over the pages of a book. Suddenly he looked up, and began to declaim, in a clear, sweet voice:—

> "He's speaking now,
> Or murmuring, 'Where's my serpent of old Nile?'
> For so he calls me. Now I feed myself
> With most delicious poison!"

Just then there came the sharp rattle of machinery borne on the wind; he recollected himself, shut the volume, and rose from his seat. "The men have finished luncheon," he said; "I must go and see how things are getting on." The Indian officer, after one glance back at the house, went with him. There was a private footpath through the plantation of trees, and down this the two disappeared. Soon afterwards the piano ceased, and a lady came slowly across the lawn, still humming the air she had been playing. She was the farmer's sister, and was engaged to the officer. The wife looked up from the book which she had taken from the table, with a smile of welcome. But the smile faded as she said—"They have gone out to the reapers. Oh, this farm will worry him out of his life! How I wish he had never bought it! Don't let Alick have anything to do with farms or land, dear, when you are married."

The girl laughed, sat down, took her hand, and asked if matters were really so serious.

"It is not so much the money I trouble about," said the wife. "It is Cecil himself. His nature is too fine for these dull clods. You know him, dear; his mind is full of art—look at these glasses—of music and pictures. Why, he has just been reading 'Antony and Cleopatra,' and now he's gone to look after reapers. Then, he is so fiery and quick, and wants everything done in a minute, like the men of business in the 'City.' He keeps his watch timed to a second, and expects the men to be there. They are so slow. Everything agricultural is so slow. They say we shall have fine seasons in two or three years; only think, *years*. That is what weighs on Cecil."

By this time the two men had walked through the plantation, and paused at a small gate that opened on the fields. The ground fell rapidly away, sloping down for half a mile, so that every portion of the fields below was visible at once. The house and gardens were situate on the hill; the farmer had only to stand on the edge to overlook half his place.

"What a splendid view!" said the officer. The entire slope was yellow with wheat—on either hand, and in front the surface of the crop extended unbroken by hedge, tree, or apparent division. Two reaping-machines were being driven rapidly round and round, cutting as they went; one was a self-binder and threw the sheaves off already bound; the other only laid the corn low, and it had afterwards to be gathered up and bound by hand-labour. There was really a small army of labourers in the field; but it was so large they made but little show.

"You have a first-rate crop," said the visitor; "I see no weeds, or not more than usual; it is a capital crop."

"Yes," replied the farmer, "it is a fine crop; but just think what it cost me to produce it, and bear in mind, too, the price I shall get for it." He took out his pocket-book, and began to explain.

While thus occupied he looked anything but a farmer. His dress was indeed light and careless, but it was the carelessness of breeding, not slovenliness. His hands were brown, but there were clean white cuffs on his wrist and gold studs; his neck was brown, but his linen spotless. The face was too delicate, too refined with all its bronze; the frame was well developed, but too active; it lacked the heavy thickness and the lumbering gait of the farmer bred to the plough. He might have conducted a great financial operation; he might have been the head of a great mercantile house; he might have been on 'Change; but that stiff clay there, stubborn and unimpressionable, was not in his style.

Cecil had gone into farming, in fact, as a "commercial speculation," with the view of realising cent. per cent. He began at the time when it was daily announced that old-fashioned farming was a thing of the past. Business maxims and business practice were to be the rule of the future. Farming was not to be farming; it was to be emphatically "business," the same as iron, coal, or cotton. Thus managed, with steam as the motive power, a fortune might be made out of the land, in the same way as out of a colliery or a mine. But it must be done in a commercial manner; there must be no restrictions upon the employment of capital, no fixed rotation of crops, no clauses forbidding the sale of any products. Cecil found, however, that the possessors of large estates would not let him a farm on these conditions. These ignorant people (as he thought them) insisted upon keeping up the traditionary customs; they would not contract themselves out of the ancient form of lease.

But Cecil was a man of capital. He really had a large sum of money, and this shortsighted policy (as he termed it) of the landlords only made him the more eager to convince them how mistaken they were to refuse anything to a man who could put capital into the soil. He resolved to be his own landlord, and ordered his agents to find him a small estate and to purchase it outright. There was not much difficulty in finding an estate, and Cecil bought it. But he was even then annoyed and disgusted with the formalities, the investigation of title, the completion of deeds, and astounded at the length of the lawyer's bill.

Being at last established in possession Cecil set to work, and at the same time set every agricultural tongue wagging within a radius of twenty miles. He grubbed up all the hedges, and threw the whole of his arable land into one vast field, and had it levelled with the theodolite. He drained it six feet deep at an enormous cost. He built an engine-shed with a centrifugal pump, which forced water from the stream that ran through the lower ground over the entire property, and even to the topmost storey of his house. He laid a light tramway across the widest part of the estate, and sent the labourers to and fro their work in trucks. The chaff-cutters, root-pulpers, the winnowing-machine—everything was driven by steam. Teams of horses and waggons seemed to be always going to the canal wharf for coal, which he ordered from the pit wholesale.

A fine set of steam-ploughing tackle was put to work, and, having once commenced, the beat of the engines never seemed to cease. They were for ever at work tearing up the subsoil and bringing it to the surface. If he could have done it, he would have ploughed ten feet deep. Tons of artificial manure came by canal boat—positively boat loads—and were stored in the warehouse. For he put up a regular warehouse for the storage of materials; the heavy articles on the ground floor, the lighter above, hoisted up by a small crane. There was, too, an office, where the "engineer" attended every morning to take his orders, as the bailiff might at the back-door of an old farmhouse. Substantial buildings were erected for the short-horn cattle.

The meadows upon the estate, like the corn-fields, were all thrown together, such divisions as were necessary being made by iron railings. Machines of every class and character were provided—reaping-machines, mowing-machines, horse-hoes, horse-rakes, elevators—everything was to be done by ma-chinery. That nothing might be incomplete, some new and well-designed cottages were erected for the skilled artisans —they could scarcely be called labourers—who were engaged to work these engines. The estate had previously consisted of several small farms: these were now thrown all into one, otherwise there would not have been room for this great enterprise.

A complete system of booking was organised. From the sale of a bullock to the skin of a calf, everything was put down on paper. All these entries, made in books specially prepared and conveniently ruled for the purpose, came under Cecil's eye weekly, and were by him re-entered in his ledgers. This writing took up a large part of his time, and the labour was sometimes so severe that he could barely get through it: yet he would not allow himself a clerk, being economical in that one thing only. It was a saying in the place that not a speck of dust could be blown on to the estate by the wind, or a straw blown off, without it being duly entered in the master's books.

Cecil's idea was to excel in all things. Some had been famous for shorthorns before him, others for sheep, and others again for wheat. He would be celebrated for all. His shorthorns should fetch fabulous prices; his sheep should be known all over the world; his wheat should be the crop of the season. In this way he invested his capital in the soil with a thorough-ness unsurpassed. As if to prove that he was right, the success of his enterprise seemed from the first assured. His crops of wheat, in which he especially put faith, and which he grew year after year upon the same land, totally ignoring the ancient rotations, were the wonder of the neighbourhood. Men came from far and near to see them. Such was the effect of draining, turning up the subsoil, continual ploughing, and the consequent atmospheric action upon the exposed earth, and of liberal manure, that here stood such crops of wheat as had never previously been seen. These he sold, as they stood, by auction; and no sooner had the purchasers cleared the ground than the engines went to work again, tearing up the earth. His meadow lands were irrigated by the centrifugal pump, and yielded three crops instead of one. His shorthorns began to get known—for he spared no expense upon them—and already one or two profitable sales had been held. His sheep prospered; there was not so much noise made about them, but, perhaps, they really paid better than anything.

Meantime, Cecil kept open house, with wine and refreshments, and even beds for everybody who chose to come and inspect his place. Nothing gave him such delight as to conduct visitors over the estate and to enter into minute details of his system. As for the neighbouring farmers they were only too welcome. These things became noised abroad, and people arrived from strange and far off places, and were shown over this Pioneer's Farm, as Cecil loved to call it. His example was triumphantly quoted by every one who spoke on agricultural progress. Cecil himself was the life and soul of the farmers' club in the adjacent market town. It was not so much the speeches he made as his manner. His enthusiasm was contagious. If a scheme was started, if an experiment was suggested, Cecil's cheque-book came out directly, and the thing was set on foot without delay. His easy, elastic step, his bright eye, his warm, hearty handshake, seemed to electrify people— to put some of his own spirit into them. The circle of his influence was ever increasing—the very oldest fogeys, who had prophesied every kind of failure, were being gradually won over.

Cecil himself was transcendently happy in his work; his mind was in it; no exertion, no care or trouble, was too much. He worked harder than any navvy, and never felt fatigue. People said of him—"What a wonderful man!" He was so genuine, so earnest, so thorough, men could not choose but believe in him. The sun shone brightly, the crops ripened, the hum of the threshing-machine droned on the wind—all was life and happiness. In the summer evenings pleasant groups met upon the lawn; the song, the jest went round; now and then an informal dance, arranged with much laughter, whiled away the merry hours till the stars appeared above the trees and the dew descended.

Yet to-day, as the two leaned over the little gate in the

plantation and looked down upon the reapers, the deep groove which continual thought causes was all too visible on Cecil's forehead. He explained to the officer how his difficulties had come about. His first years upon the farm or estate—it was really rather an estate than a farm—had been fairly prosperous, notwithstanding the immense outlay of capital. A good per-centage, in some cases a high rate of per-centage, had been returned upon the money put into the soil. The seasons were good, the crops large and super-abundant. Men's minds were full of confidence, they bought freely, and were launching out in all directions.

They wanted good shorthorn cattle—he sold them cattle; they wanted sheep—he sold them sheep. They wanted wheat, and he sold them the standing crops, took the money, and so cleared his profit and saved himself trouble. It was, in fact, a period of inflation. Like stocks and shares, everything was going up; everybody hastening to get rich. Shorthorns with a strain of blue blood fetched fancy prices; corn crops ruled high; every single thing sold well. The dry seasons suited the soil of the estate, and the machinery he had purchased was rapidly repaying its first cost in the saving of labour. His whole system was succeeding, and he saw his way to realise his cent. per cent.

But by degrees the dream faded. He attributed it in the first place to the stagnation, the almost extinction, of the iron trade, the blowing out of furnaces, and the consequent cessation of the demand for the best class of food on the part of thousands of operatives and mechanics, who had hitherto been the farmers' best customers. They would have the best of everything when their wages were high; as their wages declined their purchases declined. In a brief period, far briefer than would be imagined, this shrinking of demand reacted upon agriculture. The English farmer made his profit upon superior articles—the cheaper class came from abroad so copiously that he could not compete against so vast a supply.

When the demand for high-class products fell, the English farmer felt it directly. Cecil considered that it was the dire distress in the manufacturing districts, the stagnation of trade and commerce, and the great failures in business centres, that were the chief causes of low prices and falling agricultural markets. The rise of labour was but a trifling item. He had always paid good wages to good men, and always meant to. The succession of wet seasons was more serious, of course;

it lowered the actual yield, and increased the cost of procuring the yield; but as his lands were well drained, and had been kept clean, he believed he could have withstood the seasons for awhile.

The one heavy cloud that overhung agriculture, in his opinion, was the extraordinary and almost world-spread depression of trade, and his argument was very simple. When men prospered they bought freely, indulged in luxurious living, kept horses, servants, gave parties, and consumed indirectly large quantities of food. As they made fortunes they bought estates and lived half the year like country gentlemen —that competition sent up the price of land. The converse was equally true. In times of pressure households were reduced, servants dismissed, horses sold, carriages suppressed. Rich and poor acted alike in different degrees; but as the working population was so much more numerous it was through the low wages of the working population in cities and manufacturing districts that the farmers suffered most.

It was a period of depression—there was no confidence, no speculation. For instance, a year or two since the crop of standing wheat then growing on the very field before their eyes was sold by auction, and several lots brought from £16 to £18 per acre. This year the same wheat would not fetch £8 per acre; and, not satisfied with that price, he had determined to reap and thresh it himself. It was the same with the shorthorns, with the hay, and indeed with everything except sheep, which had been a mainstay and support to him.

"Yet even now," concluded Cecil, shutting his pocketbook, "I feel convinced that my plan and my system will be a success. I can see that I committed one great mistake—I made all my improvements at once, laid out all my capital, and crippled myself. I should have done one thing at a time. I should, as it were, have grown my improvements—one this year, one next. As it was, I denuded myself of capital. Had the times continued favourable it would not have mattered, as my income would have been large. But the times became adverse before I was firmly settled, and, to be plain, I can but just keep things going without a loan—dear Bella will not be able to go to the sea this year; but we are both determined not to borrow.

"In a year or two I am convinced we shall flourish again; but the waiting, Alick, the waiting, is the trial. You know I am impatient. Of course, the old-fashioned people, the farmers, all expect me to go through the Bankruptcy Court. They always said these new-fangled plans would not answer, and now they are sure they were right. Well, I forgive them their croaking, though most of them have dined at my table and drank my wine. I forgive them their croaking, for so they were bred up from childhood. Were I ill-natured, I might even smile at them, for they are failing and leaving their farms by the dozen, which seems a pretty good proof that their anti-quated system is at best no better than mine. But I can see what they cannot see—signs of improvement. The steel industry is giving men work; the iron industry is reviving; the mines are slowly coming into work again; America is pur-chasing of us largely; and when other nations purchase of us, part, at least, of the money always finds its way to the farmer. Next season, too, the weather may be more propitious.

"I shall hold on, Alick—a depression is certain to be fol-lowed by a rise. That has been the history of trade and agricul-ture for generations. Nothing will ever convince me that it was intended for English agriculturists to go on using wooden ploughs, to wear smock-frocks, and plod round and round in the same old track for ever. In no other way but by science, by steam, by machinery, by artificial manure, and, in one word, by the exercise of intelligence, can we compete with the world. It is ridiculous to suppose we can do so by return-ing to the ignorance and prejudice of our ancestors. No; we must beat the world by superior intelligence and superior energy. But intelligence, mind, has ever had every obstacle to contend against. Look at M. Lesseps and his wonderful Suez Canal. I tell you that to introduce scientific farming into England, in the face of tradition, custom, and prejudice, is a far harder task than overcoming the desert sand."

CHAPTER IV

GOING DOWNHILL

AN aged man, coming out of an arable field into the lane, pauses to look back. He is shabbily clad, and there is more than one rent in his coat; yet it is a coat that has once been a good one, and of a superior cut to what a labourer would purchase. In the field the ploughman to whom he has been speaking has started his team again. A lad walks beside the horses, the iron creaks, and the ploughman holding the handles seems now to press upon them with his weight, and now to be himself bodily pulled along. A dull November cloud overspreads the sky, and misty skits of small rain sweep across the landscape. As the old man looks back from the gate, the chill breeze whistles through the boughs of the oak above him, tearing off the brown dry leaves, and shaking out the acorns to fall at his feet. It lifts his grey hair, and penetrates the threadbare coat. As he turns to go, something catches his eye on the ground, and from the mud in the gateway he picks up a cast horse-shoe. With the rusty iron in his hand he passes slowly down the lane, and, as he goes, the bitter wind drives the fallen leaves that have been lying beside the way rustling and dancing after him.

From a farmer occupying a good-sized farm he had descended to be a farmer's bailiff in the same locality. But a few months since he was himself a tenant, and now he is a bailiff at 15s. a week and a cottage. There is nothing dramatic, nothing sensational, in the history of his descent; but it is, perhaps, all the more full of bitter human experiences. As a man going down a steep hill, after a long while finds himself on the edge of a precipitous chalk pit, and topples in one fall to the bottom, so, though the process of going downhill occupied so long, the actual finish came almost suddenly. Thus it was that from being a master he found himself a servant. He does not complain, nor appeal for pity. His back is a little more bowed, he feels the cold a little more, his step is yet more spiritless. But all he says about it is that "Hard work never made any money yet."

He has worked exceedingly hard all his life-time. In his youth, though the family were then well-to-do, he was not permitted to lounge about in idleness, but had to work with the rest in the fields. He dragged his heavy nailed shoes over the furrows with the plough; he reaped and loaded in harvest time; in winter he trimmed the hedgerows, split logs, and looked after the cattle. He enjoyed no luxurious education —luxurious in the sense of scientifically arranged dormitories, ample meals, and vacations to be spent on horseback, or with the breechloader. Trudging to and fro the neighbouring country town, in wind, and wet, and snow, to school, his letters were thrashed into him. In holiday time he went to work—his holidays, in fact, were so arranged as to fall at the time when the lad could be of most use in the field. If an occasion arose when a lad was wanted, his lessons had to wait while he lent a hand. He had his play, of course, as boys in all ages have had; but it was play of a rude character with the plough lads, and the almost equally rough sons of farmers, who worked like ploughmen.

In those days the strong made no pretence to protect the weak, or to abnegate their natural power. The biggest lad used his thews and sinews to knock over the lesser without mercy, till the lesser by degrees grew strong enough to retaliate. To be thrashed, beaten, and kicked was so universal an experience that no one ever imagined it was not correct, or thought of complaining. They accepted it as a matter of course. As he grew older his work simply grew harder, and in no respect differed from that of the labourers, except that he directed what should be done next, but none the less assisted to do it.

Thus the days went on, the weeks, and months, and years. He was close upon forty years old before he had his own will for a single day. Up to almost that age he worked on his father's farm as a labourer among the labourers, as much under parental authority as when he was a boy of ten. When the old man died it was not surprising that the son, so long held down in bondage—bondage from which he had not the spirit to escape—gave way for a short period to riotous living. There was hard drinking, horse-racing, and card-playing, and waste of substance generally.

But it was not for long, for several reasons. In the first place, the lad of forty years, suddenly broken forth as it were from school, had gone past the age when youth plunges beyond recall. He was a grown man, neither wise nor clever; but with a man's sedateness of spirit and a man's hopes. There was no innate evil in his nature to lead him into unrighteous courses. Perhaps his fault rather lay in his inoffensive disposition—he submitted too easily. Then, in the second place, there was not much money, and what there was had to meet many calls.

The son found that the father, though reputed a substantial man, and a man among farmers of high esteem and good family, had been anything but rich. First there were secret debts that had run on for fully thirty years—sums of from fifty to one hundred pounds—borrowed in the days of his youth, when he, too, had at last been released in a similar manner from similar bondage, to meet the riotous living in which he also had indulged. In those earlier days there had been more substance in cattle and corn, and he had had no difficulty in borrowing ready money from adjoining farmers, who afterwards helped him to drink it away. These boon companions had now grown old. They had never pressed their ancient comrade for the principal, the interest being paid regularly. But now their ancient comrade was dead they wanted their money, especially when they saw the son indulging himself, and did not know how far he might go. Their money was paid, and reduced the balance in hand materially.

Now came a still more serious matter. The old man, years ago, when corn farming paid so handsomely, had been induced by the prospect of profit to take a second and yet larger farm, nearly all arable. To do this he was obliged, in farming phrase, to "take up"—*i.e.*, to borrow—a thousand pounds, which was advanced to him by the bank. Being a man of substance, well reputed, and at that date with many friends, the thousand pounds was forthcoming readily, and on favourable terms. The enterprise, however, did not prosper; times changed, and wheat was not so profitable. In the end he had the wisdom to accept his losses and relinquish the second farm before it ate him up. Had he only carried his wisdom a little farther and repaid the whole of the bank's advance, all might yet have been well. But he only repaid five hundred pounds, leaving five hundred pounds still owing. The bank having regularly received the interest, and believing the old gentleman upright—as he was—was not at all anxious to have the money back, as it was earning fair interest. So the five hundred remained on loan, and, as it seemed, for no very definite purpose.

Whether the old gentleman liked to feel that he had so much money at command (a weakness of human nature common enough), or whether he thought he could increase the produce of his farm by putting it in the soil, it is not possible to say. He certainly put the five hundred out of sight somewhere, for when his son succeeded him it was nowhere to be found. After repaying the small loans to his father's old friends, upon looking round the son saw cattle, corn, hay, and furniture, but no five hundred pounds in ready money. The ready money had been muddled away—simply muddled away, for the old man had worked hard, and was not at all extravagant.

43

The bank asked for the five hundred, but not in a pressing manner, for the belief still existed that there was money in the family. That belief was still further fostered because the old friends whose loans had been repaid talked about that repayment, and so gave a colour to the idea. The heir, in his slow way, thought the matter over and decided to continue the loan. He could only repay it by instalments—a mode which, to a farmer brought up in the old style, is almost impossible, for though he might meet one he would be sure to put off the next—or by selling stock (equivalent to giving up his place), or by borrowing afresh. So he asked and obtained a continuation of the loan of the five hundred, and was accommodated, on condition that some one "backed" him. Some one in the family did back him, and the fatal mistake was committed of perpetuating this burden. A loan never remains at the same sum; it increases if it is not reduced. In itself the five hundred was not at all a heavy amount for the farm to carry, but it was the nucleus around which additional burdens piled themselves up. By a species of gravitation such a burden attracts others, till the last straw breaks the camel's back. This, however, was not all.

The heir discovered another secret which likewise contributed to sober him. It appeared that the farm, or rather the stock and so on, was really not all his father's. His father's brother had a share in it—a share of which even the most inquisitive gossips of the place were ignorant. The brother being the eldest (himself in business as a farmer at some distance) had the most money, and had advanced a certain sum to the younger to enable him to start his farm, more than a generation since. From that day to this not one shilling of the principal had been repaid, and the interest only partially and at long intervals. If the interest were all claimed it would now amount to nearly as much as the principal. The brother—or, rather, the uncle—did not make himself at all unpleasant in the matter. He only asked for about half the interest due to him, and at the same time gave the heir a severe caution not to continue the aforesaid riotous living. The heir, now quite brought down to earth after his momentary exaltation, saw the absolute necessity of acquiescence. With a little management he paid the interest—leaving himself with barely enough to work the farm. The uncle, on his part, did not act unkindly; it was he who "backed" the heir up at the bank in the matter of the continuation of the loan of the five hundred pounds. This five hundred pounds the heir had never seen and never would see; so far as he was concerned it did not exist; it was a mere figure, but a figure for which he must pay. In all these circumstances there was nothing at all exceptional.

At this hour throughout the width and breadth of the country there are doubtless many farmers' heirs stepping into their fathers' shoes, and at this very moment looking into their affairs. It may be safely said that few indeed are those fortunate individuals who find themselves clear of similar embarrassments. In this particular case detailed above, if the heir's circumstances had been rigidly reduced to figures—if a professional accountant had examined them—it would have been found that, although in possession of a large farm, he had not got one scrap of capital.

But he was in possession of the farm, and upon that simple fact of possession he henceforth lived, like so many, many more of his class. He returned to the routine of labour, which was a part of his life. After a while he married, as a man of forty might naturally wish to, and without any imputation of imprudence so far as his own age was concerned. The wife he chose was one from his own class, a good woman, but, as is said to be often the case, she reflected the weakness of her husband's character. He now worked harder than ever—a labourer with the labourers. He thus saved himself the weekly expense of the wages of a labourer—perhaps, as labourers do not greatly exert themselves, of a man and a boy. But while thus slaving with his hands and saving this small sum in wages, he could not walk round and have an eye upon the other men. They could therefore waste a large amount of time, and thus he lost twice what he saved. Still, his intention was commendable, and his persistent, unvarying labour really wonderful. Had he but been sharper with his men he might still have got a fair day's work out of them while working himself. From the habit of associating with them from boyhood he had fallen somewhat into their own loose, indefinite manner, and had lost the prestige which attaches to a master. To them he seemed like one of themselves, and they were as much inclined to argue with him as to obey. When he met them in the morning he would say, "Perhaps we had better do so and so," or "Suppose we go and do this or that." They often thought otherwise; and it usually ended in a compromise, the master having his way in part, and the men in part.

45

This lack of decision ran through all, and undid all that his hard work achieved. Everything was muddled from morn till night, from year's end to year's end. As children came the living indoors became harder, and the work out of doors still more laborious.

If a farmer can put away fifty pounds a year, after paying his rent and expenses, if he can lay by a clear fifty pounds of profit, he thinks himself a prosperous man. If this farmer, after forty years of saving, should chance to be succeeded by a son as thrifty, when he too has carried on the same process for another twenty years, then the family may be, for village society, wealthy, with three or even four thousand pounds, besides goods and gear. This is supposing all things favourable, and men of some ability, making the most of their opportunities. Now reverse the process. When children came, as said before, our hard-working farmer found the living indoors harder, and the labour without heavier. Instead of saving fifty pounds a year, at first the two sides of the account (not that he ever kept any books) about balanced. Then, by degrees, the balance dropped the wrong way. There was a loss of twenty or thirty pounds on the year, and presently of forty or fifty pounds, which could only be made good by borrowing, and so increasing the payment of interest.

Although it takes sixty years—two generations—to accumulate a village fortune by saving fifty pounds a year, it does not occupy so long to reduce a farmer to poverty when half that sum is annually lost. There was no strongly marked and radical defect in his system of farming to account for it; it was the muddling, and the muddling only, that did it. His work was blind. He would never miss giving the pigs their dinner. He rose at half-past three in the morning, and foddered the cattle in the grey dawn, or milked a certain number of cows, with unvarying regularity. But he had no foresight, and no observation whatever. If you saw him crossing a field, and went after him, you might walk close behind, placing your foot in the mark just left by his shoe, and he would never know it. With his hands behind his back, and his eyes upon the ground, he would plod across the field, perfectly unconscious that any one was following him. He carried on the old rotation of cropping in the piece of arable land belonging to the farm, but in total oblivion of any advantage to be obtained by local change of treatment. He could plan nothing out for next year. He spent nothing, or next to nothing, on improved implements; but, on the other hand, he saved nothing, from a lack of resource and contrivance.

As the years went by he fell out of the social life of the times; that is, out of the social life of his own circle. He regularly fed the pigs; but when he heard that the neighbours were all going in to the town to attend some important agricultural meeting, or to start some useful movement, he put his hands behind his back and said that he should not go; he did not understand anything about it. There never used to be anything of that sort. So he went in to luncheon on bread and cheese and small ale. Such a course could only bring him into the contempt of his fellow-men. He became a nonentity. No one had any respect for or confidence in him. Otherwise, possibly, he might have obtained powerful help, for the memory of what his family had been had not yet died out.

Men saw that he lived and worked as a labourer; they gave him no credit for the work, but they despised him for the meanness and churlishness of his life. There was neither a piano nor a decanter of sherry in his house. He was utterly out of accord with the times. By degrees, after many years, it became apparent to all that he was going downhill. The stock upon the farm was not so large nor of so good a character as had been the case. The manner of men visibly changed towards him. The small dealers, even the very carriers along the road, the higglers, and other persons who call at a farm on petty business, gave him clearly to know in their own coarse way that they despised him. They flatly contradicted him, and bore him down with loud tongues. He stood it all meekly, without showing any spirit; but, on the other hand, without resentment, for he never said ill of any man behind his back.

It was put about now that he drank, because some busybody had seen a jar of spirits carried into the house from the wine merchant's cart. A jar of spirits had been delivered at the house at intervals for years and years, far back into his father's time, and every one of those who now expressed their disgust at his supposed drinking habits had sipped their tumblers in that house without stint. He did not drink—he did not take one half at home what his neighbours imbibed without injury at markets and auctions every week of their lives. But he was growing poor, and they called to mind that brief spell of extravagance years ago, and pointed out to their acquaintances how the sin of the Prodigal was coming home to him.

No man drinks the bitter cup of poverty to the dregs like the declining farmer. The descent is so slow; there is time to drain every drop, and to linger over the flavour. It may be eight, or ten, or fifteen years about. He cannot, like the bankrupt tradesman, even when the fatal notice comes, put up his shutters at once, and retire from view. Even at the end, after the notice, six months at least elapse before all is over—before the farm is surrendered, and the sale of household furniture and effects takes place. He is full in public view all that time. So far as his neighbours are concerned he is in public view for years previously. He has to rise in the morning and meet them in the fields. He sees them in the road; he passes through groups of them in the market-place. As he goes by they look after him, and perhaps audibly wonder how long he will last. These people all knew him from a lad, and can trace every inch of his descent. The labourers in the field know it, and by their manner show that they know it.

His wife—his wife who worked so hard for so many, many years—is made to know it too. She is conspicuously omitted from the social gatherings that occur from time to time. The neighbours' wives do not call; their well-dressed daughters, as they rattle by to the town in basket-carriage or dog-cart, look askance at the shabby figure walking slowly on the path beside the road. They criticise the shabby shawl; they sneer at the slow step which is the inevitable result of hard work, the cares of maternity, and of age. So they flaunt past with an odour of perfume, and leave the "old lady" to plod unrecognised.

The end came at last. All this blind work of his was of no avail against the ocean steamer and her cargo of wheat and meat from the teeming regions of the West. Nor was it of avail against the fall of prices, and the decreased yield consequent upon a succession of bad seasons. The general lack of confidence pressed heavily upon a man who did not even attempt to take his natural place among his fellow-men. The loan from the bank had gradually grown from five to seven or eight hundred by thirties, and forties, and fifties added to it by degrees; and the bank—informed, perhaps, by the same busybodies who had discovered that he drank—declined further assistance, and notified that part, at least, of the principal must be repaid. The landlord had long been well aware of the state of affairs, but refrained from action out of a feeling for the old family. But the land, from the farmer's utter lack of capital, was now going from bad to worse. The bank having declined to advance further, the rent began to fall into arrear. The landlord caused it to be conveyed to his tenant that if he would quit the farm, which was a large one, he could go into a smaller, and his affairs might perhaps be arranged. The old man—for he was now growing old—put his hands behind his back and said nothing, but went on with his usual routine of work. Whether he had become dulled and deadened and cared nothing, whether hope was extinct, or he could not wrench himself from the old place, he said nothing. Even then some further time elapsed—so slow is the farmer's fall that he might almost be excused for thinking that it would never come. But now came the news that the old uncle who had "backed" him at the bank had been found dead in bed of sheer old age. Then the long-kept secret came out at last. The dead man's executors claimed the money advanced so many, many years ago.

This discovery finished it. The neighbours soon had food for gossip in the fact that a load of hay which he had sold was met in the road by the landlord's agent and turned back. By the strict letter of his agreement he could not sell hay off the farm; but it had been permitted for years. When they heard this they knew it was all over. The landlord, of course, put in his claim; the bank theirs. In a few months the household furniture and effects were sold, and the farmer and his aged wife stepped into the highway in their shabby clothes.

He did not, however, starve; he passed to a cottage on the outskirts of the village, and became bailiff for the tenant of that very arable farm to work which years ago his father had borrowed the thousand pounds that ultimately proved their ruin. He made a better bailiff than a farmer, being at home with every detail of practice, but incapable of general treatment. His wife does a little washing and charing; not much, for she is old and feeble. No charity is offered to them—they have outlived old friends—nor do they appeal for any. The people of the village do not heed them nor reflect upon the spectacle in their midst. They are merged and lost in the vast multitude of the agricultural poor. Only two of their children survive; but these, having early left the farm and gone into a city, are fairly well-to-do. That, at least, is a comfort to the old folk.

It is, however, doubtful whether the old man, as he walks down the lane with his hands behind his back and the dead leaves driven by the November breeze rustling after, has much feeling of any kind left. Hard work and adversity have probably deadened his finer senses. Else one would think he could never endure to work as a servant upon that farm of all others, nor to daily pass the scenes of his youth. For yonder, well in sight as he turns a corner of the lane, stands the house where he dwelt so many, many years; where the events of his life came slowly to pass; where he was born; where his bride came home; where his children were born, and from whose door he went forth penniless.

Seeing this every day, surely that old man, if he have but one spark of feeling left, must drink the lees of poverty to the last final doubly bitter dregs.

CHAPTER V

THE BORROWER AND THE GAMBLER

"WHERE do he get the money from, you?" "It be curious, bean't it; I minds when his father drove folks' pigs to market." These remarks passed between two old farmers, one standing on the sward by the roadside, and the other talking to him over the low hedge, as a gentleman drove by in a Whitechapel dog-cart, groom behind. The gentleman glanced at the two farmers, and just acknowledged their existence with a careless nod, looking at the moment over their heads and far away.

There is no class so jealous of a rapid rise as old-fashioned farming people. They seem to think that if a man once drove pigs to market he should always continue to do so, and all his descendants likewise. Their ideas in a measure approximate to those of caste among the Hindoos. It is a crime to move out of the original groove; if a man be lowly he must remain lowly, or never be forgiven. The lapse of time makes not the least difference. If it takes the man thirty years to get into a fair position he is none the less guilty. A period equal to the existence of a generation is not sufficient excuse for him. He is not one whit better than if he had made his money by a lucky bet on a racehorse. Nor can he ever hope to live down this terrible social misdemeanour, especially if it is accompanied by the least ostentation.

Now, in the present day a man who gets money shows off more than ever was the case. In the olden time the means of luxury were limited, and the fortunate could do little more than drink, and tempt others to drink. But to-day the fortunate farmer in the dog-cart, dressed like a gentleman, drove his thoroughbred, and carried his groom behind. Frank D——, Esq., in the slang of the time, "did the thing grand!" The dog-cart was a first-rate article. The horse was a high-stepper, such as are not to be bought for a song; the turn-out was at the first glance perfect. But if you looked keenly at the groom, there was a suspicion of the plough in his face and attitude. He did not sit like a man to the manner born. He was lumpy; he lacked the light, active style characteristic of the thoroughbred groom, who is as distinct a breed as the thoroughbred horse. The man looked as if he had been taken from the plough and was conscious of it. His feet were in top-boots, but he could not forget the heavy action induced by a long course of walking in wet furrows. The critics by the hedge were not capable of detecting these niceties. The broad facts were enough for them. There was the gentleman in his ulster, there was the resplendent turn-out, there was the groom, and there was the thoroughbred horse. The man's father drove their pigs to market, and they wanted to know where he got the money from.

Meantime Mr. D——, having carelessly nodded, had gone on. Half a mile farther some of his own fields were contiguous to the road, yet he did not, after the fashion of the farmer generally, pause to gaze at them searchingly; he went on with the same careless glance. This fact, which the old-fashioned folk had often observed, troubled them greatly. It seemed so unnatural, so opposite to the old ideas and ways, that a man should take no apparent interest in his own farm. They said that Frank was nothing of a farmer; he knew nothing of farming. They looked at his ricks; they were badly built, and still worse thatched. They examined his meadows, and saw wisps of hay lying about, evidence of neglect; the fields had not been properly raked. His ploughed fields were full of weeds, and not half worked enough. His labourers had acquired a happy-go-lucky style, and did their work anyhow or not at all, having no one to look after them. So, clearly, it was not Frank's good farming that made him so rich, and enabled him to take so high and leading a position.

Nor was it his education or his "company" manners. The old folk noted his boorishness and lack of the little refinements which mark the gentleman. His very voice was rude and hoarse, and seemed either to grumble or to roar forth his meaning. They had frequently heard him speak in public—he was generally on the platform when any local movement was in progress—and could not understand why he was put up there to address the audience, unless it was for his infinite brass. The language he employed was rude, his sentences disjointed, his meaning incoherent; but he had a knack of an *apropos* jest, not always altogether savoury, but which made a mixed assembly laugh. As his public speeches did not seem very brilliant, they supposed he must have the gift of persuasion in private. He did not even ride well to hounds—an accomplishment that has proved a passport to a great landlord's favour before now—for he had an awkward, and to the eye not too secure a seat in the saddle.

Nor was it his personal appearance. He was very tall and ungainly, with a long neck and a small round head on the top of it. His features were flat, and the skin much wrinkled; there seemed nothing in his countenance to recommend him to the notice of the other sex. Yet he had been twice married; the last time to a comparatively young lady with some money, who dressed in the height of fashion.

Frank had two families—one, grown up, by his first wife, the second in the nursery—but it made no difference to him. All were well dressed and well educated; the nursery maids and the infants went out for their airings in a carriage and pair. Mrs. D——, gay as a Parisian belle, and not without pretensions to beauty, was seen at balls, parties, and every other social amusement. She seemed to have the *entrée* everywhere in the county. All this greatly upset and troubled the old folk, whose heads Frank looked over as he carelessly nodded them good morning driving by. The cottage people from whose ranks his family had so lately risen, however, had a very decided opinion upon the subject, and expressed it forcibly. "'Pend upon it," they said, "'pend upon it, he have zucked zumbody in zumhow."

This unkind conclusion was perhaps not quite true. The fact was, that Frank, aided by circumstances, had discovered the ease with which a man can borrow. That was his secret—

his philosopher's stone. To a certain extent, and in certain ways, he really was a clever man, and he had the luck to begin many years ago when farming was on the ascending side of the cycle. The single solid basis of his success was his thorough knowledge of cattle—his proficiency in dealership. Perhaps this was learnt while assisting his father to drive other folks' pigs to market. At all events, there was no man in the county who so completely understood cattle and sheep, for buying and selling purposes, as Frank. At first he gained his reputation by advising others what and when to buy; by degrees, as people began to see that he was always right, they felt confidence in him, and assisted him to make small investments on his own account. There were then few auctioneers, and cattle were sold in open market. If a man really was a judge, it was as good to him as a reputation for good ale is to an innkeeper. Men flock to a barrel of good ale, no matter whether the inn be low class or high class. Men gather about a good judge of cattle, and will back him up. By degrees D—— managed to rent a small farm, more for the purpose of having a place to turn his cattle into than for farming proper—he was, in fact, a small dealer.

Soon afterwards there was an election. During the election, Frank gained the good will of a local solicitor and political agent. He proved himself an active and perhaps a discreetly unscrupulous assistant. The solicitor thought he saw in Frank talent of a certain order—a talent through which he (the solicitor) might draw unto himself a share of other people's money. The lawyer's judgment of men was as keen as Frank's judgment of cattle. He helped Frank to get into a large farm, advancing the money with which to work it. He ran no risk; for, of course, he had Frank tight in the grasp of his legal fist, and he was the agent for the landlord. The secret was this—the lawyer paid his clients four per cent. for the safe investment of their money. Frank had the money, worked a large farm with it, and speculated in the cattle markets, and realised some fifteen or perhaps twenty per cent., of which the lawyer took the larger share. Something of this sort has been done in other businesses besides farming. Frank, however, was not the man to remain in a state of tutelage, working for another. His forte was not saving—simple accumulation was not for him; but he looked round the district to discover those who had saved.

Now, it is a fact that no man is so foolish with his money

as the working farmer in a small way, who has put by a little coin. He is extremely careful about a fourpenny piece, and will wrap a sovereign up in several scraps of paper lest he should lose it; but with his hundred or two hundred pounds he is quite helpless. It has very likely occupied him the best part of his lifetime to add one five pound note to another, money most literally earned in the sweat of his brow; and at last he lends it to a man like Frank, who has the wit to drive a carriage and ride a thoroughbred. With the strange inconsistency so characteristic of human nature, a half-educated, working farmer of this sort will sneer in his rude way at the pretensions of such a man, and at the same time bow down before him.

Frank knew this instinctively, and, as soon as ever he began to get on, set up a blood-horse and a turn-out. By dint of such vulgar show and his own plausible tongue he persuaded more than one such old fellow to advance him money. Mayhap these confiding persons, like a certain Shallow, J.P., have since earnestly besought him in vain to return them five hundred of their thousand. In like manner one or two elderly maiden ladies—cunning as magpies in their own conceit—let him have a few spare hundreds. They thought they could lay out this money to better advantage than the safe family adviser "uncle John," with his talk of the Indian railways and a guaranteed five per cent. They thought (for awhile) that they had done a very clever thing on the sly in lending their spare hundreds to the great Mr. Frank D—— at a high rate of interest, and by this time would perhaps be glad to get the money back again in the tea-caddy.

But Frank was not the man to be satisfied with such small game. After a time he succeeded in getting at the "squire." The squire had nothing but the rents of his farms to live upon and was naturally anxious for an improving tenant who would lay out money and put capital into the soil. He was not so foolish as to think that Frank was a safe man, and of course he had legal advice upon the matter. The squire thought, in fact, that although Frank himself had no money, Frank could get it out of others, and spend it upon his place. It did not concern the squire where or how Frank got his money, provided he had it—he as landlord was secure in case of a crash, because the law gave him precedence over all other creditors. So Frank ultimately stepped into one of the squire's largest farms and cut a finer dash than ever.

There are distinct social degrees in agriculture. The man who occupies a great farm under a squire is a person of much more importance than he who holds a little tenancy of a small proprietor. Frank began to take the lead among the farmers of the neighbourhood, to make his appearance at public meetings, and to become a recognised politician—of course upon the side most powerful in that locality, and most likely to serve his own interest. His assurance, and, it must be owned, his ready wit, helped him in coming to the front. When at the front, he was invited to the houses of really well-to-do country people. They condoned his bluff manners—they were the mark of the true, solid British agriculturist. Some perhaps in their hearts thought that another day they might want a tenant, and this man would serve their turn. As a matter of fact, Frank took every unoccupied farm which he could get at a tolerably reasonable rent. He never seemed satisfied with the acreage he held, but was ever desirous of extending it. He took farm after farm, till at last he held an area equal to a fine estate. For some years there has been a disposition on the part of landlords to throw farms together, making many small ones into one large one. For the time, at all events, Frank seemed to do very well with all these farms to look after. Of course the same old-fashioned folk made ill-natured remarks, and insisted upon it that he merely got what he could out of the soil, and did not care in the least how the farming was done. Nevertheless, he flourished—the high prices and general inflation of the period playing into his hand.

Frank was now a very big man, the biggest man thereabout. And it was now that he began to tap another source of supply —to, as it were, open a fresh cask—*i.e.*, the local bank. At first he only asked for a hundred or so, a mere bagatelle, for a few days—only a temporary convenience. The bank was glad to get hold of what really looked like legitimate business, and he obtained the bagatelle in the easiest manner—so easily that it surprised him. He did not himself yet quite know how completely his showy style of life, his large acreage, his speeches, and politics, and familiarity with great people, had imposed upon the world in which he lived. He now began to realise that he was somebody. He repaid the loan to the day, waited awhile and took a larger one, and from that time the frequency and the amount of his loans went on increasing.

We have seen in these latter days bank directors bitterly complaining that they could not lend money at more than $\frac{7}{8}$

or even ½ per cent., so little demand was there for accommodation. They positively could not lend their money; they had millions in their tills unemployed, and practically going a-begging. But here was Frank paying seven per cent. for short loans, and upon a continually enlarging amount. His system, so far as the seasons were concerned, was something like this. He took a loan (or renewed an old one) at the bank on the security of the first draught of lambs for sale, say, in June. This paid the labourers and the working expenses of the hay harvest, and of preparing for the corn. He took the next upon the second draught of lambs in August, which paid the reapers. He took a third on the security of the crops, partly cut, or in process of cutting, for his Michaelmas rent. Then for the fall of the year he kept on threshing out and selling as he required money, and had enough left to pay for the winter's work. This was Frank's system—the system of too many farmers, far more than would be believed. Details of course vary, and not all, like Frank, need three loans at least in the season to keep them going. It is not every man who mortgages his lambs, his ewes (the draught from a flock for sale), and the standing crops in succession.

But of late years farming has been carried on in such an atmosphere of loans, and credit, and percentage, and so forth, that no one knows what is or what is not mortgaged. You see a flock of sheep on a farm, but you do not know to whom they belong. You see the cattle in the meadow, but you do not know who has a lien upon them. You see the farmer upon his thoroughbred, but you do not know to whom in reality the horse belongs. It is all loans and debt. The vendors of artificial manure are said not to be averse sometimes to make an advance on reasonable terms to those enterprising and deserving farmers who grow so many tons of roots, and win the silver cups, and so on, for the hugest mangold grown with their particular manure. The proprietors of the milkwalks in London are said to advance money to the struggling dairymen who send them their milk. And latterly the worst of usurers have found out the farmers—*i.e.* the men who advance on bills of sale of furniture, and sell up the wretched client who does not pay to the hour. Upon such bills of sale English farmers have been borrowing money, and with the usual disastrous results. In fact, till the disastrous results became so conspicuous, no one guessed that the farmer had descended so far. Yet, it is a fact, and a sad one.

All the while the tradespeople of the market-towns—the very people who have made the loudest outcry about the depression and the losses they have sustained—these very people have been pressing their goods upon the farmers, whom they must have known were many of them hardly able to pay their rents. Those who have not seen it cannot imagine what a struggle and competition has been going on in little places where one would think the very word was unknown, just to persuade the farmer and the farmer's family to accept credit. But there is another side to it. The same tradesman who to-day begs—positively begs—the farmer to take his goods on any terms, in six months' time sends his bill, and, if it be not paid immediately, puts the County Court machinery in motion.

Now this to the old-fashioned farmer is a very bitter thing. He has never had the least experience of the County Court; his family never were sued for debt since they can remember. They have always been used to a year's credit at least—often two, and even three. To be threatened with public exposure in the County Court because a little matter of five pounds ten is not settled instantly is bitter indeed. And to be sued so arbitrarily by the very tradesman who almost stuffed his goods down their throats is more bitter still.

Frank D——, Esq.'s coarse grandeur answered very well indeed so long as prices were high. While the harvests were large and the markets inflated; while cattle fetched good money; while men's hearts were full of mirth—all went well. It is whispered now that the grand Frank has secretly borrowed £25 of a little cottage shopkeeper in the adjacent village —a man who sells farthing candles and ounces of tea—to pay his reapers. It is also currently whispered that Frank is the only man really safe, for the following reason—they are all "in" so deep they find it necessary to keep him going. The squire is "in," the bank is "in," the lawyer is "in," the small farmers with two hundred pounds capital are "in," and the elderly ladies who took their bank-notes out of their tea-caddies are "in." That is to say, Mr. Frank owes them so much money that, rather than he should come to grief (when they must lose pretty well all), they prefer to keep him afloat. It is a noticeable fact, that Frank is the only man who has not raised his voice and shouted "Depression." Perhaps the squire thinks that so repellant a note, if struck by a leading man like Frank, might not be to his interest, and has conveyed that thought to the gentleman in the dog-cart with the groom behind. There are, however, various species of the façade farmer.

"What kind of agriculture is practised here?" the visitor from town naturally asks his host, as they stroll towards the turnips (in another district) with shouldered guns. "Oh, you had better see Mr. X——," is the reply. "He is our leading agriculturist; he'll tell you all about it." Everybody repeats the same story, and once Mr. X——'s name is started everybody talks of him. The squire, the clergyman—even in casually calling at a shop in the market town, or at the hotel (there are few inns now)—wherever he goes the visitor hears from all of Mr. X——. A successful man—most successful, progressive, scientific, intellectual. "Like to see him? Nothing easier. Introduction? Nonsense. Why he'd be delighted to see you. Come with me."

Protesting feebly against intruding on privacy, the visitor is hurried away, and expecting to meet a solid, sturdy, and somewhat gruff old gentleman of the John Bull type, endeavours to hunt up some ideas about shorthorns and bacon pigs. He is a little astonished upon entering the pleasure grounds to see one or more gardeners busy among the parterres and shrubberies, the rhododendrons, the cedar deodaras, the laurels, the pampas grass, the "carpet gardening" beds, and the glass of distant hot-houses glittering in the sun. A carriage and pair, being slowly driven by a man in livery from the door down to the extensive stabling, passes—clearly some of the family have just returned. On ringing, the callers are shown through a spacious hall with a bronze or two on the marble table, into a drawing-room, elegantly furnished. There is a short iron grand open with a score carelessly left by the last player, a harp in the corner, half hidden by the curtains, some pieces of Nankin china on the side tables.

Where are the cow-sheds? Looking out of window a level lawn extends, and on it two young gentlemen are playing tennis, in appropriate costume. The laboured platitudes that had been prepared about shorthorns and bacon pigs are quite forgotten, and the visitor is just about to risk the question if his guide has not missed the farm-house and called at the squire's, when Mr. X—— comes briskly in, and laughs all apology about intrusion to the winds in his genial manner. He insists on his friends taking some refreshment, will not take refusal; and such is the power of his vivacity, that they find themselves sipping Madeira and are pressed to come and dine in the evening, before one at least knows exactly where he is. "Just a homely spread, you know; pot-luck; a bit of fish and a glass of Moet; now *do* come." This curious mixture of bluff cordiality, with unexpected snatches of refinement, is Mr. X——'s great charm. "Style of farming; tell you with pleasure." (Rings the bell.) "John" (to the man servant), "take this key and bring me account book No. 6 B, Copse Farm; that will be the best way to begin."

If the visitor knows anything of country life, he cannot help recollecting that, if the old type of farmer was close and mysterious about anything, it was his accounts. Not a word could be got out of him of profit or loss, or revenue; he would barely tell you his rent per acre, and it was doubtful if his very wife ever saw his pass-book. Opening account book No. 6 B, the explanation proceeds.

" My system of agriculture is simplicity itself, sir. It is all founded on one beautiful commercial precept. Our friends round about here (with a wave of the hand, indicating the country side)—our old folks—whenever they got a guinea put it out of sight, made a hoard, hid it in a stocking or behind a brick in the chimney. Ha! ha! Consequently their operations were always restricted to the same identical locality—no scope, sir, no expansion. Now my plan is—invest every penny. Make every shilling pay for the use of half a crown, and turn the half-crown into seven and sixpence. Credit is the soul of business. There you have it. Simplicity itself. Here are the books; see for yourself. I publish my balance half-yearly—like a company. Then the public see what you are doing. The earth, sir, as I said at the dinner the other day (the idea was much applauded) the earth is like the Bank of England—you may draw on it to any extent; there's always a reserve to meet you. You positively can't overdraw the account. You see there's such a solid security behind you. The fact is, I bring commercial principles into agriculture; the result is, grand success. However, here's the book; just glance over the figures."

The said figures utterly bewilder the visitor, who in courtesy runs his eye from top to bottom of the long columns—farming accounts are really the most complicated that can be imagined—so he, meantime, while turning over the pages, mentally absorbs the personality of the commercial agriculturist. He sees a tall, thin farmer, a brown face and neck, long restless sinewy hands, perpetually twiddling with a cigar or a gold pencil-case—generally the cigar, or rather the extinct stump of it, which he every now and then sucks abstractedly, in total oblivion as to its condition. His dress would pass muster in towns—well cut, and probably from Bond Street. He affects a frock and high hat one day, and knickerbockers and sun helmet the next. His pockets are full of papers, letters, etc., and as he searches amid the mass for some memorandum to show, glimpses may be seen of certain oblong strips of blue paper with an impressed stamp.

"Very satisfactory," says the visitor, handing back No. 6 B; "may I inquire how many acres you occupy?"

Out comes a note-book, "Hum! There's a thousand down in the vale, and fifteen hundred upland, and the new place is about nine hundred, and the meadows—I've mislaid the meadows—but it's near about four thousand. Different holdings, of course. Great nuisance that, sir; transit, you see, costs money. City gentlemen know that. Absurd system in this country—the land parcelled out in little allotment gardens of two or three hundred acres. Why, there's a little paltry hundred and twenty acre freehold dairy farm lies between my vale and upland, and the fellow won't let my waggons or ploughing-tackle take the short cut. Ridiculous. Time it was altered, sir. Shooting? Why, yes; I have the shooting. Glad if you'd come over."

Then more Madeira, and after it a stroll through the gardens and shrubberies and down to the sheds, a mile, or nearly, distant. There, a somewhat confused vision of "grand shorthorns," and an inexplicable jumble of pedigrees, grand-dams, and "g-g-g-g-g-g-dams," as the catalogues have it; handsome hunters paraded, steam-engines pumping water, steam-engines slicing up roots, distant columns of smoke where steam-engines are tearing up the soil. All the while a scientific disquisition on ammonia and the constituent parts and probable value of town sewage as compared with guano. And at intervals, and at parting, a pressing invitation to dinner (when pineapples or hot-house grapes are certain to make their appearance at dessert)—such a flow of genial eloquence surely was never heard before!

It requires a week at least of calm reflection, and many questions to his host, before the visitor—quite carried away—can begin to arrange his ideas, and to come slowly to the opinion that though Mr. X—— is as open as the day and frank to a fault, it will take him a precious long time to get to the bottom of Mr. X—— 's system; that is to say, if there is any bottom at all to it.

Mr. X—— is, in brief, a gambler. Not in a dishonest, or even suspicious sense, but a pure gambler. He is a gigantic agricultural speculator; his system is, as he candidly told you, credit. Credit not only with the bank, but with everybody. He has actually been making use of you, his casual and unexpected visitor, as an instrument. You are certain to talk about him; the more he is talked of the better, it gives him a reputation, which is beginning to mean a great deal in agriculture as it has so long in other pursuits. You are sure to tell everybody who ever chooses to converse with you about the country of Mr. X——, and Mr. X——'s engines, cattle, horses, profuse hospitality, and progressive science.

To be socially popular is a part of his system; he sows corn among society as freely as over his land, and looks to some grains to take root, and bring him increase a hundredfold, as indeed they do. Whatever movement is originated in the neighbourhood finds him occupying a prominent position. He goes to London as the representative of the local agricultural chamber; perhaps waits upon a Cabinet Minister as one of the deputation. He speaks regularly at the local chamber meetings; his name is ever in the papers. The press are invited to inspect his farms, and are furnished with minute details. Every now and then a sketch of his life and doings, perhaps illustrated with a portrait, appears in some agricultural periodical. At certain seasons of the year parties of gentlemen are conducted over his place. In parochial or district matters he is a leading man.

Is it a cottage flower-show, a penny reading, a cricket club, a benefit society—it does not matter what, his subscriptions, his name, and his voice are heard in it. He is the life and soul of it; the energy comes from him, though others higher in the scale may be the nominal heads. And the nominal heads, knowing that he can be relied upon politically, are grateful, and give him their good word freely. He hunts, and is a welcome companion—the meet frequently takes place at his house, or some of the huntsmen call for lunch; in fact, the latter is an invariable thing. Everybody calls for lunch who happens to pass near any day; the house has a reputation for hospitality. He is the clergyman's right hand—as in managing the school committee. When the bishop comes to the confirmation, he is introduced as "my chief lay supporter." At the Rural Diaconal Conference, "my chief supporter" is one of the lay speakers. Thus he obtains every man's good word whose good word is worth anything. Social credit means commercial credit. Yet he is not altogether acting a part—he really likes taking the lead and pushing forward, and means a good deal of what he says.

He is especially quite honest in his hospitality. All the same, so far as business is concerned, it is pure gambling, which may answer very well in favourable times, but is not unlikely to end in failure should the strain of depression become too severe. Personal popularity, however, will tide him over a great deal. When a man is spoken highly of by gentry, clergy, literally everybody, the bank is remarkably accommodating. Such a man may get for his bare signature—almost pressed on him, as if his acceptance of it were a favour—what another would have to deposit solid security for.

In plain language, he borrows money and invests it in every possible way. His farms are simply the basis of his credit. He buys blood shorthorns, he buys blood horses, and he sells them again. He buys wheat, hay, etc., to dispose of them at a profit. If he chose, he could explain to you the meaning of contango, and even of that mysterious term to the uninitiated, "backwardation." His speculations for the "account" are sometimes heavy. So much so, that occasionally, with thousands invested, he has hardly any ready money. But, then, there are the crops; he can get money on the coming crops. There is, too, the live stock—money can be borrowed on the stock.

Here lies the secret reason of the dread of foreign cattle disease. The increase of our flocks and herds is, of course, a patriotic cry (and founded on fact); but the secret pinch is this—if foot and mouth, pleuro-pneumonia, or rinderpest threaten the stock, the tenant-farmer cannot borrow on that security. The local bankers shake their heads—three cases of rinderpest are equivalent to a reduction of 25 per cent. in the borrowing power of the agriculturist. The auctioneers and our friend have large transactions—"paper" here again. With certain members of the hunt he books bets to a high amount; his face is not unknown at Tattersall's, or at the race-meetings. But he does not flourish the betting-book in the face of society. He bets—and holds his tongue. Some folks have an ancient and foolish prejudice against betting; he respects sincere convictions.

Far and away he is the best fellow, the most pleasant company in the shire, always welcome everywhere. He has read widely, is well educated; but, above all, he is ever jolly, and his jollity is contagious. Despite his investments and speculations, his brow never wears that sombre aspect of gloomy care, that knitted concentration of wrinkles seen on the face of the City man, who goes daily to his "office." The out-of-door bluffness, the cheery ringing voice, and the upright form only to be gained in the saddle over the breezy uplands, cling to him still. He wakes everybody up, and, risky as perhaps some of his speculations are, is socially enlivening.

The two young gentlemen, by-the-bye, observed playing lawn-tennis from the drawing-room window, are two of his pupils, whose high premiums and payments assist to keep up the free and generous table, and who find farming a very pleasant profession. The most striking characteristic of their tutor is his Yankee-like fertility of resource and bold innovations—the very antipodes of the old style of "clod-compeller."

CHAPTER VI

AN AGRICULTURAL GENIUS
—OLD STYLE

TOWARDS the hour of noon Harry Hodson, of Up-court Farm, was slowly ascending the long slope that led to his dwelling. In his left hand he carried a hare, which swung slightly to and fro as he stepped out, and the black-tipped ears rubbed now and then against a bunch of grass. His double-barrel was under his right arm. Every day at the same hour Harry turned towards home, for he adhered to the ways of his fathers and dined at half-past twelve, except when the stress of harvest, or some important agricultural operation, disturbed the usual household arrangements. It was a beautiful October day, sunny and almost still, and, as he got on the high ground, he paused and looked round. The stubbles stretched far away on one side, where the country rose and fell in undulations. On the distant horizon a column of smoke, broadening at the top, lifted itself into the sky; he

knew it was from the funnel of a steam-plough, whose furnace
had just been replenished with coal. The appearance of the
smoke somewhat resembled that left by a steamer at sea when
the vessel is just below the horizon. On the other hand were
wooded meadows, where the rooks were cawing—some on the
oaks, some as they wheeled round in the air. Just beneath him
stood a row of wheat ricks—his own. His gaze finally rested
upon their conical roofs with satisfaction, and he then resumed his walk.

Even as he moved he seemed to bask in the sunshine; the
sunshine pouring down from the sky above, the material sunshine of the goodly wheat ricks, and the physical sunshine of
personal health and vigour. His walk was the walk of a strong,
prosperous man—each step long, steady, and firm, but quite
devoid of haste. He was, perhaps, forty years of age, in the
very prime of life, and though stooping a little, like so many
countrymen, very tall, and built proportionately broad across
the shoulders and chest. His features were handsome—perhaps
there was a trace of indolence in their good-humoured expression—and he had a thick black beard just marked with
one thin wavy line of grey. That trace of snow, if anything,
rather added to the manliness of his aspect, and conveyed the
impression that he was at the fulness of life when youth and
experience meet. If anything, indeed, he looked too comfortable, too placid. A little ambition, a little restlessness, would
perhaps have been good for him.

By degrees he got nearer to the house; but it was by degrees
only, for he stayed to look over every gate, and up into almost
every tree. He stopped to listen as his ear caught the sound of
hoofs on the distant road, and again at the faint noise of a
gun fired a mile away. At the corner of a field a team of horses
—his own—were resting awhile as the carter and his lad ate
their luncheon. Harry stayed to talk to the man, and yet again
at the barn door to speak to his men at work within with the
winnowing machine. The homestead stood on an eminence,
but was hidden by elms and sycamores, so that it was possible
to pass at a distance without observing it.

On entering the sitting-room Harry leaned his gun against
the wall in the angle between it and the bureau, from which
action alone it might have been known that he was a bachelor,
and that there were no children about the house to get into
danger with fire-arms. His elderly aunt, who acted as housekeeper, was already at table waiting for him. It was spread

with a snow-white cloth, and almost equally snow-white platter for bread—so much and so well was it cleaned. They ate home-baked bread; they were so many miles from a town or baker that it was difficult to get served regularly, a circumstance which preserved that wholesome institution. There was a chine of bacon, small ale, and a plentiful supply of good potatoes. The farmer did full justice to the sweet picking off the chine, and then lingered over an old cheese. Very few words were spoken.

Then, after his dinner, he sat in his arm-chair—the same that he had used for many years—and took a book. For Harry rather enjoyed a book, provided it was not too new. He read works of science, thirty years old, solid and correct, but somewhat behind the age; he read histories, such as were current in the early part of the present century, but none of a later date than the end of the wars of the First Napoleon. The only thing modern he cared for in literature was a "society" journal, sent weekly from London. These publications are widely read in the better class of farmsteads now. Harry knew something of most things, even of geology. He could show you the huge vertebrae of some extinct saurian, found while draining was being done. He knew enough of archaeology to be able to tell any enthusiastic student who chanced to come along where to find the tumuli and the earthworks on the Downs. He had several Roman coins, and a fine bronze spearhead, which had been found upon the farm. These were kept with care, and produced to visitors with pride. Harry really did possess a wide fund of solid, if quiet, knowledge. Presently, after reading a chapter or two, he would drop off into a siesta, till some message came from the men or the bailiff, asking for instructions.

The farmstead was, in fact, a mansion of large size, an old manor-house, and had it been situate near a fashionable suburb and been placed in repair would have been worth to let as much per annum as the rent of a small farm. But it stood in a singularly lonely and outlying position, far from any village of size, much less a town, and the very highway even was so distant that you could only hear the horse's hoofs when the current of air came from that direction. This was his aunt's—the housekeeper's—great complaint, the distance to the highway. She grumbled because she could not see the carriers' carts and the teams go by; she wanted to know what was going on.

Harry, however, seemed contented with the placid calm of the vast house that was practically empty, and rarely left it, except for his regular weekly visit to market. After the fashion of a thoroughbred farmer he was often rather late home on market nights. There were three brothers, all in farms, and all well to do; the other two were married, and Harry was finely plagued about being a bachelor. But the placid life at the old place—he had succeeded to his father—somehow seemed to content him. He had visitors at Christmas, he read his books of winter evenings and after dinner; in autumn he strolled round with his double-barrel and knocked over a hare or so, and so slumbered away the days. But he never neglected the farming—everything was done almost exactly as it had been done by his father.

Old Harry Hodson was in his time one of the characters of that country side. He was the true founder of the Hodson family. They had been yeomen in a small way for generations, farming little holdings, and working like labourers, plodding on, and never heard of outside their fifty-acre farms. So they might have continued till this day had not old Harry Hodson arose to be the genius—the very Napoleon—of farming in that district. When the present Harry, the younger, had a visitor to his taste—*i.e.* one who was not in a hurry—he would, in the evening, pull out the books and papers and letters of his late father from the bureau (beside which stood the gun), and explain how the money was made. The logs crackled and sparkled on the hearth, the lamp burnt clear and bright; there was a low singing sound in the chimney; the elderly aunt nodded and worked in her arm-chair, and woke up and mixed fresh spirits and water, and went off to sleep again; and still Harry would sit and smoke and sip and talk. By and by, the aunt would wish the visitor good night, draw up the clock, and depart, after mixing fresh tumblers and casting more logs upon the fire, for well she knew her nephew's ways. Harry was no tippler, he never got intoxicated; but he would sit and smoke and sip and talk with a friend, and tell him all about it till the white daylight came peeping through the chinks in the shutters.

Old Harry Hodson, then, made the money, and put two of his sons in large farms, and paid all their expenses, so that they started fair, besides leaving his own farm to the third. Old Harry Hodson made the money, yet he could not have done it had he not married the exact woman. Women have made the fortunes of Emperors by their advice and assistance, and the greatest men the world has seen have owned that their success was owing to feminine counsel. In like manner a woman made the policy of an obscure farmer a success. When the old gentleman began to get well to do, and when he found his teeth not so strong as of yore, and his palate less able to face the coarse, fat, yellowy bacon that then formed the staple of the household fare, he actually ventured so far as to have one joint of butcher's meat, generally a leg of mutton, once a week. It was cooked for Sunday, and, so far as that kind of meat was concerned, lasted till the next Sunday. But his wife met this extravagant innovation with furious opposition. It was sheer waste; it was something almost unpardonably prodigal. They had eaten bacon all their lives, often bacon with the bristles thick upon it, and to throw away money like this was positively wicked. However, the old gentleman, being stubborn as a horse-nail, persisted; the wife, still grumbling, calmed down; and the one joint of meat became an institution. Harry, the younger, still kept it up; but it had lost its significance in his day, for he had a fowl or two in the week, and a hare or a partridge, and, besides, had the choicest hams.

Now, this dispute between the old gentleman and his wife —this dispute as to which should be most parsimonious—was typical of their whole course of life. If one saved cheese-parings, the other would go without cheese at all, and be content with dry bread. They lived, indeed, harder than their own labourers, and it sometimes happened that the food they thought good enough was refused by a cottager. When a strange carter, or shepherd, or other labourer came to the house from a distance, perhaps with a waggon for a load of produce or with some sheep, it was the custom to give them some lunch. These men, unaccustomed even in their own cottages to such coarse food, often declined to eat it, and went away empty, but not before delivering their opinion of the fare, expressed in language of the rudest kind.

No economy was too small for old Hodson; in the house his wife did almost all the work. Now-a-days a farmer's house alone keeps the women of one, or even two, cottages fully employed. The washing is sent out, and occupies one cottage woman the best part of her spare time. Other women come in to do the extra work, the cleaning up and scouring, and so on. The expense of employing these women is not great; but still it is an expense. Old Mrs. Hodson did everything herself, and the children roughed it how they could, playing in the mire with the pigs and geese. Afterwards, when old Hodson began to get a little money, they were sent to a school in a market town. There they certainly did pick up the rudiments, but lived almost as hard as at home. Old Hodson, to give an instance of his method, would not even fatten a pig, because it cost a trifle of ready money for "toppings," or meal, and nothing on earth could induce him to part with a coin that he had once grasped. He never fattened a pig (meaning for sale), but sold the young porkers directly they were large enough to fetch a sovereign a-piece, and kept the money.

The same system was carried on throughout the farm. The one he then occupied was of small extent, and he did a very large proportion of the work himself. He did not purchase stock at all in the modern sense; he grew them. If he went to a sale he bought one or two despicable-looking cattle at the lowest price, drove them home, and let them gradually gather condition. The grass they ate grew almost as they ate it—in his own words, "They cut their own victuals"—*i.e.* with their teeth. He did not miss the grass blades, but had he paid a high price then he would have missed the money.

Here he was in direct conflict with modern farming. The theory of the farming of the present day is that time is money, and, according to this, Hodson made a great mistake. He should have given a high price for his stock, have paid for cake, etc., and fattened them up as fast as possible, and then realised. The logic is correct, and in any business or manufacture could not be gainsaid. But Hodson did just the reverse. He did not mind his cattle taking a little time to get into condition, provided they cost him no ready money. Theoretically, the grass they ate represented money, and might have been converted to a better use. But in practice the reverse came true. He succeeded, and other men failed. His cattle and his sheep, which he bought cheap and out of condition, quietly improved (time being no object), and he sold them at a profit, from which there were no long bills to deduct for cake.

He purchased no machinery whilst in this small place— which was chiefly grass land—with the exception of a second-hand hay-making machine. The money he made he put out at interest on mortgage of real property, and it brought in about 4 per cent. It was said that in some few cases where the security was good he lent it at a much higher rate to other farmers of twenty times the outward show. After a while he went into the great farm now occupied by his son Harry, and commenced operations without borrowing a single shilling. The reason was because he was in no hurry. He slowly grew his money in the little farm, and then, and not till then, essayed the greater. Even then he would not have ventured had not the circumstances been peculiarly favourable. Like the present, it was a time of depression generally, and in this particular case the former tenant had lived high and farmed bad. The land was in the worst possible state, the landlord could not let it, and Hodson was given to understand that he could have it for next to nothing at first.

Now it was at this crisis of his life that he showed that in his own sphere he possessed the true attribute of genius. Most men who had practised rigid economy for twenty years, whose hours, and days, and weeks had been occupied with little petty details, how to save a penny here and a fourpenny bit yonder, would have become fossilised in the process. Their minds would have become as narrow as their ways. They would have shrunk from any venture, and continued in the old course to the end of their time.

Old Hodson, mean to the last degree in his way of living, narrow to the narrowest point where sixpence could be got, nevertheless had a mind. He saw that his opportunity had come, and he struck. He took the great corn farm, and left his little place. The whole country side at once pronounced him mad, and naturally anticipated his failure. The country side did not yet understand two things. They did not know how much money he had saved, and they did not know the capacity of his mind. He had not only saved money, and judiciously invested it, but he had kept it a profound secret, because he feared if his landlord learnt that he was saving money so fast the rent of the little farm would have been speedily raised. Here, again, he was in direct conflict with the modern farmer. The modern man, if he has a good harvest or makes a profit, at once buys a "turn-out," and grand furniture, and in every way "exalts his gate." When landlords saw their tenants living in a style but little inferior to that they themselves kept up, it was not really very surprising that the rents a few years back began to rise so rapidly. In a measure tenants had themselves to blame for that upward movement.

Old Hodson carried his money to a long distance from home

to invest, so anxious was he that neither his landlord nor any
one else should know how quickly he was getting rich. So he
entered upon his new venture—the great upland farm, with
its broad cornfields, its expanse of sheep walk and down, its
meadows in the hollow, its copses (the copses alone almost as
big as his original holding), with plenty of money in his
pocket, and without being beholden to bank or lawyer for
a single groat. Men thought that the size of the place, the big
manor-house, and so on, would turn his head. Nothing of the
kind; he proceeded as cautiously and prudently as previously.
He began by degrees. Instead of investing some thousand
pounds in implements and machinery at a single swoop,
instead of purchasing three hundred sheep right off with a
single cheque, he commenced with one thing at a time. In this
course he was favoured by the condition of the land, and by
the conditions of the agreement. He got it, as it were, gradually
into cultivation, not all at once; he got his stock together, a
score or two at a time, as he felt they would answer. By the
year the landlord was to have the full rent the new tenant was
quite able to pay it, and did pay it without hesitation at the
very hour it was due. He bought very little machinery, nothing
but what was absolutely necessary—no expensive steam-
plough. His one great idea was still the same, *i.e.* spend no
money.

Yet he was not bigoted or prejudiced to the customs of his
ancestors—another proof that he was a man of mind. Hodson
foresaw, before he had been long at Upcourt Farm, that corn
was not going in future to be so all in all important as it had
been. As he said himself, "We must go to our flocks now for
our rent, and not to our barn doors." His aim, therefore,
became to farm into and through his flock, and it paid him
well. Here was a man at once economical to the verge of meanness, prudent to the edge of timidity, yet capable of venturing
when he saw his chance; and above all, when that venture
succeeded, capable of still living on bacon and bread and
cheese, and putting the money by.

In his earlier days Hodson was as close of speech as of
expenditure and kept his proceedings a profound secret.
As he grew older and took less active exercise—the son resident at home carrying out his instructions—he became more
garrulous and liked to talk about his system. The chief topic
of his discourse was that a farmer in his day paid but one rent,
to the landlord, whereas now, on the modern plan, he paid

eight rents, and sometimes nine. First, of course, the modern farmer paid his landlord (1); next he paid the seedsman (2); then the manure manufacturer (3); the implement manufacturer (4); the auctioneer (5); the railroad, for transit (6); the banker, for short loans (7); the lawyer or whoever advanced half his original capital (8); the schoolmaster (9).

To begin at the end, the rent paid by the modern farmer to the schoolmaster included the payment for the parish school; and, secondly, and far more important, the sum paid for the education of his own children. Hodson maintained that many farmers paid as much hard cash for the education of their children, and for the necessary social surroundings incident to that education, as men used to pay for the entire sustenance of their households. Then there was the borrowed capital, and the short loans from the banker; the interest on these two made two more rents. Farmers paid rent to the railroad for the transit of their goods. The auctioneer, whether he sold cattle and sheep, or whether he had a depot for horses, was a new man whose profits were derived from the farmers. There were few or no auctioneers or horse depositories when he began business; now the auctioneer was everywhere, and every country town of any consequence had its establishment for the reception and sale of horses. Farmers sunk enough capital in steam-ploughs and machinery to stock a small farm on the old system, and the interest on this sunk capital represented another rent. It was the same with the artificial manure merchant and with the seedsman. Farmers used to grow their own seed, or, at most, bought from the corn dealers or a neighbour if by chance they were out. Now the seedsman was an important person, and a grand shop might be found, often several shops, in every market town, the owners of which shops must likewise live upon the farmer. Here were eight or nine people to pay rent to instead of one.

No wonder farming nowadays was not profitable. No wonder farmers could not put their sons into farms. Let any one look round their own neighbourhood and count up how many farmers had managed to do that. Why, they were hardly to be found. Farmers' sons had to go into the towns to get a livelihood now. Farming was too expensive a business on the modern system—it was a luxury for a rich man, who could afford to pay eight or nine landlords at once. The way he had got on was by paying one landlord only. Old Hodson always

71

finished his lecture by thrusting both hands into his breeches pockets, and whispering to you confidentially that it was not the least use for a man to go into farming now unless he had got ten thousand pounds.

It was through the genius of this man that his three sons were doing so well. At the present day, Harry, the younger, took his ease in his arm-chair after his substantial but plain dinner, with little care about the markets or the general depression. For much of the land was on high ground and dry, and the soil there benefited by the wet. At the same time sheep sold well, and Harry's flocks were large and noted. So he sauntered round with his gun, and knocked over a hare, and came comfortably home to dinner, easy in his mind, body, and pocket.

Harry was not a man of energy and intense concentrated purpose like his father. He could never have built up a fortune, but, the money being there, Harry was just the man to keep it. He was sufficiently prudent to run no risk and to avoid speculation. He was sufficiently frugal not to waste his substance on riotous living, and he was naturally of a placid temperament, so that he was satisfied to silently and gradually accumulate little by little. His knowledge of farming, imbibed from his father, extended into every detail. If he seldom touched an implement now, he had in his youth worked like the labourers, and literally followed the plough. He was constantly about on the place, and his eye, by keeping the men employed, earned far more money than his single arm could have done. Thus he dwelt in the lonely manor-house, a living proof of the wisdom of his father's system.

Harry is now looking, in his slow complacent way, for a wife. Being forty years of age, he is not in a great hurry, and is not at all inclined to make a present of himself to the first pretty face he meets. He does not like the girl of the period; he fears she would spend too much money. Nor, on the other hand, does he care for the country hoyden, whose mind and person have never risen above the cheese-tub, with red hands, awkward gait, loud voice, and limited conversation. He has read too much, in his quiet way, and observed too much, in his quiet way also, for that. He wants a girl well educated, but not above her station, unaffected and yet comely, fond of home and home duties, and yet not homely. And it would be well if she had a few hundreds—a very small sum would do —for her dower. It is not that he wants the money, which can be settled on herself; but there is a vein of the old, prudent common sense running through Harry's character. He is in no hurry; in time he will meet with her somewhere.

CHAPTER VII

THE GIG AND THE FOUR-IN-HAND—A BICYCLE FARMER

Two vehicles were gradually approaching each other from opposite directions on a long, straight stretch of country road, which, at the first glance, appeared level. The glare of the August sunshine reflected from the white dust, the intense heat that caused a flickering motion of the air like that which may be seen over a flue, the monotonous low cropped hedges, the scarcity of trees, and boundless plain of cornfields, all tended to deceive the eye. The road was not really level, but rose and fell in narrow, steep valleys, that crossed it at right angles—the glance saw across these valleys without recognising their existence. It was curious to observe how first one and then the other vehicle suddenly disappeared, as if they had sunk into the ground, and remained hidden for some time. During the disappearance the vehicle was occupied in cautiously going down one steep slope and slowly ascending the other. It then seemed to rapidly come nearer till another hollow intervened, and it was abruptly checked. The people who were driving could observe each other from a long distance, and might naturally think that they should pass directly, instead of which they did not seem to get much nearer. Some miles away, where the same road crossed the Downs, it looked from afar like a white line drawn perpendicularly up the hill.

The road itself was narrow, hardly wider than a lane, but on either side was a broad strip of turf, each strip quite twice the width of the metalled portion. On the verge of the dust the red pimpernel opened its flowers to the bright blue cloudless sky, and the lowly convolvulus grew thickly among the tall dusty bennets. Sweet short clover flowers stood but a little way back; still nearer the hedges the grass was coarser, long, and wire-like. Tall thistles stood beside the water

73

furrows and beside the ditch, and round the hawthorn bushes that grew at intervals on the sward isolated from the hedge. Loose flints of great size lay here and there among the grass, perhaps rolled aside surreptitiously by the stone-breakers to save themselves trouble. Everything hot and dusty. The clover dusty, the convolvulus dusty, the brambles and hawthorn, the small scattered elms all dusty, all longing for a shower or for a cool breeze.

The reapers were at work in the wheat, but the plain was so level that it was not possible to see them without mounting upon a flint heap. Then their heads were just visible as they stood upright, but when they stooped to use the hook they disappeared. Yonder, however, a solitary man in his shirt-sleeves perched up above the corn went round and round the field, and beside him strange awkward arms seemed to beat down the wheat. He was driving a reaping machine, to which the windmill-like arms belonged. Beside the road a shepherd lingered, leaning on a gate, while his flock, which he was driving just as fast and no faster than they cared to eat their way along the sward, fed part on one side and part on the other. Now and then two or three sheep crossed over with the tinkling of a bell. In the silence and stillness and brooding heat, the larks came and dusted themselves in the white impalpable powder of the road. Farther away the partridges stole quietly to an anthill at the edge of some barley. By the white road, a white milestone, chipped and defaced, stood almost hidden among thistles and brambles. Some white railings guarded the sides of a bridge, or rather a low arch over a dry watercourse. Heat, dust, a glaring whiteness, and a boundless expanse of golden wheat on either hand.

After a while a towering four-in-hand coach rose out of the hollow where it had been hidden, and came bowling along the level. The rapid hoofs beat the dust, which sprang up and followed behind in a cloud, stretching far in the rear, for in so still an atmosphere the particles were long before they settled again. White parasols and light dust coats—everything that could be contrived for coolness—gay feathers and fluttering fringes, whose wearers sat in easy attitudes enjoying the breeze created by the swift motion. Upon such a day the roof of a coach is more pleasant than the thickest shade, because of that current of air, for the same leaves that keep off the sun also prevent a passing zephyr from refreshing the forehead. But the swifter the horses the sweeter the fresh wind to fan the delicate cheek and drooping eyelid of indolent beauty. So idle were they all that they barely spoke, and could only smile instead of laugh if one exerted himself to utter a good jest. The gentleman who handled the ribbons was the only one thoroughly awake.

His eyes were downcast, indeed, because they never left his horses, but his ears were sharply alive to the rhythmic beat of the hoofs and the faint creak and occasional jingle of the harness. Had a single shoe failed to send forth the proper sound as it struck the hard dry road, had there been a creak or a jingle too many, or too few, those ears would instantly have detected it. The downcast eyes that looked neither to the right nor left—at the golden wheat or the broad fields of barley—were keenly watching the ears of the team, and noting how one of the leaders lathered and flung white froth upon the dust. From that height the bowed backs of the reapers were visible in the corn. The reapers caught sight of the coach, and stood up to look, and wiped their brows, and a distant hurrah came from the boys among them. In all the pomp and glory of paint and varnish the tall coach rolled on, gently swaying from side to side as the springs yielded to the irregularities of the road. It came with a heavy rumble like far-away thunder over the low arch that spanned the dry watercourse.

Meantime the vehicle approaching from the opposite direction had also appeared out of a hollow. It was a high narrow gig of ancient make, drawn by a horse too low for the shafts and too fat for work. In the gig sat two people closely pressed together by reason of its narrow dimensions. The lady wore a black silk dress, of good and indeed costly material, but white with the dust that had settled upon it. Her hands were covered with black cotton gloves, and she held a black umbrella. Her face was hidden by a black veil; thin corkscrew curls fringed the back of her head. She was stout, and sat heavily in the gig. The man wore a grey suit, too short in the trousers—at least they appeared so as he sat with his knees wide apart, and the toe of one heavy boot partly projecting at the side of the dash-board. A much-worn straw hat was drawn over his eyes, and he held a short whip in his red hand. He did not press his horse, but allowed the lazy animal to go jog-trot at his own pace. The panels of the gig had lost their original shining polish; the varnish had cracked and worn, till the surface was rough and grey. The

75

harness was equally bare and worn, the reins mended more than once. The whole ramshackle concern looked as if it would presently fall to pieces, but the horse was in much too good a condition.

When the four-in-hand had come within about a hundred yards, the farmer pulled his left rein hard, and drew his gig right out of the road on to the sward, and then stopped dead, to give the coach the full use of the way. As it passed he took off his straw hat, and his wife stooped low, as a makeshift for bowing. An outsider might have thought that the aristocratic coach would have gone by this extremely humble couple without so much as noticing it. But the gentleman who was driving lifted his hat to the dowdy lady, with a gesture of marked politeness, and a young and elegantly-dressed lady, his sister, nodded and smiled, and waved her hand to her. After the coach had rolled some fifty yards away, the farmer pulled into the road, and went on through the cloud of dust it had left behind it, with a complacent smile upon his hard and weather-worn features. "A' be a nice young gentleman, the Honourable be," said he presently. "So be Lady Blanche," replied his wife, lifting her veil and looking back after the four-in-hand. "I'm sure her smile's that sweet it be a pleasure for to see her."

Half a mile farther the farmer drew out of the road again, drove close to the hedge, stopped, and stood up to look over. A strongly-built young man, who had been driving the reaping machine in his shirt-sleeves, alighted from his seat and came across to the hedge.

"Goes very well to-day," he said, meaning that the machine answered.

"You be got into a good upstanding piece, John," replied the old man sharply in his thin jerky voice, which curiously contrasted with his still powerful frame. "You take un in there and try un"—pointing to a piece where the crop had been beaten down by a storm, and where the reapers were at work. "You had better put the rattletrap thing away, John, and go in and help they. Never wasted money in all my life over such a thing as that before. What be he going to do all the winter? Bide and rust, I 'spose. Can you put un to cut off they nettles along the ditch among they stones?"

"It would break the knives," said the son.

"But you could cut um with a hook, couldn't you?" asked the old man, in a tone that was meant to convey withering contempt of a machine that could only do one thing, and must perforce lie idle ten months of the year.

"That's hardly a fair way of looking at it," the son ventured.

"John," said his mother, severely, "I can't think how you young men can contradict your father. I'm sure young men never spoke so in my time; and I'm sure your father has been prospered in his farming (she felt her silk dress), and has done very well without any machines, which cost a deal of money—and Heaven knows there's a vast amount going out every day."

A gruff voice interrupted her—one of the reapers had advanced along the hedge, with a large earthenware jar in his hand.

"Measter," he shouted to the farmer in the gig, "can't you send us out some better tackle than this yer stuff?"

He poured some ale out of the jar on the stubble with an expression of utter disgust.

"It be the same as I drink myself," said the farmer, sharply, and immediately sat down, struck the horse, and drove off.

His son and the labourer—who could hardly have been distinguished apart so far as their dress went—stood gazing after him for a few minutes. Then they turned, and each went back to his work without a word.

The farmer drove on steadily homewards at the same jog-trot pace that had been his wont these forty years. The house stood a considerable distance back from the road: it was a gabled building of large size, and not without interest. It was approached by a drive that crossed a green, where some ducks were waddling about, and entered the front garden, which was surrounded by a low wall. Within was a lawn and an ancient yew tree. The porch was overgrown with ivy, and the trees that rose behind the grey tiles of the roof set the old house in a frame of foliage. A fine old English homestead, where any man might be proud to dwell. But the farmer did not turn up the drive. He followed the road till he came to a gate leading into the rickyard, and, there getting out of the gig, held the gate open while the horse walked through. He never used the drive or the front door, but always came in and went out at the back, through the rickyard.

The front garden and lawn were kept in good order, but no one belonging to the house ever frequented it. Had any stranger driven up to the front door, he might have hammered away with the narrow knocker—there was no bell—for half an hour before making any one hear, and then probably it would have been by the accident of the servant going by the passage, and not by dint of noise. The household lived in the back part of the house. There was a parlour well furnished, sweet with flowers placed there fresh daily, and with the odour of those in the garden, whose scent came in at the ever open window; but no one sat in it from week's end to week's end. The whole life of the inmates passed in two back rooms—a sitting-room and kitchen.

With some slight concessions to the times only, Farmer M—— led the life his fathers led before him, and farmed his tenancy upon the same principles. He did not, indeed, dine with the labourers, but he ate very much the same food as they did. Some said he would eat what no labourer or servant would touch; and, as he had stated, drank the same smallest of small beer. His wife made a large quantity of home-made wine every year, of which she partook in a moderate degree, and which was the liquor usually set before visitors. They rose early, and at once went about their work. He saw his men, and then got on his horse and rode round the farm. He returned to luncheon, saw the men again, and again went out and took a turn of work with them. He rode a horse because of the distance—the farm being large—not for pleasure. Without it he could not have visited his fields often enough to satisfy himself that the labourers were going on with their work. He did not hunt, nor shoot—he had the right, but never exercised it; though occasionally he was seen about the newly-sown fields with a single-barrel gun, firing at the birds that congregated in crowds. Neither would he allow his sons to shoot or hunt.

One worked with the labourers, acting as working bailiff—it was he who drove the reaping machine, which after long argument and much persuasion the farmer bought, only to grumble at and abuse every day afterwards. The other was apprenticed as a lad to a builder and carpenter of the market town, and learned the trade exactly as the rest of the men did there. He lodged in the town in the cheapest of houses, ate hard bread and cheese with the carpenters and masons and bricklayers, and was glad when the pittance he received was raised a shilling a week. Once now and then he walked over to the farm on Sundays or holidays—he was not allowed to come too often. They did not even send him in a basket of apples from the great orchard; all the apples were carefully gathered and sold.

These two sons were now grown men, strong and robust, and better educated than would have been imagined—thanks to their own industry and good sense, and not to any schooling they received. Two finer specimens of physical manhood it would have been difficult to find, yet their wages were no more than those of ordinary labourers and workmen. The bailiff, the eldest, had a pound a week, out of which he had to purchase every necessary, and from which five shillings were deducted for lodgings. It may be that he helped himself to various little perquisites, but his income from every source was not equal to that of a junior clerk. The other nominally received more, being now a skilled workman; but as he had to pay for his lodgings and food in town, he was really hardly so well off. Neither of these young men had the least chance of marrying till their father should die; nothing on earth would induce him to part with the money required to set the one up in business or the other in a separate farm. He had worked all his time under his father, and it seemed to him perfectly natural that his sons should work all their time under him.

There was one daughter, and she, too, was out at work. She was housekeeper to an infirm old farmer; that is to say, she superintended the dairy and the kitchen, and received hardly as much as a cook in a London establishment. Like the sons, she was finely developed physically, and had more of the manners of a lady than seemed possible under the circumstances.

Her father's principles of farming were much the same as his plan of housekeeping and family government. It consisted of never spending any money. He bought no machines. The reaping machine was the one exception, and a bitter point with the old man. He entered on no extensive draining works, nor worried his landlord to begin them. He was content with the old tumbledown sheds till it was possible to shelter cattle in them no longer. Sometimes he was compelled to purchase a small quantity of artificial manure, but it was with extreme reluctance. He calculated to produce sufficient manure in the stalls, for he kept a large head of fattening cattle, and sheep to the greatest extent possible. He would rather let a field lie fallow, and go without the crop from it, till nature had restored the exhausted fertility, than supply that fertility at the cost of spending money. The one guiding motto of his life was "Save, not invest." When once he got hold of a sovereign he parted with it no more; not though all the scientific professors in the world came to him with their analyses, and statistics, and discoveries. He put it in the bank, just as his father would have put it into a strong box under his bed. There it remained, and the interest that accrued, small as it was, was added to it.

Yet it was his pride to do his land well. He manured it well, because he kept cattle and sheep, especially the latter, to the fullest capacity of his acreage; and because, as said before, he could and did afford to let land lie fallow, when necessary. He was in no hurry. He was not anxious for so much immediate percentage upon an investment in artificial manure or steam-plough. He might have said, with a greater man, "Time and I are two." It was Time, the slow passage of the years, that gave him his profit. He was always providing for the future; he was never out of anything, because he was never obliged to force a sale of produce in order to get the ready cash to pay the bank its interest upon borrowed money. He never borrowed; neither did he ever make a speech, or even so much as attend a farmer's club, to listen to a scientific lecture. But his teams of horses were the admiration of the country side—no such horses came into the market town. His rent was paid punctually, and always with country bank-notes—none of your clean, new-fangled cheques, or Bank of England crisp paper, but soiled, greasy country notes of small denomination.

Farmer M—— never asked for a return or reduction of his rent. The neighbours said that he was cheaply rented: that was not true in regard to the land itself. But he certainly was cheaply rented if the condition of the farm was looked at. In the course of so many long years of careful farming he had got his place into such a state of cultivation that it could stand two or three bad seasons without much deterioration. The same bad seasons quite spoiled the land of such of his neighbours as had relied upon a constant application of stimulants to the soil. The stimulating substances being no longer applied, as they could not afford to buy them, the land fell back and appeared poor.

Farmer M——, of course, grumbled at the weather, but the crops belied his lips. He was, in fact, wealthy—not the wealth that is seen in cities, but rich for a countryman. He could have started both his sons in business with solid capital. Yet he drank small beer which the reapers despised, and drove about in a rusty old gig, with thousands to his credit at that old country bank. When he got home that afternoon, he carefully put away some bags of coin for the wages of the men, which he had been to fetch, and at once started out for the rickyard, to see how things were progressing. So the Honourable on the tall four-in-hand, saluted with marked emphasis the humble gig that pulled right out of the road to give him the way, and the Lady Blanche waved her hand to the dowdy in the dusty black silk with her sweetest smile. The Honourable, when he went over the farm with his breechloader, invariably came in and drank a glass of the small beer. The Lady Blanche, at least once in the autumn, rode up, alighted, and drank one glass of the home-made wine with the dowdy. Her papa, the landlord, was an invalid, but he as invariably sent a splendid basket of hot-house grapes. But Farmer M—— was behind the age.

Had he looked over the hedge in the evening, he might have seen a row of reapers walking down the road at the sudden sound of a jingling bell behind them, open their line, and wheel like a squad, part to the right and part to the left, to let the bicycle pass. After it had gone by they closed their rank, and trudged on toward the village. They had been at work all day in the uplands among the corn, cutting away with their hooks low down the yellow straw. They began in the early morning, and had first to walk two miles or more up to the harvest field. Stooping, as they worked, to strike low enough, the hot sun poured his fierce rays upon their shoulders and the backs of their necks. The sinews of the right arm had continually to drive the steel through straw and tough weeds entangled in the wheat. There was no shadow to sit under for luncheon, save that at the side of the shocks, where the sheaves radiated heat and interrupted the light air, so that the shadow was warmer than the sunshine. Coarse cold bacon and bread, cheese, and a jar of small beer, or a tin can of weak cold tea, were all they had to supply them with fresh strength for further labour.

At last the evening came, the jackets so long thrown aside were resumed, and the walk home began. After so many hours of wearisome labour it was hardly strange that their natural senses were dulled—that they did not look about them, nor converse gaily. By mutual, if unexpressed consent, they intended to call at the wayside inn when they reached it, to rest on the hard bench outside, and take a quart of stronger ale. Thus trudging homewards after that exhausting day, they did not hear the almost silent approach of the bicycle behind till the rider rang his bell. When he had passed, the rider worked his feet faster, and swiftly sped away along the dry and dusty road. He was a tall young gentleman, whose form was well set off and shown by the tight-fitting bicycle costume. He rode well and with perfect command—the track left in the dust was straight, there was no wobbling or uncertainty.

"That be a better job than ourn, you," said one of the men, as they watched the bicycle rapidly proceeding ahead.

"Ay," replied his mate, "he be a vine varmer, he be."

Master Phillip, having a clear stretch of road, put on his utmost speed, and neither heard the comments made upon him, nor would have cared if he had. He was in haste, for he was late, and feared every minute to hear the distant dinner bell. It was his vacation, and Master Phillip, having temporarily left his studies, was visiting a gentleman who had taken a country mansion and shooting for the season. His host had accumulated wealth in the "City," and naturally considered himself an authority on country matters. Master Phillip's "governor" was likewise in a large way of business, and possessed of wealth, and thought it the correct thing for one of his sons to "go in" for agriculture—a highly genteel occupation, if rightly followed, with capital and intelligence. Phillip liked to ride his bicycle in the cool of the evening, and was supposed in these excursions to be taking a survey of the soil and the crops, and to be comparing the style of agriculture in the district to that to which he had been trained while pursuing his studies. He slipped past the wayside inn; he glided by the cottages and gardens at the outskirts of the village; and then, leaving the more thickly inhabited part on one side, went by a rickyard. Men were busy in the yard putting up the last load of the evening, and the farmer in his shirt-sleeves was working among and directing the rest. The bicyclist without a glance rode on, and shortly after reached the lodge gates. They were open, in anticipation of his arrival.

He rode up the long drive, across the park, under the old elms, and alighted at the mansion before the dinner bell rang, much to his relief; for his host had more than one daughter, and Phillip liked to arrange his toilet to perfection before he joined their society. His twenty-five guinea dressing-case, elaborately fitted up—too completely, indeed, for he had no use for the razor—soon enabled him to trim and prepare for the dining-room. His five-guinea coat, elegant studs, spotless shirt and wristbands, valuable seal ring on one finger, patent leather boots, keyless watch, eye-glass, gold toothpick in one pocket, were all carefully selected, and in the best possible style. Mr. Phillip—he would have scorned the boyish "master" —was a gentleman, from the perfumed locks above to the polished patent leather below. There was *ton* in his very air, in the "ah, ah," of his treble London tone of voice, the antithesis of the broad country bass. He had a firm belief in the fitness of things—in the unities, so to speak, of suit, action, and time.

When his team were struggling to force the ball by kick, or other permitted means, across the tented field, Phillip was arrayed in accurate football costume. When he stood on the close-mown lawn within the white-marked square of tennis and faced the net, his jacket was barred or striped with scarlet. Then there was the bicycle dress, the morning coat, the shooting jacket, and the dinner coat, not to mention the Ulster or Connaught overcoat, the dust coat, and minor items innumerable. Whether Phillip rolled in the mire at football, or bestrode a bicycle, or sat down to snow-white tablecloth and napkin, he conscientiously dressed the part. The very completeness of his prescribed studies—the exhaustive character of the curriculum—naturally induced a frame of mind not to be satisfied with anything short of absolute precision, and perhaps even apt to extend itself into dilettantism.

Like geology, the science of agriculture is so vast, it embraces so wide a range, that one really hardly knows where it begins or ends. Phillip's knowledge was universal. He understood all about astronomy, and had prepared an abstract of figures proving the connection of sun-spots, rainfall, and the price of wheat. Algebra was the easiest and at the same time the most accurate mode of conducting the intricate calculations arising out of the complicated question of food—of flesh formers and heat generators—that is to say, how much a sheep increased in weight by gnawing a turnip. Nothing could be more useful than botany—those who could not distinguish between a dicotyledon and a monocotyledon could certainly never rightly grasp the nature of a hedgerow. *Bellis perennis* and *Sinapis arvensis* were not to be confounded, and

Triticum repens was a sure sign of a bad farmer. Chemistry proved that too small a quantity of silicate made John Barley-corn weak in the knee; ammonia, animal phosphates, nitrogen, and so on, were mere names to many ignorant folk. The various stages and the different developments of insect life were next to be considered.

As to the soil and strata—the very groundwork of a farm —geology was the true guide to the proper selection of suit-able seed. Crops had been garnered by the aid of the electric light, the plough had been driven by the Gramme machine; electricity, then, would play a foremost part in future farming, and should be studied with enthusiasm. Without mathematics nothing could be done; without ornithological study, how know which bird revelled on grain and which destroyed in-jurious insects? Spectrum analysis detected the adulteration of valuable compounds; the photographer recorded the exact action of the trotting horse; the telephone might convey orders from one end of an estate to the other; and thus you might go through the whole alphabet, the whole cyclopædia of science, and apply every single branch to agriculture.

It is to be hoped that Phillip's conversational account of his studies has been correctly reproduced here. The chemical terms look rather weak, but the memory of an ordinary listener can hardly be expected to retain such a mass of technicalities. He had piles of strongly-bound books, the reward of successful examinations, besides diplomas and cer-tificates of proficiency. These subjects could be pursued under cover, but there was besides the field work, which had a more practical sound; model farms to be visited; steam-engines to be seen at work; lectures to be listened to on the spot; deep-drainage operations, a new drill, or a new sheaf-binder to be looked at. Then there were the experimental plots—some-thing like the little *parterres* seen at the edge of lawns.

One plot was sown without manure, another was sown with manure, a third had a different kind of manure. The dozen mangolds grown in one patch were pulled up and carefully weighed. The grains of wheat in an ear standing in an adjacent patch were counted and recorded. As these plots were about a yard wide, and could be kept clean, no matter what the weather; and as a wheel-barrow load of clay, or chalk, or sand thrown down would alter the geological formation, the results obtained from them were certainly instructive, and would be very useful as a guide to the cultivation of a thousand acres. There was also a large, heavy iron roller, which the scholars could if they chose drag round and round the gravel path.

Architecture, again, touches the agriculturist nearly. He requires buildings for the pigs, cattle, horses, labourers, engine and machinery, lastly, for himself. Out of doors almost any farmhouse that could be visited might be made by a lecturer an illustrative example of what ought to be avoided. Scarcely one could be found that was not full of mistakes—utterly wrong, and erected regardless of design and utility. Within doors, with ink, tracing paper, compasses, straight-edge and ruler, really valuable ground plans, front elevations, and so on, could be laid down. Altogether, with this circle of science to study, the future farmer had very hard work to face. Such exhaustive mental labour induced a certain nervousness that could only be allayed by relaxation. The bicycle afforded a grateful change. Mounted upon the slender, swift-revolving wheel, Mr. Phillip in the cool of the evening, after the long day of study, sometimes proceeded to stretch his limbs. The light cigar soothed his weary and over-strained mind.

The bicycle by-and-by, as if drawn by the power of gravitation, approached more and more nearly to the distant town. It threaded the streets, and finally stopped in the archway of an inn. There, leaned against the wall, under the eye of the respectful ostler, the bicycle reposed. The owner strolled upstairs, and in the company of choice spirits studied the laws of right angles, of motion, and retarding friction, upon the level surface of the billiard table. Somewhere in a not much frequented street there could be seen a small window in which a coloured plate of fashions was always displayed. There were also some bonnets, trimmings, and tasteful feathers. Nothing could be more attractive than this window. The milliner was young and pretty, and seemed to have a cousin equally young and pretty. Poor lonely, friendless creatures, it was not surprising they should welcome a little flirtation. The bicycle which so swiftly carries the young man of the present day beyond the penetrating vision of his aunt or tutor has much to answer for.

But, as pointed out previously, such exhaustive scientific training naturally tends to make the mind mathematical. It cannot be satisfied unless its surroundings—the substantial realisation of the concrete—are perfect. So Mr. Phillip had a suit for every purpose—for football, cricket, tennis, bicycle, shooting, dining, and strolling about. In the same way he possessed a perfect armoury of athletic and other useful implements. There were fine bats by the best makers for cricket, rods for trout fishing, splendid modified choke-bores, saddles, jockey caps, and so on. A gentleman like this could hardly long remain in the solitary halls of learning—society must claim him for parties, balls, dinners, and the usual round. It was understood that his "governor" was a man of substantial wealth; that Phillip would certainly be placed in an extensive farm, to play the pleasant part of a gentleman farmer. People with marriageable daughters looked upon the clever scholar as a desirable addition to their drawing-rooms. Phillip, in short, found himself by degrees involved in a whirl of festivities, and was never at a loss where to go for amusement when he could obtain leave to seek relaxation. If such social adulation made him a little vain, if it led to the purchase of a twenty-five-guinea dressing-case, and to frequent consultations with the tailor, it really was not Phillip's fault. He felt himself popular, and accepted the position.

When the vacation came, gathering up a fresh pile of grandly-bound prize books, broad sheets of diplomas, and certificates, Phillip departed to his friend's mansion for the partridge shooting. Coming down the road on the bicycle he overtook the reapers, and sprang his bell to warn them. The reapers thought Phillip's job better than theirs.

At dinner, while sipping his claret, Phillip delivered his opinion upon the agriculture of the district, which he had surveyed from his bicycle. It was incomplete, stationary, or retrograde. The form of the fields alone was an index to the character of the farmers who cultivated them. Not one had a regular shape. The fields were neither circles, squares, parallelograms, nor triangles. One side, perhaps, might be straight; the hedgerow on the other had a dozen curves, and came up to a point. With such irregular enclosures it was impossible that the farmer could plan out his course with the necessary accuracy. The same incompleteness ran through everything —one field was well tilled, the next indifferently, the third full of weeds. Here was a good modern cattle-shed, well designed for the purpose; yonder was a tumble-down building, with holes in the roof and walls.

So, too, with the implements—a farmer never seemed to have a complete set. One farmer had, perhaps, a reaping machine, but he had not got an elevator; another had an elevator, but no steam-plough. No one. had a full set of machinery. If they drained, they only drained one field; the entire farm was never by any possibility finished straight off. If the farmer had two new light carts of approved construction, he was sure to have three old rumbling waggons, in drawing which there was a great waste of power. Why not have all light carts? There was no uniformity. The farming mind lacked breadth of view, and dwelt too much on detail. It was not, of course, the fault of the tenants of the present day, but the very houses they inhabited were always put in the wrong place. Where the ground was low, flat, and liable to be flooded, the farmhouse was always built by a brook. When the storms of winter came the brook overflowed, and the place was almost inaccessible. In hilly districts, where there was not much water, the farmhouse was situate on the slope, or perhaps on the plateau above, and in summer very likely every drop of water used had to be drawn up there from a distance in tanks.

The whole of rural England, in short, wanted rearranging upon mathematical principles. To begin at the smallest divisions, the fields should be mapped out like the squares of a chessboard; next, the parishes; and, lastly, the counties. You ought to be able to work steam-ploughing tackle across a whole parish, if the rope could be made strong enough. If you talked with a farmer, you found him somehow or other quite incapable of following a logical sequence of argument. He got on very well for a few sentences, but, just as one was going to come to the conclusion, his mind seized on some little paltry detail, and refused to move any farther. He positively could not follow you to a logical conclusion. If you, for instance, tried to show him that a certain course of cropping was the correct one for certain fields, he would listen for a while, and then suddenly declare that the turnips in one of the said fields last year were a failure. That particular crop of turnips had nothing at all to do with the system at large, but the farmer could see nothing else.

What had struck him most, however, in that particular district, as he traversed it on the bicycle, was the great loss of time that must result from the absence of rapid means of communication on large farms. The distance across a large farm might, perhaps, be a mile. Some farms were not very broad, but extended in a narrow strip for a great way. Hours were occupied in riding round such farms, hours which might be saved by simple means. Suppose, for example, that a gang of labourers were at work in the harvest-field, three-quarters of a mile from the farmhouse. Now, why not have a field telegraph, like that employed in military operations? The cable or wire was rolled on a drum like those used for watering a lawn. All that was needed was to harness a pony, and the drum would unroll and lay the wire as it revolved. The farmer could then sit in his office and telegraph his instructions without a moment's delay. He could tap the barometer, and wire to the bailiff in the field to be expeditious, for the mercury was falling. Practically, there was no more necessity for the farmer to go outside his office than for a merchant in Mincing Lane. The merchant did not sail in every ship whose cargo was consigned to him: why should the farmer watch every waggon loaded? Steam could drive the farmer's plough, cut the chaff, pump the water, and, in short, do everything. The field telegraph could be laid down to any required spot with the greatest ease, and thus, sitting in his office chair, the farmer could control the operations of the farm without once soiling his hands. Mr. Phillip, as he concluded his remarks, reached his glass of claret, and thus incidentally exhibited his own hand, which was as white as a lady's.

CHAPTER VIII

HAYMAKING—"THE JUKE'S COUNTRY"

A RATTLING, thumping, booming noise, like the beating of their war drums by savages, comes over the hedge where the bees are busy at the bramble flowers. The bees take no heed, they pass from flower to flower, seeking the sweet honey to store at home in the hive, as their bee ancestors did before the Roman legions marched to Cowey Stakes. Their habits have not changed; their "social" relations are the same; they have not called in the aid of machinery to enlarge their liquid wealth, or to increase the facility of collecting it. There is a low murmur rather than a buzz along the hedgerow; but over it the hot summer breeze brings the thumping, rattling, booming sound of hollow metal striking against the ground or in contact with other metal. These ringing noises, which so little accord with the sweet-scented hay and green hedgerows, are caused by the careless handling of milk tins dragged hither and thither by the men who are getting the afternoon milk ready for transit to the railway station miles away. Each tin bears a brazen badge engraved with the name of the milkman who will retail its contents in distant London. It may be delivered to the countess in Belgravia, and reach her dainty lip in the morning chocolate, or it may be eagerly swallowed up by the half-starved children of some back court in the purlieus of the Seven Dials.

Sturdy milkmaids may still be seen in London, sweeping the crowded pavement clear before them as they walk with swinging tread, a yoke on their shoulders, from door to door. Some remnant of the traditional dairy thus survives in the stony streets that are separated so widely from the country. But here, beside the hay, the hedgerows, the bees, the flowers that precede the blackberries—here in the heart of the meadows the romance has departed. Everything is mechanical or scientific. From the refrigerator that cools the milk, the thermometer that tests its temperature, the lactometer that proves its quality, all is mechanical precision. The tins themselves are metal—wood, the old country material for almost every purpose, is eschewed—and they are swung up into a waggon specially built for the purpose. It is the very antithesis of the jolting and cumbrous waggon used for generations in the hay-fields and among the corn. It is light, elegantly proportioned, painted, varnished—the work rather of a coachbuilder than a cartwright. The horse harnessed in it is equally unlike the cart-horse. A quick, wiry horse, that may be driven in a trap or gig, is the style—one that will rattle along and catch the train.

The driver takes his seat and handles the reins with the air of a man driving a tradesman's van, instead of walking, like the true old carter, or sitting on the shaft. The vehicle rattles off to the station, where ten, fifteen, or perhaps twenty such converge at the same hour, and then ensues a scene of bustle, chaff, and rough language. The tins are placed in the van specially reserved for them, the whistle sounds, the passengers—who have been wondering why on earth there was all this noise and delay at a little roadside station without so much as a visible steeple—withdraw their heads from the windows; the wheels revolve, and, gathering speed, the train disappears round the curve, hastening to the metropolis. Then the empty tins returned from town have to be conveyed home with more rattling, thumping, and booming of hollow tin—there to be carefully cleansed, for which purpose vast quantities of hot water must be ready, and coal, of course, must be consumed in proportion.

This beautiful afternoon the booming seems to sound more than usual; it may perhaps be the wind that carries the noise along. But Mr. George, the farmer, who has been working among the haymakers, steps out from the rank, and going some way aside pauses awhile to consider. You should not address him as Farmer George. Farmer as an affix is not the thing now; farmers are "Mr. So-and-so." Not that there is any false pride about the present individual; his memory goes back too far, and he has had too much experience of the world. He leans on his prong—the sharp forks worn bright as silver from use—stuck in the sward, and his chest pressing on the top of the handle, or rather on both hands, with which he holds it. The handle makes an angle of forty-five degrees with his body, and thus gives considerable support and relief while he reflects.

He leans on his prong, facing to windward, and gazing straight into the teeth of the light breeze, as he has done these forty and odd summers past. Like the captain of a sailing ship, the eye of the master haymaker must be always watching the horizon to windward. He depends on the sky, like the mariner, and spreads his canvas and shapes his course by the clouds. He must note their varying form and drift; the height and thickness and hue; whether there is a dew in the evenings; whether the distant hills are clearly defined or misty; and what the sunset portends. From the signs of the sunset he learns, like the antique Roman husbandman—

> When the south projects a stormy day,
> And when the clearing north will puff the clouds away.

According as the interpretation of the signs be favourable, adverse, or doubtful, so he gives his orders.

This afternoon, as he stands leaning on the prong, he marks the soft air which seems itself to be heated, and renders the shade, if you seek it for coolness, as sultry as the open field. The flies are numerous and busy—the horses can barely stand still, and nod their heads to shake them off. The hills seem near, and the trees on the summit are distinctly visible. Such noises as are heard seem exaggerated and hollow. There is but little cloud, mere thin flecks; but the horizon has a brassy look, and the blue of the sky is hard and opaque. Farmer George recollects that the barometer he tapped before coming out showed a falling mercury; he does not like these appearances, more especially the heated breeze. There is a large quantity of hay in the meadow, much of it quite ready for carting, indeed, the waggons are picking it up as fast as they can, and the rest, if left spread about through next day —Sunday—would be fit on Monday.

On Sunday there are no wages to pay to the labourers; but the sun, if it shines, works as hard and effectually as ever. It is always a temptation to the haymaker to leave his half-made hay spread about for Sunday, so that on Monday morning he may find it made. Another reason why he hesitates is because he knows he will have trouble with the labourers, who will want to be off early as it is Saturday. They are not so ready to work an hour or two overtime as when he was a boy. On the other hand, he recollects that the weather cablegrams from America foretell the arrival of a depression. What would his grandfather have thought of adjusting the work in an English meadow to the tenour of news from the other side of the Atlantic?

Suddenly, while he ponders, there arises a shout from the labourers. The hay in one spot, as if seized by an invisible force, lifts itself up and revolves round and round, rising higher every turn. A miniature cyclone is whirling it up—a column of hay twisting in a circle and rising above the trees. Then the force of the whirlwind spends itself; some of the hay falls on the oaks, and some drifts with the breeze across the field before it sinks.

This decides him at once. He resolves to have all the hay carted that he can, and the remainder put up into haycocks. The men grumble when they hear it; perhaps a year ago they would have openly mutinied, and refused to work beyond the usual hour. But, though wages are still high, the labourers feel that they are not so much the masters as they were—they grumble, but obey. The haycocks are put up, and the rick-cloth unfolded over the partly made rick. Farmer George himself sees to it that the cloth does not touch the rick at the edges, or the rain, if it comes, will go through instead of shooting off, and that the ropes are taut and firmly belayed. His caution is justified in the night by a violent thunderstorm, and in the morning it is raining steadily.

It rains again on Monday, Tuesday, and Wednesday. Thursday it does not rain, but the hedges are wet, the ground is soaked, the grass hung with raindrops, the sky heavy with masses of drifting cloud. The hay cannot be touched; it must lie a day till sufficiently dry. Friday is more hopeful. He walks out into the fields, and kicks a haycock half over. The hay is still wet, but he congratulates himself that not much damage is done. Saturday is warm and fine—work goes on again. But Sunday is near. Sunday is fiery hot. Monday, the rain pours down with tropical vehemence.

Thus the monotonous, heart-breaking days go by and lengthen into weeks, and the weeks extend into months. The wheat is turning colour, and still the hay lies about, and the farmer has ceased even to tap the barometer. Those fields that are not cut are brown as brown can be—the grass has seeded and is over ripe. The labourers come every day, and some trifling job is found for them—the garden path is weeded, the nettles cut, and such little matters done. Their wages are paid every week in silver and gold—harvest wages for which no stroke of harvest work has been done. He must keep them on, because any day the weather may brighten, and then they will be wanted. But the weather does not brighten, and the drain of ready cash continues. Besides the men, the mowing machine is idle in the shed. Even if the rain ceases, the crops are so laid that it is doubtful if it can be employed. The horse rake is idle, the elevator is idle, the haymaking machine is idle, and these represent capital, if not to a large amount. He notes the price of hay at the market. For months past it has been low—so low that it has hardly paid to sell that portion of old hay which he felt he could spare. From October of last year to June of this (1879) the price remained about the same. It is now rising, but he has no more old hay to part with, and the new is not yet made. He has to bear in mind that his herd of cows has to be kept in high feed all the winter, to supply an unvarying quantity of milk to the London purchaser.

These wet days, forcing him unwillingly to stay within doors, send him to his books and accounts, and they tell a story somewhat at variance with the prevalent belief that dairy-farming is the only branch of farming that is still profitable. First, as to the milk-selling. Cows naturally yield a larger supply in the summer than in winter, but by the provisions of the contract between the farmer and the milkman the quantity sent in summer is not to exceed, and the quantity in winter not to fall short of, a stipulated amount.[1] The price received in summer is about fivepence or fivepence-halfpenny per imperial gallon, afterwards retailed in London at about one shilling and eightpence. When the cost of conveyance to the station, of the horses, of the wear and tear, of the men who have to be paid for doing nothing else but look after the milk, is deducted, the profit to the farmer is but small. He thinks, too, that he notices a decided falling-off in the demand for milk even at this price.

Some dairies find a difficulty in disposing of the milk—they cannot find a purchaser. He has himself a considerable surplus over and above what the contract allows him to send. This must either be wasted entirely or made into butter and cheese. In order to make cheese, the plant, the tubs, vats, presses, and so on, must be kept in readiness, and there must be an experienced person to superintend the work. This person must be paid a salary, and lodge and board in the house, representing therefore a considerable outlay. The cheese, when made and sent to market, fluctuates of course in price: it may be as low as fourpence a pound wholesale; it may go as high as sixpence. Fourpence a pound wholesale will not pay for the making; sixpence will leave a profit; but of late the price has gone rather to the lower than the higher figure. A few years since, when the iron industries flourished, this kind of cheese had a good and ready sale, and there was a profit belonging to it; but since the iron trade has been in so depressed a condition this cheese has sold badly. The surplus milk consequently brings no profit, and is only made into cheese because it shall not be wasted, and in the hope that possibly a favourable turn of the cheese market may happen. Neither the summer cheese nor the summer milk is bringing him in a fortune.

Meantime the hay is spoiling in the fields. But a few years ago, when agricultural prices were inflated, and men's minds were full of confidence, he recollects seeing standing grass

---

[1] An improvement upon this system has been introduced by the leading metropolitan dairy company. The farmer is asked to fix a minimum quantity which he will engage to supply daily, but he can send as much more as he likes. This permits of economical and natural management in a dairy, which was very difficult under the rigid rule mentioned above.

crops sold by auction for £5 the acre, and in some cases even higher prices were realised. This year similar auctions of standing grass crops hardly realised 30s. an acre, and in some instances a purchaser could not be found even at that price. The difference in the value of grass represented by these prices is very great.

He has no pigs to sell, because, for a long while past, he has had nothing upon which to feed them, the milk being sold. The pig-sties are full of weeds; he can hardly fatten one for his own use, and has scarcely better facilities for keeping pigs than an agricultural labourer. The carriage of the milk to the station requires at least two quick horses, and perhaps more; one cannot do it twice a day, even with a very moderate load. The hard highway and the incessant work would soon knock a single horse up. The mowing machine and the horse-rake must be drawn by a similar horse, so that the dairy farm may be said to require a style of horse like that employed by omnibus proprietors. The acreage being limited, he can only keep a certain number of horses, and, therefore, has no room for a brood mare.

Farmer George is aware that nothing now pays like a brood cart mare with fair good luck. The colt born in April is often sold six months afterwards, in September, for £20 or £25, and even up to £30, according to excellence. The value of cart-horse colts has risen greatly, and those who are fortunately able to maintain a brood mare have reaped the profit. But Mr. George, selling the milk, and keeping a whole stud of nags for the milk cart, the mowing machine, the horse-rake, and so forth, cannot maintain a brood mare as well. In the winter, it is true, the milk may sell for as high as 10d. per gallon of four quarts, but then he has a difficulty in procuring the quantity contracted for, and may perhaps have to buy of neighbours to keep up the precise supply.

His herd must also be managed for the purpose, and must be well fed, and he will probably have to buy food for them in addition to his hay. The nag horses, too, that draw the milk waggon, have to be fed during the winter, and are no slight expense. As for fattening a beast in a stall, with a view to take the prize at Christmas at the local show, he has abandoned that, finding that it costs more to bring the animal up to the condition required than he can afterwards sell it for. There is no profit in that. America presses upon him hard, too—as hard, or harder, than on the wheat-grower. Cases have been known of American cheese being sold in manufacturing towns as low as 2d. per pound retail—given away by despairing competition.

How, then, is the dairyman to succeed when he cannot, positively cannot, make cheese to sell at less than 4d. per pound wholesale? Of course such instances are exceptional, but American cheese is usually sold a penny or more a pound below the English ordinary, and this cuts the ground from under the dairyman's feet; and the American cheese too is acquiring a reputation for richness, and, price for price, surpasses the English in quality. Some people who have long cherished a prejudice against the American have found, upon at last being induced to try the two, that the Canadian cheddar is actually superior to the English cheddar, the English selling at 10d. per pound and the Canadian at 7d.

Mr. George finds he pays a very high rent for his grass land —some 50s. per acre—and upon reckoning up the figures in his account-books heaves a sigh. His neighbours perchance may be making fortunes, though they tell quite a different tale, but he feels that he is not growing rich. The work is hard, or rather it is continuous. No one has to attend to his duties so regularly all the year round as the man who looks after cows. They cannot be left a single day from the 1st of January to the 31st of December. Nor is the social state of things altogether pleasant to reflect on. His sons and daughters have all left home; not one would stay and take to the dairy work. They have gone into the towns, and found more congenial employment there. He is himself growing in years. His wife, having once left off making cheese when the milk selling commenced, and having tasted the sweets of rest, is unwilling to return to that hard labour. When it is done he must pay some one to do it.

In every way ready money is going out of the house. Cash to pay the haymakers idling about in the sheds out of the rain; cash to pay the men who manage the milk; cash to pay the woman who makes the cheese out of the surplus milk; cash to pay the blacksmith for continually re-shoeing the milkcart nags and for mending machines; cash to pay the brewer and the butcher and the baker, neither of whom took a sovereign here when he was a lad, for his father ate his own bacon, brewed his own beer, and baked his own bread; cash to pay for the education of the cottagers' children; cash, a great deal of cash, to pay the landlord.

Mr. George, having had enough of his accounts, rises and goes to the window. A rain cloud sweeping along the distant hills has hidden them from sight, and the rack hurries overhead driven before the stormy wind. There comes a knock at the door. It is the collector calling the second time for the poor rates, which have grown heavier of late.

But, however delayed, the haymaking is finished at last, and by-and-by, when the leaves have fallen and the hunting commences, a good run drives away for the time at least the memory of so unpropitious a season. Then Mr. George some mild morning forms one of a little group of well-mounted farmers waiting at a quiet corner while the hounds draw a great wood. Two of them are men long past middle age, whose once tawny beards are grizzled, but who are still game, perhaps more so than the rising generation. The rest have followed them here, aware that these old hands know every inch of the country, and are certain to be in the right place. The spot is not far from the park wall, where the wood runs up into a wedge-shaped point, and ends in a low mound and hedge. Most of the company at the meet in the park have naturally cantered across the level sward, scattering the sheep as they go, and are now assembled along the side of the wood, near where a green "drive" goes through it, and apparently gives direct access to the fields beyond. From thence they can see the huntsman in the wood occasionally, and trace the exact course the hounds are taking in their search.

A gallant show it is by the wood! Horsemen and horsewomen, late comers hastening up, restless horses, a throng for ever in motion, and every now and then the blast of a horn rising up from the trees beneath. A gallant show indeed, but the two old cunning ones and their followers have slipped away down to this obscure corner, where they can see nothing of it, and are themselves hidden. They know that the wood is triangular in shape, and that from this, the apex, they have merely to pass the low hedge in front, and, turning to the left, ride along the lower side, and so bisect the course the fox will probably take. They know that the "drive," which offers so straight and easy a descent through the wood from the park, is pleasant enough till the lower ground is reached. There the soft, oozy earth, which can never dry under the trees, is poached into a slough through which even timber carriages cannot be drawn. Nor can a horseman slip aside, because of the ash poles and thorn thickets. Those who are trapped there must return to the park and gallop all round the wood outside unless they like to venture a roll in that liquid mud. Any one can go to a meet, but to know all the peculiarities of the covers is only given to those who have ridden over the country these forty years. In this corner a detached copse of spruce fir keeps off the wind—the direction of which they have noted—and in this shelter it is almost warm.

The distant crack of a whip, the solitary cry of a hound, a hollow shout, and similar sounds, come frequently, and now and then there is an irrepressible stir in the little group as they hear one of the many false alarms that always occur in drawing a great wood. To these noises they are keenly sensitive, but utterly ignore the signs of other life around them. A pheasant, alarmed by the hounds, comes running quietly, thinking to escape into the line of isolated copses that commences here; but, suddenly confronted by the horsemen just outside, rises with an uproar, and goes sailing down over the fields. Two squirrels, happy in the mild weather, frisk out of the copse into the dank grass, till a curvet of one of the horses frightens them up into the firs again.

Horses and men are becoming impatient. "That dalled keeper has left an earth open," remarks one of the riders. His companion points with his whip at the hedge just where it joins the wood. A long slender muzzle is thrust for a moment cautiously over the bare sandy mound under cover of a thorn stole. One sniff, and it is withdrawn. The fox thought also to steal away along the copses, the worst and most baffling course he could choose. Five minutes afterwards, and there is this time no mistake. There comes from the park above the low, dull, rushing roar of hundreds of hoofs, that strike the sward together, and force by sheer weight the reluctant earth to resound. The two old hands lead over the hedge, and the little company, slipping along below the wood, find themselves well on the track, far in front of the main body. There is a block in the treacherous "drive," those who were foremost struggling to get back, and those behind struggling to come down. The rest at last, learning the truth, are galloping round the outside, and taking it out of their horses before they get on the course at all.

It is a splendid burst, and the pace is terrible. The farmers' powerful horses find it heavy going across the fresh ploughed furrows and the wet "squishey" meadows, where the double mounds cannot be shirked. Now a lull, and the two old hands,

a little at fault, make for the rising ground, where are some
ricks, and a threshing machine at work, thinking from thence
to see over the tall hedgerows. Upon the rick the labourers
have stopped work, and are eagerly watching the chase, for
from that height they can see the whole field. Yonder the main
body have found a succession of fields with the gates all open:
some carting is in progress, and the gates have been left open
for the carter's convenience. A hundred horsemen and eight
or ten ladies are galloping in an extended line along this route,
riding hardest, as often happens, when the hounds are quiet,
that they may be ready when the chiding recommences.

Suddenly the labourers exclaim and point, the hounds open,
and the farmers, knowing from the direction they point where
to ride, are off. But this time the fox has doubled, so that the
squadrons hitherto behind are now the closest up, and the
farmers in the rear: thus the fortune of war changes, and the
race is not to the swift. The labourers on the rick, which stands
on the side of a hill, are fully as excited as the riders, and they
can see what the hunter himself rarely views, *i.e.*, the fox slipping ahead before the hounds. Then they turn to alternately
laugh at, and shout directions to a disconsolate gentleman,
who, ignorant of the district, is pounded in a small meadow.
He is riding frantically round and round, afraid to risk the
broad brook which encircles it, because of the treacherous
bank, and maddened by the receding sound of the chase. A
boy gets off the rick and runs to earn sixpence by showing a
way out. So from the rick Hodge has his share of the sport, and
at that elevation can see over a wide stretch of what he—
changing the "d" into a "j"—calls "the juke's country."

It is a famous land. There are spaces, which on the map look
large, and yet have no distinctive character, no individuality as
it were. Such broad expanses of plain and vale are usefully
employed in the production of cattle and corn. Villages, hamlets, even towns are dotted about them, but a list of such places
would not contain a single name that would catch the eye.
Though occupying so many square miles, the district, so far as
the world is concerned, is non-existent. It is socially a blank.
But "the juke's country" is a well-known land. There are
names connected with it which are familiar not only in
England, but all the world over, where men—and where do
they not?—converse of sport. Something beyond mere utility,
beyond ploughing and sowing, has given it within its bounds
a species of separate nationality. The personal influence of an

acknowledged leader has organised society and impressed it with a quiet enthusiasm. Even the bitterest Radical forgives the patrician who shoots or rides exceptionally well, and hunting is a pursuit which brings the peer and the commoner side by side.

The agricultural population speak as one man upon the subject. The old farmer will tell you with pride how his advice was sought when disease entered the kennels, and how his remedy saved the lives of valuable hounds. The farmer's son, a mere lad, whose head barely rises to his saddle, talks of "the duke" as his hero. This boy knows the country, and can ride straight, better than many a gentleman with groom, and second horse behind. Already, like his elders, he looks forward impatiently to the fall of the leaf. The tenants' wives and daughters allude with pleasure to the annual social gatherings at the mansion, and it is apparent that something like a real bond exists between landlord and tenant. No false pride separates the one from the other—intercourse is easy, for a man of high and ancient lineage can speak freely to the humblest labourer without endangering his precedence. It needs none of the parvenu's *hauteur* and pomp to support his dignity. Every tenant is treated alike.

On small estates there is sometimes a complaint that the largest tenant is petted while the lesser are harshly treated. Nothing of that is known here. The tenants are as well content as it is possible for men to be who are passing under the universal depression. *Noblesse oblige*—it would be impossible for that ancient house to stoop to meanness. The head rides to the hunt, as his ancestors rode to battle, with a hundred horsemen behind him. His colours are like the cockades of olden times. Once now and then even Royalty honours the meet with its presence. Round that ancient house the goodwill of the county gathers; and when any family event—as a marriage —takes place, the hearty congratulations offered come from far beyond the actual property. His pastime is not without its use—all are agreed that hunting really does improve the breed of horses. Certainly it gives a life, a go, a social movement to the country which nothing else imparts.

It is a pleasant land withal—a land of hill and vale, of wood and copse. How well remembered are the copses on the hills, and the steeples, those time-honoured landmarks to wandering riders! The small meadows with double mounds have held captive many a stranger. The river that winds through them enters by-and-by a small but ancient town, with its memories of the fierce Danes, and its present talk of the hunt. About five o'clock on winter afternoons there is a clank of spurs in the courtyard of the old inn, and the bar is crowded with men in breeches and top-boots. As they refresh themselves there is a ceaseless hum of conversation, how so-and-so came a cropper, how another went at the brook in style, or how some poor horse got staked and was mercifully shot. A talk, in short, like that in camp after a battle, of wounds and glory. Most of these men are tenant farmers, and reference is sure to be made to the price of cheese, and the forthcoming local agricultural show.

This old market town has been noted for generations as a great cheese centre. It is not, perhaps, the most convenient situation for such a market, and its population is inconsiderable; but the trade is, somehow or other, a tradition of the place, and traditions are hard to shake. Efforts have been made to establish rival markets in towns nearer to the modern resorts of commerce, but in vain. The attempt has always proved a failure, and to this day the prices quoted at this place rule those of the adjoining counties, and are watched in distant cities. The depression made itself felt here in a very practical manner, for prices fell to such an extent that the manufacture of the old style of cheese became almost a dead loss. Some farmers abandoned it, and at much trouble and expense changed their system, and began to produce Cheddar and Stilton. But when the Stilton was at last ready, there was no demand for it. Almost suddenly, however, and quite recently, a demand sprang up, and the price of that cheese rose. They say here in the bar that this probably saved many from difficulties; large stocks that had been lying on hand unsaleable for months going off at a good price. They hope that it is an omen of returning prosperity, and do not fail to observe the remarkable illustration it affords of the close connection between trade and agriculture. For no sooner did the iron trade revive than the price of cheese responded. The elder men cannot refrain from chuckling over the altered tone of the inhabitants of cities towards the farmers. "Years ago," they say, "we were held up to scorn, and told that we were quite useless; there was nothing so contemptible as the British farmer. Now they have discovered that, after all, we are some good, and even Manchester sympathises with us."

It is now hoped that the forthcoming local show—largely

patronised and promoted by the chief of the hunting field—
will be better than was at one time anticipated. Those who
would like to see the real working of an agricultural show such
as this should contrive to visit the yard early in the morning
of the opening day, some few hours before the public are admitted. The bustle, the crush of excited exhibitors, the cries of
men in charge of cattle, the apparently inextricable confusion,
as if everything had been put off to the last moment—the
whole scene is intensely agricultural. Every one is calling for
the secretary. A drover wants to know where to put his fat
cattle; a carter wants to ask where a great cart-horse is to
stand—he and his horse together are hopelessly floundering
about in the crowd. The agent of a firm of implement manu-
facturers has a telegram that another machine is coming, and
is anxious for extra space; the representative of an artificial
manure factory is vainly seeking a parcel that has got mislaid.
The seedsman requires permission to somewhat shift his stall;
wherever is the secretary?

When he appears, a clergyman at once pounces on him, to
apply for tickets for the dinner, and is followed by a farmer,
who must have a form and an explanation how to fill it up.
One of his labourers has decided at the last minute to enter
for a prize—he has had a year to make up his mind in. A
crowd of members of the Society are pushing round for a
private view, and watching the judges at their work. They all
turn to the secretary to ask where such and such an exhibit
may be found, and demand why on earth the catalogues are
not ready? Mr. Secretary, a stout tenant farmer, in breeches
and top-boots, whose broad face beams with good nature
(selected, perhaps, for that very quality), pants and wipes his
forehead, for, despite the cold, the exertion and the universal
flurry have made him quite hot. He gives every enquirer a civil
answer, and affably begs the eager folk that press upon him to
come up into the committee-room.

At this a satisfied smile replaces the troubled expression
upon their faces. They feel that their difficulties are at an end;
they have got hold of the right man at last—there is something
in the very sound of the committee-room. When they get up
into this important apartment they find it quite empty. There
is a blazing fire in the grate, and littered on the long table is a
mass of forms, letters, lists, and proofs of the catalogue waiting for the judges' decision to be entered. After half an hour
or so their hopes begin to fall, and possibly someone goes

down to try and haul the secretary up into his office. The messenger finds that much-desired man in the midst of an excited group; one has him by the arm pulling him forward, another by the coat dragging him back, a third is bawling at him at the top of a powerful voice.

By-and-by, however, the secretary comes panting up into the committee-room with a letter in his hand and a pleased expression on his features. He announces that he has just had a note from his Grace, who, with his party, will be here early, and who hopes that all is going on well. Then to business, and it is surprising how quickly he disposes of it. A farmer himself, he knows exactly what is wanted, and gives the right order without a moment's hesitation. It is no new experience to him, and despite all this apparent confusion, everything presently falls into its place.

After the opening of the show there is a meeting, at which certain prizes are distributed, among them rewards to the best ploughman in the "juke's country," and to those labourers who have remained longest in the service of one master. For the graceful duty of presentation a marchioness has been selected, who, with other visitors of high social rank, has come over from that famous hunting mansion. To meet that brilliant party the whole agricultural interest has assembled. The room is crowded with tenant farmers, the entire hunting field is present. Every clergyman in the district is here, together with the gentry, and many visitors for the hunting season. Among them, shoulder to shoulder, are numbers of agricultural labourers, their wives, and daughters, dressed in their best for the occasion. After some speeches, a name is called, and an aged labourer steps forward.

His grandchildren are behind him; two of his sons, quite elderly themselves, attend him almost to the front, so that he may have to make but a few steps unsupported. The old man is frosted with age, and moves stiffly, like a piece of mechanism rather than a living creature, nor is there any expression—neither smile nor interest—upon his absolutely immobile features. He wears breeches and gaiters, and a blue coat cut in the style of two generations since. There is a small clear space in the midst of the well-dressed throng. There he stands, and for the moment the hum is hushed.

For sixty years that old man laboured upon one farm; sixty years of ploughing and sowing, sixty harvests. What excitement, what discoveries and inventions—with what giant strides

102

the world has progressed while he quietly followed the plough!
An acknowledgment has been publicly awarded to him for
that long and faithful service. He puts forth his arm; his dry,
horny fingers are crooked, and he can neither straighten nor
bend them. Not the least sign appears upon his countenance
that he is even conscious of what is passing. There is a quick
flash of jewelled rings ungloved to the light, and the reward is
placed in that claw-like grasp by the white hand of the
marchioness.

Not all the gallant cavalry of the land fearlessly charging
hedge and brook can, however, repel the invasion of a foe
mightier than their chief. Frost sometimes comes and checks
their gaiety. Snow falls, and levels every furrow, and then
Hodge going to his work in the morning can clearly trace the
track of one of his most powerful masters, Squire Reynard,
who has been abroad in the night, and, likely enough, throttled
the traditional grey goose. The farmer watches for the frozen
thatch to drip; the gentleman visiting the stable looks up dis-
consolately at the icicles dependent from the slated eave with
the same hope. The sight of a stray seagull wandering inland
is gladly welcomed, as the harbinger of drenching clouds
sweeping up on soft south-westerly gales from the nearest
coast.

The hunt is up once more, and so short are the hours of the
day in the dead of the year, that early night often closes round
the chase. From out of the gloom and the mist comes the
distant note of the horn, with a weird and old-world sound.
By-and-by the labourer, trudging homeward, is overtaken by
a hunter whose horse's neck droops with weariness. His boots
are splashed with mud, his coat torn by the thorns. He is a
visitor, vainly trying to find his way home, having come some
ten or fifteen miles across country since the morning. The
labourer shows the route—the longest way round is the
shortest at night—and as they go listens eagerly to the hunter's
tale of the run. At the cross roads they part with mutual goodwill towards each other, and a shilling, easily earned, pays
that night for the cottager's pipe and glass of ale.

CHAPTER IX

THE FINE LADY FARMER — COUNTRY GIRLS

A PAIR of well-matched bays in silver-plated harness, and driven by a coachman in livery, turn an easy curve round a corner of the narrow country road, forcing you to step on the sward by the crimson-leafed bramble bushes, and sprinkling the dust over the previously glossy surface of the newly fallen horse-chestnuts. Two ladies, elegantly dressed, lounge in the carriage with that graceful idleness—that indifferent indolence—only to be acquired in an atmosphere of luxury. Before they pass out of sight round another turn of the road it is possible to observe that one at least possesses hair of the fashionable hue, and a complexion delicately brilliant—whether wholly natural or partly aided by art. The other must be pronounced a shade less rich in the colours of youth but is perhaps even more expensively dressed. An experienced observer would at once put them down as mother and daughter, as, indeed, they are.

The polished spokes of the wheels glitter in the sun, the hoofs of the high-stepping pair beat the firm road in regular cadence, and smoothly the carriage rolls on till the brown beech at the corner hides it. But a sense of wealth, of social station, and refinement—strange and in strong contrast to the rustic scene—lingers behind, like a faint odour of perfume. There are the slow teams pulling stolidly at the ploughs—they were stopped, of course, for the carters to stare at the equipage; there are the wheat ricks; yonder a lone farmstead, and black cattle grazing in the pasture. Surely the costly bays, whose hoofs may even now be heard, must belong to the lordly owner of these broad acres—this undulating landscape of grass and stubble, which is not beautiful, but evidently fertile!

A very brief inquiry at the adjacent market town disposes of this natural conclusion. It is the carriage of a tenant farmer —but what a tenant! The shopkeepers here are eloquent, positively gratefully eloquent, in the praise of his wife and daughter. Customers!—no such customers had been known in the old borough from time immemorial. The tradesman as he speaks involuntarily pulls out his till, glances in, and shuts it up with a satisfied bang. The old style of farmer, solid and substantial enough, fumbling at the bottom of his canvas bag for silver and gold, was a crusty curmudgeon where silk and satin, kid gloves, and so forth were concerned. His wife had to look sharp after her poultry, geese, and turkeys, and such similar perquisites, in order to indulge in any innocent vanity, notwithstanding that the rent was paid and a heavy balance at the bank.

Then he would have such a length of credit—a year at least —and nowadays a shopkeeper, though sure of his money, cannot wait long for it. But to ask for the account would give mortal offence. The bill would be paid with the remark, intended to be intensely sarcastic, "Suppose you thought we was a-going to run away—eh?" and the door would never again be darkened by those antique breeches and gaiters. As for the common run of ordinary farmers, their wives bought a good deal, but wanted it cheap, and, looking at the low price of corn and the "paper" there was floating about, it did not do to allow a long bill to be run up. But the Grange people— ah! the Grange people put some life into the place. 'Money! they must have heaps of money (lowering his voice to a whisper). Why, Mrs. —— brought him a fortune, sir; why, she's got a larger income than our squire (as if it were rank treason to say so). Mr. —— has got money too, and, bless you, they holds their heads as high as their landlord's, and good reason they should. They spend as much in a week as the squire do in a month, and don't cheapen nothing, and your cheque just whenever you like to ask for it. That's what I calls gentlefolks.' For till and counter gauge long descent and heraldic quarterings, and ancestral Crusaders, far below the chink of ready money, that synonym for all the virtues.

The Grange people, indeed, are so conspicuous, that there is little secrecy about them or their affairs. The house they reside in—it cannot be called a farmstead—is a large villa-like mansion of recent erection, and fitted with every modern convenience. The real farmstead which it supplanted lies in a hollow at some distance, and is occupied by the head bailiff, for there are several employed. As the architecture of the villa is consonant with modern "taste," so too the interior is furnished in the "best style," of course under the supervision of the mistress. Mrs. —— has filled it with rosewood and ormolu, with chairs completely gilt, legs, back, seat, and all, with luxurious ottomans, "occasional" tables inlaid with mother-o'-pearl, soft carpets, polished brazen grate-fittings, semi-ecclesiastical, semi-mediæval, and so forth.

Everywhere the glitter of glass, mirrors over the mantel-pieces, mirrors let into panels, glass chiffoniers, and pendant prisms of glass round the ornamental candlesticks. Mixed with this some of the latest productions of the new English Renaissance—stiff, straight-back, plain oak chairs, such as men in armour may have used—together with Japanese screens. In short, just such a medley of artistic styles as may be seen in scores of suburban villas where money is of little account, and even in houses of higher social pretensions. There is the usual illustrated dining-room literature, the usual *bric-à-brac*, the usual cabinet series of poets. There are oil paintings on the walls; there is an immense amount of the most expensive electroplate on the dinner table; the toilet accessories in the guest chambers are "elegant" and *recherché*. The upholsterer has not been grudged.

For Mrs. —— is the daughter of a commercial man, one of the principals of a great firm, and has been accustomed to these things from her youth upwards. She has no sympathies with the past, that even yet is loth to quit its hold of the soil and of those who are bred upon it. The ancient simplicity and plainness of country life are positively repulsive to her; she associates them with poverty. Her sympathies are with warm, well-lighted rooms, full of comfort, shadowless because of the glare of much gas. She is not vulgar, just the reverse—she is a thorough lady, but she is not of the country and its traditions. She is the city and the suburb transplanted to the midst of corn, and grass, and cattle. She has her maid, skilled in the toilet, her carriage and pair and pony carriage, grooms, foot-men, just exactly as she would have done had she brought her magnificent dowry to a villa at Sydenham.

In the season, with her daughter, she goes to town, and drives daily in the park, just the same as to-day she has driven through the leaf-strewn country lane to the market town. They go also to the sea-side, and now and then to the Continent. They are, of course, invited to the local balls, and to many of the best houses on more private occasions. The ramifications of finance do not except the proudest descendants of the Crusaders, and "the firm" has its clients even among them. Bonnets come down from Madame Louise, boxes of novels from Mudie's; "Le Follet" is read in the original, and many a Parisian romance as well. Visitors are continually coming

106

and going—the carriage is perpetually backwards and forwards to the distant railway station. Friends come to the shooting, the hunting, the fishing; there is never any lack of society.

The house is full of servants, and need be, to wait upon these people. Now, in former days, and not such a great while since, the best of servants came from the country. Mistresses sought for them, and mourned when, having imbibed town ways and town independence, they took their departure to "better" themselves. But that is a thing of the past; it is gone with the disappearance of the old style of country life. Servant girls in farmhouses when young used to have a terribly hard life: hard work, hard fare, up early of a morning, stone flags under foot by day, bare boards under foot upstairs, small pay, and hard words too often. But they turned out the best of women, the healthiest and strongest, the most sought after. Now they learn a great deal about Timbuctoo, and will soon, no doubt, about Cyprus; but the "servant from the country" is no more. Nothing less will suit them to begin with than the service of the parish clergyman, then they aspire to the Grange, get there, and receive a finishing education, and can never afterwards condescend to go where a footman is not kept. They become, in short, fine ladies, whose fathers are still at the plough—ladies who at home have been glad of bread and bacon, and now cannot possibly survive without hot butcher's meat every day, and game and fish in their seasons.

But to return. Mrs. —— and her daughter have also their saddle horses. They do not often hunt, but frequently go to the meet. They have, it is true, an acceptable excuse for preferring riding to walking—the fashion of tying the dress back so tightly makes it extremely difficult for a lady to get over a country stile. The rigours of winter only enable them to appear even yet more charming in furs and sealskin. In all this the Grange people have not laid themselves open to any reproach as to the extravagance or pretension of their doings. With them it is genuine, real, unaffected: in brief, they have money, and have a right to what it can purchase.

Mr. —— is not a tenant farmer from necessity; personally he is not a farmer at all, and knows no more of shorthorns than the veriest "City" man. He has a certain taste for country life, and this is his way of enjoying it—and a very acute way, too, when you come to analyse it. The major portion of his capital is, with his wife's, in the "firm"; it is administered and employed for him by men whose family interests and his are identical, whose knowledge of business is profound, whose own capital is there too. It is a fortunate state of things, not brought about in a day, but the growth of more than one generation. Now this man, as has been remarked, has a taste for country life—that is to say, he is an enthusiast over horses—not betting, but horses in their best form. He likes to ride and drive about, to shoot, and fish, and hunt. There is nothing despicable in this, but, after the manner of men, of course he must find an excuse.

He found it in the children when they were young—two boys and one girl. It was better for them to have country air, to ride about the country lanes, and over the hills. The atmosphere altogether was more healthy, more manly than in the suburbs of a city. The excuse is a good one. Now come the means; two plans are open to him. He can buy an estate, or he can rent a large farm, or rather series of farms. If he purchases a fine estate he must withdraw his capital from business. In the first place, that would be inconvenient to old friends, and even unjust to them; in the second place, it would reduce his income most materially. Suppose we say, not for absolute exactness, but for the sake of present contrast, that capital well invested in business brings in ten per cent. The same capital invested in land brings in, say, three per cent. nominally; but is it as much in reality if you deduct those expensive improvements upon which tenants insist nowadays, and the five per cents. and ten per cents. allowed off the rent in bad years? At all events, it is certain that landlords, as a class, are investing more and more every year in business, which looks as if they did not consider land itself sufficiently remunerative. In addition, when you have bought your estate, should you subsequently wish to realise, the difficulties and delays are very trying. You cannot go down to your broker and say, "Sell me a thousand acres this morning." Capital in land is locked up.

Mr. ——, having been trained in traditions of ready money and easy transfer, does not like this prospect. But as the tenant of a great farm it is quite another matter. The larger part of his capital still remains in the "firm," and earns him a handsome income. That which is invested in stock, cattle, horses, implements, etc., is in a sense readily negotiable if ever he should desire to leave. Instead of having to pet and pamper discontented tenants, his landlord has to pet and pamper him.

He has, in fact, got the upper hand. There are plenty of land-lords who would be only too glad to get the rich Mr. —— to manure and deep-plough their lands; but there are compara-tively few Mr. ——'s whose rent-day payments can be im-plicitly relied on. Mr. ——, in point of fact, gets all the sweets of the country gentleman's life, and leaves the owner all the sour. He has no heir presumptive to check his proceedings; no law of entail to restrain him; no old settlements to bind him hand and foot; none of those hundred and one family interests to consult which accumulate in the course of years around a landed estate, and so seriously curtail the freedom of the man in possession, the head of the family. So far as liberty and financial considerations go, he is much better off than his landlord, who perhaps has a title.

Though he knows nothing of farming, he has the family instinct of accounts and figures; he audits the balance-sheets and books of his bailiff personally, and is not easily cheated. Small peculations of course go on, but nothing serious. The farms pay their way, and contribute a trifle towards the house-hold expenses. For the rest, it is taken out in liberty, out-of-door life, field sports, and unlimited horses. His wife and daughter mix in the best society the county affords, besides their annual visits to town and the sea-side: they probably enjoy thrice the liberty and pleasure they would elsewhere. Certainly they are in blooming health. The eldest son is study-ing for the law, the younger has the commercial instinct more strongly developed, and is already with the "firm." Both of them get the full benefit of country life whenever they wish; both of them feel that there is plenty of capital behind them, and not the slightest jealousy exists on account of primo-geniture. Of course they have their troubles—what family has not its troubles?—but on the whole their position is an en-viable one.

When Mrs. —— and her daughter rustle into their pew at church—placed next in honour to that of the proprietor of the soil—all eyes are turned upon them. The old-fashioned farmer's wife, who until her years pressed heavily upon her made the cheese and butter in her husband's dairy, is not so old but that her eyes can distinguish the colour of a ribbon. She may talk of such things as vanities, and unknown in her day, but for all that a pair of keen eyes criticise skirt, and trimmings, and braidings, and so forth, as displayed up in the Grange pew. Her daughter, who is quite young—for in her

mother's time farming people did not marry till late in life—
brings a still keener pair of eyes to bear in the same direction.

The bonnets from Regent Street are things to think over and
talk of. The old lady disinters her ancient finery; the girl, by
hook or crook, is determined to dress in the fashion. If one
farmer's wife is a fine lady, why not another? Do not even
the servant girls at the Grange come out twenty times finer
than people who have a canvas bag full of sovereigns at home,
and many such bags at the bank? So that the Grange people,
though they pay their way handsomely, and plough deep and
manure lavishly, and lead the van of agriculture, are not, perhaps, an unmixed good. They help on that sapping and undermining of the ancient, sturdy simplicity, the solid oak of country
character, replacing it with veneer. It is not, of course, all, or
a tenth part, their fault, or in any way traceable to them. It is
part and parcel of the widespread social changes which have
gradually been proceeding.

But the tenant farmer's wife who made the butter and
cheese, and even helped to salt bacon, where is she now?
Where are the healthy daughters that used to assist her? The
wife is a fine lady—not, indeed, with carriage and pair, but
with a dandy dog-cart at least; not with three-guinea bonnets,
but with a costly sealskin jacket. There are kid gloves on her
hands; there is a suspicion of perfume about her; there is a
rustling of silk and satin, and a waving of ostrich feathers.
The daughter is pale and interesting, and interprets Beethoven,
and paints the old mill; while a skilled person, hired at a high
price, rules in the dairy. The son rides a-hunting, and is glib
on the odds. The "offices"—such it is the fashion to call the
places in which work was formerly done—are carefully kept
in the background. The violets and snowdrops and crocuses
are rooted up, all the sweet and tender old flowers ruthlessly
eradicated, to make way for a blazing parterre after the manner
of the suburban villa—gay in the summer, in the spring a
wilderness of clay, in the autumn a howling desert of musty
evergreens.

The "civilisation" of the town has, in fact, gone out and
taken root afresh in the country. There is no reason why the
farmer should not be educated; there is no reason why his
wife should not wear a sealskin jacket, or the daughter interpret Beethoven. But the question arises, Has not some of the
old stubborn spirit of earnest work and careful prudence gone
with the advent of the piano and the oil painting? While wear-

ing the dress of a lady, the wife cannot tuck up her sleeves and
see to the butter, or even feed the poultry, which are down at
the pen across "a nasty dirty field." It is easy to say that
farming is gone to the dogs, that corn is low, and stock uncertain, and rents high, and so forth. All that is true, but
difficulties are nothing new; nor must too much be expected
from the land.

A moderate-sized farm, of from 200 to 300 acres, will no
more enable the mistress and the misses to play the fine lady
to-day than it would two generations ago. It requires work
now the same as then—steady, persevering work—and, what
is more important, prudence, economy, parsimony if you like;
nor do these necessarily mean the coarse manners of a former
age. Manners may be good, education may be good, the intellect and even the artistic sense may be cultivated, and yet
extravagance avoided. The proverb is true still: "You cannot
have your hare and cook him too." Now so many cook their
hares in the present day without even waiting to catch them
first. A euphuism has been invented to cover the wrongfulness
of this system; it is now called "discounting." The fine lady
farmers discount their husbands' corn and fat cattle, cheese
and butter, before they reach the market. By-and-by the
plough stops in the furrow, and the team is put up to auction,
and farewell is said to the old homestead for evermore.

There was no warmer welcome to be met with in life than
used to be bestowed upon the fortunate visitor to an old house
in the country where the people were not exactly farmers in
the ordinary sense, because they were sufficiently well off to
be independent, and yet made no pretence to gentility. You
dropped in quite unexpectedly and informally after a pleasant
stroll about the fields with a double-barrel, untrammelled by
any attendant. The dogs were all over cleavers sticking to their
coats, and your boots had to be wiped with a wisp of straw;
your pocket was heavy with a couple of rabbits or a hare, and
your hands black enough from powder and handling gates
and stiles. But they made you feel immediately that such
trifles were not of the slightest account.

The dogs were allowed to rush in anyhow and set to work
to lick their paws by the fire as if the house was their own.
Your apology about your boots and general state of disorder
was received with a smile by the mistress, who said she had
sons of her own, and knew their ways. Forthwith one sturdy
son seized the double-barrel, and conveyed it to a place of

safety; a second took the rabbits or the hare, that you might not be incommoded by such a lump in your pocket, and sent the game on home to your quarters by a labourer; a third relieved you of your hat. As many tall young ladies rose to offer you a seat, so that it was really difficult to know which way to turn, besides which the old grandfather with silvery hair pressed you to take his chair by the fire.

They had just sat down to the old-fashioned tea at half-past four, and in a moment there was a cup and plate ready. The tea had a fragrant scent, warm and grateful after the moist atmosphere of the meadows, smelling of decaying leaves. The mistress suggested that a nip of brandy might improve it, thinking that tea was hardly strong enough for a man. But that was declined; for what could be more delicious than the sweet, thick cream poured in by a liberal hand? A fine ham had already been put on the table, as if by magic—the girls really seemed to anticipate everything you could possibly want. As for the butter, it was exquisite, and so, too, the home-baked bread, the more so because only touched in the processes of preparing by the whitest and softest of hands. Such simple things become luxuries when brought to perfection by loving care. The old dog on the hearthrug came thrusting his nose into your hands, making almost too great friends, being perfectly well aware (cunning old fellow) that he could coax more out of a visitor than one of the family, who knew how he had stuffed all day.

Over all there was an atmosphere of welcome, a genial brightness. The young men were anxious to tell you where the best sport could be got. The young ladies had a merry, genuine, unaffected smile—clearly delighted to see you, and not in the least ashamed of it. They showed an evident desire to please, without a trace of an *arrière pensée*. Tall, well-developed, in the height of good health, the bloom upon the cheek and the brilliant eyes formed a picture irresistibly charming. But it was the merry laugh that so long dwelt in the memory—nothing so thoroughly enchants one as the woman who laughs from her heart in the joyousness of youth. They joined freely in the conversation, but did not thrust themselves forward. They were, of course, eager for news of the far away world, but not a hint was breathed of those social scandals which now form our favourite gossip. From little side remarks concerning domestic matters it was evident that they were well acquainted with household duties. Indeed, they assisted to

112

remove the things from the table without any consciousness that it was a menial task.

It was not long after tea before, drawing round the fire, pipes were produced, and you were asked to smoke. Of course you declined on account of the ladies, but it was none the less pleasant to be asked. There was the great secret of it all—the genuine, liberal, open-handed and open-hearted proffering of all the house contained to the guest. And it was none the less an amusing conversation because each of the girls candidly avowed her own opinions upon such topics as were started— blushing a little, it is true, if you asked the reason for the opinion, for ladies are not always quite ready with the why and wherefore. But the contrast of character, the individuality displayed, gave a zest and interest to the talk; so that the hour wore late before you were aware of it. Then, if you would go, two, at least, of the three boys piloted you by the best and cleanest route, and did not wish you farewell till you were in the straight road. This was not so many years ago.

To-day, if you call at such a country house, how strangely different is the reception! None of the family come to the door to meet you. A servant shows you into a parlour—drawing-room is the proper word now—well carpeted and furnished in the modern style. She then takes your name—what a world of change is shown in that trifling piece of etiquette! By-and-by, after the proper interval, the ladies enter in morning costume, not a stray curl allowed to wander from its stern bands, nature rigidly repressed, decorum—"Society"—in every flounce and trimming. You feel that you have committed a solecism coming on foot, and so carrying the soil on your boots from the fields without into so elegant an apartment. Visitors are obviously expected to arrive on wheels, and in correct trim for company. A remark about the crops falls on barren ground; a question concerning the dairy, ignorantly hazarded, is received with so much *hauteur* that at last you see such subjects are considered vulgar. Then a touch of the bell, and decanters of port and sherry are produced, and your wine presented to you on an electro salver, together with sweet biscuits. It is the correct thing to sip one glass and eat one biscuit.

The conversation is so insipid, so entirely confined to the merest platitudes, that it becomes absolutely a relief to escape. You are not pressed to stay and dine, as you would have been in the old days—not because there is a lack of hospitality, but because they would prefer a little time for preparation in order that the dinner might be got up in polite style. So you depart —chilled and depressed. No one steps with you to open the gate and exchange a second farewell, and express a cordial wish to see you again there. You feel that you must walk in measured step and place your hat precisely perpendicular, for the eyes of "Society" are upon you. What a comfort when you turn a corner behind the hedge and can thrust your hands into your pockets and whistle!

The young ladies, however, still possess one thing which they cannot yet destroy—the good constitution and the rosy look derived from ancestors whose days were spent in the field under the glorious sunshine and the dews of heaven. They worry themselves about it in secret and wish they could appear more ladylike—*i.e.* thin and white. Nor can they feel quite so languid and indifferent, and *blasé* as they desire. Thank Heaven they cannot! But they have succeeded in obliterating the faintest trace of character, and in suppressing the slightest approach to animation. They have all got just the same opinions on the same topics—that is to say, they have none at all; the idea of a laugh has departed. There is a dead line of uniformity. But if you are sufficiently intimate to enter unto the inner life of the place it will soon be apparent that they either are or wish to appear up to the "ways of the world."

They read the so-called social journals, and absorb the gossip, tittle-tattle, and personalities—absorb it because they have no means of comparison or of checking the impression it produces of the general loose tone of society. They know all about it, much more than you do. No turn of the latest divorce case or great social exposure has escaped them, and the light, careless way in which it is the fashion nowadays to talk openly of such things, as if they were got up like a novel—only with living characters—for amusement, has penetrated into this distant circle. But then they have been to half the leading watering-places—from Brighton to Scarborough; as for London, it is an open book to them; the railways have long dissipated the pleasing mysteries that once hung over the metropolis. Talk of this sort is, of course, only talk; still it is not a satisfactory sign of the times. If the country girl is no longer the hoyden that swung on the gates and romped in the hay, neither has she the innocent thought of the olden days.

At the same time our friends are greatly devoted to the Church—old people used to attend on Sundays, as a sacred and time-honoured duty, but the girls leave them far behind, for they drive up in a pony carriage to the distant church at least twice a week besides. They talk of matins and even-song; they are full of vestments, and have seen "such lovely things" in that line. At Christmas and Easter they are mainly instrumental in decorating the interior till it becomes perfectly gaudy with colour, and the old folk mutter and shake their heads. Their devotion in getting hothouse flowers is quite touching. One is naturally inclined to look with a liberal eye upon what is capable of a good construction. But is all this quite spontaneous? Has the new curate nothing at all to do with it? Is it not considered rather the correct thing to be "High" in views, and even to manifest an Ultramontane tendency? There is a rather too evident determination to go to the extreme—the girls are clearly bent upon thrusting themselves to the very front of the parish, so that no one shall be talked of but the Misses ——. Anything is seized upon that will afford an opening for posing before the world of the parish, whether it be an extreme fashion in dress or in ritual.

And the parish is splitting up into social cliques. These girls, the local leaders of fashion, hold their heads far above those farmers' sons who bear a hand in the field. No one is eligible who takes a share in manual work; not even to be invited to the house, or even to be acknowledged if met in the road. The Misses ——, whose papa is well-to-do, and simply rides round on horseback to speak to the men with his steam-plough, could not possibly demean themselves to acknowledge the existence of the young men who actually handle a fork in the haymaking time. Nothing less than the curate is worthy of their smile. A very great change has come over country society in this way. Of course, men (and women) with money were always more eligible than those without; but it is not so very long ago that one and all—well-to-do and poor—had one bond in common. Whether they farmed large or small acres, all worked personally. There was no disgrace in the touch of the plough—rather the contrary; now it is contamination itself.

The consequence is that the former general goodwill and acquaintanceship is no more. There are no friendly meetings; there is a distinct social barrier between the man and the woman who labours and the one who does not. These fashionable young ladies could not possibly even go into the hayfield because the sun would spoil their complexion, they refresh them-

selves with aërated waters instead. They could not possibly
enter the dairy because it smells so nasty. They would not
know their father's teams if they met them on the road. As
for speaking to the workpeople—the idea would be too
absurd!

Once on a time a lift in the waggon just across the wet turf
to the macadamised road—if it chanced to be going that way
—would have been looked upon as a fortunate thing. The
Misses —— would indeed stare if one of their papa's carters
touched his hat and suggested that they should get up. They
have a pony carriage and groom of their own. He drives the
milk-cart to the railway station in the morning; in the afternoon he dons the correct suit and drives the Misses —— into
the town to shopping. Now there exists a bitter jealousy
between the daughters of the tradesmen in the said town and
these young ladies. There is a race between them as to which
shall be first in fashion and social rank. The Misses —— know
very well that it galls their rivals to see them driving about so
grandly half the afternoon up and down the streets, and to see
the big local people lift their hats, as the banker, with whom,
of course, the large farmer has intimate dealings. All this is
very little; on paper it reads mean and contemptible; but in
life it is real—in life these littlenesses play a great part. The
Misses —— know nothing of those long treasured recipes
formerly handed down in old country houses, and never enter
the kitchen. No doubt, if the fashion for teaching cooking
presently penetrates into the parish, they will take a leading
part, and with much show and blowing of trumpets instruct
the cottager how to boil the pot. Anything, in short, that
happens to be the rage will attract them, but there is little that
is genuine about them, except the eagerness for a new excitement.

What manner of men shall accept these ladies as their
future helpmates? The tenant farmers are few and far between
that could support their expenditure upon dress, the servants
they would require, and last, but not least, the waste which
always accompanies ignorance in household management.
Nor, indeed, do they look for tenant farmers, but hope for
something higher in the scale.

The Misses —— are fortunate in possessing a "papa"
sufficiently well-to-do to enable them to live in this manner.
But there are hundreds of young ladies whose fathers have not
got so much capital in their farms, while what they have is

perhaps borrowed. Of course these girls help cheerfully in
the household, in the dairy, and so forth? No. Some are forced
by necessity to assist in the household with unwilling hands;
but few, indeed, enter the dairy. All dislike the idea of manual
labour, though never so slight. Therefore they acquire a
smattering of knowledge, and go out as governesses. They earn
but a small stipend in that profession, because they have
rarely gone through a sufficiently strict course of study themselves. But they would rather live with strangers, accepting a
position which is often invidious, than lift a hand to work at
home, so great is the repugnance to manual labour. These,
again, have no domestic knowledge (beyond that of teaching
children), none of cooking, or general household management. If they marry a tenant farmer of their own class, with
but small capital, they are too often a burden financially.
Whence comes this intense dislike to hard work—this preference for the worst paid head work? It is not confined, of
course, to the gentler sex. No more striking feature of modern
country life can be found.

You cannot blame these girls, whether poor or moderately
well-to-do, for thinking of something higher, more refined,
and elevating than the cheese-tub or the kitchen. It is natural,
and it is right, that they should wish to rise above that old,
dull, dead level in which their mothers and grandmothers
worked from youth to age. The world has gone on since then
—it is a world of education, books, and wider sympathies.
In all this they must and ought to share. The problem is
how to enjoy the intellectual progress of the century and yet
not forfeit the advantages of the hand labour and the thrift
of our ancestors? How shall we sit up late at night, burning
the midnight oil of study, and yet rise with the dawn, strong
from sweet sleep, to guide the plough? One good thing must
be scored down to the credit of the country girls of the day.
They have done much to educate the men. They have shamed
them out of the old rough, boorish ways; compelled them to
abandon the former coarseness, to become more gentlemanly
in manner. By their interest in the greater world of society,
literature, art, and music (more musical publications probably
are now sold for the country in a month than used to be in a
year), they have made the somewhat narrow-sighted farmer
glance outside his parish. If the rising generation of tenant
farmers have lost much of the bigoted provincial mode of
thought, together with the provincial pronunciation, it is

undoubtedly due to the influence of the higher ideal of woman-hood that now occupies their minds. And this is a good work to have accomplished.

CHAPTER X

MADEMOISELLE, THE GOVER-NESS

A COUNTRY "roadside" railway station seemed deserted upon a warm August afternoon. It was all but concealed on that level ground by the hedges and trees of the fields with which it was surrounded. There was no sound of man or wheels, and nothing moving upon the platform. On the low green banks of the rail, where the mast-like telegraph poles stood, the broad leaves of the coltsfoot almost covered the earth, and were dusty with the sand whirled up an hour since behind the rushing express. By the footpath, higher up under the close-cropped hedge, the yarrow flourished, lifting its white flower beside the trodden soil. The heavy boots of the platelayers walking to and fro to their work on the permanent way brushed against it, and crushed the venturous fibres of the creeping cinquefoil that stretched into the path. From the yellow standing wheat the sparrows rose in a bevy, and settled upon the hedge, chirping merrily. Farther away, where a meadow had been lately mown, the swallows glided to and fro, but just above the short grass, round and round, under the shadow of the solitary oaks. Over the green aftermath is the swallow's favourite haunt when the day, though passing fair, does not look like settled weather. For lack of such weather the reapers have not yet entered the ripening corn.

But, for the hour, the sun shines brightly, and a narrow line along the upper surfaces of the metals, burnished by the polishing friction of a thousand wheels, glints like silver under the rays. The red brick of the booking-office looks redder and more staring under the fierce light. The door is locked, and there is no waiting-room in which to take shelter; nothing but a projecting roof over a part of the platform. On the lintel is the stationmaster's name painted in small white letters, like the name of the landlord over the doorway of an inn. Two corded boxes lie on the platform, and near them stand half a dozen rusty milk tins, empty. With the exception of a tortoiseshell cat basking in the sunshine, there seems nothing living in the station, and the long endless rails stretching on either side in a straight line are vacant. For hours during the day the place slumbers, and a passenger gliding by in the express may well wonder why a station was built at all in the midst of trees and hedges without so much as a single visible house.

But by night and very early in the morning there is bustle enough. Then the white painted cattle pen yonder, from which the animals are forced into the cattle trucks, is full of frightened beasts, lowing doubtfully, and only goaded in by the resounding blows upon their backs. Then the sheep file in in more patient ranks, but also doubtful and bleating as they go. An engine snorts to and fro, shunting coal waggons on to the siding—coal for the traction engines, and to be consumed in threshing out the golden harvest around. Signalmen, with red and green lights, rush hither and thither, the bull's-eyes now concealed by the trucks, and now flashing out brightly like strange will-o'-the-wisps. At intervals long and heavy goods trains go by, causing the solid earth to tremble.

Presently the sun rises over the distant hills, and the red arms of the signals stand out clearly defined, and then the noise of wheels, the shouts of the drivers, and the quick sound of hoofs betoken the approach of the milk carts with their freight for the early morning train. From the platform it is out of sight; but a few yards from the gate a small inn is hidden under the tall elms of the hedgerow. It has sprung up since the railway came, and is called the Railway Hotel. It proffers good stabling, and even a fly and posting for the passenger who finds himself set down at that lonely place—a mere road—without the certainty of a friendly carriage meeting him. The porter may, perhaps, be taking his glass within. The inspector, or stationmaster (whichever may be technically correct), now that the afternoon express has gone safely through, has strolled up the line to his garden to see how his potatoes are getting on. He knows full well that the slow, stopping train despatched just after it will not reach his station for at least an hour.

Outside the "Hotel" stands a pony cart—a gaily coloured

travelling rug lies across the seat, and the pony, a perfect little beauty, is cropping the grass by the hedge side. By and by a countryman comes up the road, evidently a labourer dressed in his best—he hastens to the "Hotel," instead of to the station, and finds from the porter that he is at least twenty minutes too soon. Then a waggon arrives, and stops while the carter drinks. Presently the porter and the labourer stroll together over to the platform, and after them a young fellow —a farmer's son, not yet a man but more than a boy—comes out and rearranges the travelling rug in the pony cart. He then walks on to the platform, whistling defiantly with his hands in his pockets, as if he had got an unpleasant duty to perform, but was not going to be intimidated. He watches the station-master unlock the booking-office, and follows him in out of idle curiosity.

It is booking-office, parcel-office, waiting-room and all combined, and the telegraph instrument is there, too, some of the needles blocked over with a scrap of paper. The place is crammed with sacks, bags, boxes, parcels and goods mixed together, such as ironwork for agricultural machines, and in a corner lies a rick-cloth smelling strongly of tar like the rigging of a ship. On the counter, for there is no sliding window as usual at large stations, stands the ticket-stamping machine, surrounded with piles of forms, invoices, notices, letters, and the endless documents inseparable from railway business, all printed on a peculiar paper with a faint shade of yellow.

Somebody says "A' be coming," and the young farmer walks out to watch the white steam now just visible far away over the trees. The train runs round the curve on to the straight, and the engine in front grows gradually larger and larger as it comes nearer, visibly vibrating till the brake draws it up at the platform.

Master Jack has no difficulty in identifying the passenger he has come to meet. His sister, a governess, coming home for a holiday, is the only person that alights, and the labourer, dressed for the occasion, is the only one who gets in. No sooner is he in than he gapes out of the window open-mouthed at Miss S——. She wears a light Ulster to protect her dress from the dust and dirt of travel. Her fashionable hat has an air of the West End; her gloved hand holds a dainty little bag; she steps as those must do who wear tight dresses and high heels to their boots. Up goes her parasol instantly to shade her delicate complexion from the glaring sun. Master Jack does

not even take her hand, or kiss her; he looks her up and down
with a kind of contemptuous admiration, nods, and asks how
much luggage? He has, you see, been repulsed for "gush"
on previous occasions. Mademoiselle points to her luggage,
which the porter, indeed, has already taken out. He worked in
his boyhood on her father's farm, and attends upon her with
cheerful alacrity. She gives him a small coin, but looks the
other way, without a sign of recognition. The luggage is
placed in the pony cart.

Mademoiselle gets in without so much as patting the beautiful little creature in the shafts. Her ticket is the only first-class
ticket that has been given up at that lonely station all the week.
"Do make haste," she remarks petulantly as her brother
pauses to speak to a passing man who looks like a dealer.
Master Jack turns the pony cart, and away they go rattling
down the road. The porter, whilom an agricultural labourer,
looks after them with a long and steady stare. It is not the
first time he has seen this, but he can hardly take it in yet.

"She do come the lady grandish, don't her?" the dealer
remarks meditatively. "Now her father——"

"Ay," interrupts the porter, "he be one of the old sort;
but she——" he cannot get any further for lack of an appropriate illustration. The arrival of mademoiselle periodically
takes their breath away at that little place.

As the pair rattle along in the pony trap there is for a time
a total silence. Mademoiselle looks neither to the right nor
the left, and asks after nobody. She does not note the subtle
tint of bronze that has begun to steal over the wheat, nor the
dark discoloured hay, witness of rough weather, still lying
in the meadows. Her face—it is a very pretty face—does not
light up with any enthusiasm as well-remembered spots come
into sight. A horseman rides round a bend of the road, and
meets them—he stares hard at her—she takes no heed. It is a
young farmer, an old acquaintance, anxious for some sign
of recognition. After he has passed he lifts his hat, like a true
countryman, unready at the moment. As for the brother, his
features express gathering and almost irrepressible disgust.
He kicks with his heavy boots, he whistles, and once now and
then gives a species of yell. Mademoiselle turns up her pretty
nose, and readjusts her chevron gloves.

"Have you not got any cuffs, Jack?" she asks, "your wrists
look so bare without them."

Jack makes no reply. Another silence. Presently he points

with an expression meant to be sardonic at a distant farm-house with his whip.

"Jenny's married," he says, full well aware that this announcement will wake her up, for there had been of old a sort of semi-feud or rivalry between the two girls, daughters of neighbouring farmers, and both with pretensions to good looks.

"Who to?" she asks eagerly.

"To old Billy L——; lots of tin."

"Pshaw!" replies mademoiselle. "Why, he's sixty, a nasty, dirty old wretch."

"He has plenty of money," suggests Jack.

"What *you* think plenty of money, perhaps. He is nothing but a farmer," as if a farmer was quite beneath her notice.

Just then a farmer rode out into the road from the gateway of a field, and Jack pulled up the pony. The farmer was stout, elderly, and florid; he appeared fairly well-to-do by his dress, but was none too particular to use his razor regularly. Yet there was a tenderness—almost a pathos—in the simple words he used:—"Georgie, dear, come home?" "Yes, papa," and she kissed his scrubby chin as he bent down from his horse. He would not go to the station to meet her; but he had been waiting about behind the hedge for an hour to see her come along. He rode beside the pony cart, but Georgie did not say anything more, or ask after any one else.

As they turned a corner the farmer pointed ahead. "There's your mother, Georgie, looking over the garden wall." The yearning mother had been there these two hours, knowing that her darling could not arrive before a certain time, and yet unable in her impatience to stay within. Those old eyes were dim with tears under the spectacles as Georgie quietly kissed her forehead, and then suddenly with something like generous feeling, her lips.

They went in, an old pointer, whose days in the stubble were nearly over, following close at Georgie's heels, but without obtaining a pat for his loving memory. The table was spread for tea—a snowy cloth, the whitest of bread, the most delicious golden butter, the ham fresh cooked, as Georgie might be hungry, the thick cream, the silver teapot, polished for Georgie, and the bright flowers in the vase before her plate. The window was open, with its view of the old, old hills, and a breath of summer air came in from the meadow.

The girl glanced round, frowned, and went upstairs to her room without a word, passing on the landing the ancient clock in its tall case, ticking loud and slow.

And this was "home." The whole place jarred upon her, fresh as she was from a fine house in Belgravia. The sitting-room beneath, which she had so quickly left, looked cheerful and homely, but it was that very homeliness that jarred upon her. The teapot was real silver, but it was of old-fashioned shape. Solid as the furniture was, and still after so many years of service worth money, yet it was chipped by kicks from iron-shod boots, which had also worn the dingy carpet bare. There was an absence of the nick-nacks that strew the rooms of people in "Society." There was not even a bell-handle to pull; if you wanted the maid of all work, you must open the door and call to her. These little things, trifles as they may be, repelled her. It was a bitter cup to her to come "home."

Mr. S—— was a farmer of fair means, and, compared with many of his neighbours, well-to-do, and well connected. But he was still a yeoman only, and personally made pretensions to nothing more. Though he himself had received little or no education, he quite saw the value of it, and was determined that his children should be abreast of the times. Accordingly, so soon as Georgie grew old enough, a governess with high recommendations, and who asked what the farmer then thought a high price (he knows more about such things now!) was had down from London. Of course the rudimentary A B C of learning could just as well have been imparted by an ordinary person, but Mr. and Mrs. S—— had a feeling which they could not perhaps have expressed in words, that it was not so much the actual reading and writing, and French and music, and so on, as a social influence that was needed to gradually train the little country girl into a young lady fit to move in higher society.

The governess did her work thoroughly. Georgie was not allowed to walk in the wet grass, to climb up the ladder on to the half-completed hayrick, and romp under the rick-cloth, to paddle with naked feet in the shallow brook, or any other of the things that country children have done from time immemorial. Such things she was taught were not ladylike, and, above all, she was kept away from the cottage people. She was not permitted to enter their doors, to converse with the women, or to watch the carter with his horses. Such vulgar folk and their vulgar dialect were to be carefully avoided. Nor

must she get into a hedge after a bird's nest, lest she should tear her frock.

It was not long before the governess really ruled the house. The farmer felt himself totally unable to interfere in these matters; they were outside his experience altogether. His wife did not like it, but for Georgie's sake she gave up her former habits, and endeavoured to order the house according to the ideas of the governess from London. The traditions, as it were, of the place were upset. It was not a solitary instance, the same thing has happened in scores of farmhouses to a more or less degree. Mr. S—— all his life had ridden on horseback, or driven a gig, which did very well for him and his wife. But the governess thought Georgie ought to learn to ride and drive, and gigs were so much out of fashion. So the pony cart and pony were purchased for her, and in this she went into the distant market town twice or more weekly. Sometimes it was for shopping, sometimes to fetch household goods, sometimes to see friends; any excuse answered very well. The governess said, and really believed, that it was better for Georgie to be away from the farm as much as possible, to see town people (if only a country town), and to learn their ways.

The many cheap illustrated papers giving the last details of fashionable costumes were, of course, brought home to be carefully read in the evenings. These publications have a large circulation now in farmhouses. Naturally Georgie soon began to talk about, and take an interest—as girls will do—in the young gentlemen of the town, and who was and who was not eligible. As for the loud-voiced young farmers, with their slouching walk, their ill-fitting clothes, and stupid talk about cows and wheat, they were intolerable. A banker's clerk at least—nothing could be thought of under a clerk in the local banks; of course, his salary was not high, but then his "position." The retail grocers and bakers and such people were quite beneath one's notice—low, common persons. The "professional tradesmen" (whatever that may be) were decidedly better, and could be tolerated. The solicitors, bank managers, one or two brewers (wholesale—nothing retail), large corn factors or coal merchants, who kept a carriage of some kind—these formed the select society next under, and, as it were, surrounding the clergy and gentry. Georgie at twelve years old looked at least as high as one of these; a farmhouse was to be avoided above all things.

124

As she grew older her mind was full of the local assembly ball. The ball had been held for forty years or more, and had all that time been in the hands of the exclusive upper circles of the market town. They only asked their own families, relations (not the poor ones), and visitors. When Georgie was invited to this ball it was indeed a triumph. Her poor mother cried with pleasure over her ball dress. Poor woman, she was a good, a too good, mother, but she had never been to a ball. There were, of course, parties, picnics, and so on, to which Georgie, having entered the charmed circle, was now asked; and thus her mind from the beginning centred in the town. The sheep-fold, the cattle-pen, the cheese-tub, these were thrust aside. They did not interest her, she barely understood the meaning when her father took the first prize at an important cattle show. What So-and-so would wear at the flower show, where all the select would come, much more nearly concerned her.

At the high-class academy where her education was finished the same process went on. The other girls quickly made her thoroughly understand (a bitter knowledge) that the great people in the little market town, the very richest of them, were but poor in comparison with their papas. Their papas were in the "City," or on "'Change," and had as many thousands a year as the largest farmer she knew could reckon hundreds. Georgie felt ashamed of her papa, recollecting his crumpled old hat, and his scrubby chin. Being really a nice girl, under the veneer that was so industriously placed upon her, she made friends among her fellow scholars, and was invited to more than one of their grand homes in Kensington and the suburbs of London. There she learned all the pomp of villa life, which put into the shade the small incomes which displayed their miserable vanities in the petty market town. Footmen, butlers, late dinners, wines, carriages, the ceaseless gossip of "Society" were enough to dazzle the eyes of a girl born so near the cowshed. The dresses she had to wear to mix with these grand friends cost a good deal—her parents sacrificing their own comforts for her advantage—and yet, in comparison with the beautiful costumes she saw, they seemed shabby.

Georgie was so far fortunate as to make friends of some of the elder people, and when she had passed her examinations, and obtained the diplomas and certificates which are now all essential, through their interest she obtained at starting a

very high salary. It was not long before she received as much as sixty or seventy pounds a year. It was not only that she really was a clever and accomplished girl, but her recommendations were influential. She was employed by wealthy people, who really did not care what they paid so long as their children were in good hands. Now to the old folk at home, and to the neighbours, this seemed an immense salary for a girl, especially when the carriage, the footmen, the wines, and late dinners, and so on, were taken into consideration. The money, however, was of very little use to her. She found it necessary to dress equal to her place. She had to have several dresses to wear, according to the time of day, and she had to have new ones very often, or she might be told petulantly and pointedly by her mistress that "one gets so weary of seeing the same dresses every day." Instead of the high salary leaving a handsome profit, her father had occasionally to pay a stiff bill for her. But then the "position"—look at the "position" and the society.

Georgie, in process of time, went to Scotland, to Paris, the South of France, to Rome, and Naples. Being a discreet girl, and having a winning manner, she became as much a companion to her mistress as governess, and thus saw and heard more of the world than she would otherwise have done. She saw some very grand people indeed occasionally. After this, after the Continent, and, above all, London in the season, the annual visit to the old farmhouse came to be a bitter time of trial. Georgie had come home now for a few days only, to ask for money, and already before she had scarcely spoken had rushed upstairs to hide her feeling of repulsion in the privacy of her room.

Her welcome had been warm, and she knew that under the rude exterior it was more than warm; but the absence of refinement jarred upon her. It all seemed so uncouth. She shrank from the homely rooms; the very voice of her mother, trembling with emotion, shocked her ear, unaccustomed to country pronunciation. She missed the soft accents of the drawing-room. From her window she could see nothing but the peaceful fields—the hateful green trees and hedges, the wheat, and the hateful old hills. How miserable it was not to be born to Grosvenor Square!

Georgie's case was, of course, exceptional in so far as her "success" was concerned. She possessed good natural parts, discretion, and had the advantage of high-class recommendations. But apart from her "success," her case was not exceptional. The same thing is going on in hundreds of farmhouses. The daughters from the earliest age are brought up under a system of education the practical tendency of which is to train their minds out of the associations of farming. When later on they go out to teach they are themselves taught by the social surroundings of the households into which they enter to still more dislike the old-fashioned ways of agriculture. Take twenty farmers' families, where there are girls, and out of that twenty fifteen will be found to be preparing for a scholastic life. The farmer's daughter does not like the shop-counter, and, as she cannot stay at home, there is nothing left to her but the profession of governess. Once thoroughly imbued with these "social" ideas, and a return to the farm is almost impossible. The result is a continuous drain of women out of agriculture—of the very women best fitted in the beginning to be the helpmate of the farmer. In no other calling is the assistance of the wife so valuable; it is not too much to say that part at least of the decadence of agriculture is owing to the lack of women willing to devote themselves as their mothers did before them. It follows that by degrees the farming caste is dying out. The sons go to the city, the daughters go to the city; in a generation, or little more, a once well-known farming family becomes extinct so far as agriculture is concerned.

How could such a girl as poor Georgie, looking out of window at the hateful fields, and all at discord with the peaceful scene, settle down as the mistress of a lonely farmhouse?

CHAPTER XI

FLEECEBOROUGH—A "DESPOT"

AN agricultural district, like a little kingdom, has its own capital city. The district itself is as well defined as if a frontier line had been marked out around it, with sentinels and barriers across the roads, and special tolls and duties. Yet an ordinary traveller, upon approaching, fails to perceive the difference, and may, perhaps, drive right through the territory without knowing it. The fields roll on and rise into the hills, the hills sink again into a' plain, just the same as elsewhere; there are cornfields and meadows; villages and farmsteads, and no visible boundary. Nor is it recognised upon the map. It does not fit into any political or legal limit; it is neither a county, half a county, a hundred, or police division. But to the farmer it is a distinct land. If he comes from a distance he will at once notice little peculiarities in the fields, the crops, the stock, or customs, and will immediately inquire if it be not such and such a place that he has heard of. If he resides within thirty miles or so he will ever since boyhood have heard "the uplands" talked of as if it were a separate country, as distinct as France. Cattle from the uplands, sheep, horses, labourers, corn or hay, or anything and anybody from thence, he has grown up accustomed to regard almost as foreign.

There is good reason, from an agricultural point of view, for this. The district, with its capital city, Fleeceborough, really is distinct, well marked, and defined. The very soil and substrata are characteristic. The products are wheat, and cattle, and sheep, the same as elsewhere, but the proportions of each, the kind of sheep, the traditionary methods and farm customs are separate and marked. The rotation of crops is different, the agreements are on a different basis, the very gates to the fields have peculiar fastenings, not used in other places. Instead of hedges, the fields, perhaps, are often divided by dry stone walls, on which, when they have become old, curious plants may sometimes be found. For the flora, too, is distinct; you may find herbs here that do not exist a little way off, and on the other hand, search how you will, you will not discover one single specimen of a simple flower which strews the meadows elsewhere.

Here the very farmhouses are built upon a different plan, and with different materials; the barns are covered with old stone slates, instead of tiles or thatch. The people are a nation amongst themselves. Their accent is peculiar and easily recognised, and they have their own folklore, their own household habits, particular dainties, and way of life. The tenant farmers, the millers, the innkeepers, and every Hodge within "the uplands" (not by any means all hills)—in short, every one is a citizen of Fleeceborough. Hodge may tend his flock on distant pastures, may fodder his cattle in far-away meadows, and dwell in little hamlets hardly heard of, but all the same he is a

Fleeceborough man. It is his centre; thither he looks for everything.

The place is a little market town, the total of whose population in the census records sounds absurdly small; yet it is a complete world in itself; a capital city, with its kingdom and its ruler, for the territory is practically the property of a single family. Enter Fleeceborough by whichever route you will, the first object that fixes the attention is an immensely high and endless wall. If you come by carriage one way, you skirt it for a long distance; if you come the other, you see it as you pass through the narrow streets every now and then at the end of them, closing the prospect and overtopping the lesser houses. By railway it is conspicuous from the windows; and if you walk about the place, you continually come upon it. It towers up perpendicular and inaccessible, like the curtain wall of an old fortification: here and there the upper branches of some great cedar or tall pine just show above it. One or more streets for a space run conterminous with it—the wall on one side, the low cottage-houses on the other, and their chimneys are below the coping. It does not really encircle the town, yet it seems everywhere, and is the great fact of the place.

If you wander about examining this wall, and wondering where it begins and where it ends, and what is inside, you may perchance come upon a gateway of noble proportions. It is open, but one hesitates to pass through, despite the pleasant vista of trees and green sward beyond. There is a watchman's wooden hut, and the aged sentinel is reading his newspaper in the shadow, his breast decorated with medal and clasp, that tell of honourable service. A scarlet-coated soldier may, too, be strolling thereabout, and the castellated top of a barrack-like building near at hand is suggestive of military force. You hesitate, but the warden invites you to walk at your leisure under the old trees, and along the endless glades. If you enter, you pass under the metal scrollwork of the iron gates, and, above, the gilded circle of a coronet glistens in the sunshine. These are the private demesnes of a prince and ruler of Hodge—the very highest and most powerful of his masters in that part of the country. The vast wall encloses his pleasure-grounds and mansion; the broad iron gates give access to mile after mile of park and wood, and the decorated warden or pensioner has but to open them for the free entry of all Fleeceborough and her citizens. Of course the position of the barrack is a mere accident, yet it gives an air of power and authority—the place is really as open, the beautiful park as common and accessible as the hill-top under the sky. A peer only at Westminster, here he is a prince, whose dominions are almost co-extensive with the horizon; and this, the capital city, is for the most part his.

Far away stretches that little kingdom, with its minor towns of villages, hamlets, and farms. Broad green meadows, where the cattle graze beside the streams and in the plains; rolling uplands, ploughed and sown, where the barley flourishes; deep rich wheatlands; high hills and shadowy woods; grey church towers; new glaring schools; quiet wayside inns, and ancient farmhouses tenanted for generations by the same families.

Farmers have long since discovered that it is best to rent under a very large owner, whether personal as in this case, or impersonal as a college or corporation. A very large owner like this can be, and is, more liberal. He puts up sheds, and he drains, and improves, and builds good cottages for the labourers. Provided, of course, that no serious malpractice comes to light, he, as represented by his steward, never interferes, and the tenant is personally free. No one watches his goings out and comings in; he has no sense of an eye for ever looking over the park wall. There is a total absence of the grasping spirit sometimes shown. The farmer does not feel that he will be worried to his last shilling. In case of unfavourable seasons the landlord makes no difficulty in returning a portion of the rent; he anticipates such an application. Such immense possessions can support losses which would press most heavily upon comparatively small properties. At one side of the estate the soil perchance is light and porous, and is all the better for rain; on the other, half across the county, or quite, the soil is deep and heavy and naturally well watered and flourishes in dry summers. So that there is generally some one prospering if another suffers, and thus a balance is maintained.

A reserve of wealth has, too, slowly accumulated in the family coffers, which, in exceptional years, tides the owner over with little or no appreciable inconvenience. With an income like this, special allowances, even generous allowances, can be and are made, and so the tenants cease to feel that their landlord is living out of their labour. The agreements are just; there is no rapacity. Very likely the original lease or arrangement has expired half a century since; but no one troubles to renew it. It is well understood that no change

will be effected. The tenure is as steady as if the tenant had
an Act of Parliament at his back.

When men have once settled, they and their descendants
remain, generation after generation. By degrees their sons and
sons' descendants settle too, and the same name occurs perhaps
in a dozen adjacent places. It is this fixed unchangeable
character of the district which has enabled the mass of the
tenants not indeed to become wealthy, but to acquire a solid,
substantial standing. In farming affairs money can be got
together only in the slow passage of years; experience has
proved that beyond a doubt. These people have been stationary for a length of time, and the moss of the proverb has
grown around them. They walk sturdily, and look all men in
the face; their fathers put money in the purse. Times are hard
here as everywhere, but if they cannot, for the present
season, put more in that purse, its contents are not, at all
events, much diminished, and enable them to maintain the
same straightforward manliness and independence. By and
by, they know there will come the chink of the coin again.

When the tenant is stationary, the labourer is also. He stays
in the same cottage on the same farm all his life, his descendants remain and work for the same tenant family. He can
trace his descent in the locality for a hundred years. From
time immemorial both Hodge and his immediate employers
have looked towards Fleeceborough as their capital. Hodge
goes in to the market in charge of his master's sheep, his wife
trudges in for household necessaries. All the hamlet goes in
to the annual fairs. Every cottager in the hamlet knows somebody in the town; the girls go there to service, the boys to get
employment. The little village shops obtain their goods from
thence. All the produce—wheat, barley, oats, hay, cattle, and
sheep—is sent into the capital to the various markets held
there. The very ideas held in the villages by the inhabitants
come from Fleeceborough; the local papers published there
are sold all round, and supply them with news, arguments, and
the politics of the little kingdom. The farmers look to Fleeceborough just as much or more. It is a religious duty to be seen
there on market days. Not a man misses being there; if he is
not visible, his circle note it, and guess at various explanations.

Each man has his own particular hostelry, where his father,
and his grandfather, put up before him, and where he is expected to dine in the same old room, with the pictures of
famous rams, that have fetched fabulous prices, framed

against the walls, and ram's horns of exceptional size and peculiar curve fixed up above the mantelpiece. Men come in in groups of two or three, as dinner time approaches, and chat about sheep and wool, and wool and sheep; but no one finally settles himself at the table till the chairman arrives. He is a stout, substantial farmer, who has dined there every market day for the last thirty or forty years.

Everybody has his own particular seat, which he is certain to find kept for him. The dinner itself is simple enough, the waiters perhaps still more simple, but the quality of the viands is beyond praise. The mutton is juicy and delicious, as it should be where the sheep is the very idol of all men's thoughts; the beef is short and tender of grain; the vegetables, nothing can equal them, and they are all here, asparagus and all, in profusion. The landlord grows his own vegetables—every householder in Fleeceborough has an ample garden—and produces the fruit from his own orchards for the tarts. Ever and anon a waiter walks round with a can of ale and fills the glasses, whether asked or not. Beef and mutton, vegetables, and fruit tarts, and ale are simple and plain fare, but when they are served in the best form, how will you surpass them? The real English cheese, the fresh salads, the exquisite butter —everything on the table is genuine, juicy, succulent, and rich. Could such a dinner be found in London, how the folk would crowd thither! Finally, comes the waiter with his two clean plates, the upper one to receive the money, the lower to retain what is his. If you are a stranger, and remember what you have been charged elsewhere in smoky cities for tough beef, stringy mutton, waxy potatoes, and the very bread black with smuts, you select half a sovereign and drop it on the upper plate. In the twinkling of an eye eight shillings are returned to you; the charge is a florin only.

They live well in Fleeceborough, as every fresh experience of the place will prove; they have plentiful food, and of the best quality; poultry abounds, for every resident having a great garden (many, too, have paddocks) keeps fowls; fresh eggs are common; as for vegetables and fruit, the abundance is not to be described. A veritable cornucopia—a horn of plenty —seems to for ever pour a shower of these good things into their houses. And their ale! To the first sight it is not tempting. It is thick, dark, a deep wine colour; a slight aroma arises from it like that which dwells in bonded warehouses. The first taste is not pleasing; but it induces a second, and a third. By and by the flavour grows upon the palate; and now beware, for if a small quantity be thrown upon the fire it will blaze up with a blue flame like pure alcohol. That dark vinous-looking ale is full of the strength of malt and hops; it is the brandy of the barley. The unwary find their heads curiously queer before they have partaken, as it seems to them, of a couple of glasses. The very spirit and character of Fleeceborough is embodied in the ale; rich, strong, genuine. No one knows what English ale is till he has tried this.

After the market dinner the guests sit still—they do not hurry away to counter and desk; they rest awhile, and dwell as it were on the flavour of their food. There is a hum of pleasant talk, for each man is a right boon companion. The burden of that talk has been the same for generations—sheep and wool, wool and sheep. Occasionally mysterious allusions are made to "he," what "he" will do with a certain farm, whether "he" will support such and such a movement, or subscribe to some particular fund, what view will "he" take of the local question of the day? Perhaps some one has had special information of the step "he" is likely to take; then that favoured man is an object of the deepest interest, and is cross-questioned all round the table till his small item of authentic intelligence has been thoroughly assimilated. "He" is the resident within those vast and endless walls, with the metal gates and the gilded coronet above—the prince of this kingdom and its capital city. To rightly see the subjects loyally hastening hither, let any one ascend the church tower on market day.

It is remarkably high, and from thence the various roads converging on the town are visible. The province lies stretched out beneath. There is the gleam of water—the little river, with its ancient mills—that flows beside the town; there are the meadows, with their pleasant footpaths. Yonder the ploughed fields and woods, and yet more distant the open hills. Along every road, and there are many, the folk are hastening to their capital city, in gigs, on horseback, in dog-traps and four-wheels, or sturdily trudging afoot. The breeze comes sweet and exhilarating from the hills and over the broad acres and green woods; it strikes the chest as you lean against the parapet, and the jackdaws suspend themselves in mid-air with outstretched wings upheld by its force. For how many years, how many centuries, has this little town and this district around it been distinct and separate? In the days before the arrival of the Roman legions it was the country of a distinct tribe, or nation, of the original Britons. But if we speak of history we shall never have done, for the town and its antique abbey (of which this tower is a mere remnant) have mingled more or less in every change that has occurred, down from the earthwork camp yonder on the hills to to-day—down to the last puff of the locomotive there below, as its driver shuts off steam and runs in with passengers and dealers for the market, with the papers, and the latest novel from London.

Something of the old local patriotism survives, and is vigorous in the town here. Men marry in the place, find their children employment in the place, and will not move, if they can help it. Their families—well-to-do and humble alike—have been there for so many, many years. The very carter, or the little tailor working in his shop-window, will tell you (and prove to you by records) that his ancestor stood to the barricade with pike or matchlock when the army of King or Parliament, as the case may be, besieged the sturdy town two hundred years ago. He has a longer pedigree than many a titled dweller in Belgravia. All these people believe in Fleeceborough. When fate forces them to quit—when the young man seeks his fortune in New Zealand or America—he writes home the fullest information, and his letters published in the local print read curiously to an outsider, so full are they of local inquiries, and answers to friends who wished to know this or that. In the end he comes back—should he succeed in getting the gold which tempted him away—to pass his latter days gossiping round with the dear old folk, and to marry amongst them. Yet, with all their deep local patriotism, they are not bigoted or narrow-minded; there is too much literature abroad for that, and they have the cosiest reading-room wherein to learn all that passes in the world. They have a town council held now and then in an ancient wainscoted hall, with painted panels and coats of arms, carved oaken seats black with age, and narrow windows from which men once looked down into the street, wearing trunk hose and rapier.

But they have at least two other councils that meet much more often, and that meet by night. When his books are balanced, when his shop is shut, after he has strolled round his garden, and taken his supper, the tradesman or shopkeeper walks down to his inn, and there finds his circle assembled. They are all there, the rich and the moderately well-to-do, the struggling, and the poor. Each delivers his opinion over the social glass, or between the deliberate puffs of his cigar or pipe. The drinking is extremely moderate, the smoking not quite so temperate; but neither the glass nor the cigar are the real attractions. It is the common hall—the informal place of meeting.

It is here that the real government of the town is planned— the mere formal resolutions voted in the ancient council-room are the outcome of the open talk, and the quiet whisper here. No matter what subject is to the front, the question is always heard—What will "he" do? What will "he" say to it? The Volunteers compete for prizes which "he" offers. The cottage hospital; the flower show; the cattle show, or agricultural exhibition; the new market buildings arose through his subscriptions and influence: the artesian well, sunk that the town might have the best of water, was bored at his expense; and so on through the whole list of town affairs. When "he" takes the lead all the lesser gentry—many of whom, perhaps, live in his manor houses—follow suit, and with such powerful support to back it a movement is sure to succeed, yet "he" is rarely seen; his hand rarely felt; everything is done, but without obtrusiveness. At these nightly councils at the chief hostelries the farmers of the district are almost as numerous as the townsmen. They ride in to hear the news and exchange their own small coin of gossip. They want to know what "he" is going to do, and little by little of course it leaks out.

But the town is not all so loyal. There is a section which is all the more vehemently rebellious because of the spectacle of its staid and comfortable neighbours. This section is very small, but makes a considerable noise. It holds meetings and utters treasonable speeches, and denounces the "despot" in fiery language. It protests against a free and open park; it abhors artesian wells; it detests the throwing open of nut woods that all may go forth a-nutting; it waxes righteously indignant at every gift, be it prizes for the flower show or a new market site. It scorns those mean-spirited citizens that cheer these kindly deeds. It asks why? Why should we wait till the park gates are open? Why stay till the nut woods are declared ready? Why be thankful for pure water? Why not take our own? This one man has no right to these parks and woods and pleasure grounds and vast walls; these square miles of ploughed fields, meadows and hills. By right they should all be split up into little plots to grow our potatoes. Away with gilded coronet and watchman, batter down these walls, burn the ancient deeds and archives, put pick and lever to the tall church tower; let us have the rights of man! These violent ebullitions make not the least difference. All the insults they can devise, all the petty obstructions they can set up, the mud they can fling, does not alter the calm course of the "despot" one jot. The artesian well is bored, and they can drink pure water or not, as pleases them. The prizes are offered, and they can compete or stand aloof. Fleeceborough smiles when it meets at night in its council-rooms, with its glass and pipe; Fleeceborough knows that the traditional policy of the Hall will continue, and that policy is acceptable to it.

What manner of man is this "despot" and prince behind his vast walls? Verily his physique matters nothing; whether he be old or of middle age, tall or short, infirm or strong. The policy of the house keeps the actual head and owner rather in the background. His presence is never obtruded; he is rarely seen; you may stay in his capital for months and never catch a glimpse of him. He will not appear at meetings, that every man may be free, nor hesitate to say his say, and abuse what he lists to abuse. The policy is simply perfect freedom, with support and substantial assistance to any and to every movement set on foot by the respectable men of Fleeceborough, or by the tenant farmers round about. This has been going on for generations; so that the *personnel* of the actual owner concerns little. His predecessors did it, he does it, and the next to come will do it. It is the tradition of the house. Nothing is left undone that a true princely spirit could do to improve, to beautify, or to preserve.

The antiquities of the old, old town are kept for it, and not permitted to decay; the ancient tesselated pavements of Roman villas carefully protected from the weather; the remnants of the enclosing walls which the legions built for their defence saved from destruction; the coins of the emperors and of our own early kings collected; the spurs, swords, spearheads, all the fragments of past ages arranged for inspection and study by every one who desires to ponder over them. Chipped flints and arrowheads, the bones of animals long extinct, and the strange evidences of yet more ancient creatures that swam in the seas of the prehistoric world, these too are preserved at his cost and expense. Archæologists, geologists, and other men of science come from afar to see these things and to carry away their lessons. The memories of the place are cherished. There was a famous poet who sang in the woods about the park; his hermitage remains, and nothing is lost that was his. Art-treasures there are, too, heirlooms to be seen behind those vast walls by any who will be at the trouble of asking.

Such is the policy of Hodge's own prince, whose silent influence is felt in every household for miles about, and felt, as all must admit, however prejudiced against the system, in this case for good. His influence reaches far beyond the bounds even of that immense property. The example communicates itself to others, and half the county responds to that pleasant impulse. It is a responsible position to hold; something, perhaps, a little like that of the Medici at Florence in the olden times. But here there is no gonfalon, no golden chain of office, no velvet doublet, cloak, and rapier, no guards with arquebuss or polished cross-bow. An entire absence of state and ceremony marks this almost unseen but powerful sway. The cycle of the seasons brings round times of trial here as over the entire world, but the conditions under which the trial is sustained could scarcely in our day, and under our complicated social and political system, be much more favourable.

CHAPTER XII

THE SQUIRE'S "ROUND ROBIN"

A COCK pheasant flies in frantic haste across the road, beating the air with wide-stretched wings, and fast as he goes, puts on yet a faster spurt as the shot comes rattling up through the boughs of the oak beneath him. The ground is, however, unfavourable to the sportsman, and the bird escapes. The fir copse from which the pheasant rose covers a rather sharp descent on one side of the highway. On the level above are the ploughed fields, but the slope itself is too abrupt for agricultural operations, and the soil perhaps thin and worthless. It is therefore occupied by a small plantation. On the opposite side of the road there grows a fine row of oaks in a hedge, under whose shade the dust takes long to dry when once damped by a shower. The sportsman who fired stands in the road; the beaters are above, for they desire the game to fly in a certain direction; and what with the narrow space between the firs and the oaks, the spreading boughs, and the uncertainty of the spot where the pheasant would break cover, it is not surprising that he missed.

The shot, after tearing through the boughs, rises to some height in the air, and, making a curve, falls of its own weight only, like pattering hail—and as harmless—upon an aged woman, just then trudging slowly round the corner. She is a cottager, and has been to fetch the weekly dole of parish bread that helps to support herself and infirm husband. She wears a long cloak that nearly sweeps the ground on account of her much-bowed back, and carries a flag basket full of bread in one hand, and a bulging umbrella, which answers as a walking stick, in the other. The poor old body, much startled, but not in the least injured, scuttles back round the corner, exclaiming, "Lor! it be Filbard a-shooting; spose a'had better bide a bit till he ha' done." She has not long to wait. The young gentleman standing in the road gets a shot at another cock; this time the bird flies askew, instead of straight across, and so gives him a better opportunity. The pheasant falls crash among the nettles and brambles beside the road. Then a second and older gentleman emerges from the plantation, and after a time a keeper, who picks up the game.

The party then proceed along the road, and coming round the corner the great black retriever runs up to the old woman with the most friendly intentions, but to her intense confusion, for she is just in the act of dropping a lowly curtsey when the dog rubs against her. The young gentleman smiles at her alarm and calls the dog; the elder walks on utterly indifferent. A little way up the road the party get over the gate into the meadows on that side, and make for another outlying plantation. Then, and not till then, does the old woman set out again upon her slow and laborious journey. "Filbard be just like a gatepost," she mutters; "a' don't take no notice of anybody." Though she had dropped the squire so lowly a curtsey, and in his presence would have behaved with profound respect, behind his back and out of hearing she called him by his family name without any prefix. The cottagers thereabout almost always did this in speaking among themselves of their local magnate. They rarely said "Mr."; it was generally "Filbard," or, even more familiarly, "Jim Filbard." Extremes

meet. They hardly dared open their mouths when they saw
him, and yet spoke of him afterwards as if he sat with them
at bacon and cabbage time.

Squire Filbard and one of his sons were walking round the
outlying copses that October day with the object of driving
the pheasants in towards the great Filbard wood, rather than
of making a bag. The birds were inclined to wander about,
and the squire thought a little judicious shooting round the
outskirts would do good, and at the same time give his son
some sport without disturbing the head of game he kept up
in the wood itself. The squire was large made, tall, and well
proportioned, and with a bearded, manly countenance. His
neck was, perhaps, a little thick and apoplectic-looking, but
burnt to a healthy brick-dust colour by exposure to the sun.
The passing years had drawn some crows'-feet round the eyes,
but his step was firm, his back straight, and he walked his
ancestral acres every inch the master. The defect of his features
was the thinness of the lips, and a want of character in a nose
which did not accord with a good forehead. His hands, too,
were very large and puffy; his finger-nails (scrupulously clean)
were correspondingly large, and cut to a sharp point, that
seemed to project beyond the tip of the finger, and gave it a
scratchy appearance.

The chimneys of Filbard Hall showed for some distance
above the trees of the park, for the house stood on high
ground. It was of red brick, somewhat square in style, and
had little of the true Elizabethan character—it was doubtless
later in date, though not modern. The chimneys, however,
had a pleasing appearance over the trees; they were in stacks,
and rather larger, or broader apparently at the top than where
they rose from the roof. Such chimneys are not often seen on
recent buildings. A chimney seems a simple matter, and yet
the aspect of a house from a distance much depends upon its
outline. The mansion was of large size, and stood in an extensive park, through which carriage drives swept up to the
front from different lodge gates. Each of the drives passed
under avenues of trees—the park seemed to stretch on either
hand without enclosure or boundary—and the approach was
not without a certain stateliness. Within the apartments were
commodious, and from several there were really beautiful
views. Some ancient furniture, handed down generation after
generation, gave a character to the rooms; the oak staircase
was much admired, and so was the wainscoting of one part.

The usual family portraits hung on the walls, but the present squire had rather pushed them aside in favour of his own peculiar hobby. He collected antique Italian pictures—many on panels—in the pre-Raphaelite style. Some of these he had picked up in London, others he had found and purchased on the Continent. There were saints with glories or *nimbi* round their heads, Madonnas and kneeling Magi, the manger under a kind of penthouse, and similar subjects—subjects the highest that could be chosen. The gilding of the *nimbi* seemed well done certainly, and was still bright, but to the ordinary eye the stiffness of the figures, the lack of grace, the absence of soul in the composition was distressingly apparent. It was, however, the squire's hobby, and it must be admitted that he had very high authority upon his side. Some sensitive persons rather shrank from seeing him handle these painted panels with those peculiar scratchy finger-nails; it set their teeth on edge. He gave considerable sums of money for many of these paintings, the only liberality he permitted himself, or was capable of.

His own room or study was almost bare, and the solitary window looked on a paved passage that led to the stables. There was nothing in it but a large table, a bookcase, and two or three of the commonest horsehair chairs; the carpet was worn bare. He had selected this room because there was a door close by opening on the paved passage. Thus the bailiff of the Home Farm, the steward, the gamekeeper, the policeman, or any one who wished to see him on business, could come to the side door from the back and be shown in to him without passing through the mansion. This certainly was a convenient arrangement; yet one would have thought that he would have had a second and more private study in which to follow his own natural bent of mind. But the squire received the gardener and gave him directions about the cucumbers—for he descended even to such minutiæ as that—sitting at the same table on which he had just written to an Italian art collector respecting a picture, or to some great friend begging him to come and inspect a fresh acquisition. The bookcase contained a few law books, a manual for the direction of justices—the squire was on the commission—a copy of Burke, and in one corner of a shelf a few musty papers referring to family history. These were of some value, and the squire was proud of showing them to those who took an interest in archæology; yet he kept them much as if they had been receipts for the footman's livery, or a dozen bottles of stable medicine. He wrote with a quill pen, and as it went up and down it scratched the paper as if it had been those sharp projecting finger-nails.

In this study he spent many hours when at home—he rose late, and after breakfast repaired hither. The steward was usually in attendance. He was a commonplace man, but little above the description of a labourer. He received wages not much superior to those a labourer takes in summer time, but as he lived at the Home Farm (which was in hand) there were of course some perquisites. A slow, quiet man, of little or no education, he pottered about and looked after things in general. One morning perhaps he would come in to talk with the squire about the ash wood they were going to cut in the ensuing winter, or about the oak bark which had not been paid for. Or it might be the Alderney cow or the poultry at the Home Farm, or a few fresh tiles on the roof of the pigsty, which was decaying. A cart wanted a new pair of wheels or a shaft. One of the tenants wanted a new shed put up, but it did not seem necessary; the old one would do very well if people were not so fidgety. The wife or daughter of one of the cottage people was taking to drink and getting into bad ways. This or that farmer had had some sheep die. Another farmer had bought some new silver-mounted harness, and so on, through all the village gossip.

Often it was the gamekeeper instead of the steward who came in or was sent for. The squire kept a large head of pheasants for certain reasons, but he was not over-anxious to pay for them. The keeper grumbled about his wages, that he had no perquisites, and that the shooting season never brought him any fees—unless the squire let the place; he only wished he let it every year. This, of course, was said aside; to the squire he was hat in hand. He had to produce his vouchers for food for the pheasants and dogs, and to give particulars why a certain gate on the plantation wanted renewing. The steward had seen it, and thought it might be repaired; why did the keeper think it ought to be renewed altogether? And was there not plenty of larch timber lying about, that had been thrown and not sold, that would make a very good spar-gate, without purchasing one? Why couldn't old Hooker, the hedge carpenter, knock it up cheap?

Next came the coachman—the squire did not keep up anything of a stud, just enough to work the carriage, and some ordinary riding horses and a pony for the children. The coachman had to explain why a new lock was wanted on the stable door; why the blacksmith's bill was so much for shoes; after which there was a long gossip about the horses of a gentleman who had come down and rented a place for the season. The gardener sometimes had an interview about the quantity of apples that might be sold from the orchard, and twenty other peddling details, in which the squire delighted. As for the butler, time at last had brought him to bear with patience the inquisition about the waste corks and the empty bottles.

The squire would have had the cook in and discussed the stock-pot with her for a full hour, but the cook set up her back. She wouldn't, no, that she wouldn't; and the squire found that the cook was mistress of the situation. She was the only personage who did not pass him with deference. She tossed her head, and told her fellow-servants audibly that he was a poor, mean-spirited man; and as for missis, she was a regular Tartar—there! In this they thoroughly agreed. The coachman and footman, when out with the carriage, and chancing to get a talk with other coachmen and footmen, were full of it. He was the meanest master they had ever known; yet they could not say that he paid less wages, or that they were ill-fed—it was this meddling, peddling interference they resented. The groom, when he rode into town for the letter-bag, always stopped to tell his friends some fresh instance of it. All the shopkeepers and tradesmen, and everybody else, had heard of it. But they were none the less obsequious when the squire passed up the street. The servants were never so glad as when young master came home with the liberal views imbibed in modern centres of learning, and with a free, frank mode of speech. But miss, the sole daughter, they simply hated; she seemed to have ten times the meanness of her papa, and had been a tell-tale from childhood. The kitchen said she saved her curl papers to sell as waste paper.

The "missis" was as haughty, as unapproachable, and disdainful as the master was inquisitive; she never spoke to, looked at, nor acknowledged any one—except the three largest tenants and their wives. To these, who paid heavily, she was gracious. She dressed in the very extreme and front of fashion—the squire himself quite plainly, without the least pretence of dandyism. Hateful as the village folk thought her *hauteur* and open contempt for them, they said she was more the lady than the squire was the gentleman.

The squire's time, when at home, like everything else, was peddled away. He rode into market one day of the week; he went to church on Sundays with unfailing regularity, and he generally attended the petty sessional bench on a third day. Upon the bench, from the long standing of his family, he occupied a prominent position. His mind invariably seized the minutiæ of the evidence, and never seemed to see the point or the broad bearings of the case. He would utterly confuse a truthful witness, for instance, who chanced to say that he met the defendant in the road. ''But you said just now that you and he were both going the same way, how, then could you meet him?'' the squire would ask, frowning sternly. Whether the witness overtook or met the defendant mattered nothing to the point at issue; but the squire, having got a satisfactory explanation, turned aside, with an aggravating air of cleverness. For the rest of the week the squire could not account for his time. He sometimes, indeed, in the hunting season, rode to the meet; but he rarely followed. He had none of the enthusiasm that makes a hunter; besides, it made the horse in such a heat, and would work him out too quick for economy.

He went out shooting, but not in regular trim. He would carry his gun across to the Home Farm, and knock over a rabbit on the way; then spend two hours looking at the Alderney cow, the roof of the pigstye, and the poultry, and presently stroll across a corner of the wood, and shoot a pheasant. The head of game was kept up for the purpose of letting the mansion from time to time when the squire or his lady thought it desirable to go on the Continent, that the daughter might acquire the graces of travel. A visit to London in the season, a visit to the seaside, and then home in the autumn to peddle about the estate, made up the year when they did not go abroad. There was a broad park, noble trees, a great mansion, a stately approach; but within it seemed all littleness of spirit.

The squire's own private study—the morning-room of the owner of this fine estate—was, as previously observed, next the passage that led to the stables, and the one window looked out on a blank wall. It was in this room that he conducted his business and pleasure, and his art researches. It was here that he received the famous ''Round Robin'' from his tenants. The estate was not very large—something between 3,000 and 4,000 acres—but much of it was good and fertile, though heavy land, and highly rented. Had the squire received the whole of his rents for his own private use he would have been well off as squires go. But there was a flaw or hitch somewhere in the right, or title, or succession. No one knew the precise circumstances, because, like so many similar family disputes, when the lawyers were ready, and the case had come before the tribunal, a compromise was arrived at, the terms of which were only known to the tribunal and the parties directly concerned.

But everybody knew that the squire had to pay heavy pensions to various members of another branch of the family; and it was imagined that he did not feel quite fixed in the tenure—that possibly the case might, under certain circumstances, be heard of again—since it was noticed that he did not plant trees, or make improvements, or in any way proceed to increase the permanent attractions of the estate. It seemed as if he felt he was only lodging there. He appeared to try and get all he could off the place—without absolute damage—and to invest or spend nothing. After all these payments had been made the squire's income was much reduced, and thus, with all these broad acres, these extensive woods, and park, and mansion, pleasure grounds, game, and so forth, he was really a poor man. Not poor in the sense of actual want, but a man in his position had, of course, a certain appearance to keep up. Horses, carriages—even cooks—are not to be had for nothing, and are absolutely essential to those who are compelled to maintain any kind of dignity. Sons with liberal ideas are expensive; a daughter is expensive; a wife who insists on dressing in the fashion is expensive.

Now, taking all these things into consideration, and remembering, too, that the squire as a good father (which he was admittedly) wished to make provision for the future of his children, it may perhaps, after all, be questioned whether he really was so mean and little of spirit as appeared. Under the circumstances, if he wished to save, the only way open to him was to be careful in little things. Even his hobby—the pre-Raphaelite pictures—was not without its advantage in this sense; the collection was certainly worth more than he gave for it, for he got it all by careful bargaining, and it could be sold again at a profit. The careful superintendence of the Alderney cow, the cucumber frames, and the rabbits, might all be carried out for the very best of objects, the good of his children.

Now, the squire was, of course, very well aware of the troubles of agriculture, the wetness of the seasons—which played havoc with the game—the low prices, and the loud talk that was going on around him. But he made no sign. He might have been deaf, dumb, and blind. He walked by the wheat, but did not see the deficiency of the crop, nor the extraordinary growth of weeds. There were voices in the air like the mutterings of a coming storm, but he did not hear them. There were paragraphs in the papers—how So-and-so had liberally reduced the rents or returned a percentage; but he did not read them, or did not understand. Rent days came and went, and no sign was made. His solicitor received the rents, but nothing could be got out of him by the farmers. The little farmers hardly liked to take the lead: some of them did not dare. The three largest farmers looked at each other and wondered which would speak first. They were awkwardly situated. The squire's wife acknowledged their wives and daughters, and once now and then deigned to invite them to the mansion. The squire himself presented them with specimens of a valuable breed of poultry he was bringing up at the Home Farm. It was difficult to begin unpleasant business.

Meantime the solicitor gathered up the cheques, wished them good afternoon and departed. Another rent day came round, and still no sign. The squire's policy was, in fact, to ignore. He ignored the depression altogether—could not see that it existed in that county at all. Recollect, it was the only policy open to him. Whether the rents paid to him were large or small, his expenses would be the same. There were the members of the other branch of the family to be paid in full. There were the carriages, the servants, the gamekeepers, and so on. He could reduce nothing; no wonder that he was slow to acknowledge that he must be himself reduced. The fatal day—so long dreaded—came at last.

A large letter lay on the table in the study one morning, along with the other letters. He did not recognise the handwriting, and naturally opened it first. It was a ''Round Robin'' from the tenants. All had signed a memorial, setting forth the depression, and respectfully, even humbly, asking that their case be taken into consideration, and that a percentage be returned, or the rent reduced. Their heavy land, they pointed out, had been peculiarly difficult to work in such seasons. They had suffered exceptionally, and they trusted he would take no offence. But there was an unmistakeable hint that they were in earnest. All signed it—from the ungrateful largest tenants, who had had presents of fancy poultry, and whose wives had been smiled upon, down to the smallest working farmer, who could hardly be distinguished from his own labourers.

The squire read the names over twice, pointing to each with his sharp, scratchy finger-nail. There were other letters from the members of the other branch of the family whose pensions were just due in full. Suppose he returned ten per cent. of the rents to the tenants, that would not be like ten per cent. upon the entire rental, but perhaps twenty-five or thirty per cent. upon that portion of the rental which actually went into his own pocket. A man can hardly be expected to cheerfully tender other people a third of his income. But sprawling and ill-written as many of the signatures were to the "Round Robin"—the pen held by heavy hands—yet they were genuine, and constituted a very substantial fact, that must be yielded to.

CHAPTER XIII

AN AMBITIOUS SQUIRE

PERHAPS the magistrate most regular in his attendance at a certain country Petty Sessional Court is young Squire Marthorne. Those who have had business to transact at such Courts know the difficulty that often arises from the absence of a second magistrate, there being a numerous class of cases with which one justice of the peace is not permitted to deal. There must be two, and it sometimes happens that only one is forthcoming. The procedure adopted varies much in different divisions, according to the population and the percentage of charges brought up. Usually a particular day is appointed when it is understood that a full bench will be present, but it not unfrequently happens that another and less formal meeting has to be held, at which the attendance is uncertain. The district in which Mr. Marthorne resides chances to be somewhat populous, and to include one or two turbulent places that furnish a steady supply of offenders. The practice therefore is to hold two Courts a week; at one of these, on the Saturday, the more important cases are arranged to be heard, when there are always plenty of magistrates. At the other, on the Tuesday, remands and smaller matters are taken, and there then used to be some delay.

One justice thought his neighbour would go, another thought the same of his neighbour, and the result was nobody went. Having tacitly bound themselves to attend once a week, the justices, many of whom resided miles away, did not care formally to pledge themselves to be invariably present on a second day. Sometimes the business on that second day was next to nothing, but occasionally serious affairs turned up, when messengers had to be despatched to gather a quorum.

But latterly this uncertainty has been put an end to through the regular attendance of young Squire Marthorne, of Marthorne House. The Marthornes are an old family, and one of the best connected in the county, though by no means rich, and, whether it was the lack of great wealth or a want of energy, they had until recently rather dropped out of the governing circle. When, however, the young squire, soon after his accession to the property, in the natural course of events, was nominated to the Commission of the Peace, he began to exhibit qualities calculated to bring him to the front. He developed an aptitude for business, and at the same time showed a personal tact and judgment which seemed to promise a future very different from the previous stagnation of his family.

These qualities came first into play at the Petty Sessions, which, apart from the criminal business, is practically an informal weekly Parliament of local landowners. Marthorne, of course, was well known to the rest long before his appearance among them as a colleague. He had gained some reputation at college; but that had long since been forgotten in the prestige he had attained as a brilliant foxhunter. Even in the days before his accession, when his finances were notoriously low, he had somehow contrived to ride a first-rate horse. Everybody likes a man who rides a good horse. At the same time there was nothing horsey about him; he was always the gentleman. Since his succession the young squire, as he was familiarly described—most of the others being elderly—had selected his horses with such skill that it was well known a very great man had noticed them, so that when he came to the Bench, young as he was, Marthorne escaped the unpleasant process of finding his level—*i.e.* being thoroughly put down.

If not received quite as an equal by that assemblage of elderly gentlemen, he was made to feel that at all events they would listen to what he had to say. That is a very great point gained. Marthorne used his advantage with judgment. He displayed a modesty highly commendable in a young man. He listened, and only spoke for the purpose of acquiring information. Nothing is so pleasing as to find a man of intelligence willingly constituting himself your pupil. They were all anxious to teach him the business of the county, and the more he endeavoured to learn from them the cleverer they thought him.

Now, the business of the county was not very intricate; the details were innumerable, but the general drift was easy to acquire. Much more complicated to see through were all the little personal likings, dislikings, petty spites, foibles, hobbies, secret understandings, family jars, and so forth, which really decide a man's vote, or the scale into which he throws his influence. There were scores of squires dotted over the county, each of whom possessed local power more or less considerable, and each of whom might perchance have private relations with men who held high office in the State. Every family had its history and its archives containing records of negotiations with other families. People who met with all outward friendliness, and belonged to the same party, might have grudges half a century old, but not yet forgotten. If you made friends with one, you might mortally offend the other. The other would say nothing, but another day a whisper to some great authority might destroy the hopes of the aspirant. Those who would attain to power must study the inner social life, and learn the secret motives that animate men. But to get at the secret behind the speech, the private thought behind the vote, would occupy one for years.

Marthorne, of course, having been born and bred in the circle, knew the main facts; but, when he came to really set himself to work, he quickly felt that he was ignorant, and that at any moment he might irritate some one's hidden prejudice. He looked round for an older man who knew all about it, and could inform him. This man he found in the person of the Vice-Chairman of the Petty Sessions. The nominal Chairman, like many other unpaid officials, held the place because of old family greatness, not from any personal ability—family greatness which was in reality a mere tradition. The Vice-Chairman was the true centre and spirit of the circle.

A man of vast aptitude for details, he liked county business for its own sake, and understood every technicality. With little or no personal ambition, he had assisted in every political and social movement in the county for half a century, and knew the secret motives of every individual landowner. With large wealth, nothing to do, and childless, he took a liking to young Marthorne. The old man wished for nothing better than to talk; the young squire listened attentively. The old man was delighted to find some one who would sit with him through the long hours of Petty Sessional business. Thus it was that the people who had to attend the Local Board, whether it was a Saturday, the principal day, or whether it was a Tuesday, that had previously been so trying, found their business facilitated by the attendance of two magistrates. The Vice-Chairman was always there, and Mr. Marthorne was always there. It sometimes happened that while Hodge the lately intoxicated, or Hodge the recent pugilist, was stolidly waiting for his sentence, the two justices in the retiring room were convulsed with laughter; the one recounting, the other imbibing, some curious racy anecdote concerning the family history of a local magnate.

Meantime, the young squire was steadily gaining a reputation for solid qualities, for work and application. Not only at the Bench, but at the Board of Guardians and at other Boards where the Justice of the Peace is *ex officio* a member, he steadily worked at details, sat patiently upon committees, audited endless accounts, read interminable reports, and was never weary of work. The farmers began to talk about him, and to remark to each other what a wonderful talent for business he possessed, and what a pleasant-speaking young gentleman he was. The applause was well earned, for probably there is no duller or more monotonous work than that of attending Boards which never declare dividends. He next appeared at the farmers' club, at first as a mere spectator, and next, though with evident diffidence, as a speaker.

Marthorne was no orator; he felt when he stood up to speak an odd sensation in the throat, as if the glottis had contracted. He was, in fact, very nervous, and for the first two or three sentences had not the least idea what he had said. But he forced himself to say it—his will overruled his physical weakness. When said it was not much—only a few safe platitudes—but it was a distinct advance. He felt that next time he should do better, and that his tongue would obey his mind. His remarks appeared in the local print, and he had started as a speaker. He was resolved to be a speaker, for it is evident to all that, without frequent public speech, no one can now be a representative man. Marthorne, after this, never lost an opportunity of speaking—if merely to second a resolution, to propose a toast, he made the most of it. One rule he laid down for himself, namely, never to say anything original. He was not speaking to propound a new theory, a new creed, or view of life. His aim was to become the mouthpiece of his party. Most probably the thought that seemed to him so clever might, if publicly expressed, offend some important people. He, therefore, carefully avoided anything original. High authorities are now never silent; when Parliament closes they still continue to address the public, and generally upon more or less stirring questions of the time.

In those addresses, delivered by the very leaders of his own party, Marthorne found the material, and caught from their diligent perusal the spirit in which to use it. In this way, without uttering a single original idea of his own, and with very little originality of expression, the young orator succeeded perfectly in his aim. First, he became recognised as a speaker, and, therefore, extremely useful; secondly, he was recognised as one of the soundest exponents of politics in the county. Marthorne was not only clever, but "safe." His repute for the latter quality was of even more service to him than for talent; to be "safe" in such things is a very great recommendation. Personal reputation is of slow growth, but it does grow. The Vice-Chairman, Marthorne's friend and mentor, had connections with very high people indeed. He mentioned Marthorne to the very high people. These, in their turn, occasionally cast a glance at what Marthorne was doing. Now and then they read a speech of his, and thought it extremely good, solid, and well put. It was understood that a certain M.P. would retire at the next election; and they asked themselves whom they had to take his place?

While this important question was exercising the minds of those in authority, Marthorne was energetically at work gaining the social suffrage. The young squire's lady—he had married in his minority for beauty and intelligence, and not for money—was discovered to be a very interesting young person. Her beauty and intelligence, and, let it be added, her true devotion to her husband's cause, proved of fifty times more value to him than a dowry of many manors. Her tact smoothed the way everywhere; she made friends for him in all directions, especially perhaps during the London season. Under the whirl and glitter of that fascinating time there are latent possibilities of important business. Both Marthorne and his lady had by birth and connections the *entrée* into leading circles; but many who have that *entrée* never attain to more influence in society than the furniture of the drawing-room.

These two never for a moment lost sight of the country while they enjoyed themselves in town. Everything they said or did was said and done with a view to conciliate people who might have direct or indirect influence in the country. In these matters, ladies of position still retain considerable power in their hands. The young squire and his wife put themselves to immense trouble to get the good will of such persons, and being of engaging manners they in time succeeded. This was not effected at once, but three or four years are a very short time in which to develop personal influence, and their success within so brief a period argues considerable skill.

At home again in the autumn the same efforts were diligently continued. The mansion itself was but of moderate size and by no means convenient, but the squire's lady transformed it from a gaunt, commonplace country house into an elegant and charming residence. This she contrived without great expense by the exercise of good taste and a gift of discriminating between what was and what was not *àpropos*. The exterior she left alone—to alter an exterior costs a heavy sum and often fails. But the interior she gradually fitted in a novel style, almost entirely after her own design. The gardens, too, under her supervision, became equally inviting. The house got talked about, and was itself a social success.

On his part, the squire paid as much attention to the estate. It was not large, far from sufficient of itself, indeed, to support any social or political pretensions without the most rigid economy. And the pair were rigidly economical. The lady dressed in the height of the fashion, and drove the most beautiful horses, and yet she never wasted a shilling upon herself. Her own little private whims and fancies she resolutely refused to gratify. Every coin was spent where it would produce effect. In like manner, the squire literally never had half a sovereign in his pocket. He selected the wines in his

cellar with the greatest care, and paid for them prices which
the wine merchant, in these days of cheap wines, was unaccustomed to receive from men of thrice his income. The
squire paid for the very best wine, and in private drank a
cheap claret. But his guests, many of them elderly gentlemen,
when once they had dined with him never forgot to come
again. His bins became known throughout the county; very
influential people indeed spoke of them with affection. It
was in this way that the squire got a high value out of his by
no means extensive rents.

He also looked after the estate personally. Hodge, eating
his luncheon under the hedge in October, as he slowly
munched his crust, watched the squire strolling about the
fields, with his gun under his arm, and wondered why he did
not try the turnips. The squire never went into the turnip
field, and seemed quite oblivious that he carried a gun, for
when a covey rose at his feet he did not fire, but simply
marked them down. His mind, in fact, was busy with more
important matters, and, fond as he was of shooting, he wanted
the birds for some one else's delectation. After he had had
the place a little while, there was not a square inch of waste
ground to be found. When the tenants were callous to hints,
the squire gave them pretty clearly to understand that he
meant his land to be improved, and improved it was. He himself of his own free motive and initiative ordered new buildings to be erected where he, by personal inspection, saw that
they would pay. He drained to some extent, but not very
largely, thinking that capital sunk in drains, except in particular soils, did not return for many years.

Anxious as he was to keep plenty of game, he killed off the
rabbits, and grubbed up many of the small covers at the
corners and sides of arable fields which the tenants believed
injurious to crops. He repaired labourers' cottages, and added
offices to farmsteads. In short, he did everything that could
be done without too heavy an expenditure. To kill off the
rabbits, to grub the smaller coverts, to drain the marshy spots,
to thatch the cottages, put up cattle sheds, and so on, could
be effected without burdening the estate with a loan. But,
small as these improvements were in themselves, yet, taken
together, they made an appreciable difference.

There was a distinct increase in the revenue of the estate
after the first two years. The increase arose in part from the
diminished expenses, for it had been found that a tumble-

down place is more costly to maintain than one in good repair. The tenants at first were rather alarmed, fearing lest the change should end in a general rise of rents. It did not. The squire only asked an increase when he had admittedly raised the value of the land, and then only to a moderate amount. By degrees he acquired a reputation as the most just of landlords. His tenantry were not only satisfied, but proud of him; for they began to foresee what was going to happen.

Yet all these things had been done for his own interest— so true is it that the interest of the landlord and the tenant are identical. The squire had simply acted judiciously, and from personal inspection. He studied his estate, and attended to it personally. Of course he could not have done these things had he not succeeded to a place but little encumbered with family settlements. He did them from interested motives, and not from mere sentiment. But, nevertheless, credit of a high order was justly accorded to him. So young a man might naturally have expended his income on pleasure. So young a wife might have spent his rents in frivolity. They worked towards an end, but it was a worthy end—for ambition, if not too extravagant, is a virtue. Men with votes and influence compared this squire in their minds with other squires, whose lives seemed spent in a slumberous do-nothingness.

Thus, by degrees, the young squire's mansion and estate added to his reputation. The labour which all this represented was immense. Both the squire and his wife worked harder than a merchant in his office. Attending Boards and farmers' clubs, making speeches, carrying on correspondence, looking after the estate, discharging social duties, filled up every moment of his time. Superintending the house, the garden, corresponding, and a hundred other labours, filled up every moment of hers. They were never idle; to rise socially and politically requires as great or greater work than for a poor man to achieve a fortune.

Ultimately the desired result began to be apparent. There grew up a general feeling that the squire was the best man for the place in Parliament which, in the course of events, must ere long be vacant. There was much heartburning and jealousy secretly felt among men twice his age, who had waited and hoped for years for such an opening, till at last they had rusted and become incapable of effort. But, cynical as they might be in private, they were too wise to go openly against the stream. A few friendly words spoken in season by a great man whose good will had been gained decided the matter. At an informal meeting of the party—how much more is effected at informal than at formal assemblies!—Marthorne was introduced as the successor to the then representative. The young squire's estate could not, of course, bear the heavy pecuniary strain which must arise; but before those who had the control of these things finally selected him they had ascertained that there would be no difficulty with respect to money. Marthorne's old friend and mentor, the wealthy Vice-Chairman of the Petty Sessions, who had inducted him into the county business, announced that he should bear the larger part of the expense. He was not a little proud of his *protégé*.

The same old friend and mentor, wise with the knowledge and experience which long observation of men had given him, advised the young squire what to do when the depression first came upon agriculture. The old man said, "Meet it; very likely it will not last two years. What is that in the life of an estate?" So the young squire met it, and announced at once that he should return a percentage of his rents. "But not too high a percentage," said the old man; "let us ascertain what the rest of the landowners think, else by a too liberal reduction you may seem to cast a reflection upon them." The percentage was returned, and continued, and the young squire has tided over the difficulty.

His own tenantry and the farming interest generally are proud of him. Hodge, who, slow as he is, likes a real man, says, "He beant such a bad sort of a veller, you; a' beant above speaking to we!" When the time comes the young squire will certainly be returned.

CHAPTER XIV

THE PARSON'S WIFE

IT is pleasant on a sunny day to walk through a field of wheat when the footpath is bordered on either side by the ripening crop, without the intervention of hedge or fence. Such a footpath, narrow, but well kept, leads from a certain country churchyard to the highway road, and passes on the way a wicket gate in a thick evergreen shrubbery which surrounds the vicarage lawn and gardens. This afternoon the wheat stands still and upright, without a motion, in the burning sunshine, for the sun, though he has sloped a little from his highest meridian altitude, pours an even fiercer beam than at the exact hour of noon. The shadeless field is exposed to the full glare of the brilliant light. There are no trees in the field itself, the hedges are cut low and trimmed to the smallest proportions, and are devoid of timber; and, as the ground is high and close to the hills, all the trees in sight are beneath, and can be overlooked. Whether in sunshine or storm there is no shelter—no medium; the wind rushes over with its utmost fury, or the heat rests on it undisturbed by the faintest current. Yet, sultry as it is, the footpath is a pleasant one to follow.

The wheat ears, all but ripe—to the ordinary eye they are ripe, but the farmer is not quite satisfied—rise to the waist or higher, and tempt the hand to pluck them. Butterflies flutter over the surface, now descending to some flower hidden beneath, now resuming their joyous journey. There is a rich ripe feeling in the very atmosphere, the earth is yielding her wealth, and a delicate aroma rises from her generous gifts. Far as the eye can see, the rolling plains and slopes present various tints of yellow—wheat in different stages of ripeness, or of different kinds; oats and barley—till the hedges and woods of the vale conceal the farther landscape on the one hand, and the ridge of the hills upon the other.

Nothing conveys so strong an impression of substantial wealth as the view of wheat-fields. A diamond ornament in a window may be ticketed as worth so many hundreds of pounds; but the glittering gem, and the sum it represents, seem rather abstract than real. But the wheat, the golden wheat, is a great fact that seizes hold of the mind; the idea comes of itself that it represents solid wealth.

The tiles of the vicarage roof—all of the house visible above the shrubbery—look so hot and dry in the glaring sunshine that it does not seem possible for vegetation to exist upon them; yet they are tinted with lichen. The shrubbery has an inviting coolness about it—the thick evergreens, the hollies on which the berries are now green, the cedars and ornamental trees planted so close together that the passer-by cannot see through, must surely afford a grateful shade—a contrast with the heat of the wheat-field and the dust of the

155

highway below. Just without the wicket gate a goat standing upon his hind legs, his fore legs placed against the palings, is industriously nibbling the tenderest leaves of the shrubs and trees which he can reach. Thus extended to his full length he can reach considerably higher than might be supposed, and is capable of much destruction. Doubtless he has got out of bounds.

Inside the enclosure the reverend gentleman himself reclines in an arm-chair of canework placed under the shade of the verandah, just without the glass door or window opening from the drawing-room upon the lawn. His head has fallen back and a little to one side, and an open book lies on his knee; his soft felt hat is bent and crumpled; he has yielded to the heat and is slumbering. The blinds are partly down the window, but a glimpse can be obtained of a luxurious, carpet, of tables in valuable woods and inlaid, of a fine piano, of china, and the thousand and one nicknacks of highly civilised life. The reverend gentleman's suit of black, however, is not new; it is, on the contrary, decidedly rusty, and the sole of one of his boots, which is visible, is much worn. Over his head the roses twine round the pillars of the verandah, and there is a *parterre* of brilliant flowers not far from his feet.

His wife sits, a few yards distant, under a weeping ash, whose well-trained boughs make a perfect tent, and shield her from the sun. She has a small table before her, and writing materials, and is making notes with the utmost despatch from some paper or journal. She is no longer young, and there are the marks of much care and trouble on her forehead; but she has still a pleasing expression upon her features, her hands are exquisitely white, and her figure, once really good, retains some of the outline that rendered it beautiful. Wherever you saw her you would say, That is a lady. But her dress, tasteful though it be, is made of the cheapest material, and looks, indeed, as if it had been carefully folded away last summer, and was now brought out to do duty a second time.

The slow rumble of waggon wheels goes down the road, close to the lawn, but concealed by the trees, against whose boughs the sheaves of the load rustle as they go past. Wealth rolling by upon the waggon, wealth in the well-kept garden, in the smart lawn, in the roses, the bright flowers, the substantial well-furnished house, the luxurious carpet, and the china; wealth, too, all around in the vast expanse of ripening wheat. He has nothing to do but to slumber in the cane chair and receive his tithe of the harvest. She has nothing to do but to sit under the shadow of the weeping ash and dream dreams, or write verses. Such, at least, might be the first impression.

The publication from which she is so earnestly making notes is occupied with the management of bees, and she is so busy because the paper is only borrowed, and has to be returned. Most of the papers and books that come to the vicarage have to be hastily read for the same reason. Mrs. F——is doing her very best and hardest to increase the Rev. F——'s income; she has tried to do so for some years, and despite repeated failures is bravely, perhaps a little wearily, still trying. There is not much left for her to experiment with. The goat surreptitiously nibbling the valuable shrubs outside the palings is a member of a flock that once seemed to promise fair. Goats at one time (she was persuaded) were the means of ready wealth—they could live anywhere, on anything (the shrubs to wit), and yielded such rich milk; it far surpassed that of the shorthorn; there was the analysis to prove it! Such milk must of course be worth money, besides which there were the kids, and the cheese and butter.

Alas! the goats quickly obtained so evil a reputation, worse than that of the rabbits for biting off the shooting vegetation, that no one would have them on the land. The milk was all the analysis declared it, but in that outlying village, which did not contain two houses above the quality of a farmstead, there was no one to buy it. There was a prejudice against the butter which could not be got over; and the cheese—well, the cheese resembled a tablet of dark soap. Hodge would not eat it at a gift; he smelt it, picked a morsel off on the tip of his clasp knife, and threw it aside in contempt. One by one the goats were got rid of, and now but two or three remained; she could not make up her mind to part with all, for living creatures, however greatly they have disappointed, always enlist the sympathies of women.

Poultry was the next grand discovery—they ate their heads off, refused to lay eggs, and, when by frequent purchases they became numerous and promised to pay, quietly died by the score, seized with an epidemic. She learnt in visiting the cottagers how profitable their allotment gardens were to them, and naturally proceeded to argue that a larger piece of ground would yield a proportionately larger profit if cultivated on the same principle. If the cottagers could pay a rent or an acre which, in the aggregate, was three times that given by the ordinary farmer, and could even then make a good thing of it, surely intelligence and skill might do the same on a more extended scale. How very foolish the farmers were! they might raise at least four times the produce they did, and they might pay three times the rent. As the vicar had some hundred and fifty acres of glebe let at the usual agricultural rent, if the tenants could be persuaded or instructed to farm on the cottagers' system, what an immense increase it would be to his income! The tenants, however, did not see it. They shrugged their shoulders, and made no movement. The energetic lady resolved to set an example, and to prove to them that they were wrong.

She rented an acre of arable land (at the side of the field), giving the tenant a fair price for it. First it had to be enclosed so as to be parted off from the open field. The cost of the palings made the vicar wince; his lady set it duly down to debit. She planted one-half potatoes, as they paid thirty pounds per acre, and on the rest put in hundreds of currant bushes, set a strawberry bed and an asparagus bed, on the principle that luxuries of that kind fetch a high price and occupy no more space than cabbages. As the acre was cultivated entirely by the spade, the cost of the labour expended upon it ran up the figures on the debit side to an amount which rather startled her. But the most dispiriting part of the commencement was the length of time to wait before a crop came. According to her calculations that represented so much idle capital sunk, instead of being rapidly turned over. However she consoled herself with the pigstye, in which were half a dozen animals, whose feeding she often personally superintended.

The potatoes failed, and did not pay for the digging; the currant bushes were blighted; the strawberries were eaten by snails, and, of course, no asparagus could be cut for three years; a little item, this last, quite overlooked. The pigs returned exactly the sum spent upon them; there was neither profit nor loss, and there did not appear any chance of making a fortune out of pork. The lady had to abandon the experiment quite disheartened and found that, after all her care and energy, her books showed a loss of fifteen pounds. It was wonderful it was not more; labour was so expensive, and no doubt she was cheated right and left.

She next tried to utilise her natural abilities, **and to turn** her accomplishments to account. She painted; she illuminated texts; she undertook difficult needlework of various kinds, in answer to advertisements which promised ample remuneration for a few hours' labour. Fifteen hours' hard work she found was worth just threepence, and the materials cost one shilling: consequently she laboriously worked herself poorer by ninepence.

Finally, she was studying bees, which really seemed to hold out some prospect of success. Yonder were the hills where they could find thyme in abundance; the fields around supplied clover; and the meadows below were full of flowers. So that hot summer day, under the weeping ash, she was deep in the study of the "Ligurian queen," the "super" system, the mysteries of "driving," and was making sketches of patent hives. Looking up from her sketch she saw that her husband had fallen asleep, and stayed to gaze at him thoughtfully.

He looked worn, and older than he really was; as if rest or change would do him good; as if he required luxuries and petting. She sighed, and wondered whether the bees would enable her to buy him such things, for though the house was well furnished and apparently surrounded with wealth, they were extremely poor. Yet she did not care for money for their own household use so much as to give him the weight in parish affairs he so sadly needed. She felt that he was pushed aside, treated as a cipher, and that he had little of the influence that properly belonged to him. Her two daughters, their only children, were comfortably, though not grandly, married and settled; there was no family anxiety. But the work, the parish, the people, all seemed to have slipped out of her husband's hands. She could not but acknowledge that he was too quiet and yielding, that he lacked the brazen voice, the personal force that imposes upon men. But surely his good intentions, his way of life, his gentle kindness should carry sway. Instead of which the parish seemed to have quite left the Church, and the parson was outside the real modern life of the village. No matter what he did, even if popular, it soon seemed to pass out of his hands.

There was the school, for instance. He could indeed go across and visit it, but he had no control, no more than the veriest stranger that strolled along the road. He had always been anxious for a good school, and had done the best he could with means so limited before the new Acts came into operation. When they were passed he was the first to endeavour to carry them out and to save the village the cost and the possible quarrelling of a school board. He went through all the preliminary work, and reconciled, as far as possible, the jarring interests that came into play. The two largest landlords of the place were unfortunately not on good terms. Whatever the one did the other was jealous of, so that when one promised the necessary land for the school, and it was accepted, the other withdrew his patronage, and declined to subscribe. With great efforts the vicar, nevertheless, got the school erected, and to all appearance the difficulty was surmounted.

But when the Government inspection took place it was found that, though not nearly filled with scholars, there was not sufficient cubic space to include the children of a distant outlying hamlet, which the vicar had hoped to manage by a dame school. These poor children, ill fed and young, could hardly stand walking to and from the village school—a matter of some five miles daily, and which in winter and wet weather was, in itself, a day's work for their weary little limbs. As the vicar could not raise money enough to pay a certificated teacher at the proposed branch, or dame school, the scheme had to be abandoned. Then, according to red tape, it was necessary to enlarge the village school to accommodate these few children, and this notwithstanding that the building was never full. The enlargement necessitated a great additional expenditure. The ratepayers did, indeed, after much bickering and much persuasion, in the end pay off the deficiency; but, in the meantime, the village had been brought to the verge of a school board.

Religious differences came to the front—there was, in fact, a trial of force between the denominations. Till then for many years these differences had slumbered and been almost forgotten; they were now brought into collision, and the social quiet of the place was upset. A council of the chief farmers and some others was ultimately formed, and, as a matter of fact, really did represent the inhabitants fairly well. But while it represented the parish, it left the vicar quite outside. He had a voice, but nothing more. He was not the centre—the controlling spirit.

He bore it meekly enough, so far as he was personally concerned; but he grieved about it in connection with his deep religious feelings and his Church. The Church was not in the front of all, as it should be. It was hard after all his labour;

the rebuffs, the bitter remarks, the sneers of those who had divergent views, and, perhaps worse than all, the cold indifference and apathy of those who wished things to remain in the old state, ignoring the fact that the law would not suffer it. There were many other things besides the school, but they all went the same way. The modern institution was introduced, championed by the Church, worked for by the Church, but when at last it was successful, somehow or other it seemed to have severed itself from the Church altogether. The vicar walked about the village, and felt that, though nominally in it, he was really out of it.

His wife saw it too, still more clearly than he did. She saw that he had none of the gift of getting money out of people. Some men seem only to have to come in contact with others to at once receive the fruits of their dormant benevolent feelings. The rich man writes his cheque for £100, the middle-class well-to-do sends his bank notes for £20, the comfortable middle-class man his sovereigns. A testimonial is got up, an address engrossed on vellum, speeches are made, and a purse handed over containing a draft for so many hundreds, "in recognition, not in reward, of your long continued and successful ministrations." The art of causing the purse-strings to open is an art that is not so well understood, perhaps, among the orthodox as by the unorthodox. The Rev. F—— either could not, or would not, or did not know how to ask, and he did not receive.

Just at present his finances were especially low. The tenants who farmed the glebe land threatened to quit unless their rents were materially reduced, and unless a considerable sum was expended upon improvements. To some very rich men the reduction of rents has made a sensible difference; to the Rev. F—— it meant serious privations. But he had no choice; he had to be satisfied with that or nothing. Then the vicarage house, though substantial and pleasant to look at, was not in a good state within. The rain came through in more places than one, and the ancient woodwork of the roof was rotten. He had already done considerable repairing, and knew that he must soon do more. The nominal income of the living was but moderate; but when the reductions were all made nothing but a cheese-paring seemed left. From this his subscriptions to certain ecclesiastical institutions had to be deducted.

Lastly, he had received a hint that a curate ought to be kept now that his increasing age rendered him less active than before. There was less hope now than ever of anything being done for him in the parish. The landowners complained of rent reductions, of farms idle on their hands, and of increasing expenses. The farmers grumbled about the inclement seasons, their continual losses, and the falling markets. It was not a time when the churlish are almost generous, having such overflowing pockets. There was no testimonial, no address on vellum, no purse with banker's draft for the enfeebled servant of the Church slumbering in the cane chair in the verandah.

Yet the house was exquisitely kept, marvellously kept considering the class of servants they were obliged to put up with. The garden was bright and beautiful with flowers, the lawn smooth, there was an air of refinement everywhere. So the clergyman slept, and the wife turned again to her sketch of the patent hive, hoping that the golden honey might at last bring some metallic gold. The waggon rumbled down the road, and Hodge, lying at full length on the top of the load, could just see over the lowest part of the shrubbery, and thought to himself what a jolly life that parson led, sleeping the hot hours away in the shade.

CHAPTER XV

A MODERN COUNTRY CURATE

"He can't stroddle thuck puddle, you: can a'?"

"He be going to try: a' will leave his shoe in it."

Such were the remarks that passed between two agricultural women who from behind the hedge were watching the approach of the curate along a deep miry lane. Where they stood the meadow was high above the level of the lane, which was enclosed by steep banks thickly overgrown with bramble, briar, and thorn. The meadows each side naturally drained into the hollow, which during a storm was filled with a rushing torrent, and even after a period of dry weather was still moist, for the over-hanging trees prevented evaporation. A row of sarsen stones at irregular intervals were intended to afford firm footing to the wayfarer, but they were nothing more than traps for the unwary. Upon placing the foot on the smooth rounded surface it immediately slipped, and descended at an angle into a watery hole. The thick, stiff, yellow clay held the water like a basin; the ruts, quite two feet deep, where waggon wheels had been drawn through by main force, were full to the brim. In summer heats they might have dried, but in November, though fine, they never would.

Yet if the adventurous passenger, after gamely struggling, paused awhile to take breath, and looked up from the mud, the view above was beautiful. The sun shone, and lit up the oaks, whose every leaf was brown or buff; the gnats played in thousands in the mild air under the branches. Through the coloured leaves the blue sky was visible, and far ahead a faintly bluish shadow fell athwart the hollow. There were still blackberries on the bramble, beside which the brown fern filled the open spaces, and behind upon the banks the mosses clothed the ground and the roots of the trees with a deep green. Two or more fieldfares were watching in an elm some distance down; the flock to which they belonged was feeding, partly in the meadow and partly in the hedge. Every now and then the larks flew over, uttering their call note. Behind a bunch of rushes a young rabbit crouched in the ditch on the earth thrown out from the hole hard by, doubtful in his mind whether to stay there or to enter the burrow.

It was so still and mild between the banks, where there was not the least current of air, that the curate grew quite warm with the exertion. His boots adhered to the clay, in which they sank at every step; they came out with a "sock, sock." He now followed the marks of footsteps, planting his step where the weight of some carter or shepherd had pressed the mud down firm. Where these failed he was attracted by a narrow grass-grown ridge, a few inches wide, between two sets of ruts. In a minute he felt the ridge giving beneath him as the earth slipped into the watery ruts. Next he crept along the very edge of the ditch, where the briars hooked in the tail of his black frock-coat, and an unnoticed, projecting bough quietly lifted his shovel-hat off, but benevolently held it suspended, instead of dropping it in the mud. Still he made progress, though slow; now with a giant stride across an exceptionally doubtful spot, now zig-zagging from side to side. The lane was long, and he seemed to make but little advance.

But there was a spirit in him not to be stayed by mud, or clay, or any other obstacle. It is pleasant to see an enthusiast, whether right or wrong, in these cynical days. He was too young to have acquired much worldly wisdom, but he was full of the high spirit which arises from thorough conviction and the sense of personal consecration conferred by the mission on the man. He pushed on steadily till brought to a stop by a puddle, broad, deep, and impassable, which extended right across the lane, and was some six or eight yards long. He tried to slip past at the side, but the banks were thick with thorns, and the brambles overhung the water; the outer bushes coated with adhesive mud. Then he sounded the puddle with his stick as far as he could reach, and found it deep and the bottom soft, so that the foot would sink into it. He considered, and looked up and down the lane.

The two women, of whose presence he was unconscious, watched him from the high and dry level of the meadow, concealed behind the bushes and the oaks. They wore a species of smock frock gathered in round the waist by a band over their ordinary dress; these smock frocks had once been white, but were now discoloured with dirt and the weather. They were both stout and stolid-looking, hardy as the trees under which they stood. They were acorn picking, searching for the dropped acorns in the long rank grass by the hedge, under the brown leaves, on the banks, and in the furrows. The boughs of the oak spread wide—the glory of the tree is its head—and the acorns are found in a circle corresponding with the outer circumference of the branches. Some are still farther afield, because in falling they strike the boughs and glance aside. A long slender pole leaning against the hedge was used to thrash the boughs within reach, and so to knock down any that remained.

A sack half filled was on the ground close to the trunk of the oak, and by it was a heap of dead sticks, to be presently carried home to boil the kettle. Two brown urchins assisted them, and went where the women could not go, crawling under the thorns into the hedge, and creeping along the side of the steep bank, gathering acorns that had fallen into the mouths of the rabbit holes, or that were lying under the stoles. Out of sight under the bushes they could do much as they liked, looking for fallen nuts instead of acorns, or eating a stray blackberry, while their mothers routed about among the grass and leaves of the meadow. Such continual stooping would be weary work for any one not accustomed to it. As they worked from tree to tree they did not observe the colours of the leaves, or the wood-pigeons, or the pheasant looking along the edge of the ditch on the opposite side of the field. If they paused it was to gossip, or to abuse the boys for not bringing more acorns to the sack.

But when the boys, hunting in the hedge, descried the curate in the distance and came back with the news, the two women were suddenly interested. The pheasants, the wood-pigeons, or the coloured leaves were not worthy of a glance. To see a gentleman up to his ankles in mud was quite an attraction. The one stood with her lap half-full of acorns; the other with a basket on her arm. The two urchins lay down on the ground, and peered from behind a thorn stole, their brown faces scarcely distinguishable from the brown leaves, except for their twinkling eyes. The puddle was too wide to step across, as the women had said, nor was there any way round it.

The curate looked all round twice, but he was not the man to go back. He tucked up his trousers nearly to the knee—he wore them short always—and stepped into the water. At this the urchins could barely suppress a shout of delight—they did, however, suppress it—and craned forward to see him splash. The curate waded slowly to the middle, getting deeper and deeper, and then suddenly found firmer footing, and walked the rest of the way with the water barely over his boots. After he was through he cleansed his boots on a wisp of grass, and set off at a good pace, for the ground past the pool began to rise, and the lane was consequently drier. The women turned again to their acorns, remarking, in a tone with something like respect in it, "He didn't stop for the mud: did a'?"

Presently the curate reached the highway with its hard surface, and again increased his pace. The hedges here were cut each side, and as he walked rapidly, leaning forward, his shovel-hat and shoulders were visible above them, and his coat tails floated in the breeze of his own progress. His heavy boots—they were extremely thick and heavy, though without nails—tramped, tramped, on the hard road. With a stout walking-stick in one hand, and in the other a book, he strode forward, still more swiftly as it seemed at every stride. A tall young man, his features seemed thin and almost haggard; out of correspondence with a large frame, they looked as if asceticism had drawn and sharpened them. There was earnestness and eagerness—almost feverish eagerness—in the expression of his face. He passed the meadows, the stubble fields, the green root crops, the men at plough, who noticed his swift walk, contrasting with their own slow motion; and as he went his way now and then consulted a little slip of paper, upon which he had jotted memoranda of his engagements. Work, work, work—ceaseless work. How came this? What could there be to do in a sparsely-populated agricultural district with, to appearance, hardly a cottage to a mile?

After nearly an hour's walking he entered the outskirts of a little country town, slumbering outside the railway system, and, turning aside from the street, stopped at the door of the ancient vicarage. The resident within is the ecclesiastical head of two separate hamlets lying at some miles' distance from his own parish. Each of these hamlets possesses a church, though the population is of the very sparsest, and in each he maintains a resident curate. A third curate assists him in the duties of the home parish, which is a large one, that is in extent. From one of these distant hamlets the curate, who struggled so bravely through the mire, has walked in to consult with his superior. He is shown into the library, and sinks not unwillingly into a chair to wait for the vicar, who is engaged with a district visitor, or lay sister.

This part of the house is ancient, and dates from mediæval times. Some have conjectured that the present library and the adjoining rooms (the partitions being modern) originally formed the refectory of a monastic establishment. Others assign it to another use; but all agree that it is monastic and antique. The black oak rafters of the roof, polished as it were by age, meet overhead unconcealed by ceiling. Upon the wall in one place a figure seems at the first glance to be in the act to glide forth like a spectre from the solid stone. The effect is caused by the subdued colouring, which is shadowy and indistinct. It was perhaps gaudy when first painted; but when a painting has been hidden by a coat or two of plaster, afterwards as carefully removed as it was carelessly laid on, the tints lose their brilliancy. Some sainted woman in a flowing robe, with upraised arm, stands ever in the act to bless. Only half one of the windows of the original hall is in this apartment—the partition wall divides it. There yet remain a few stained panes in the upper part; few as they are and small, yet the coloured light that enters through them seems to tone the room.

The furniture, of oak, is plain and spare to the verge of a gaunt severity, and there is not one single picture-frame on the wide expanse of wall. On the table are a few books and some letters, with foreign postmarks, and addressed in the crabbed handwriting of Continental scholars. Over the table a brazen lamp hangs suspended by a slender chain. In a corner are some fragments of stone mouldings and wood carvings like the panel of an ancient pew. There are no shelves and no bookcase. Besides those on the table, one volume lies on the floor, which is without carpet or cover ng, but absolutely clean; and by the wall, not far from the fireplace, is an open chest, ancient and ponderous, in which are the works of the Fathers. The grate has been removed from the fireplace and the hearth restored; for in that outlying district there is plenty of wood. Though of modern make, the heavy brass fire-irons are of ancient shape. The fire has gone out—the logs are white with the ash that forms upon decaying embers; it is clear that the owner of this bare apartment, called a library, but really a study, is not one who thinks of his own personal comfort. If examined closely the floor yonder bears the marks of feet that have walked monotonously to and fro in hours of thought. When the eye has taken in these things, as the rustle of the brown leaves blown against the pane without in the silence is plainly audible, the mind seems in an instant to slip back four hundred years.

The weary curate has closed his eyes, and starts as a servant enters bringing him wine, for the vicar, utterly oblivious of his own comfort, is ever on the watch for that of others. His predecessor, a portly man, happy in his home alone, and, as report said, loving his ease and his palate, before he was preferred to a richer living, called in the advice of architects as to converting the ancient refectory to some use. In his time it was a mere lumber-room, into which all the odds and ends of the house were thrown. Plans were accordingly prepared for turning one part of it into a cosy breakfast parlour, and the other into a conservatory. Before any steps, however, were taken he received his preferment—good things flow to the rich—and departed leaving behind him a favourable memory. If any inhabitant were asked what the old vicar did, or said, and what work he accomplished, the reply invariably was, "Oh! hum! he was a very good sort of man: he never interfered with anybody or anything!"

Accustomed to such an even tenour of things, all the *vis inertiae* of the parish revolted when the new vicar immediately evinced a determination to do his work thoroughly. The restless energy of the man alone set the stolid old folk at once against him. They could not "a-bear to see he a-flying all over the parish: why couldn't he bide at home?" No one is so rigidly opposed to the least alteration in the conduct of the service as the old farmer or farmer's wife, who for forty years and more has listened to the same old hymn, the same sing-song response, the same style of sermon. It is vain to say that the change is still no more than what was contemplated by the Book of Common Prayer. They naturally interpret that book by what they have been accustomed to from childhood. The vicar's innovations were really most inoffensive, and well within even a narrow reading of the rubric. The fault lay in the fact that they were innovations, so far as the practice of that parish was concerned. So the old folk raised their voices in a chorus of horror, and when they met gossiped over the awful downfall of the faith. All that the vicar had yet done was to intone a part of the service, and at once many announced that they should stay away.

Next he introduced a choir. The sweet voices of the white-robed boys rising along the vaulted roof of the old church melted the hearts of those who, with excuses for their curiosity to their neighbours, ventured to go and hear them. The vicar had a natural talent, almost a genius, for music. There was a long struggle in his mind whether he might or might not permit himself an organ in his library. He decided it against himself, mortifying the spirit as well as the flesh, but in the service of the Church he felt that he might yield to his inclination. By degrees he gathered round him the best voices of the parish; the young of both sexes came gladly after awhile to swell the volume of song. How powerful is the influence of holy music upon such minds as are at all inclined to serious devotion! The church filled more and more every Sunday, and people came from the farthest corners of the parish, walking miles to listen. The young people grew enthusiastic, and one by one the old folk yielded and followed them.

At the same time the church itself seemed to change. It had been cold and gloomy, and gaunt within, for so many generations, that no one noticed it. A place of tombs, men hurried away from it as quickly as possible. Now, little touches here and there gradually gave it the aspect of habitation. The new curtains hung at the door of the vestry, and drawn, too, across the main entrance when service began, the *fleur-de-lys* on the crimson ground, gave an impression of warmth. The old tarnished brazen fittings of the pews were burnished up, a new and larger stove (supplied at the vicar's expense) diffused at least some little heat in winter. A curate came, one who worked heart and soul with the vicar, and the service became very nearly choral, the vicar now wearing the vestment which his degree gave him the strict right to assume. There were brazen candlesticks behind the altar, and beautiful flowers. Before, the interior was all black and white. Now there was a sense of colour, of crimson curtains, of polished brass, of flowers, and rich toned altar cloth. The place was lit up with a new light. After the first revolt of the old folk there was little opposition, because the vicar, being a man who had studied human nature and full of practical wisdom as well as learning, did all things gradually. One thing was introduced at a time, and the transition—after the first start— was effected imperceptibly. Nor was any extravagant ritual thrust upon the congregation; nor any suspicious doctrine broached.

In that outlying country place, where men had no knowledge of cathedrals, half the offices of the Church had been forgotten. The vicar brought them back again. He began early morning services; he had the church open all day for private prayer. He reminded the folk of Lent and Eastertide, which, except for the traditional pancakes, had almost passed out of their lives. Festivals, saints' days, midnight service, and above all the Communion, were insisted upon and brought home to them. As in many other country districts, the Communion had nearly dropped into disuse. At first he was alone, but by and by a group of willing lay helpers grew up around him. The churchwardens began to work with him; then a few of the larger tenant farmers. Of the two great landed proprietors, one was for him from the first, the other made no active opposition, but stood aloof. When, in the autumn, the family of the one that was for him came home, a fresh impetus was given. The ladies of the mansion came forward to join in the parish and Church work, and then other ladies, less exalted, but fairly well-to-do, who had only been waiting for a leader, crowded after.

For the first time in the memory of man the parish began to be "visited." Lay sisters accepted the charge of districts; and thus there was not a cottage, nor an old woman, but had the change brought home to her. Confirmation, which had been almost forgotten, was revived, and it was surprising what a number of girls came forward to be prepared. The

Bishop, who was not at all predisposed to view the "movement" with favour, when he saw the full church, the devotional congregation, and after he had visited the vicarage and seen into what was going on personally, expressed openly a guarded approval, and went away secretly well pleased. Rightly or wrongly, there was a "movement" in the parish and the outlying hamlets: and thus it was that the curate, struggling through the mire, carried in his face the expression of hard work. Work, work, work; the vicar, his three curates, and band of lay helpers worked incessantly.

Besides his strictly parochial duties, the vicar wrote a manual for use in the schools, he attended the Chambers of Agriculture, and supported certain social movements among the farmers, he attended meetings, and, both socially and politically, by force of character, energy, and the gift of speech, became a power in the country side. Still striving onwards, he wrote in London periodicals, he published a book; he looked from the silence of his gaunt study towards the great world, and sometimes dreamed of what he might have done had he not been buried in the country, and of what he might even yet accomplish. All who came in contact with him felt the influence of his concentrated purpose; one and all, after they had worked their hardest, thought they had still not done so much as he would have done.

The man's charm of manner was not to be resisted; he believed his office far above monarchs, but there was no personal pretension. That gentle, pleasing manner, with the sense of intellectual power behind it, quite overcame the old folk. They all spoke with complacent pride of "our vicar"; and, what was more, opened their purses. The interior of the church was restored, and a noble organ built. When its beautiful notes rose and fell, when sweet voices swelled the wave of sound, then even the vicar's restless spirit was soothed in the fulfilment of his hope. A large proportion of the upper and middle class of the parish was, without a doubt, now gathered around him; and there was much sympathy manifested from adjacent parishes with his objects, sympathy which often took the form of subscriptions from distant people.

But what said Hodge to it all? Hodge said nothing. Some few young cottage people who had good voices, and liked to use them, naturally now went to church. So did the old women and old men, who had an eye to charity. But the strong, sturdy men, the carters and shepherds, stood aloof; the bulk and backbone of the agricultural labouring population were not in the least affected. They viewed the movement with utter indifference. They cleaned their boots on a Sunday morning while the bells were ringing, and walked down to their allotments, and came home and ate their cabbage, and were as oblivious of the vicar as the wind that blew. They had no present quarrel with the Church; no complaint whatever; nor apparently any old memory or grudge; yet there was a something, a blank space as it were, between them and the Church. If anything, the "movement" rather set them against going.

Agricultural cottagers have a strong bias towards Dissent in one form or another; village chapels are always well filled. Dissent, of course, would naturally rather dislike a movement of the kind. But there was no active or even passive opposition. The cottage folk just ignored the Church; nothing more and nothing less. No efforts were spared to obtain their good will and to draw them into the fold, but there was absolutely no response. Not a labourer's family in that wide district was left unvisited. The cottages were scattered far apart, dotted here and there, one or two down in a narrow coombe surrounded on three sides by the green wall of the hills. Others stood on the bleak plains, unsheltered by tree or hedge, exposed to the keen winds that swept across the level, yet elevated fields. A new cottage built in modern style, with glaring red brick, was perched on the side of a hill, where it was visible miles away. An old thatched one stood in a hollow quite alone, half a mile from the highway, and so hidden by the oaks that an army might have ravaged the country and never found it. How many, many miles of weary walking such rounds as these required!

Though they had, perhaps, never received a "visitor" before, it was wonderful with what skill the cottage women especially—the men being often away at work—adapted themselves to the new *régime*. Each time they told a more pitiful tale, set in such a realistic framing of hardship and exposure that a stranger could not choose but believe. In the art of encouraging attentions of this sort no one excels the cottage women; the stories they will relate, with the smallest details inserted in the right place, are something marvellous. At first you would exclaim with the deepest commiseration, such a case of suffering and privation as this cannot possibly be equalled by any in the parish; but calling at the next cottage, you are presented with a yet more moving relation, till you find the whole population are plunged in misery and afflicted with incredible troubles. They cannot, surely, be the same folk that work so sturdily at harvest. But when the curate has administered words of consolation and dropped the small silver dole in the palm, when his shovel-hat and black frock-coat tails have disappeared round the corner of the copse, then in a single second he drops utterly out of mind. No one comes to church the more. If inquiries are made why they did not come, a hundred excuses are ready; the rain, a bad foot, illness of the infant, a cow taken ill and requiring attention, and so on.

After some months of such experience the curate's spirits gradually decline; his belief in human nature is sadly shaken. Men who openly oppose, who argue and deny, are comparatively easy to deal with; there is the excitement of the battle with evil. But a population that listens, and apparently accepts the message, that is so thankful for little charities, and always civil, and yet turns away utterly indifferent, what is to be done with it? Might not the message nearly as well be taken to the cow at her crib, or the horse at his manger? They too, would receive a wisp of sweet hay willingly from the hand.

But the more bitter the experience, the harder the trial, the more conscientiously the curate proceeds upon his duty, struggling bravely through the mire. He adds another mile to his daily journey; he denies himself some further recreation. The cottages in the open fields are comparatively pleasant to visit, the sweet fresh air carries away effluvia. Those that are so curiously crowded together in the village are sinks of foul smell, and may be of worse—places where, if fever comes, it takes hold and quits not. His superior requests him earnestly to refrain awhile and to take rest, to recruit himself with a holiday—even orders him to desist from overmuch labour. The man's mind is in it, and he cannot obey. What is the result?

Some lovely autumn day, at a watering-place, you may perchance be strolling by the sea, with crowds of well-dressed, happy people on the one side, and on the other the calm sunlit plain where boats are passing to and fro. A bath-chair approaches, and a young man clad in black gets out of it, where some friendly iron railings afford him a support for his hand. There, step by step, leaning heavily on the rails, he essays to walk as a child. The sockets of his joints yield beneath him, the limbs are loose, the ankle twists aside; each step is an enterprise, and to gain a yard a task. Thus day by day the convalescent strives to accustom the sinews to their work. It is a painful spectacle; how different, how strangely altered, from the upright frame and the swift stride that struggled through the miry lane, perhaps even then bearing the seeds of disease imbibed in some foul village den, where duty called him!

His wan, white face seems featureless; there is nothing but a pair of deep-set eyes. But as you pass, and momentarily catch their glance, they are bright and burning still with living faith.

CHAPTER XVI

THE SOLICITOR

IN glancing along the street of a country town, a house may sometimes be observed of a different and superior description to the general row of buildings. It is larger, rises higher, and altogether occupies more space. The façade is stylish, in the architectural fashion of half a century since. To the modern eye it may not perhaps look so interesting as the true old gabled roofs which seem so thoroughly English, nor, on the other hand, so bright and cheerful as the modern suburban villa. But it is substantial, and roomy within. The weather has given the front a sombre hue, and the windows are dingy, as if they rarely or never knew the care of a housemaid. On the ground floor the windows that would otherwise look on to the street are blocked to almost half their height with a wire blind so closely woven that no one can see in, and it is not easy to see out. The doorway is large, with stone steps and porch—the doorway of a gentleman's house. There is business close at hand—shops and inns, and all the usual offices of a town—but, though in the midst, this house wears an air of separation from the rest of the street.

When it was built—say fifty years ago, or more—it was, in fact, the dwelling-house of an independent gentleman. Similar houses may be found in other parts of the place, once inhabited by retired and wealthy people. Such persons no

longer live in towns of this kind—they build villas with lawns
and pleasure grounds outside in the environs, or, though still
retaining their pecuniary interest, reside at a distance. Like
large cities, country towns are now almost given over to
offices, shops, workshops, and hotels. Those who have made
money get away from the streets as quickly as possible.
Upon approaching nearer to this particular building the street
door will be found to be wide open to the public, and, if you
venture still closer, a name may be seen painted in black
letters upon the side of the passage wall, after the manner of
the brokers in the courts off Throgmorton Street, or of the
lawyers in the Temple. It is, in fact, the office of a country
solicitor—most emphatically one of Hodge's many masters
—and is admirably suited for his purpose, on account of its
roomy interior.

The first door within opens on the clerks' room, and should
you modestly knock on the panels instead of at once turning
the handle, a voice will invite you to "Come in." Half of the
room is partitioned off for the clerks, who sit at a long high
desk, with a low railing or screen in front of them. Before
the senior is a brass rail, along which he can, if he chooses,
draw a red curtain. He is too hard at work and intent upon
some manuscript to so much as raise his head as you enter.
But the two younger men, eager for a change, look over the
screen, and very civilly offer to attend to your business. When
you have said that you wish to see the head of the firm, you
naturally imagine that your name will be at once shouted
up the tube, and that in a minute or two, at farthest, you will
be ushered into the presence of the principal. In that small
country town there cannot surely be much work for a lawyer,
and a visitor must be quite an event. Instead, however, of
using the tube they turn to the elder clerk, and a whispered
conversation takes place, of which some broken sentences
may be caught—"He can't be disturbed," "It's no use,"
"Must wait." Then the elder clerk looks over his brass rail
and says he is very sorry, but the principal is engaged, the
directors of a company are with him, and it is quite impossible
to say exactly when they will leave. It may be ten minutes, or
an hour. But if you like to wait (pointing with his quill to a
chair) your name shall be sent up directly the directors leave.

You glance at the clock, and elect to wait. The elder clerk
nods his head, and instantly resumes his writing. The chair is
old and hard—the stuffing compressed by a generation of

weary suitors; there are two others at equal distances along the wall. The only other furniture is a small but solid table, upon which stands a brass copying-press. On the mantelpiece there are scales for letter-weighing, paper clips full of papers, a county Post-office directory, a railway time-table card nailed to the wall, and a box of paper fasteners. Over it is a map, dusty and dingy, of some estate laid out for building purposes, with a winding stream running through it, roads crossing at right angles, and the points of the compass indicated in an upper corner.

On the other side of the room, by the window, a framed advertisement hangs against the wall, like a picture, setting forth the capital and reserve and the various advantages offered by an insurance company, for which the firm are the local agents. Between the chairs are two boards fixed to the wall with some kind of hook or nail for the suspension of posters and printed bills. These boards are covered with such posters, announcing sales by auction, farms to be let, houses to be had on lease, shares in a local bank or gas works for sale, and so on, for all of which properties the firm are the legal representatives. Though the room is of fair size the ceiling is low, as is often the case in old houses, and it has, in consequence, become darkened by smoke and dust, thereby, after a while, giving a gloomy, oppressive feeling to any one who has little else to gaze at. The blind at the window rises far too high to allow of looking out, and the ground glass above it was designed to prevent the clerks from wasting their time watching the passers-by in the street. There is, however, one place where the glass is worn and transparent, and every now and then one of the two younger clerks mounts on his stool and takes a peep through to report to his companion.

The restraint arising from the presence of a stranger soon wears off; the whisper rises to a buzz of talk; they laugh, and pelt each other with pellets of paper. The older clerk takes not the least heed. He writes steadily on, and never lifts his head from the paper—long hours of labour have dimmed his sight, and he has to stoop close over the folio. He may be preparing a brief, he may be copying a deposition, or perhaps making a copy of a deed; but whatever it is, his whole mind is absorbed and concentrated on his pen. There must be no blot, no erasure, no interlineation. The hand of the clock moves slowly, and the half-heard talk and jests of the junior clerks —one of whom you suspect of making a pen and ink sketch

175

of you—mingle with the ceaseless scrape of the senior's pen,
and the low buzz of two black flies that circle for ever round
and round just beneath the grimy ceiling. Occasionally noises
of the street penetrate; the rumble of loaded waggons, the
tramp of nailed shoes, or the sharp quick sound of a trotting
horse's hoofs. Then the junior jumps up and gazes through
the peep-hole. The directors are a very long time upstairs.
What can their business be? Why are there directors at all
in little country towns?

Presently there are heavy footsteps in the passage, the door
slowly opens, and an elderly labourer, hat in hand, peers in.
No one takes the least notice of him. He leans on his stick and
blinks his eyes, looking all round the room; then taps with
the stick and clears his throat—"Be he in yet?" he asks, with
emphasis on the "he." "No, he be not in," replies a junior,
mocking the old man's accent and grammar. The senior looks
up, "Call at two o'clock, the deed is not ready," and down
goes his head again. "A' main bit o' bother about this yer
margidge" (mortgage), the labourer remarks, as he turns to
go out, not without a complacent smile on his features, for
the law's delays seem to him grand, and he feels important.
He has a little property—a cottage and garden—upon which
he is raising a small sum for some purpose, and this "margidge" is one of the great events of his life. He talked about
it for two or three years before he ventured to begin it; he has
been weeks making up his mind exactly what to do after his
first interview with the solicitor—he would have been months
had not the solicitor at last made it plain that he could waste
no more time—and when it is finally completed he will talk
about it again till the end of his days. He will be in and out
asking for "he" all day long at intervals, and when the interview takes place it will be only for the purpose of having
everything already settled explained over to him for the
fiftieth time. His heavy shoes drag slowly down the passage
—he will go to the street corner and talk with the carters
who come in, and the old women, with their baskets, a-
shopping, about "this yer law job."

There is a swifter step on the lead-covered staircase, and a
clerk appears, coming from the upper rooms. He has a telegram and a letter in one hand, and a bundle of papers in the
other. He shows the telegram and the letter to his fellow clerks
—even the grave senior just glances at the contents silently,
elevates his eyebrows, and returns to his work. After a few

minutes' talk and a jest or two the clerk rushes upstairs
again.

Another caller comes. It is a stout, florid man, a young
farmer or farmer's son, riding-whip in hand, who produces
a red-bound rate-book from a pocket in his coat made on
purpose to hold the unwieldy volume. He is a rate-collector
for his parish, and has called about some technicalities. The
grave senior clerk examines the book, but cannot solve the
difficulties pointed out by the collector, and, placing it on one
side, recommends the inquirer to call in two hours' time.
Steps again on the stairs, and another clerk comes down
leisurely, and after him still another. Their only business is
to exchange a few words with their friends, for pastime, and
they go up again.

As the morning draws on, the callers become more numerous, and it is easy to tell the positions they occupy by the
degree of attention they receive from the clerks. A tradesman calls three or four times, with short intervals between—
he runs over from his shop; the two juniors do not trouble
to so much as look over the screen, and barely take the
trouble to answer the anxious inquiry if the principal is yet
disengaged. They know, perhaps, too much about his bills
and the state of his credit. A builder looks in—the juniors are
tolerably civil, and explain to him that it is no use calling for
yet another hour at least. The builder consults his watch, and
decides to see the chief clerk (who is himself an attorney,
having passed the examination), and is forthwith conducted
upstairs. A burly farmer appears, and the grave senior puts
his head up to answer, and expresses his sorrow that the
principal is so occupied. The burly farmer, however, who is
evidently a man of substance, thinks that the chief clerk can
also do what he wants, and he, too, is ushered upstairs.
Another farmer enters—a rather rougher-looking man—and,
without saying a word, turns to the advertisement boards on
which the posters of farms to be let, etc., are displayed.
These he examines with the greatest care, pointing with his
forefinger as he slowly reads, and muttering to himself.
Presently he moves to go. "Anything to suit you, sir?" asks
the senior clerk. "Aw, no; I knows they be too much money,"
he replies, and walks out.

A gentleman next enters, and immediately the juniors sink
out of sight, and scribble away with eager application; the
senior puts down his pen and comes out from his desk. It is

a squire and magistrate. The senior respectfully apologises
for his employer being so occupied. The gentleman seems a
little impatient. The clerk rubs his hands together deprecat-
ingly, and makes a desperate venture. He goes upstairs, and
in a few minutes returns; the papers are not ready, but shall
be sent over that evening in any case. With this even the squire
must fain be satisfied and depart. The burly farmer and the
builder come downstairs together amicably chatting, and after
them the chief clerk himself. Though young, he has already
an expression of decision upon his features, an air of business
about him; in fact, were he not thoroughly up to his work he
would not remain in that office long. To hold that place is a
guarantee of ability. He has a bundle of cheques, drafts, etc.,
in his hand, and after a few words with the grave senior at
the desk, strolls across to the bank.

No sooner has the door closed behind him than a shoal of
clerks come tripping down on tip-toe, and others appear
from the back of the house. They make use of the opportunity
for a little gossip. Voices are heard in the passage, and an aged
and infirm labouring man is helped in by a woman and a
younger man. The clerks take no notice, and the poor old
fellow props himself against the wall, not daring to take a
chair. He is a witness. He can neither read nor write, but he
can recollect "thuck ould tree," and can depose to a fact
worth perhaps hundreds of pounds. He has come in to be
examined; he will be driven in a week or two's time from the
village to the railway station in a fly, and will talk about it and
his visit to London till the lamp of life dies out.

A footman calls with a note, a groom brings another, the
letters are carelessly cast aside, till one of the juniors, who has
been watching from the peephole, reports that the chief clerk
is coming, and everybody scuttles back to his place. Callers
come still more thickly; another solicitor, well-to-do, and
treated with the utmost deference; more tradesmen; farmers;
two or three auctioneers, in quick succession; the well-
brushed editor of a local paper; a second attorney, none too
well dressed, with scrubby chin and face suspiciously cloudy,
with an odour of spirits and water and tobacco clinging to
his rusty coat. He belongs to a disappearing type of country
lawyer, and is the wreck, perhaps, of high hopes and good
opportunities. Yet, wreck as he is, when he gets up at the
Petty Sessions to defend some labourer, the bench of magistrates listen to his maundering argument as deferentially as

if he were a Q.C. They pity him, and they respect his cloth.
The scrubby attorney whistles a tune, and utters an oath when
he learns the principal is engaged. Then he marches out, with
his hat on one side of his head, to take another "refresher."

Two telegrams arrive, and are thrown aside; then a gentleman appears, whom the senior goes out to meet with an air
of deference, and whom he actually conducts himself upstairs
to the principal's room. It is a local banker, who is thus
admitted to the directors' consultation. The slow hand of the
clock goes round, and, sitting wearily on the hard chair, you
wonder if ever it will be possible to see this much-sought man.
By-and-by a door opens above, there is a great sound of
voices and chatting and half-a-dozen gentlemen—mostly
landed proprietors from their appearance—come downstairs.
They are the directors, and the consultation is over. The senior
clerk immediately goes to the principal, and shortly afterwards
reappears and asks you to come up.

As you mount the lead-covered stairs you glance down and
observe the anxious tradesman, the ancient labourer, and
several others who have crowded in, all eyeing you with
jealous glances. But the senior is holding the door open—you
enter, and it closes noiselessly behind you. A hand with a pen
in it points to a chair, with a muttered "Pardon—half a
moment," and while the solicitor just jots down his notes you
can glance round the apartment. Shelves of calf-bound law
books; piles of japanned deed-boxes, some marked in white
letters "Trustees of," or "Executors of," and pigeon-holes
full of papers seem to quite hide the walls. The floor is
covered with some material noiseless to walk on (the door,
too, is double, to exclude noise and draught); the furniture
is solid and valuable; the armchair you occupy capacious and
luxurious. On the wall hangs a section of the Ordnance map
of the district. But the large table, which almost fills the centre
of the room, quickly draws the attention from everything else.

It is on that table that all the business is done; all the
energies of the place are controlled and directed from thence.
At the first glance it appears to support a mere chaotic mass
of papers. They completely conceal it, except just at the edge.
Bundles of letters tied with thin red tape, letters loose, letters
unopened; parchment deeds with the seals and signature just
visible; deeds with the top and the words "This indenture,"
alone showing out from the confusion; deeds neatly folded;
broad manuscript briefs; papers fastened with brass fasteners;

papers hastily pinned together; old newspapers marked and
underlined in red ink; a large sectional map, half unrolled
and hanging over the edge; a small deed-box, the lid open,
and full of blue paper in oblong strips; a tall porcupine-quill
pen handle sticking up like a spire; pocket-books; books open;
books with half-a-dozen papers in them for markers; altogether an utter chaos. But the confusion is only apparent; the
master mind knows the exact position of every document, and
can lay his hand on it the moment it is wanted.

The business is such that even that master mind can barely
keep pace with it. This great house can hardly contain it; all
the clerks we saw rushing about cannot get through the work,
and much of the mechanical copying or engrossing goes to
London to be done. The entire round of country life comes
here. The rolling hills where the shepherd watches his flock,
the broad plains where the ploughman guides the share, the
pleasant meadows where the roan cattle chew the cud, the
extensive parks, the shady woods, sweet streams, and hedges
overgrown with honeysuckle, all have their written counter-
part in those japanned deed boxes. Solid as is the land over
which Hodge walks stolid and slow, these mere written words
on parchment are the masters of it all. The squire comes here
about intricate concerns of family settlements which in their
sphere are as hard to arrange as the diplomatic transactions
of Governments. He comes about his tenants and his rent;
he comes to get new tenants.

The tenants resort to the solicitor for farms, for improvements, reductions, leases, to negotiate advances, to insure, for
the various affairs of life. The clergyman comes on questions
that arise out of his benefice, the churchyard, ecclesiastical
privileges, the schools, and about his own private property.
The labourer comes about his cottage and garden—an estate
as important to him as his three thousand acres to the squire—
or as a witness. The tradesman, the builder, the banker come
for financial as well as legal objects. As the town develops, and
plots are needed for houses and streets, the resort to the
solicitor increases tenfold. Companies are formed and require
his advice. Local government needs his assistance. He may
sit in an official position in the County Court, or at the bench
of the Petty Sessions. Law suits—locally great—are carried
through in the upper courts of the metropolis; the counsel's
name appears in the papers, but it is the country solicitor
who has prepared everything for him, and who has mar-

shalled that regiment of witnesses from remote hamlets of the earth. His widening circle of landlord clients have each their attendant circles of tenants, who feel confidence in their leader's legal adviser. Parochial officers come to him; overseer, rate-collector, churchwarden, tithing-man.

The all-important work of registering voters fills up the space between one election and another. At the election his offices are like the head-quarters of an army. He may represent some ancient college, or corporation with lands of vast extent. Ladies with a little capital go home content when he has invested their money in mortgage of real property. Still the work goes on increasing; additional clerks have to be employed; a fresh wing has to be built to the old house. He has, too, his social duties; he is, perhaps, the head or mainspring of a church movement—this is not for profit, but from conviction. His lady is carried to and fro in the brougham, making social visits. He promotes athletic clubs, reading-rooms, shows, exhibitions. He is eagerly seized upon by promoters of all kinds, because he possesses the gift of organisation. It becomes a labour merely to catalogue his engagements like this. Let the rain rain, or the sun shine, the pen never stays work.

Personally he is the very antithesis of what might be predicated of the slow, comfortable, old-fashioned lawyer. He is in the prime of life, physically full of vigour, mentally persevering with untiring perseverance, the embodiment of energy, ever anxious to act, to do rather than to delay. As you talk with him you find his leading idea seems to be to arrange your own half-formed views for you; in short, to show you what you really do want, to put your desire into shape. He interprets you. Many of the clients who come to him are the most impracticable men in the world. A farmer, for instance, with a little money, is in search of a farm. Find him twenty farms just the size for his capital, he will visit them all and discover a fault in each, and waver and waver till the proper season for entering on possession is past. The great problem with country people is how to bring them to the point. You may think you have got all your witnesses ready for the train for London, and, as the bell rings, find that one has slipped away half-a-mile to talk with the blacksmith about the shoeing of his mare. Even the squire is trying, when he talks of this or that settlement. Of course, as he is educated, no lengthy and oft-repeated explanations are needed; but the squire forgets that time is valuable, and lingers merely to chat. He has so much time to spare, he is apt to overlook that the solicitor has none. The clergyman will talk, talk, talk in rounded periods, and nothing will stop him; very often he drives his wife in with him from the village, and the wife must have her say. As for Hodge and his mortgage, ten years would not suffice for his business were he allowed to wander on. The problem is to bring these impracticable people to the point with perfect courtesy. As you talk with him yourself, you feel tempted to prolong the interview—so lucid an intellect exercises an indefinable charm.

Keen and shrewd as he is, the solicitor has a kindly reputation. Men say that he is slow to press them, that he makes allowances for circumstances; that if the tenant is honestly willing to discharge his obligation he need fear no arbitrary selling up. But he is equally reputed swift of punishment upon those who would take shelter behind mere shallow pretence, or attempt downright deceit. Let a man only be straightforward, and the solicitor will wait rather than put the law in force. Therefore, he is popular, and people have faith in him. But the labour, the incessant supervision, the jotting down of notes, the ceaseless interviews, the arguments, the correspondence, the work that is never finished when night comes, tell even upon that physical vigour and mental elasticity. Hodge sleeps sound and sees the days go by with calm complacency. The man who holds that solid earth, as it were, in the japanned boxes finds a nervous feeling growing upon him despite his strength of will. Presently nature will have her way; and, weary and hungry for fresh air, he rushes off for a while to distant trout-stream, moor, or stubble.

CHAPTER XVII

"COUNTY-COURT DAY"

THE monthly sitting of the County Court in a country market town is an event of much interest in all the villages around, so many of the causes concerning agricultural people. "County-Court Day" is looked upon as a date in the calendar by which to recollect when a thing happened, or to arrange for the future.

As the visitor enters the doorway of the Court, at a distance the scene appears imposing. Brass railings and red curtains partition off about a third of the hall, and immediately in the rear of this the Judge sits high above the rest on a raised and carpeted dais. The elevation and isolation of the central figure adds a solemn dignity to his office. His features set, as it were, in the wig, stand out in sharp relief—they are of a keenly intellectual cast, and have something of the precise clearness of an antique cameo. The expression is that of a mind in continuous exercise—of a mind accustomed not to slow but to quick deliberation, and to instant decision. The definition of the face gives the eyes the aspect of penetration, as if they saw at once beneath the surface of things.

If the visitor looks only at the Judge he will realise the dignity of the law; the law which is the outcome and result of so many centuries of thought. But if he glances aside from the central figure the impression is weakened by the miserable, hollow, and dingy framing. The carpet upon the dais and the red curtains before it conceal the paltry substructure. It is composed of several large tables, heavy and shapeless as benches, placed side by side to form a platform. The curtains are dingy and threadbare; the walls dingy, the ceiling, though lofty, dingy; the boxes on either side for Plaintiff and Defendant are scratched and defaced by the innumerable witnesses who have blundered into them, kicking their shoes against the woodwork. The entire apparatus is movable, and can be taken to pieces in ten minutes, or part of it employed for meetings of any description. There is nothing appropriate or convenient; it is a makeshift, and altogether unequal to the pretensions of a Court now perhaps the most useful and most resorted to of any that sit in the country.

Quarter sessions and assizes come only at long intervals, are held only in particular time-honoured places, and take cognisance only of very serious offences which happily are not numerous. The County Court at the present day has had its jurisdiction so enlarged that it is really, in country districts, the leading tribunal, and the one best adapted to modern wants, because its procedure is to a great extent free from obsolete forms and technicalities. The Plaintiff and the Defendant literally face their Judge, practically converse with him, and can tell their story in their own simple and natural way. It is a fact that the importance and usefulness of the country County Court has in most places far outgrown the arrangements made for it. The Judges may with reason complain that while their duties have been enormously added to, their convenience has not been equally studied, nor their salaries correspondingly increased.

In front, and below the Judge's desk, just outside the red curtain, is a long and broad table, at which the High Bailiff sits facing the hall. By his side the Registrar's clerk from time to time makes notes in a ponderous volume which contains a minute and exact record of every claim. Opposite, and at each end, the lawyers have their chairs and strew the table with their papers.

As a rule a higher class of lawyers appear in the County Court than before the Petty Sessional Bench. A local solicitor of ability no sooner gets a "conveyancing" practice than he finds his time too valuable to be spent arguing in cases of assault or petty larceny. He ceases to attend the Petty Sessions, unless his private clients are interested or some exceptional circumstances induce him. In the County Court cases often arise which concern property, houses and lands, and the fulfilment of contracts. Some of the very best lawyers of the district may consequently be seen at that table, and frequently a barrister or two of standing specially retained is among them.

A low wooden partition, crossing the entire width of the hall, separates the "bar" from the general public, Plaintiff and Defendant being admitted through a gangway. As the hall is not carpeted, nor covered with any material, a new comer must walk on tip-toe to avoid raising the echo of hollow boards, or run the risk of a reproof from the Judge, anxiously endeavouring to catch the accents of a mumbling witness. Groups of people stand near the windows whispering, and occasionally forgetting in the eagerness of the argument, that talking is prohibited. The room is already full, but will be crowded when the "horse case" comes on again. Nothing is of so much interest as a "horse case." The issues raised concern almost every countryman, and the parties are generally well known. All the idlers of the town are here, and among them many a rascal who has been through the processes, and comes again to listen and possibly learn a dodge by which to delay the execution of judgment. Some few of the more favoured and respectable persons have obtained entrance to the space allotted to the solicitors, and have planted themselves in a solid circle round the fire, effectually preventing

the heat from benefiting any one else. Another fire, carefully
tended by a bailiff, burns in the grate behind the Judge, but, as
his seat is so far from it, without adding much to his comfort.
A chilly draught sweeps along the floor, and yet at the same
time there is a close and somewhat fetid atmosphere at the
height at which men breathe. The place is ill warmed and
worse ventilated; altogether without convenience, and com-
fortless.

To-day the Judge, to suit the convenience of the solicitors
engaged in the "horse case," who have requested permission
to consult in private, has asked for a short defended cause to
fill up the interval till they are ready to resume. The High
Bailiff calls "Brown v. Jones," claim 8s. for goods supplied.
No one at first answers, but after several calls a woman in
the body of the court comes forward. She is partly deaf, and
until nudged by her neighbours did not hear her husband's
name. The Plaintiff is a small village dealer in tobacco, snuff,
coarse groceries, candles, and so on. His wife looks after the
little shop, and he works with horse and cart, hauling and
doing odd jobs for the farmers. Instead of attending himself
he has sent his wife to conduct the case. The Defendant is
a labourer living in the same village, who, like so many of
his class, has got into debt. He, too, has sent his wife to represent him. This is the usual course of the cottagers, and of
agricultural people who are better off than cottagers. The men
shirk out of difficulties of this kind by going off in the morning
early to their work with the parting remark, "Aw, you'd
better see about it; I don't knaw nothing about such jobs."

The High Bailiff has no easy task to swear the Plaintiff's representative. First, she takes the book and kisses it before the
formula prescribed has been repeated. Then she waits till
the sentence is finished and lifts the book with the left hand
instead of the right. The Registrar's clerk has to go across to
the box and shout an explanation into her ear. "Tell the
truth," says the old lady, with alacrity; "why, that's what I
be come for." The Judge asks her what it is she claims, and
she replies that that man, the Registrar's clerk, has got it all
written down in his book. She then turns to the Defendant's
wife, who stands in the box opposite, and shouts to her, "You
knows you ain't paid it."

It is in vain that the Judge endeavours to question her, in
vain that the High Bailiff tries to calm her, in vain that the
clerk lays his hand on her arm—she is bent on telling the de-

185

fendant a bit of her mind. The Court is perforce compelled to wait till it is over, when the Judge, seeing that talking is of no avail, goes at once to the root of the matter and asks to see her books. A dirty account book, such as may be purchased for threepence, is handed up to him; the binding is broken, and some of the leaves are loose. It is neither a day-book, a ledger, nor anything else—there is no system whatever and indeed the Plaintiff admits that she only put down about half of it, and trusted to memory for the rest. Here is a date, and after it some figures, but no articles mentioned, neither tea nor candles. Next come some groceries, and the price, but no one's name, so that it is impossible to tell who had the goods. Then there are pages with mysterious dots and strokes and half strokes, which ultimately turn out to mean ounces and half ounces of tobacco. These have neither name nor value attached. From end to end nothing is crossed off, so that whether an account be paid or not cannot be ascertained.

While the Judge laboriously examines every page, trying by the light of former experience to arrive at some idea of the meaning, the Defendant's wife takes up her parable. She chatters in return at the Plaintiff, then she addresses the High Bailiff, who orders her to remain quiet, and, finally, turns round and speaks to the crowd. The Judge, absorbed in the attempt to master the account book, does not for the moment notice this, till, as he comes to the conclusion that the book is utterly valueless, he looks up and finds the Defendant with her back turned gesticulating and describing her wrongs to the audience. Even his command of silence is with reluctance obeyed, and she continues to mutter to herself. When order is restored the Judge asks for her defence, when the woman immediately produces a receipt, purporting to be for this very eight shillings' worth. At the sight of this torn and dirty piece of paper the Plaintiff works herself into a fury, and speaks so fast and so loud (as deaf people will) that no one else can be heard. Till she is made to understand that she will be sent out of Court she does not desist. The Judge looks at the receipt, and finds it correct; but still the Plaintiff positively declares that she has never had the money. Yet she admits that the receipt is in her handwriting. The Judge asks the Defendant who paid over the cash, and she replies that it was her husband. The account-book contains no memorandum of any payment at all. With difficulty the Judge again obtains silence, and once more endeavours to understand a page of the account-book to which the Plaintiff persists in pointing. His idea is now to identify the various articles mentioned in the receipt with the articles put down on that particular page.

After at least three-quarters of an hour, during which the book is handed to and fro by the clerk from Judge to Plaintiff, that she may explain the meaning of the hieroglyphics, some light at last begins to dawn. By dint of patiently separating the mixed entries the Judge presently arrives at a partial comprehension of what the Plaintiff has been trying to convey. The amount of the receipted bill and the amount of the entries in the page of the account book are the same; but the articles entered in the book and those admitted to be paid for are not. The receipt mentions candles; the account book has no candles. Clearly they are two different debts, which chanced to come to the same figure. The receipt, however, is not dated, and whether it is the Defendant who is wilfully misrepresenting, or whether the Plaintiff is under a mistaken notion, the Judge for the time cannot decide. The Defendant declares that she does not know the date and cannot fix it—it was a ''main bit ago,'' and that is all she can say.

For the third time the Judge, patient to the last degree, wades through the account book. Meanwhile the hands of the clock have moved on. Instead of being a short case, this apparently simple matter has proved a long one, and already as the afternoon advances the light of the dull winter's day declines. The solicitors engaged in the horse case, who retired to consult, hoping to come to a settlement, returned into Court fully an hour ago, and have since been sitting at the table waiting to resume. Besides these some four or five other lawyers of equal standing are anxiously looking for a chance of commencing their business. All their clients are waiting, and the witnesses; they have all crowded into the Court, the close atmosphere of which is almost intolerable.

But having begun the case the Judge gives it his full and undivided attention. Solicitors, clients, witnesses, cases that interest the public, causes that concern valuable property, or important contracts must all be put aside till this trifling matter is settled. He is as anxious as any, or more so, to get on, because delay causes business to accumulate—the adjourned causes, of course, having to be heard at next Court, and thus swelling the list to an inordinate length. But, impatient as he may be, especially as he is convinced that one or other of the parties is keeping back a part of the truth, he is determined

187

that the subject shall be searched to the bottom. The petty village shopkeeper and the humble cottager obtain as full or fuller attention than the well-to-do Plaintiffs and Defendants who can bring down barristers from London.

"What have you there?" the Registrar's clerk demands of the Plaintiff presently. She has been searching in her pocket for a snuff-box wherewith to refresh herself, and, unable to immediately discover it, has emptied the contents of the pocket on the ledge of the witness-box. Among the rest is another little account book.

"Let me see that," demands the Judge, rather sharply, and no wonder. "Why did you not produce it before?"

"Aw, he be last year's un; some of it be two years ago," is the reply.

Another long pause. The Judge silently examines every page of the account book two years old. Suddenly he looks up. "This receipt," he says, "was given for an account rendered eighteen months ago. Here in this older book are the entries corresponding with it. The present claim is for a second series of articles which happened to come to the same amount, and the Defendant, finding that the receipt was not dated, has endeavoured to make it do duty for the two."

"I tould you so," interrupts the Plaintiff. "I tould you so, but you wouldn't listen to I."

The Judge continues that he is not sure he ought not to commit the Defendant, and then, with a gesture of weary disgust, throws down his pen and breaks off in the middle of his sentence to ask the High Bailiff if there are any other judgments out against the Defendant. So many years' experience of the shifts, subterfuges, paltry misrepresentations, and suppressions—all the mean and despicable side of poor humanity—have indeed wearied him, but, at the same time, taught forbearance. He hesitates to be angry, and delays to punish. The people are poor, exceedingly poor. The Defendant's wife says she has eight children; they are ignorant, and, in short, cannot be, in equity, judged as others in better circumstances. There are two other judgments against the Defendant, who is earning about 12s. a week, and the verdict is 1s. a month, first payment that day three weeks.

Then the solicitor for the Plaintiff in the "horse case" rises and informs the Judge that the parties cannot settle it, and the case must proceed. The Plaintiff and Defendant take their places, and some thirty witnesses file through the gangway to the witness-room to be out of Court. The bailiffs light the gas as the gloom deepens, and the solicitor begins his opening speech. The Judge has leant back in his chair, closed his eyes, and composed himself to listen. By the time two witnesses have been examined the hour has arrived when the Judge can sit no longer. He must leave, because on the morrow he has to hold a Court in another part of the county. The important "horse case" and the other causes must wait a month. He sits to the very last moment, then hastily stuffs deeds, documents, papers of all descriptions into a portmanteau already overflowing, and rushes to his carriage.

He will go through much the same work to-morrow; combating the irritating misrepresentations, exposing suppressions, discovering the truth under a mountain of crass stupidity and wilful deceit. Next day he will be again at work; and the same process will go on the following week. In the month there are perhaps about five days—exclusive of Sundays—upon which he does not sit. But those days are not holidays. They are spent in patiently reading a mass of deeds, indentures, contracts, vouchers, affidavits, evidence of every description and of the most voluminous character. These have been put in by solicitors, as part of their cases, and require the most careful attention. Besides causes that are actually argued out in open Court, there are others which, by consent of both parties are placed in his hands as arbitrator. Many involve nice points of law, and require a written judgment in well-chosen words.

The work of the County Court Judge at the present day is simply enormous; it is ceaseless and never finished, and it demands a patience which nothing can ruffle. No matter how much falsehood may annoy him, a Judge with arbitrary power entrusted to him must not permit indignation alone to govern his decision. He must make allowances for all.

For the County Court in country districts has become a tribunal whose decisions enter as it were into the very life of the people. It is not concerned with a few important cases only; it has to arrange and finally settle what are really household affairs. Take any village, and make inquiries how many householders there are who have not at one time or other come under the jurisdiction of the County Court? Either as Plaintiff, or Defendant, or as witness, almost every one has had such experience, and those who have not have been threatened with it. Besides those defended cases that come before the Judge, there are hundreds upon hundreds of petty claims, to which no defence is offered, and which are adjudicated upon by the Registrar at the same time that the Judge hears the defended causes.

The labourer, like so many farmers in a different way, lives on credit and is perpetually in debt. He purchases his weekly goods on the security of hoeing, harvest, or piece work, and his wages are continually absorbed in payment of instalments, just as the tenant-farmer's income is too often absorbed in the payment of interest on and instalments of his loans. No one seems ever to pay without at least a threat of the County Court, which thus occupies a position like a firm appointed to perpetually liquidate a vast estate. It is for ever collecting shillings and half-crowns.

This is one aspect of the County Court; the other is its position with respect to property. It is the great arbitrator of property—of houses and land, and deeds, and contracts. Of recent years the number of the owners of land has immensely increased—that is, of small pieces—and the litigation has correspondingly grown. There is enough work for a man of high legal ability in settling causes of this character alone, without any "horse case" with thirty witnesses, or any dispute that involves the conflict of personal testimony.

CHAPTER XVIII

THE BANK—THE OLD NEWS-PAPER

THE most imposing building in a certain country market town is the old Bank, so called familiarly to distinguish it from the new one. The premises of the old Bank would be quite unapproached in grandeur, locally, were it not for the enterprise of the new establishment. Nothing could be finer than the façade of the old Bank, which stands out clear and elegant in its fresh paint among the somewhat dingy houses and shops of the main street. It is rather larger in size, more lofty, and has the advantage of being a few yards nearer to the railway station. But the rival institution runs it very close.

It occupies a corner on the very verge of the market-place—
its door facing the farmer as he concludes his deal—and it is
within a minute of the best hotels, where much business is
done. It is equally white and clean with fresh paint, and
equally elegant in design.

A stranger, upon a nice consideration of the circumstances,
might find a difficulty in deciding on which to bestow his
patronage; and perhaps the chief recommendation of the old
establishment lies in the fact that it is the older of the two.
The value of antiquity was never better understood than in
these modern days. Shrewd men of business have observed
that the quality of being ancient is the foundation of credit.
Men believe in that which has been long established. Their
fathers dealt there, they deal themselves, and if a new comer
takes up his residence he is advised to do likewise.

A visitor desirous of looking on the outside, at least of
country banking, would naturally be conducted to the old
Bank. If it were an ordinary day, *i.e.*, not a market or fair,
he might stand on the pavement in front sunning himself
without the least inconvenience from the passenger traffic.
He would see, on glancing up and down the street, one or two
aged cottage women going in or out of the grocer's, a post-
man strolling round, and a distant policeman at the farthest
corner. A sprinkling of boys playing marbles at the side of the
pavement, and two men loading a waggon with sacks of flour
from a warehouse, complete the scene as far as human life
is concerned. There are dogs basking on doorsteps, larger
dogs rambling with idleness in the slow sway of their tails,
and overhead black swifts (whose nests are in the roofs of
the higher houses) dash to and fro, uttering their shrill screech.

The outer door of the bank is wide open—fastened back—
ostentatiously open, and up the passage another mahogany
door, closed, bears a polished brazen plate with the word
"Manager" engraved upon it. Everything within is large and
massive. The swing door itself yields with the slow motion of
solidity, and, unless you are agile as it closes in the rear,
thrusts you forward like a strong gale. The apartment is large
and lofty: there is room for a crowd, but at present there is no
one at the counter. It is long enough and broad enough for
the business of twenty customers at once; so broad that the
clerks on the other side are beyond arm's reach. But they have
shovels with which to push the gold towards you, and in a
small glass stand is a sponge kept constantly damp, across

which the cashier draws his finger as he counts the silver, the slight moisture enabling him to sort the coin more swiftly.

The fittings are perfect, as perfect as in a London bank, and there is an air of extreme precision. Yonder open drawers are full of pass-books; upon the desks and on the broad mantelpiece are piles of cheques, not scattered in disorder but arranged in exact heaps. The very inkstands are heavy and vast, and you just catch a glimpse round the edge of the semisentry box which guards the desk of the chief cashier, of a ledger so huge that the mind can hardly realise the extent of the business which requires such ponderous volumes to record it. Then beyond these a glass door, half open, apparently leads to the manager's room, for within it is a table strewn with papers, and you can see the green-painted iron wall of a safe.

The clerks, like the place, are somewhat imposing; they are in no hurry, they allow you time to look round you and imbibe the sense of awe which the magnificent mahogany counter and the brazen fittings, all the evidences of wealth, are so calculated to inspire. The hollow sound of your footstep on the floor does not seem heard; the slight "Ahem!" you utter after you have waited a few moments attracts no attention, nor the rustling of your papers. The junior clerks are adding up column after column of figures and are totally absorbed; the chief cashier is pondering deeply over a letter and annotating it. By-and-by he puts it down, and slowly approaches. But after you have gone through the preliminary ceremony of waiting, which is an institution of the place, the treatment quite changes. Your business is accomplished with practised ease, any information you may require is forthcoming on the instant, and deft fingers pass you the coin. In brief, the whole machinery of banking is here as complete as in Lombard Street. The complicated ramifications of commercial transactions are as well understood and as closely studied as in the "City." No matter what your wishes, provided, of course, that your credentials are unimpeachable, they will be conducted for you satisfactorily and without delay.

Yet the green meadows are within an arrow shot, and standing on the threshold and looking down a cross street you can see the elms of the hedgerows closing in the prospect. It is really wonderful that such conveniences should be found in so apparently insignificant a place. The intelligence and courtesy of the officials is most marked. It is clear, upon reflection, that such intelligence, such manners, and knowledge not only of business but of men (for a banker and a banker's agent has often to judge at a moment's notice whether a man be a rogue or honest), cannot be had for nothing. They must be paid for, and, in so far at least as the heads are concerned, paid liberally. It is known that the old Bank has often paid twenty and twenty-five per cent. to its shareholders. Where does all this money come from? From Hodge, toiling in the field and earning his livelihood in the sweat of his brow? One would hardly think so at first, and yet there are no great businesses or manufactories here. Somehow or other the money that pays for this courtesy and commercial knowledge, for these magnificent premises and furniture, that pays the shareholders twenty-five per cent., must be drawn from the green meadows, the cornfields, and the hills where the sheep feed.

On an ordinary day the customers that come to the bank's counter may be reckoned on the fingers. Early in the morning the Post-office people come for their cash and change; next, some of the landlords of the principal inns with their takings; afterwards, such of the tradesmen as have cheques to pay in. Later on the lawyer's clerks, or the solicitors themselves drop in; in the latter case for a chat with the manager. A farmer or two may call, especially on a Friday, for the cash to pay the labourers next day, and so the morning passes. In the afternoon one or more of the local gentry or clergy may drive up or may not—it is a chance either way—and as the hour draws near for closing some of the tradesmen come hurrying in again. Then the day, so far as the public are concerned, is over. To-morrow sees the same event repeated.

On a market-day there is a great bustle; men hustle in and out, with a bluff disregard of conventional politeness, but with no intention of rudeness. Through the open doors comes the lowing of cattle, and the baaing of sheep; the farmers and dealers that crowd in and out bring with them an odour of animals that exhales from their garments. The clerks are now none too many, the long broad counter none too large; the resources of the establishment are taxed to the utmost. The manager is there in person, attending to the more important customers.

In the crush are many ladies who would find their business facilitated by coming on a different day. But market-day is a tradition with all classes; even the gentry appear in greater numbers. If you go forth into the market-place you will find it thronged with farmers. If you go into the Corn Hall or Exchange, where the corndealers have their stands, and where business in cereals and seeds is transacted; if you walk across to the auction yard for cattle, or to the horse depository, where an auction of horses is proceeding; everywhere you have to push your way through groups of agriculturists. The hotels are full of them (the stable-yards full of their various conveyances), and the restaurant, the latest innovation in country towns, is equally filled with farmers taking a chop, and the inner rooms with ladies discussing coffee and light refreshments.

Now every farmer of all this crowd has his cheque-book in the breast pocket of his coat. Let his business be what it may, the purchase of cattle, sheep, horses, or implements, seed, or any other necessary, no coin passes. The parties, if the transaction be private, adjourn to their favourite inn, and out comes the cheque-book. If a purchase be effected at either of the auctions proceeding it is paid for by cheque, and, on the other hand, should the farmer be the vendor, his money comes to him in the shape of a cheque. With the exception of his dinner and the ostler, the farmer who comes to market carries on all his transactions with paper. The landlord of the hotel takes cash for the dinner, and the ostler takes his shilling. For the rest, it is all cheques, cheques, cheques; so that the whole business of agriculture, from the purchase of the seed to the sale of the crop, passes through the bank.

The toll taken by the bank upon such transactions as simple buying and selling is practically *nil*; its profit is indirect. But besides the indirect profit there is the direct speculation of making advances at high interest, discounting bills, and similar business. It might almost be said that the crops are really the property of the local banks, so large in the aggregate are the advances made upon them. The bank has, in fact, to study the seasons, the weather, the probable market prices, the import of grain and cattle, and to keep an eye upon the agriculture of the world. The harvest and the prices concern it quite as much as the actual farmer who tills the soil. In good seasons, with a crop above the average, the business of the bank expands in corresponding ratio. The manager and directors feel that they can advance with confidence; the farmer has the means to pay. In bad seasons and with short crops the farmer is more anxious than ever to borrow; but the bank is obliged to contract its sphere of operations.

It usually happens that one or more of the directors of a country bank are themselves farmers in a large way—gentlemen farmers, but with practical knowledge. They are men whose entire lives have been spent in the locality, and who have a very wide circle of acquaintances and friends among agriculturists. Their forefathers were stationed there before them, and thus there has been an accumulation of local knowledge. They not only thoroughly understand the soil of the neighbourhood, and can forecast the effect of particular seasons with certainty, but they possess an intimate knowledge of family history, what farmer is in a bad way, who is doubtful, or who has always had a sterling reputation. An old-established country bank has almost always one or more such confidential advisers. Their assistance is invaluable.

Since agriculture became in this way, through the adoption of banking, so intimately connected with commerce, it has responded, like other businesses, to the fluctuations of trade. The value of money in Threadneedle-street affects the farmer in an obscure hamlet a hundred miles away, whose fathers knew nothing of money except as a coin, a token of value, and understood nothing of the export or import of gold. The farmer's business is conducted through the bank, but, on the other hand, the bank cannot restrict its operations to the mere country-side. It is bound up in every possible manner with the vast institutions of the metropolis. Its private profits depend upon the rate of discount and the tone of the money market exactly in the same way as with those vast institutions. A difficulty, a crisis there is immediately felt by the country bank, whose dealings with its farmer customers are in turn affected.

Thus commerce acts upon agriculture. *Per contra*, the tradesmen of the town who go to the bank every morning would tell you with doleful faces that the condition of agriculture acts upon trade in a most practical manner. Neither the farmer, nor the farmer's wife and family expend nearly so much as they did at their shops, and consequently the sums they carry over to the bank are much diminished in amount. The local country tradesman probably feels the depression of agriculture all but as much as the farmer himself. The tradesman is perhaps supported by the bank; if he cannot meet his liabilities the bank is compelled to withdraw that support.

Much of this country banking seems to have grown up in very recent times. Any elderly farmer out yonder in the noisy
195

market would tell you that in his young days when he first did business he had to carry coin with him, especially if at a distance from home. It was then the custom to attend markets and fairs a long way off, such markets being centres where the dealers and drovers brought cattle. The dealers would accept nothing but cash; they would not have looked at a cheque had such a thing been proffered them. This old Bank prides itself upon the reputation it enjoyed, even in those days. It had the power of issuing notes, and these notes were accepted by such men, even at a great distance, the bank having so good a name. They were even preferred to the notes of the Bank of England, which at one time, in outlying country places, were looked on with distrust, a state of things which seems almost incredible to the present generation.

In those days men had no confidence. That mutual business understanding, the credit which is the basis of all commerce of the present time, did not exist. Of course this only applies to the country and to country trading; the business men of cities were years in advance of the agriculturists in this respect. But so good was the reputation of the old Bank, even in those times, that its notes were readily accepted. It is, indeed, surprising what a reputation some of the best of the country banks have achieved. Their names are scarcely seen in the money articles of the daily press. But they do a solid business of great extent, and their names in agricultural circles are names of power. So the old Bank here, though within an arrow shot of the green meadows, though on ordinary days a single clerk might attend to its customers, has really a valuable *clientèle*.

Of late years shrewd men of business discovered that the ranks of the British farmer offered a wonderful opportunity for legitimate banking. The farmer, though he may not be rich, must of necessity be the manager, if not the actual owner, of considerable capital. A man who farms, if only a hundred acres, must have some capital. It may not be his own—it may be borrowed; still he has the use of it. Here, then, a wide field opened itself to banking enterprise. Certainly there has been a remarkable extension of banking institutions in the country. Every market town has its bank, and in most cases two—branches of course, but banks to all intents and purposes. Branches are started everywhere.

The new Bank in this particular little town is not really new. It is simply a branch set up by a well-established bank whose original centre may perhaps be in another county. It is every whit as respectable as the other, and as well conducted. Its branch as yet lacks local antiquity, but that is the only difference. The competition for the farmer's business between these branches, scattered all over the length and breadth of the country, must of necessity be close. When the branch, or new Bank, came here, it was started in grand premises specially erected for it, in the most convenient situation that could be secured.

Till then the business of the old Bank had been carried on in a small and dingy basement. The room was narrow, badly lit, and still worse ventilated, so that on busy days both the clerks and the customers complained of the stuffy atmosphere. The ancient fittings had become worn and defaced; the ceiling was grimy; the conveniences in every way defective. When it was known that a new branch was to be opened the directors of the old Bank resolved that the building, which had so long been found inadequate, should be entirely renovated. They pulled it down, and the present magnificent structure took its place.

Thus this little country town now possesses two banks, whose façades could hardly be surpassed in a city. There is perhaps a little rivalry between the managers of the two institutions, in social as well as in business matters. Being so long established there the old Bank numbers among its customers some of the largest landed proprietors, the leading clergy, and solicitors. The manager coming into contact with these, and being himself a man of intelligence, naturally occupies a certain position. If any public movement is set on foot, the banks strive as to which shall be most to the fore, and, aided by its antiquity, the old Bank, perhaps, secures a social precedence. Both managers belong to the "carriage people" of the town.

Hodge comes into the place, walking slowly behind cattle or sheep, or jolting in on a waggon. His wife comes, too, on foot, through the roughest weather, to fetch her household goods. His daughter comes into the hiring fair, and stands waiting for employment on the pavement in the same spot used for the purpose from time immemorial, within sight of the stately façades of the banks. He himself has stood in the market-place with reaping hook or hoe looking for a master. Humble as he may be, it is clear that the wealth in those cellars—the notes and the gold pushed over the counters in shovels—must somehow come from the labour which he and his immediate employer—the farmer—go through in the field.

It is becoming more and more the practice for the carter, or shepherd, who desires a new situation, to advertise. Instead of waiting for the chance of the hiring fair, he trudges into the market town and calls at the office of the oldest established local paper. There his wishes are reduced to writing for him, he pays his money, and his advertisement appears. If there is any farmer advertising for a man, as is often the case, he at the same time takes the address, and goes over to offer his services. The farmer and the labourer alike look to the advertisement columns as the medium between them.

The vitality and influence of the old-fashioned local newspaper is indeed a remarkable feature of country life. It would be thought that in these days of cheap literature, these papers, charging twopence, threepence, and even fourpence per copy, could not possibly continue to exist. But, contrary to all expectation, they have taken quite a fresh start, and possess a stronger hold than ever upon the agricultural population. They enter into the old homesteads, and every member of the farmer's family carefully scans them, certain of finding a reference to this or that subject or person in whom he takes an interest.

Some such papers practically defy competition. In the outlying towns, where no factories have introduced a new element, it is vain for the most enterprising to start another. The squire, the clergyman, the lawyer, the tenant farmer, the wayside inn-keeper stick to the old weekly paper, and nothing can shake it. It is one of the institutions of agriculture.

The office is, perhaps, in a side street of the quiet market town, and there is no display to catch the casual purchaser. No mystery surrounds the editor's sanctum; the visitor has but to knock, and is at once admitted to his presence. An office could scarcely be more plainly furnished. A common table, which has, however, one great virtue—it does not shake when written on—occupies the centre. Upon one side is a large desk or bureau; the account books lying open show that the editor, besides his literary labour, has to spend much time in double entry. Two chairs are so completely hidden under "exchanges" that no one can sit upon them. Several of these "exchanges" are from the United States or Australia, for the colonists are often more interested and concerned about local affairs in the old country than they are with the doings in the metropolis. Against the wall, too, hangs a picture of a fine steamer careering under sail and steam, and near it a coloured sectional map of some new township marked out in squares. These are the advertisements of an Atlantic or Australian line, or of both; and the editor is their agent. When the young ploughman resolves to quit the hamlet for the backwoods of America or the sheepwalks of Australia, he comes here to engage his berth. When the young farmer wearies of waiting for dead men's shoes—in no other way can he hope to occupy an English farm—he calls here and pays his passage-money, and his broad shoulders and willing hands are shipped to a land that will welcome him. A single shelf supports a few books, all for reference, such as the "Clergy List," for the Church is studied, and the slightest change that concerns the district carefully recorded.

Beneath this, the ponderous volumes that contain the file of the paper for the last forty years are piled, their weight too great for a shelf resting on the floor. The series constitutes a complete and authentic local history. People often come from a distance to consult it, for it is the only register that affords more than the simple entry of birth and death.

There is a life in the villages and hamlets around, in the little places that are not even hamlets, which to the folk who dwell in them is fully as important as that of the greatest city. Farmhouses are not like the villas of cities and city suburbs. The villa has hardly any individuality; it is but one of many, each resembling the other, and scarcely separated. To-day one family occupies it, to-morrow another, next year perhaps a third, and neither of these has any real connection with the place. They are sojourners, not inhabitants, drawn thither by business or pleasure; they come and go, and leave no mark behind. But the farmhouse has a history. The same family have lived in it for, perhaps, a hundred years: they have married and inter-married, and become identified with the locality. To them all the petty events of village life have a meaning and importance: the slow changes that take place and are chronicled in the old newspaper have a sad significance, for they mark that flux of time which is carrying them, too, onwards to their rest.

These columns of the file, therefore, that to a stranger seem a blank, to the old folk and their descendants are like a mirror, in which they can see the faces of the loved ones who passed away a generation since. They are the archives of the hamlets round about: a farmer can find from them when his grandfather quitted the old farm, and read an account of the sale. Men who left the village in their youth for the distant city or the still more distant colonies, as they grow in years often feel an irresistible desire to revisit the old, old place. The home they so fondly recollect is in other hands, and yet in itself but little changed. A few lines in the plainest language found in the file here tell to such a greybeard a story that fills his eyes with tears. But even a stranger who took the trouble to turn over the folios would now and then find matter to interest him: such as curious notes of archæological discovery, accounts of local customs now fallen into disuse, and traditions of the past. Many of these are worthy of collection in more accessible form.

There is hardly anything else in the room except the waste basket under the table. As the visitor enters, a lad goes out with a roll of manuscript in his hand, and the editor looks up from his monotonous task of proof-reading, for he has that duty also to perform. Whatever he is doing, some one is certain to call and break off the thread of his thought. The bailiff or farm-steward of a neighbouring estate comes in to insert an advertisement of timber for sale, or of the auction of the ash-poles annually felled. A gamekeeper calls with a notice not to sport or trespass on certain lands. The editor has to write out the advertisement for these people, and for many of the farmers who come, for countrymen have the greatest dislike to literary effort of any kind, and can hardly be persuaded to write a letter. Even when they have written the letter they get the daughter to address the envelope, lest the Post Office should smile at their rude penmanship. The business of preparing the advertisement is not quickly concluded, for just as it is put down to their fancy, they recollect another item which has to be added. Then they stand and gossip about the family at the mansion and the affairs of the parish generally, totally oblivious of the valuable time they are wasting. Farmers look in to advertise a cottage or a house in the village to let and stay to explain the state of the crops, and the why and the wherefore of So-and-so leaving his tenancy.

The largest advertisers invariably put off their orders till the morning of the paper going to press, from sheer inattention. On that busy morning, auctioneers' clerks rush in with columns of auction sales of cattle, sheep, horses, hay, or standing crops (according to the season of the year), and every species of farm produce. After them come the solicitors' clerks, with equally important and lengthy notices of legal matters concerning the effects of farmers who have fallen into difficulties, of parochial or turnpike affairs, or "Pursuant to an Act intituled 'An Act to further amend the Law and to Relieve Trustees.'" These notices have been lying on their desks for days, but are perversely sent down at the last moment, and upset the entire make-up of the paper.

Just as the editor has arranged for these, and is in the act to rush up into the press-room, a timid knock announces a poor cottage girl, who has walked in from a hamlet six or seven miles away to inquire the address of a lady who wants a servant. This advertisement appeared at least three weeks since, for country folk could in no wise make up their minds to apply under three weeks, and necessitates a search back through the file, and a reference to divers papers. He cannot in common courtesy leave the poor girl to wait his convenience, and meantime the steam is up and the machine waiting. When the address is discovered, the girl thinks she cannot remember it, and so he has to write it down on a piece of paper for her.

He has no highly organised staff to carry on the routine work; he has to look after every department as well as the purely editorial part. Almost every one who has a scrap of news or gossip looks in at the office to chat about it with him. Farmers, who have driven in to the town from distant villages, call to tell him of the trouble they are having over the new schools, and the conflict in the parish as to whether they shall or shall not have a school board. Clergymen from outlying vicarages come to mention that a cottage flower show, a penny reading, a confirmation, or some such event, is impending, and to suggest the propriety of a full and special account. Occasionally a leading landed proprietor is closeted with him, for at least an hour, discussing local politics, and ascertaining from him the tone of feeling in the district.

Modern agricultural society insists upon publicity. The smallest village event must be chronicled, or some one will feel dissatisfied, and inquire why it was not put in the paper. This continual looking towards the paper for everything causes it to exercise a very considerable amount of influence. Perhaps the clergy and gentry are in some things less powerful than the local newspaper, for, from a variety of causes, agricultural society has become extremely sensitive to public

201

opinion. The temperate and thoughtful arguments put forward by a paper in which they have confidence directly affect the tenant-farmers. On the other hand, as expressing the views of the tenant-farmers, the paper materially influences the course taken by the landed proprietors.

In country districts the mere numerical circulation of a weekly publication is no measure of its importance. The position of the subscribers is the true test. These old established papers, in fact, represent property. They are the organs of all who possess lands, houses, stock, produce; in short, of the middle class. This is evident from the advertising columns. The lawyer, the auctioneer, the land agent, the farmer, all who have any substance, publish their business in this medium. Official county advertisements appear in it. The carter and the shepherd look down the column of situations vacant as they call at the village inn for a glass of ale, or, if they cannot read, ask some one to read for them. But they do not purchase this kind of newspaper. The cottager spells over prints advocating the disestablishment of the Church, the division of great estates, and the general subversion of the present order of things. Yet when the labourer advertises, he goes to the paper subscribed to by his master. The disappearance of such an obsolete and expensive paper is frequently announced as imminent; but the obsolete and expensive print, instead of disappearing, flourishes with renewed vitality. Solid matter, temperate argument, and genuine work, in the long run, pay the best. An editor who thus conducts his paper is highly appreciated by the local chiefs of his party, and may even help to contribute to the success of an Administration.

The personal labour involved in such editing must be great from the absence of trained assistance, and because the materials must be furnished by incompetent hands. Local news must be forwarded by local people, perhaps by a village tailor with literary tastes. Such correspondents often indulge in insinuations, or fulsome flattery, which must be carefully eliminated. From another village an account of some event comes from the schoolmaster—quite an important person nowadays!—who writes in a fair, round hand and uses the finest language and the longest words. He invariably puts "hebdomadal" for "weekly." A lawyer's clerk writes a narrative of some case, on blue foolscap, and, after the manner of legal documents, without a single stop from beginning to end.

Once a year comes the labour of preparing the sheet almanac. This useful publication is much valued by the tenants of the district, and may be found pinned against the wall for ready reference in most farmhouses. Besides the calendar it contains a list of county and other officials, dates of quarter sessions and assizes, fair days and markets, records of the prices obtained at the annual sales of rams or short-horns on leading farms, and similar agricultural information.

The editor has very likely been born in the district, and has thus grown up to understand the wants and the spirit of the farming class. He is acquainted with the family history of the neighbourhood, a knowledge which is of much advantage in enabling him to avoid unnecessarily irritating personal sus-ceptibilities. His private library is not without interest. It mainly consists of old books picked up at the farmhouse sales of thirty years. At such disposals of household effects volumes sometimes come to light that have been buried for genera-tions among lumber. Many of these books are valuable and all worth examination. A man of simple and retiring habits, his garden is perhaps his greatest solace, and next to that a drive or stroll through the green meadows around. Incessant mental labour has forced him to wear glasses before his time, and it is a relief and pleasure to the eyes to dwell on green sward and leaf. Such a man performs a worthy part in country life, and possesses the esteem of the country side.

CHAPTER XIX

THE VILLAGE FACTORY— VILLAGE VISITORS—WILLOW-WORK

IN the daytime the centre of a certain village may be said to be the shop of the agricultural machinist. The majority of the cottagers are away in the fields at work, and the place is elsewhere almost quiet. A column of smoke and a distant din guide the visitor to the spot where the hammers are clattering on the anvils.

Twisted iron, rusty from exposure, lies in confusion on the blackened ground before the shed. Coal dust and the carbon deposited from volumes of thick smoke have darkened the earth, and coated everything with a black crust. The windows of the shed are broken, probably by the accidental contact of long rods of iron carelessly cast aside, and some of the slates of the roof appear gone just above the furnace, as if removed for ventilation and the escape of the intense heat. There is a creaking of stiff leather as the bellows rise and fall, and the roar of the blast as it is forced up through the glowing coals.

A ceaseless hum of wheels in motion comes from the rear, and the peculiar crackling sound of a band in rapid revolution round the drum of the engine and the shaft. Then the grinding scrape of sharp steel on iron as the edge of the tool cuts shavings from the solid metal rotating swiftly in the lathe. As blow follows blow the red-hot "scale," driven from the surface of the iron on the anvil by the heavy sledge, flies rattling against the window in a spray of fire. The ring of metal, the clatter, the roaring, and hissing of steam, fill the air, and through it rises now and then the shrill quick calls of men in command.

Outside, and as it seems but a stone's throw distant, stands the old grey church, and about it the still, silent, green-grown mounds over those who once followed the quiet plough.

Round the corner of the village street comes a man with a grimy red flag, and over the roofs of the cottages rises a cloud of smoke, and behind it yet another. Two steam ploughing engines are returning from their work to their place beside the shed to wait fresh orders. The broad wheels of the engines block up the entire width of the street, and but just escape overthrowing the feeble palings in front of the cottage doors. Within those palings the children at play scarcely turn to look; the very infants that can hardly toddle are so accustomed to the ponderous wonder that they calmly gnaw the crusts that keep them contented. It requires a full hour to get the unwieldy engines up the incline and round the sharp turns on to the open space by the workshop. The driver has to "back," and go-a-head, and "back" again, a dozen times before he can reach the place, for that narrow bye-way was not planned out for such traffic. A mere path leading to some cottages in the rear, it was rarely used even by carts before the machinist came, and it is a feat of skill to get the engines in without, like a conqueror, entering by a breach battered in the walls. When, at last, they have been piloted into position, the steam is blown off, and the rushing hiss sounds all over the village. The white vapour covers the ground like a cloud, and the noise re-echoes against the old grey church, but the jackdaws do not even rise from the battlements.

These engines and their corresponding tackle are the chief stock-in-trade of the village machinist. He lets them out to the farmers of the district, which is principally arable; that is, he contracts to do their ploughing and scarifying at so much per acre. In the ploughing seasons the engines are for ever on the road, and with their tackle dragging behind them take up the highway like a train. One day you may hear the hum and noise from a distant field on the left; in a day or two it comes from another on the right; next week it has shifted again, and is heard farther off northwards, and so all round the compass.

The visitor, driving about the neighbourhood, cannot but notice the huge and cumbrous-looking plough left awhile on the sward by the roadside. One half of the shares stand up high in the air, the other half touch the ground, and it is so nicely balanced that boys sometimes play at see-saw on it. He will meet the iron monster which draws this plough by the bridge over the brook, pausing while its insatiable thirst is stayed from the stream. He will see it patiently waiting, with a slight curl of steam over the boiler, by the wayside inn while its attendants take their lunch.

It sometimes happens in wet weather that the engines cannot be moved from the field where they have been ploughing. The soil becomes so soft from absorbing so much water that it will not bear up the heavy weight. Logs and poles are laid down to form a temporary way, but the great wheels sink too deeply, and the engines have to be left covered with tarpaulins. They have been known to remain till the fresh green leaves of spring on the hedges and trees almost hid them from sight.

The machinist has another and lighter traction engine which does not plough, but travels from farm to farm with a threshing machine. In autumn it is in full work threshing, and in winter drives chaff-cutters for the larger farmers. Occasionally it draws a load of coal in waggons or trucks built for the purpose. Hodge's forefathers knew no rival at plough time; after the harvest they threshed the corn all the winter with the flail. Now the iron horse works faster and harder than he.

Some of the great tenant-farmers have sets of ploughing engines and tackle of their own, and these are frequently at the machinist's for repairs. The reaping, mowing, threshing, haymaking, hoeing, raking, and other machines and implements also often require mending. Once now and then a bicyclist calls to have his machine attended to, something having given way while on a tour. Thus the village factory is in constant work, but has to encounter immense competition.

Country towns of any size usually possess at least one manufactory of agricultural implements, and some of these factories have acquired a reputation which reaches over sea. The visitor to such a foundry is shown medals that have been granted for excellence of work exhibited in Vienna, and may see machines in process of construction which will be used upon the Continent; so that the village machinist, though apparently isolated, with nothing but fields around him, has in reality competitors upon every side.

Ploughing engines, again, travel great distances, and there are firms that send their tackle across a county or two. Still the village factory, being on the spot, has plenty of local work, and the clatter of hammers, the roar of the blast, and the hum of wheels never cease at the shed. Busy workmen pass to and fro, lithe men, quick of step and motion, who come from Leeds, or some similar manufacturing town, and whose very step distinguishes them in a moment from the agricultural labourer.

A sturdy ploughboy comes up with a piece of iron on his shoulder; it does not look large, but it is as much as he can carry. One edge of it is polished by the friction of the earth through which it has been forced; it has to be straightened, or repaired, and the ploughboy waits while it is done. He sits down outside the shed on a broken and rusty iron wheel, choosing a spot where the sun shines and the building keeps off the wind. There, among the twisted iron, ruins and fragments of machines, he takes out his hunch of bread and cheese, and great clasp knife, and quietly enjoys his luncheon. He is utterly indifferent to the noise of the revolving wheels, the creak of the bellows, the hiss of steam; he makes no inquiry about this or that, and shows no desire to understand the wonders of mechanics. Something in his attitude—in the immobility, the almost animal repose of limb; something in the expression of his features, the self-contained oblivion, so to say, suggests an Oriental absence of aspiration. Only by negatives and side-lights, as it were, can any idea be conveyed of his contented indifference. He munches his crust; and, when he has done, carefully, and with vast deliberation, re-laces his heavy shoe. The sunshine illumines the old grey church before him, and falls on the low green mounds, almost level with the sward, which cover his ancestors.

These modern inventions, this steam, and electric telegraph, and even the printing-press have but just skimmed the surface of village life. If they were removed—if the pressure from without, from the world around, ceased, in how few years the village and the hamlet would revert to their original condition!

On summer afternoons, towards five or six o'clock, a four-wheel carriage—useful, but not pretentious—comes slowly up the hill leading to the village. The single occupant is an elderly man, the somewhat wearied expression of whose features is caused by a continuous application to business. The horse, too well fed for work, takes his own time up the hill, and when at the summit the reins are gently shaken, makes but an idle pretence to move faster, for he knows that his master is too good-natured and forbearing to use the whip, except to fondly stroke his back. The reins are scarcely needed to guide the horse along the familiar road to a large farmhouse on the outskirts of the village, where at the gate two or more children are waiting to welcome "papa."

Though a farmhouse, the garden is laid out in the style so often seen around detached villas, with a lawn for tennis and croquet, parterres bright with summer flowers, and seats under the pleasant shade of the trees. Within it is furnished in villa fashion, and is in fact let to a well-to-do tradesman of the market town a few miles distant. He has wisely sent his family for the summer months to inhale the clear air of the hills, as exhilarating as that of the sea. There they can ride the pony and donkeys over the open sward, and romp and play at gipsying. Every evening he drives out to join them, and every morning returns to his office. The house belongs to some large tenant-farmer, who has a little freehold property, and thus makes a profit from it.

This practice of hiring a village home for the summer has become common of recent years among the leading trades-men of country towns. Such visitors are welcome to the cottage folk. They require the service of a labourer now and then; they want fresh eggs, and vegetables from the allotment gardens. The women have the family washing to do, and a girl is often needed to assist indoors, or a boy to clean the knives and shoes. Many perquisites fall to the cottage people—cast aside dresses, and so on; besides which there are little gifts and kindnesses from the lady and her children.

Towards November again, the congregation in the old church one Sunday morning find subject for speculation concerning a stranger who enters a certain well-appointed pew appropriated to The Chestnuts. He is clearly the new tenant who has taken it for the hunting season. The Chestnuts is a mansion built in modern style for a former land-owner. As it is outside the great hunting centres it is let at a low rental compared with its accommodation. The labourers are glad to see that the place is let again, for although the half-pay officer—the new occupant—who has retired, wounded and decorated, from the service of a grateful country, has probably not a third the income of the tradesman, and five times the social appearance to maintain, still there will be profit to be got from him.

What chance has such a gentleman in bargaining with the cottagers? How should he know the village value of a cabbage? How should he understand the farmyard value of a fowl? It may possibly strike him as odd that vegetables should be so dear when, as he rides about, he sees whole fields green with them. He sees plenty of fowls, and geese, and turkeys, gobbling and cackling about the farmyards, and can perhaps after a while faintly perceive that they are the perquisites of the ladies of the tenants' households, who drive him a very hard bargain. He, too, has cast aside suits, shoes, hats, and so forth, really but little worn, to give away to the poor. If married, his family require some help from the cottage women; and there are odd jobs, well paid for, on the place for the men. Thus the cottagers are glad of the arrival of their new masters, the one in the summer, the other in the winter months.

The "chapel-folk" of the place have so increased in numbers and affluence that they have erected a large and commodious building in the village. Besides the cottagers, many farmers go to the chapel, driving in from the ends of the parish. It is a curious circumstance that many of the largest dealers in agricultural produce, such as cheese, bacon, and corn, and the owners of the busiest wharves where coal and timber, slate, and similar materials are stored, belong to the Dissenting community. There are some agricultural districts where this class of business is quite absorbed by Dissenters—almost as much as money-changing and banking business is said to be the exclusive property of Jews in some Continental countries. Such dealers are often substantial and, for the country, even wealthy men. Then there are the Dissenting tradesmen of the market town. All these together form a species of guild. The large chapel in the village was built by their united subscriptions. They support each other in a marked manner in times of difficulty, so that it is rare for a tenant-farmer of the persuasion to lose his position unless by wilful misconduct. This mutual support is so very marked as to be quite a characteristic fact.

The cottagers and their families go to chapel with these masters. But sometimes the cottager, as he approaches the chapel door, finds upon it (as in the church porch) a small printed notice affixed there by the overseers. If the labourer is now recognised as a person whose opinion is to be consulted, on the other hand he finds that he is not without responsibilities. The rate-collector knocks at the cottage door as well as at the farmer's. By gradual degrees village rates are becoming a serious burden, and though their chief incidence may be upon the landlord and the tenant, indirectly they begin to come home to the labourer. The school rate is voluntary, but it is none the less a rate; the cemetery, the ancient churchyard being no more available, has had to be paid for, and, as usual, probably cost twice what was anticipated. The highways, the sanitary authority, not to speak of poor relief, all demand a share. Each in itself may be only a straw, but accumulated straws in time fill a waggon.

One side of the stable of the village inn, which faces the road, presents a broad surface for the country bill-sticker. He comes out from the market town, and travels on foot for a whole day together, from hamlet to hamlet, posting up the contents of his bag in the most outlying and lonely districts. Every villager as he passes by reads the announcements on the wall: the circus coming to the market town, some jeweller's marvellous watches, the selling off of spring or summer goods by the drapers at an immense reduction, once now and then a proclamation headed V.R., and the sales of farm stock (the tenants leaving) and of large freehold properties.

These latter are much discussed by the callers at the inn. A carter comes along perhaps with a loaded waggon from some distance, and as he stays to drink his quart talks of the changes that are proceeding or imminent in his locality. Thus the fact that changes are contemplated is often widely known before the actual advertisement is issued. The labourers who hear the carter's story tell it again to their own employer next time they see him, and the farmer meeting another farmer gossips over it again.

There has grown up a general feeling in the villages and agricultural districts that the landed estates around them are no longer stable and enduring. A feeling of uncertainty is abroad, and no one is surprised to hear that some other place, or person, is going. It is rumoured that this great landlord is about to sell as many farms as the family settlements will let him. Another is only waiting for the majority of his son to accomplish the same object. Others, it is said, are proceeding abroad to retrench. Properties are coming into the market in unexpected directions, and others are only kept back because the price of land has fallen, and there is a difficulty in selling a large estate. If divided into a number of lots, each of small size, land still fetches its value, and can be readily sold; but that is not always convenient, and purchasers hesitate to invest in extensive estates. But though kept back, efforts are being made to retrench, and, it is said, old mansions that have never been let before can now be hired for the season. Not only the tenant-farmers, but the landowners are passing through a period of depression, and their tenure too is uncertain. Such is the talk of the country side as it comes to the village inn.

Once a week the discordant note of a horn or bugle, loudly blown by a man who does not understand his instrument, is heard at intervals. It is the newspaper vendor, who, like the bill-sticker, starts from the market town on foot, and goes through the village with a terrible din. He stops at the garden gate in the palings before the thatched cottage, delivers his print to the old woman or the child sent out with the copper, and starts again with a flourish of his trumpet. His business is chiefly with the cottagers, and his print is very likely full of abuse of the landed proprietors as a body. He is a product of modern days, almost the latest, and as he goes from cottage door to cottage door, the discordant uproar of his trumpet is a sign of the times.

In some districts the osier plantations give employment to a considerable number of persons. The tall poles are made into posts and rails; the trunks of the pollard trees when thrown are cut into small timber that serves many minor purposes; the brushwood or tops that are cut every now and then make thatching sticks and faggots; sometimes hedges are made of a kind of willow wicker-work for enclosing gardens. It is, however, the plantations of withy or osier that are most important. The willow grows so often in or near to water that in common opinion the association cannot be too complete. But in the arrangement of an osier-bed water is utilised, indeed, but kept in its place—*i.e.*, at the roots, and not over the stoles. The osier should not stand in water, or rise, as it were, out of a lake—the water should be in the soil underneath, and the level of the ground higher than the surface of the adjacent stream.

Before planting, the land has to be dug or ploughed, and cleared; the weeds collected in the same way as on an arable field. The sticks are then set in rows eighteen inches apart, each stick (that afterwards becomes a stole) a foot from its neighbours of the same row. At first the weeds require keeping down, but after a while the crop itself kills them a good deal. Several willows spring from each planted stick, and at the end of twelve months the first crop is ready for cutting. Next year the stick or stole will send up still more shoots, and give a larger yield.

The sorts generally planted are called Black Spanish and Walnut Leaf. The first has a darker bark, and is a tough wood; the other has a light yellow bark, and grows smoother and without knots, which is better for working up into the manufactured article. Either will grow to nine feet high—the average height is six or seven feet. The usual time for cutting is about Good Friday—that is, just before the leaf appears. After cutting, the rods are stacked upright in water, in long trenches six inches deep prepared for the purpose, and there they remain till the leaf comes out. The power of growth displayed by the willow is wonderful—a bough has only to be stuck in the earth, or the end of a pole placed in the brook, for the sap to rise and shoots to push forth.

When the leaf shows the willows are carried to the "brakes," and the work of stripping off the bark commences. A "brake" somewhat resembles a pair of very blunt scissors permanently fixed open at a certain angle, and rigidly supported at a convenient height from the ground. The operator stands behind it, and selecting a long wand from the heap beside him places

211

it in the "brake," and pulls it through, slightly pressing it downwards. As he draws it towards him, the edges of the iron tear the bark and peel it along the whole length of the stick. There is a knack in the operation, of course, but when it is acquired the wand is peeled in a moment by a dexterous turn of the wrist, the bark falls to the ground on the other side of the brake, and the now white stick is thrown to the right, where a pile soon accumulates. The peel is handy for tying up, and when dried makes a capital material for lighting fires. This stripping of the osiers is a most busy time in the neighbourhood of the large plantations—almost like hop-picking—for men, women, and children can all help. It does not require so much strength as skill and patience.

After the peeling the sticks have to be dried by exposure to the sun; they are then sorted into lengths, and sold in bundles. If it is desired to keep them any time they must be thoroughly dried, or they will "heat" and rot and become useless. This willow harvest is looked forward to by the cottagers who live along the rivers as an opportunity for earning extra money. The quantity of osier thus treated seems immense, and yet the demand is said to be steady, and as the year advances the price of the willow rises. It is manufactured into all kinds of baskets—on farms, especially arable farms, numbers of baskets are used. Clothes baskets, market baskets, chaff baskets, bassinettes or cradles, etc., are some few of the articles manufactured from it. Large quantities of willow, too, are worked up unpeeled into hampers of all kinds. The number of hampers used in these days is beyond computation, and as they are constantly wearing out, fresh ones have to be made. An advantage of the willow is that it enables the farmer to derive a profit from land that would otherwise be comparatively valueless. Good land, indeed, is hardly fitted for osier; it would grow rank with much pith in the centre, and therefore liable to break. On common land, on the contrary, it grows just right, and not too coarse. Almost any scrap or corner does for willow, and if properly tended it speedily pays for the labour.

The digging and preparation of the ground gives employment, and afterwards the weeding and the work required to clean the channels that conduct water round and through the beds. Then there is the cutting and the peeling, and finally the basket-making; and thus the willow, though so common as to be little regarded, finds work for many hands.

CHAPTER XX

HODGE'S FIELDS

THE labourer working all the year round in the open air cannot but note to some degree those changes in tree and plant which coincide with the variations of his daily employment. Early in March, as he walks along the southern side of the hedge, where the dead oak leaves still cumber the trailing ivy, he can scarcely avoid seeing that pointed tongues of green are pushing up. Some have widened into black-spotted leaves; some are notched like the many-barbed bone harpoons of savage races. The hardy docks are showing, and the young nettles have risen up. Slowly the dark and grey hues of winter are yielding to the lively tints of spring. The blackthorn has white buds on its lesser branches, and the warm rays of the sun have drawn forth the buds on one favoured hawthorn in a sheltered nook, so that the green of the coming leaf is visible. Bramble bushes still retain their forlorn, shrivelled foliage; the hardy all but evergreen leaves can stand cold, but when biting winds from the north and east blow for weeks together even these curl at the edge and die.

The remarkable power of wind upon leaves is sometimes seen in May, when a strong gale, even from the west, will so beat and batter the tender horse-chestnut sprays that they bruise and blacken. The slow plough traverses the earth, and the white dust rises from the road and drifts into the field. In winter the distant copse seemed black; now it appears of a dull reddish brown from the innumerable catkins and buds. The delicate sprays of the birch are fringed with them, the aspen has a load of brown, there are green catkins on the bare hazel boughs, and the willows have white "pussy-cats." The horse-chestnut buds—the hue of dark varnish—have enlarged, and stick to the finger if touched; some are so swollen as to nearly burst and let the green appear. Already it is becoming more difficult to look right through the copse. In winter the light could be seen on the other side; now catkin, bud, and opening leaf have thickened and check the view. The same effect was produced not long since by the rime on the branches in the frosty mornings; while each smallest twig was thus lined with crystal it was not possible to see through. Tangled weeds float down the brook, catching against projecting branches that dip into the stream, or slowly rotating and carried apparently up the current by the eddy and back-water behind the bridge. In the pond the frogs have congregated in great numbers; their constant "croo-croo" is audible at some distance.

The meadows, so long bound by frost and covered with snow, are slowly losing their wan aspect, and assuming a warmer green as the young blades of grass come upwards. Where the plough or harrow has passed over the clods they quickly change from the rich brown of fresh-turned soil to a whiter colour, the dryness of the atmosphere immediately dissipating the moisture in the earth. So, examine what you will, from the clod to the tiniest branch, the hedge, the mound, the water—everywhere a step forward has been taken. The difference in a particular case may be minute; but it is there, and together these faint indications show how closely spring is approaching.

As the sun rises the chaffinch utters his bold challenge on the tree; the notes are so rapid that they seem to come all at once. Welcome, indeed, is the song of the first finch. Sparrows are busy in the garden—the hens are by far the most numerous now, half a dozen together perch on the bushes. One suddenly darts forth and seizes a black insect as it flies in the sunshine. The bee, too, is abroad, and once now and then a yellow butterfly. From the copse on the warmer days comes occasionally the deep hollow bass of the wood pigeon. On the very topmost branch of an elm a magpie has perched; now he looks this way, and then turns that, bowing in the oddest manner, and jerking his long tail up and down. Then two of them flutter across the field—feebly, as if they had barely strength to reach the trees in the opposite hedge. Extending their wings they float slowly, and every now and then the body undulates along its entire length. Rooks are building— they fly and feed now in pairs; the rookery is alive with them. To the steeple the jackdaws have returned and fly round and round; now one holds his wings rigid and slides down at an angle of sixty degrees at a breakneck pace, as if about to dash himself in fragments on the garden beneath.

Sometimes there come a few days which are like summer. There is an almost cloudless sky, a gentle warm breeze, and a bright sun filling the fields with a glow of light. The air, though soft and genial, is dry, and perhaps it is this quality which gives so peculiar a definition to hedge, tree, and hill. A firm, almost hard, outline brings copse and wood into clear relief; the distance across the broadest fields appears sensibly diminished. Such freedom from moisture has a deliciously exhilarating effect on those who breathe so pure an atmosphere. The winds of March differ, indeed, in a remarkable manner from the gales of the early year, which, even when they blow from a mild quarter, compel one to keep in constant movement because of the aqueous vapour they carry. But the true March wind, though too boisterous to be exactly genial, causes a joyous sense of freshness, as if the very blood in the veins were refined and quickened upon inhaling it. There is a difference in its roar—the note is distinct from the harsh sound of the chilly winter blast. On the lonely highway at night, when other noises are silent, the March breeze rushes through the tall elms in a wild cadence. The white clouds hasten over, illuminated from behind by a moon approaching the full; every now and then a break shows a clear blue sky and a star shining. Now a loud roar resounds along the hedgerow like the deafening boom of the surge; it moderates, dies away, then an elm close by bends and sounds as the blast comes again. In another moment the note is caught up and repeated by a distant tree, and so one after another joins the song till the chorus reaches its highest pitch. Then it sinks again, and so continues with pauses and deep inspirations, for March is like a strong man drawing his breath full and long as he starts to run a race.

The sky, too, like the earth, whose hedges, trees, and meadows are acquiring fresher colours, has now a more lovely aspect. At noon-day, if the clouds be absent, it is a rich azure; after sunset a ruddy glow appears almost all round the horizon, while the thrushes sing in the wood till the twilight declines. At night, when the moon does not rise till late, the heavens are brilliant with stars. In the east Arcturus is up; the Great Bear, the Lesser Bear, and Cassiopeia are ranged about the Pole. Procyon goes before the Dog; the noble constellation of Orion stretches broad across the sky; almost overhead lucent Capella looks down. Aries droops towards the west; the Bull follows with the red Aldebaran and the Pleiades. Behind these, Castor and Pollux, and next the cloud-like, nebulous Cancer. Largest of all, great Sirius is flaming in the south, quivering with the ebb and flow of his light, sometimes with an emerald scintillation like a dewdrop on which a sunbeam glances.

The busy summer, with its haymaking, reaping, and continuous succession of harvest work, passes too swiftly for reflection both for masters and men. But in the calm of autumn there is time again to look round. Then white columns of smoke rise up slowly into the tranquil atmosphere, till they overtop the tallest elms, and the odour of the burning couch is carried across the meadows from the lately-ploughed stubble, where the weeds have been collected in heaps and fired. The stubble itself, short and in regular lines, affords less and less cover every year. As the seed is now drilled in, and the plants grow in mathematically straight lines, of course when the crop is reaped, if you stand at one side of the field you can see right across between the short stubs, so that a mouse could hardly find shelter. Then quickly come the noisy steam ploughing engines, after them the couch collectors, and finally the heaps are burnt, and the strong scent of smoke hangs over the ground. Against these interruptions of their haunts and quiet ways what are the partridges to do? Even at night the place is scarcely their own, for every now and then, as the breeze comes along, the smouldering fires are fanned into bright flame, enough to alarm the boldest bird.

In another broad arable field, where the teams have been dragging the plough, but have only just opened a few furrows and gone home, a flock of sheep are feeding, or rather picking up a little, having been turned in, that nothing might be lost. There is a sense of quietness—of repose; the trees of the copse close by are still, and the dying leaf as it drops falls straight to the ground. A faint haze clings to the distant woods at the foot of the hills; it is afternoon, the best part of an autumn day, and sufficiently warm to make the stile a pleasant resting-place. A dark cloud, whose edges rise curve upon curve, hangs in the sky, fringed with bright white light, for the sun is behind it, and long, narrow streamers of light radiate from the upper part like the pointed rays of an antique crown. Across an interval of blue to the eastward a second massive cloud, white and shining as if beaten out of solid silver, fronts the sun, and reflects the beams passing horizontally through the upper ether downwards on the earth like a mirror.

The sparrows in the stubble rise in a flock and settle down again. Yonder a solitary lark is singing. Then the sun emerges, and the yellow autumn beams flood the pale stubble and the dark red earth of the furrow. On the bushes in the hedge hang the vines of the bryony, bearing thick masses of red berries. The hawthorn leaves in places have turned pale, and are touched, too, towards the stalk with a deep brown hue. The contrast of the two tints causes an accidental colour resembling that of bronze, which catches the eye at the first glance, but disappears on looking closer. Spots of yellow on the elms seem the more brilliant from the background of dull green. The drooping foliage of the birch exhibits a paler yellow; the nut-tree bushes shed brown leaves upon the ground. Perhaps the beech leaves are the most beautiful; two or three tints are blended on the topmost boughs. There is a ruddy orange hue, a tawny brown, and a bright green; the sunlight comes and mingles these together. The same leaf will sometimes show two at least of these colours—green shading into brown, or into a ruddy gold. Later on, the oaks, in a monochrome of buff, will rival the beeches. Now and then an acorn drops from the tree overhead, with a smart tap on the hard earth, and rebounds some inches high. Some of these that fall are already dark—almost black—but if opened they will be found bored by a grub. They are not yet ripe as a crop; the rooks are a good guide in that respect, and they have not yet set steadily to work upon this their favourite autumn food. Others that have fallen and been knocked out of the cup are a light yellow at the base and green towards the middle and the point; the yellow part is that which has been covered by the cup. In the sward there is a small hole from out of which creeps a wasp at intervals; it is a nest, and some few of them are still at work. But their motions are slow and lack vivacity; before long, numbers must die, and already many have succumbed after crawling miserably on the ground which they spurned a short while since, when with a brisk buzz they flew from apple to plum.

In the quiet woodland lane a covey of partridges are running to and fro on the short sward at the side, and near them two or three pheasants are searching for food. The geometrical spiders—some of them look almost as big as a nut—hang their webs spun to a regular pattern on the bushes. The fungi flourish; there is a huge specimen on the elm there, but the flowers are nearly gone.

A few steps down the lane, upon looking over a gate into a large arable field where the harrow has broken up the clods, a faint bluish tinge may be noticed on the dull earth in the more distant parts. A second glance shows that it is caused by a great flock of wood-pigeons. Some more come down out of the elms and join their companions; there must be a hundred and fifty or two hundred of them. The wood-pigeon on the ground at a distance is difficult to distinguish, or rather to define individually—the pale blue tint seems to confuse the eye with a kind of haze. Though the flock take little notice now—knowing themselves to be far out of gunshot—yet they would be quickly on the alert if an attempt were made to approach them.

Already some of the elms are becoming bare—there are gaps in the foliage where the winds have carried away the leaves. On the bramble bushes the blackberries cluster thickly, unseen and ungathered in this wild spot. The happy hearts that go a-blackberrying think little of the past: yet there is a deep, a mournful significance attached to that joyous time. For how many centuries have the blackberries tempted men, women, and children out into the fields, laughing at scratched hands and nettles, and clinging burrs, all merrily endured for the sake of so simple a treasure-trove. Under the relics of the ancient pile-dwellings of Switzerland, disinterred from the peat and other deposits, have been found quantities of blackberry seeds, together with traces of crabs and sloes; so that by the dwellers in those primeval villages in the midst of the lakes the wild fruits of autumn were sought for much as we seek them now; the old instincts are strong in us still.

The fieldfares will soon be here now, and the red-wings, coming as they have done for generations about the time of the sowing of the corn. Without an almanack they know the dates; so the old sportsmen used to declare that their pointers and setters were perfectly aware when September was approaching, and showed it by unusual restlessness. By the brook the meadows are green and the grass long still; the flags, too, are green, though numbers of dead leaves float down on the current. There is green again where the root crops are flourishing; but the brown tints are striving hard, and must soon gain the mastery of colour. From the barn comes the clatter of the winnowing machine, and the floor is covered with heaps of grain.

After the sun has gone down and the shadows are deepening, it is lighter in the open stubbles than in the enclosed meadows—the short white stubbs seem to reflect what little

218

light there is. The partridges call to each other, and after each call run a few yards swiftly, till they assemble at the well-known spot where they roost. Then comes a hare stealing by without a sound. Suddenly he perceives that he is watched, and goes off at a rapid pace, lost in the brooding shadow across the field. Yonder a row of conical-roofed wheat-ricks stand out boldly against the sky, and above them a planet shines.

Still later, in November, the morning mist lingers over gorse and heath, and on the upper surfaces of the long dank grass blades, bowed by their own weight, are white beads of dew. Wherever the eye seeks an object to dwell on, there the cloud-like mist seems to thicken as though to hide it. The bushes and thickets are swathed in the vapour; yonder, in the hollow, it clusters about the oaks and hangs upon the hedge looming in the distance. There is no sky—a motionless, colourless something spreads above; it is, of course, the same mist, but looking upwards it apparently recedes and becomes indefinite. The glance finds no point to rest on—as on the edges of clouds—it is a mere opaque expanse. But the air is dry, the moisture does not deposit itself, it remains suspended and waits but the wind to rise and depart. The stillness is utter: not a bird calls or insect buzzes by. In passing beneath the oaks the very leaves have forgotten to fall. Only those already on the sward, touched by the frost, crumble under the footstep. When green they would have yielded to the weight, but now stiffened they resist it and are crushed, breaking in pieces.

A creaking and metallic rattle, as of chains, comes across the arable field—a steady gaze reveals the dim outline of a team of horses slowly dragging the plough, their shapes indistinctly seen against the hedge. A bent figure follows, and by-and-by another distinct creak and rattle, and yet a third in another direction, show that there are more teams at work, plodding to and fro. Watching their shadowy forms, suddenly the eye catches a change in the light somewhere. Over the meadow yonder the mist is illuminated; it is not sunshine, but a white light, only visible by contrast with the darker mist around. It lasts a few moments, and then moves, and appears a second time by the copse. Though hidden here, the disk of the sun must be partly visible there, and as the white light does not remain long in one place, it is evident that there is motion now in the vast mass of vapour. Looking upwards there is the faintest suspicion of the palest blue, dull and dimmed by mist, so faint that its position cannot be fixed, and the next instant it is gone again.

But the teams at plough are growing momentarily distinct—a breath of air touches the cheek, then a leaf breaks away from the bough and starts forth as if bent on a journey, but loses the impetus and sinks to the ground. Soon afterwards the beams of the sun light up a distant oak that glows in the hedge—a rich deep buff—and it stands out, clear, distinct, and beautiful, the chosen and selected one, the first to receive the ray. Rapidly the mist vanishes—disappearing rather than floating away; a circle of blue sky opens overhead, and, finally, travelling slowly, comes the sunshine over the furrows. There is a perceptible sense of warmth—the colours that start into life add to the feeling. The bare birch has no leaf to reflect it, but its white bark shines, and beyond it two great elms, the one a pale green and the other a pale yellow, stand side by side. The brake fern is dead and withered; the tip of each frond curled over downwards by the frost, but it forms a brown background to the dull green furze which is alight here and there with scattered blossom, by contrast so brilliantly yellow as to seem like flame. Polished holly leaves glisten, and a bunch of tawny fungus rears itself above the grass.

On the sheltered sunny bank lie the maple leaves fallen from the bushes, which form a bulwark against the north wind; they have simply dropped upon the ivy which almost covers the bank. Standing here with the oaks overhead and the thick bushes on the northern side it is quite warm and genial; so much so that it is hard to realise that winter is at hand. But even in the shortest days, could we only get rid of the clouds and wind, we should find the sunshine sufficiently powerful to make the noontide pleasant. It is not that the sun is weak or low down, nor because of the sharp frosts, that winter with us is dreary and chill. The real cause is the prevalence of cloud, through which only a dull light can penetrate, and of moisture-laden winds.

If our winter sun had fair play we should find the climate very different. Even as it is, now and then comes a break in the masses of vapour streaming across the sky, and if you are only sheltered from the wind (or stand at a southern window), the temperature immediately rises. For this reason the temperatures registered by thermometers are often far from being a correct record of the real weather we have had. A bitter frost early in the morning sends the mercury below zero, but perhaps, by eleven o'clock the day is warm, the sky being clear and the wind still. The last register instituted—that of the duration of sunshine, if taken in connection with the state of the wind—is the best record of the temperature that we have actually felt. These thoughts naturally arise under the oaks here as the bright sunlight streams down from a sky the more deeply blue from contrast with the brown, and buff, and yellow leaves of the trees.

Hark! There comes a joyous music over the fields—first one hound's note, then two, then three, and then a chorus; they are opening up a strong scent. It rises and falls—now it is coming nearer, in a moment I shall see them break through the hedge on the ridge—surely that was a shout! Just in the very moment of expectation the loud tongues cease; I wait, listening breathlessly, but presently a straggling cry or two shows that the pack has turned and are spread wide trying to recover. By degrees the sounds die away; and I stroll onwards.

A thick border of dark green firs bounds the copse—the brown leaves that have fallen from the oaks have lodged on the foliage of the firs and are there supported. In the sheltered corner some of the bracken has partly escaped the frost, one frond has two colours. On one side of the rib it is green and on the other yellow. The grass is strewn with the leaves of the aspen, which have turned quite black. Under the great elms there seems a sudden increase of light—it is caused by the leaves which still remain on the branches; they are all of the palest yellow, and, as you pass under, give the impression of the tree having been lit up—illuminated with its own colour. From the bushes hang the red berries of the nightshade, and the fruit on the briars glistens in the sun. Inside the copse stand innumerable thistles shoulder high, dead and gaunt; and a grey border running round the field at the bottom of the hedge shows where the tall, strong weeds of summer have withered up. A bird flutters round the topmost boughs of the elm yonder and disappears with a flash of blue—it is a jay. Here the grass of the meadow has an undertone of grey; then an arable field succeeds, where six strong horses are drawing the heavy drill, and great bags of the precious seed are lying on the furrows.

Another meadow, where note a broken bough of elder, the leaves on which have turned black, while still on its living branches they are green, and then a clump of beeches. The trunks are full of knot-holes; after a dead bough has fallen off and the stump has rotted away, the bark curls over the orifice and seemingly heals the wound more smoothly and completely than with other trees. But the mischief is proceeding all the same, despite that flattering appearance; outwardly the bark looks smooth and healthy, but probe the hole and the rottenness is working inwards. A sudden gap in the clump attracts the glance, and there—with one great beech trunk on this side and another on that—is a view opening down on the distant valley far below. The wood beneath looks dwarfed, and the uneven tops of the trees, some green, some tinted, are apparently so close together as to hide aught else, and the shadows of the clouds move over it as over a sea. A haze upon the horizon brings plain and sky together there; on one side, in the far distance a huge block, a rude vastness stands out dusky and dimly defined—it is a spur of the rolling hills.

Out in the plain, many a mile away, the sharp, needle-like point of·a steeple rises white above the trees, which there shade and mingle into a dark mass—so brilliantly white as to seem hardly real. Sweeping the view round, there is a strange and total absence of houses or signs of habitation, other than the steeple, and now that, too, is gone. It has utterly vanished —where, but a few moments before it glowed with whiteness, is absolutely nothing. The disappearance is almost weird in the broad daylight, as if solid stone could sink into the earth. Searching for it suddenly a village appears some way on the right—the white walls stand out bright and clear, one of the houses is evidently of large size, and placed on a slight elevation is a prominent object. But as we look it fades, grows blurred and indistinct, and in another moment is gone. The whole village has vanished—in its place is nothing; so swift is the change that the mind scarcely credits the senses.

A deep shadow creeping towards us explains it. Where the sunlight falls, there steeple or house glows and shines; when it has passed, the haze that is really there, though itself invisible, instantly blots out the picture. The thing may be seen over and over again in the course of a few minutes; it would be difficult for an artist to catch so fleeting an effect. The shadow of the cloud is not black—it lacks several shades of that—there is in it a faint and yet decided tint of blue. This tone of blue is not the same everywhere—here it is almost distinct, there it fades; it is an aerial colour which rather hints

itself than shows. Commencing the descent the view is at once
lost, but we pass a beech whose beauty is not easily conveyed.
The winds have scarcely rifled it; being in a sheltered spot on
the slope, the leaves are nearly perfect. All those on the outer
boughs are a rich brown—some, perhaps, almost orange.
But there is an inner mass of branches of lesser size which
droop downwards, something after the manner of a weeping
willow; and the leaves on these are still green and show
through. Upon the whole tree a flood of sunshine pours, and
over it is the azure sky. The mingling, shading, and contrast
of these colours give a lovely result—the tree is aglow, its
foliage ripe with colour.

Farther down comes the steady sound of deliberate blows,
and the upper branches of the hedge fall beneath the steel.
A sturdy labourer, with a bill on a pole, strikes slow and
strong and cuts down the hedge to an even height. A dreadful
weapon that simple tool must have been in the old days before
the advent of the arquebus. For with the exception of the
spike, which is not needed for hedge work, it is almost an
exact copy of the brown bill of ancient warfare; it is brown
still, except where sharpened. Wielded by a sinewy arm, what
gaping gashes it must have slit through helm and mail and
severed bone! Watch the man there—he slices off the tough
thorn as though it were straw. He notes not the beauty of the
beech above him, nor the sun, nor the sky; but on the other
hand, when the sky is hidden, the sun gone, and the beautiful
beech torn by the raving winds, neither does he heed that.
Rain and tempest affect him not; the glaring heat of summer,
the bitter frost of winter are alike to him. He is built up like
an oak. Believe it, the man that from his boyhood has stood
ankle-deep in the chill water of the ditch, patiently labouring
with axe and bill; who has trudged across the furrow, hand
on plough, facing sleet and mist; who has swung the sickle
under the summer sun—this is the man for the trenches. This
is the man whom neither the snows of the North nor the sun
of the South can vanquish; who will dig and delve, and carry
traverse and covered way forward in the face of the fortress,
who will lie on the bare ground in the night. For they who go
up to battle must fight the hard earth and the tempest, as well
as face bayonet and ball. As of yore with the brown bill, so
now with the rifle—the muscles that have been trained about
the hedges and fields will not fail England in the hour of
danger.

Hark!—a distant whoop—another, a blast of a horn, and then a burst of chiding that makes the woods ring. Down drops the bill, and together, heedless of any social difference in the common joy, we scramble to the highest mound, and see the pack sweep in full cry across the furrows. Crash—it is the bushes breaking, as the first foam-flecked, wearied horse hardly rises to his leap, and yet crushes safely through, opening a way, which is quickly widened by the straggling troop behind. Ha! down the lane from the hill dashes another squadron that has crossed the chord of the arc and comes in fresher. Ay, and a third is entering at the bottom there, one by one, over the brook. Woods, field, and paths, but just before an empty solitude, are alive with men and horses. Up yonder, along the ridge, gallops another troop in single file, well defined against the sky, going parallel to the hounds. What a view they must have of the scene below! Two ladies who ride up with torn skirts cannot lift their panting horses at the double mound. Well, let us defy "wilful damage" for once. The gate, jealously padlocked, is swiftly hoisted off its hinges, and away they go with hearty thanks. We slip the gate on again just as some one hails to us across the field to wait a minute, but seeing it is only a man we calmly replace the timber and let him take his chance. He is excited, but we smile stolidly. In another minute the wave of life is gone; it has swept over and disappeared as swiftly as it came. The wood, the field, and lane seem painfully—positively painfully—empty. Slowly the hedger and ditcher goes back to his work, where in the shade under the bushes even now the dew lingers.

So there are days to be enjoyed out of doors even in much-abused November. And when the wind rises and the storm is near, if you get under the lee of a good thick copse there is a wild pleasure in the frenzy that passes over. With a rush the leaves stream outwards, thickening the air, whirling round and round; the tree-tops bend and sigh, the blast strikes them, and in an instant they are stripped and bare. A spectral rustling, as the darkness falls and the black cloud approaches, is the fallen leaves in the copse, lifted up from their repose and dashed against the underwood. Then a howl of wrath descends and fills the sense of hearing, so that for the moment it is hard to tell what is happening. A rushing hiss follows, and the rain hurtles through the branches, driving so horizontally as to pass overhead. The sheltering thorn-thicket stirs, and a long, deep, moaning roar rises from the fir-trees. Another howl that seems to stun—to so fill the ears with sound that they cannot hear—the aerial host charges the tree-ranks, and the shock makes them tremble to the root. Still another and another; twigs and broken boughs fly before it and strew the sward; larger branches that have long been dead fall crashing downwards; leaves are forced right through the thorn-thicket, and strike against the face. Fortunately, so fierce a fury cannot last; presently the billows of wind that strike the wood come at longer intervals and with less vigour; then the rain increases, and yet a little while and the storm has swept on. The very fury—the utter *abandon*—of its rage is its charm; the spirit rises to meet it, and revels in the roar and buffeting.

By-and-by they who have faced it have their reward. The wind sinks, the rain ceases, a pale blue sky shows above, and then yonder appears a majesty of cloud—a Himalaya of vapour. Crag on crag rises the vast pile—such jagged and pointed rocks as never man found on earth, or, if he found, could climb—topped with a peak that towers to the heavens, and leans—visibly leans—and threatens to fall and over-whelm the weak world at its feet. A gleam as of snow glitters on the upper rocks, the passes are gloomy and dark, the faces of the precipices are lit up with a golden gleam from the rapidly-sinking sun. So the magic structure stands and sees the great round disk go down. The night gathers around those giant mounts and dark space receives them.

CHAPTER XXI

A WINTER'S MORNING

THE pale beams of the waning moon still cast a shadow on the cottage, when the labourer rises from his heavy sleep on a winter's morning. Often he huddles on his things and slips his feet into his thick "water-tights"—which are stiff and hard, having been wet over night—by no other light than this. If the household is comparatively well managed, however, he strikes a match, and his "dip" shows at the window. But he generally prefers to save a candle, and clatters down the narrow steep stairs in the semi-darkness, takes a piece of bread and cheese, and steps forth into the sharp air. The cabbages in the garden he notes are covered with white frost, so is the grass in the fields, and the footpath is hard under foot. In the furrows is a little ice—white because the water has shrunk from beneath it, leaving it hollow—and on the stile is a crust of rime, cold to the touch, which he brushes off in getting over. Overhead the sky is clear—cloudless but pale—and the stars, though not yet fading, have lost the brilliant glitter of midnight. Then, in all their glory, the idea of their globular shape is easily accepted; but in the morning, just as the dawn is breaking, the absence of glitter conveys the impression of flatness—circular rather than globular. But yonder, over the elms, above the cowpens, the great morning star has risen, shining far brighter, in proportion, than the moon; an intensely clear metallic light—like incandescent silver.

The shadows of the trees on the frosted ground are dull. As the footpath winds by the hedge the noise of his footstep startles the blackbird roosting in the bushes, and he bustles out and flies across the field. There is more rime on the posts and rails around the rickyard, and the thatch on the haystack is white with it in places. He draws out the broad hay-knife— a vast blade, wide at the handle, the edge gradually curving to a point—and then searches for the rubber or whet-stone, stuck somewhere in the side of the rick. At the first sound of the stone upon the steel the cattle in the adjoining yard and sheds utter a few low "moos," and there is a stir among them. Mounting the ladder he forces the knife with both hands into the hay, making a square cut which bends outwards, opening from the main mass till it appears on the point of parting and letting him fall with it to the ground. But long practice has taught him how to balance himself half on the ladder, half on the hay. Presently, with a truss unbound and loose on his head, he enters the yard, and passes from crib to crib, leaving a little here and a little there. For if he fills one first, there will be quarrelling among the cows, and besides, if the crib is too liberally filled, they will pull it out and tread it under foot. The cattle that are in the sheds fattening for Christmas have cake as well, and this must be supplied in just proportion.

The hour of milking, which used to be pretty general everywhere, varies now in different places, to suit the necessities of the milk trade. The milk has, perhaps, to travel three or four miles to the railway station; near great towns, where some of the farmers deliver milk themselves from house to house, the cows are milked soon after noonday. What would their grandfathers have said to that? But where the old customs have not much altered, the milker sits down in the morning to his cow with the stars still visible overhead, punching his hat well into her side—a hat well battered and thickly coated with grease, for the skin of the cow exudes an unctuous substance. This hat he keeps for the purpose. A couple of milking pails—they are of large size—form a heavy load when filled. The milker, as he walks back to the farmhouse, bends his head under the yoke—whence so many men are round-shouldered—and steps slowly with a peculiar swaying motion of the body, which slight swing prevents it from spilling.

Another man who has to be up while the moon casts a shadow is the carter, who must begin to feed his team very early in order to get them to eat sufficient. If the manger be over-filled they spill and waste it, and at the same time will not eat so much. This is tedious work. Then the lads come and polish up the harness, and so soon as it is well light get out to plough. The custom with the horses is to begin to work as early as possible, but to strike off in the afternoon some time before the other men, the lads riding home astride. The strength of the carthorse has to be husbanded carefully, and the labour performed must be adjusted to it and to the food—*i.e.*, fuel, consumed. To manage a large team of horses, so as to keep them in good condition, with glossy coats and willing step, and yet to get the maximum of work out of them, requires long experience and constant attention. The carter, therefore, is a man of much importance on a farm. If he is up to his duties he is a most valuable servant; if he neglects them he is a costly nuisance, not so much from his pay, but because of the hindrance and disorganisation of the whole farm-work which such neglect entails.

Foggers and milkers, if their cottages are near at hand, having finished the first part of the day's work, can often go back home to breakfast, and, if they have a good woman in the cottage, find a fire and hot tea ready. The carter can rarely leave his horses for that, and, therefore, eats his breakfast in the stable; but then he has the advantage that up to the time of starting forth he is under cover. The fogger and milker, on the other hand, are often exposed to the most violent tempests. A gale of wind, accompanied with heavy rain, often reaches its climax just about the dawn. They find the soil saturated, and the step sinks into it—the furrows are full of water; the cowyard, though drained, is a pool, no drain being capable of carrying it off quick enough. The thatch of the sheds drips continually; the haystack drips; the thatch of the stack, which has to be pulled off before the hay-knife can be used, is wet; the old decaying wood of the rails and gates is wet. They sit on the three-legged milking-stool (whose rude workmanship has taken a dull polish from use) in a puddle; the hair of the cow, against which the head is placed, is wet; the wind blows the rain into the nape of the neck behind, the position being stooping. Staggering under the heavy yoke homewards, the boots sink deep into the slush and mire in the gateways, the weight carried sinking them well in. The teams do not usually work in very wet weather, and most of the out-door work waits; but the cattle must be attended to, Sundays and holidays included. Even in summer it often happens that a thunderstorm bursts about that time of the morning. But in winter, when the rain is driven by a furious wind, when the lantern is blown out, and the fogger stumbles in pitchy darkness through mud and water, it would be difficult to imagine a condition of things which concentrates more discomfort.

If, as often happens, the man is far from home—perhaps he has walked a mile or two to work—of course he cannot change his clothes, or get near a fire, unless in the farmer's kitchen. In some places the kitchen is open to the men, and on Sundays, at all events, they get a breakfast free. But the kindly old habits are dying out before the hard-and-fast money system and the abiding effects of unionism, which, even when not prominently displayed, causes a silent, sullen estrangement.

Shepherds, too, sometimes visit the fold very early in the morning, and in the lambing season may be said to be about both day and night. They come, however, under a different category to the rest of the men, because they have no regular hours, but are guided solely by the season and the work. A shepherd often takes his ease when other men are busily labouring. On the other hand, he is frequently anxiously engaged when they are sleeping. His sheep rule his life, and he has little to do with the artificial divisions of time.

Hedgers and ditchers often work by the piece, and so take their own time for meals; the ash woods, which are cut in the winter, are also usually thrown by the piece. Hedging and ditching, if done properly, is hard work, especially if there is any grubbing. Though the arms get warm from swinging the grub-axe or billhook, or cleaning out the ditch and plastering and smoothing the side of the mound with the spade, yet feet and ankles are chilled by the water in the ditch. This is often dammed up and so kept back partially, but it generally forces its way through. The ditcher has a board to stand on; there is a hole through it, and a projecting stick attached, with which to drag it into position. But the soft soil allows the board to sink, and he often throws it aside as more encumbrance than use. He has some small perquisites: he is allowed to carry home a bundle of wood or a log every night, and may gather up the remnants after the faggoting is finished. On the other hand, he cannot work in bad weather.

Other men come to the farm buildings to commence work about the time the carter has got his horses fed, groomed, and harnessed, and after the fogger and milker have completed their early duties. If it is a frosty morning and the ground firm, so as to bear up a cart without poaching the soil too much, the manure is carried out into the fields. This is plain, straightforward labour, and cannot be looked upon as hard work. If the cattle want no further attention, the foggers and milkers turn their hands after breakfast to whatever may be going on. Some considerable time is taken up in slicing roots with the machine, or chaff-cutting—monotonous work of a simple character, and chiefly consisting in turning a handle.

The general hands—those who come on when the carter is ready, and who are usually young men, not yet settled down to any particular branch—seem to get the best end of the stick. They do not begin so early in the morning by some time as the fogger, milker, carter, or shepherd; consequently, if the cottage arrangements are tolerable, they can get a comfortable breakfast first. They have no anxieties or trouble whatever; the work may be hard in itself, but there is no particular hurry (in their estimation) and they do not distress themselves. They receive nearly the same wages as the others who have the care of valuable flocks, herds, and horses; the difference is but a shilling or two, and, to make up for that, they do not work on Sundays. Now, the fogger must feed his cows, the carter his horses, the shepherd look to his sheep every day; consequently their extra wages are thoroughly well earned. The young labourer—who is simply a labourer, and professes no special branch—is, therefore, in a certain sense, the best off. He is rarely hired by the year—he prefers to be free, so that when harvest comes he may go where wages chance to be highest. He is an independent person, and full of youth, strength, and with little experience of life, is apt to be rough in his manners and not over civil. His wages too often go in liquor, but if such a young man keeps steady (and there are a few that do keep steady) he does very well indeed, having no family to maintain.

A set of men who work very hard are those who go with the steam-ploughing tackle. Their pay is so arranged as to depend in a measure on the number of acres they plough. They get the steam up as early as possible in the morning, and continue as late as they can at night. Just after the harvest, when the days are long, and, indeed, it is still summer, they work for extremely long hours. Their great difficulty lies in getting water. This must be continually fetched in carts, and, of course, requires a horse and man. These are not always forthcoming in the early morning, but they begin as soon as they can get water for the boiler, and do not stop till the field be finished or it is dark.

The women do not find much work in the fields during the winter. Now and then comes a day's employment with the threshing-machine when the farmer wants a rick of corn threshed out. In pasture or dairy districts some of them go out into the meadows and spread the manure. They wear gaiters, and sometimes a kind of hood for the head. If done carefully, it is hard work for the arms—knocking the manure into small pieces by striking it with a fork swung to and fro smartly.

In the spring, when the great heaps of roots are opened— having been protected all the winter by a layer of straw and earth—it is necessary to trim them before they are used. This is often done by a woman. She has a stool or log of wood to sit on, and arranges a couple of sacks or something of the kind, so as to form a screen and keep off the bitter winds which are then so common—colder than those of the winter proper. With a screen one side, the heap of roots the other, and the hedge on the third, she is in some sense sheltered, and, taking her food with her, may stay there the whole day long, quite alone in the solitude of the broad, open, arable fields.

From a variety of causes, the number of women working

in the fields is much less than was formerly the case; thus presenting precisely the reverse state of things to that complained of in towns, where the clerks, etc., say that they are undersold by female labour. The contrast is rather curious. The price of women's labour has, too, risen; and there does not appear to be any repugnance on their part to field-work. Whether the conclusion is to be accepted that there has been a diminution in the actual number of women living in rural places, it is impossible to decide with any accuracy. But there are signs that female labour has drifted to the towns quite as much as male—especially the younger girls. In some places it seems rare to see a young girl working in the field (meaning in winter) —those that are to be found are generally women well advanced in life. Spring and summer work brings forth more, but not nearly so many as used to be the case.

Although the work of the farm begins so soon in the morning, it is, on the other hand, in the cold months, over early. "The night cometh when no man can work" was, one would think, originally meant in reference to agricultural labour. It grows dusk before half-past four on a dull winter's day, and by five is almost, if not quite, dark. Lanterns may be moving in the cowyards and stables; but elsewhere all is quiet—the hedger and ditcher cannot see to strike his blow, the ploughs have ceased to move for some time, the labourer's workshop —the field—is not lighted by gas as the rooms of cities.

The shortness of the winter day is one of the primary reasons why, in accordance with ancient custom, wages are lowered at that time. In summer, on the contrary, the hours are long, and the pay high—which more than makes up for the winter reduction. A labourer who has any prudence can, in fact, do very well by putting by a portion of his extra summer wages for the winter; if he does not choose to exercise common sense, he cannot expect the farmer (or any manufacturer) to pay the same price for a little work and short time as for much work and long hours. Reviewing the work the labourer actually does in winter, it seems fair and just to state that the foggers, or milkers, i.e., the men who attend on cattle, the carters, and the shepherds, work hard, continuously, and often in the face of the most inclement weather. The mere labourers, who, as previously remarked, are usually younger and single men, do not work so hard, nor so long. And when they are at it—whether turning the handle of a winnowing machine in a barn, cutting a hedge, spreading manure, or digging—it must be said that they do not put the energy into it of which their brawny arms are capable.

"The least work and the most money," however, is a maxim not confined to the agricultural labourer. Recently I had occasion to pass through a busy London street in the West-end where the macadam of the roadway was being picked up by some score of men, and, being full of the subject of labour, I watched the process. Using the right hand as a fulcrum and keeping it stationary, each navvy slowly lifted his pick with the left halfway up, about on a level with his waistcoat, when the point of the pick was barely two feet above the ground. He then let it fall—simply by its own weight—producing a tiny indentation such as might be caused by the kick of one's heel. It required about three such strokes, if they could be called strokes, to detach one single small stone. After that exhausting labour the man stood at ease for a few minutes, so that there were often three or four at once staring about them, while several others lounged against the wooden railing placed to keep vehicles back.

A more irritating spectacle it would be hard to imagine. Idle as much agricultural labour is, it is rarely so lazy as that. How contractors get their work done, if that is a sample, it is a puzzle to understand. The complaint of the poor character of the work performed by the agricultural labourer seems also true of other departments, where labour—pure and simple labour of thews and sinews—is concerned. The rich city merchant, who goes to his office daily, positively works harder, in spite of all his money. So do the shopmen and assistants behind their counters; so do the girls in drapers' shops, standing the whole day and far into the evening when, as just observed, the fields have been dark for hours; so, indeed, do most men and women who earn their bread by any other means than mere bodily strength.

But the cattle-men, carters, and shepherds, men with families and settled, often seem to take an interest in their charges, in the cows, horses, or sheep: some of them are really industrious, deserving men. The worst feature of unionism is the lumping of all together, for where one man is hardly worth his salt, another is a good workman. It is strange that such men as this should choose to throw in their lot with so many who are idle—whom they must know to be idle—thus jeopardising their own position for the sake of those who are not worth one-fifth the sacrifice the agricultural cottager must be called upon to make in a strike. The hard-working carter or cattle-man, according to the union theory, is to lose his pay, his cottage, his garden, and get into bad odour with his employer, who previously trusted him, and was willing to give him assistance, in order that the day labourer, who has no responsibilities either of his own or his master's, and who has already the best end of the stick, should enjoy still further opportunities for idleness.

CHAPTER XXII

THE LABOURER'S CHILDREN — COTTAGE GIRLS

IN the coldest weather one or more of the labourer's children are sure to be found in the farmyard somewhere. After the mother has dressed her boy (who may be about three or four years old) in the morning, he is at once turned out of doors to take care of himself, and if, as is often the case, the cottage is within a short distance of the farmyard, thither he toddles directly. He stands about the stable door, watching the harnessing of the great cart-horses, which are, from the very first, the object of his intense admiration. But he has already learnt to keep out of the way, knowing that his presence would not otherwise be tolerated a moment, and occupies a position which enables him to dart quickly behind a tree, or a rick.

When the horses are gone he visits the outhouse, where the steam-engine is driving the chaff-cutter, or peers in at the huge doors of the barn, where with wide wooden shovel the grain is being moved. Or he may be met with round the hay-ricks, dragging a log of wood by a piece of tar cord, the log representing a plough. As you come upon him suddenly he draws up to the rick as if the hay was his natural protector, and looks up at you with half-frightened, half-curious gaze, and mouth open. His hat is an old one of his father's, a mile too big, coming down over his ears to his shoulders, well greased from ancient use—a thing not without its advantage, since it makes it impervious to rain. He wears what was a white jacket, but is now the colour of the prevailing soil of the place; a belt; and a pair of stumping boots, the very picture in miniature of his father's, heeled and tipped with iron. His naked legs are red with the cold, but thick and strong; his cheeks are plump and firm, his round blue eyes bright, his hair almost white, like bleached straw.

An hour or two ago his skin was clean enough, for he was sent out well washed, but it is now pretty well grimed, for he has been making himself happy in the dirt, as a boy should do if he be a boy. For one thing it is clean dirt, nothing but pure mother earth, and not the nasty unctuous filth of city courts and back lanes. If you speak to him he answers you sturdily —if you can catch the meaning of his words, doubly difficult from accent and imperfect knowledge of construction. But he means well, and if you send him on an errand will run off to find "measter" as fast as his short stature will allow. He will potter about the farmyard the whole morning, perhaps turning up at home for a lunch of a slice of bread well larded. His little sister, not so old as himself, is there, already beginning her education in the cares of maternity, looking after the helpless baby that crawls over the wooden threshold of the door with bare head, despite the bitter cold. Once during the day he may perhaps steal round the farmhouse, and peer wistfully from behind the tubs or buckets into the kitchen, when, if the mistress chances to be about, he is pretty certain to pick up some trifle in the edible line.

How those prosperous parents who dwell in highly-rented suburban villas, and send out their children for a walk with a couple of nurses and a "bow-wow" to run beside the perambulator, would be eaten up with anxiety did their well-dressed boys or girls play where this young son of toil finds his amusement! Under the very hoofs of the cart-horses—he will go out to them when they are loose in the field, three or four in a group, under a tree, when it looks as if the slightest movement on their part must crush him; down to the side of the deep broad brook to swim sticks in it for boats, where a slip on the treacherous mud would plunge him in, and where the chance of rescue—everybody being half a mile away at work—would be absolutely *nil*. The cows come trampling through the yard; the bull bellows in the meadow; great, grunting sows, savage when they have young, go by, thrusting their noses into and turning up the earth for food; steam ploughing engines pant and rumble about; carts are con-

tinually coming and going; and he is all day in the midst of it
without guardian of any kind whatsoever. The fog, and frost,
and cutting winter winds make him snivel and cry with the
cold, and yet there he is out in it—in the draughts that blow
round the ricks, and through the hedge bare of leaves. The
rain rushes down pitilessly—he creeps inside the barn or
shed, and with a stick splashes the puddles. The long glaring
days of summer see him exposed to the scorching heat in the
hay, or the still hotter harvest field. Through it all he grows
stout and strong, and seems happy enough.

He is, perhaps, more fortunate than his sister, who has to
take part in the household work from very early age. But the
village school claims them both after awhile; and the greater
number of such schools are well filled, taking into consideration the long distances the children have to come and the
frequent bad state of the roads and lanes. Both the employers
and the children's own parents get them to school as much as
possible; the former put on a mild compulsion, the latter for
the most part are really anxious for the schooling, and have
even an exaggerated idea of the value of education. In some
cases it would seem as if the parents actually educated themselves in some degree from their own children, questioning
them as to what they have been told. But, on the other hand,
the labourer objects to paying for the teaching, and thinks
the few coppers he is charged a terrible extortion.

The lads, as they grow older and leave school, can almost
always find immediate employment with their father on the
same farm, or on one close by. Though they do not now go
out to work so soon, yet, on the other hand, when they do
commence they receive higher weekly wages. The price paid
for boys' labour now is such that it becomes a very important addition to the aggregate income of the cottager.
When a man has got a couple of boys out, bringing home so
much per week, his own money, of course, goes very much
farther.

The girls go less and less into the field. If at home, they assist
their parents at harvest time when work is done by the acre,
and the more a man can cut, the better he is off; but their aim
is domestic service, and they prefer to be engaged in the
towns. They shirk the work of a farmhouse, especially if it
is a dairy, and so it has come to be quite a complaint among
farmers' wives, in many places, that servants are not to be
obtained. Those that are available are mere children, whose

mothers like them to go out anywhere at first, just to obtain an insight into the duties of a servant. The farmer's wife has the trouble and annoyance of teaching these girls the rudiments of household work, and then, the moment they are beginning to be useful, they leave, and almost invariably go to the towns. Those that remain are the slow-witted, or those who are tied in a measure by family difficulties—as a bedridden mother to attend to; or, perhaps, an illegitimate child of her own may fetter the cottage girl. Then she goes out in the daytime to work at the farmhouse, and returns to sleep at home.

Cottage girls have taken to themselves no small airs of recent years—they dress, so far as their means will go, as flashily as servants in cities, and stand upon their dignity. This foolishness has, perhaps, one good effect—it tends to diminish the illegitimate births. The girls are learning more self-respect—if they could only achieve that and eschew the other follies it would be a clear gain. It may be questioned whether purely agricultural marriages are as common as formerly. The girl who leaves her home for service in the towns sees a class of men—grooms, footmen, artisans, and workmen generally—not only receiving higher wages than the labourers in her native parish, but possessing a certain amount of comparative refinement. It is not surprising that she prefers, if possible, to marry among these.

On the other hand, the young labourer, who knows that he can get good wages wherever he likes to go, has become somewhat of a wanderer. He roams about, not only from village to village, but from county to county; perhaps works for a time as a navvy on some distant railway, and thus associates with a different class of men, and picks up a sort of coarse cynicism. He does not care to marry and settle and tie himself down to a routine of labour—he despises home pleasures, preferring to spend his entire earnings upon himself. The roaming habits of the rising generation of labourers is an important consideration, and it has an effect in many ways. Statistics are not available; but the impression left on the mind is that purely rural marriages are not so frequent, notwithstanding that wages at large have risen. When a young man does marry, he and his wife not uncommonly live for a length of time with his parents, occupying a part of the cottage.

Had any one gone into a cottage some few years back and

inquired about the family, most probably the head of the house could have pointed out all his sons and daughters engaged in or near the parish. Most likely his own father was at work almost within hail. Uncles, cousins, various relations, were all near by. He could tell where everybody was. To-day if a similar inquiry were made, the answer would often be very different. The old people might be about still, but the younger would be found scattered over the earth. One, perhaps, went to the United States or Canada in the height of the labourers' agitation some years ago, when agents were busy enlisting recruits for the Far West. Since then another has departed for Australia, taking with him his wife. Others have migrated northwards, or to some other point of the compass—they are still in the old country, but the exact whereabouts is not known. The girls are in service a hundred miles away—some married in the manufacturing districts. To the middle-aged, steady, stay-at-home labourer, the place does not seem a bit like it used to. Even the young boys are restless, and talking of going somewhere. This may not be the case with every single individual cottage family, but it is so with a great number. The stolid phalanx of agricultural labour is slowly disintegrating.

If there yet remains anything idyllic in the surroundings of rural cottage life, it may be found where the unmarried but grown-up sons—supposing these, of course, to be steady —remain at home with their parents. The father and head of the house, having been employed upon one farm for the last thirty years or more, though nominally carter, is really a kind of bailiff. The two young men work on at the same place, and lodge at home, paying a small weekly sum for board and lodging. Their sister is probably away in service; their mother manages the cottage. She occasionally bears a hand in indoor work at the farmhouse, and in the harvest time aids a little in the field, but otherwise does not labour. What is the result? Plenty to eat, good beds, fairly good furniture, sufficient fuel, and some provision for contingencies, through the benefit club. As the wages are not consumed in drink, they have always a little ready money, and, in short, are as independent as it is possible for working men to be, especially if, as is often the case, the cottage and garden is their own, or is held on a small quit-rent. If either of the sons in time desires to marry, he does not start utterly unprovided. His father's influence with the farmer is pretty sure to procure him a cottage; he has some small savings himself, and his parents in the course of years have accumulated some extra furniture, which is given to him.

If a cottage, where the occupants are steady like this, be visited in the evening, say towards seven o'clock, when dinner is on the table (labourers dining or supping after the conclusion of the day's work) the fare will often be found of a substantial character. There may be a piece of mutton—not, of course, the prime cut, but wholesome meat—cabbages, parsnips, carrots (labourers like a profusion of vegetables), all laid out in a decent manner. The food is plain, but solid and plentiful. If the sister out in service wishes to change her situation, she has a home to go to meanwhile. Should any dispute occur with the employer the cottage is still there, and affords a shelter till the difficulty is settled or other work obtained. In towns the workman who has been earning six or even ten shillings a day, and paying a high rent (carefully collected every week), no sooner gets his discharge than he receives notice to quit his lodgings, because the owner knows he will not be paid. But when the agricultural labourer has a quit-rent cottage, or one of his own, he has a permanent resource, and can look round for another engagement.

The cooking in the best cottages would not commend itself to the student of that art: in those where the woman is shiftless it would be deemed simply intolerable. Evidence of this is only too apparent on approaching cottages, especially towards the evening. Coming from the fresh air of the fields, perhaps from the sweet scent of clover or of new-mown grass, the odour which arises from the cottages is peculiarly offensive. It is not that they are dirty inside—the floor may be scrubbed, the walls brushed, the chairs clean, and the beds tidy; it is from outside that all the noisome exhalations taint the breeze. The refuse vegetables, the washings, the liquid and solid rubbish generally is cast out into the ditch, often open to the highway road, and there festers till the first storm sweeps it away. The cleanest woman indoors thinks nothing disgusting out of doors, and hardly goes a step from her threshold to cast away indescribable filth. Now, a good deal of this refuse is the remains of imperfect cooking—masses of soddened cabbage, part of which only is eaten, and the rest stored for the pig or thrown into the ditch. The place smells of soaking, saturated cabbage for yards and yards round about.

But it is much easier to condemn the cottage cook than to

show her how to do better. It is even doubtful whether professed scientific cooks could tell her what to do. The difficulty arises from the rough, coarse taste of the labourer, and the fact, which it is useless to ignore, that he must have something solid, and indeed, bulky. Thin clear soups—though proved to abound with nourishment and of delicious flavour—are utterly beside his wants. Give him the finest soup; give him *pâtés,* or even more meaty *entrées,* and his remark will be that it is very nice, but he wants "summat to eat." His teeth are large, his jaws strong, his digestive powers such as would astonish a city man; he likes solid food, bacon, butcher's meat, cheese, or something that gives him a sense of fulness, like a mass of vegetables. This is the natural result of his training and work in the fields. The materials used by the cottage cook are often quite capable of being made into agreeable dishes, but then those dishes would not suit the man. All the soups and kickshaws—though excellent in themselves—in the world are not, for his purpose, equal to a round of beef or a side of bacon. Let any one go and labour daily in the field, and they will come quickly to the same opinion. Yet something might certainly be done in the way of preventing waste. The real secret lies in the education of the women when young—that is, for the future. But, taking the present day, looking at things as they actually exist, it is no use abusing or lecturing the cottage cook. She might, perhaps, be persuaded to adopt a systematic plan of disposing of the refuse.

The Saturday half-holiday is scarcely so closely observed in rural labour as in urban. The work closes earlier, that is, so far as the day labourer is concerned, for he gets the best of this as of other things. But, half-holiday or not, cows have to be fed and milked, sheep must be looked after, and the stable attended to, so that the regular men do not get off much sooner. In winter, the days being short, they get little advantage from the short time; in summer they do. Compensation is, however, as much as possible afforded to the settled men who have gardens, by giving them a half-day now and then when work is slack to attend to them.

On Sunday morning the labourer cleans and polishes his boots (after digging the potatoes for dinner), puts on a black or dark coat, puts his hands in his pockets—a marked feature this—and rambles down to his garden or the allotment. There, if it be spring or summer, he is sure to find some acquaintances likewise "looking round." This seems to be one of the greatest pleasures of the labourer, noting the growth of a cabbage here, and the promise of potatoes yonder; he does not work, but strolls to and fro, discussing the vegetable prospect. Then back home in time for dinner—the great event of Sunday, being often the only day in the week that he can get a hot dinner in the middle of the day. It is his day at home, and though he may ramble out he never goes far.

Ladies residing in the country are accustomed to receive periodical appeals from friends in town asking their assistance in procuring servants. So frequent are such appeals that there would seem to be a popular belief that the supply is inexhaustible. The villages are supposed to be full of girls, all ready to enter service, and, though a little uncouth in manner, possessed nevertheless of sterling good qualities. The letter is usually couched in something like the following terms:— "Do you happen to know of a really good girl that would suit us? You are aware of the scale on which our household is conducted, and how very modest our requirements are. All we want is a strong, healthy, honest girl, ready and willing to work and to learn, and who will take an interest in the place, and who will not ask too extravagant a price. She can have a good home with us as long as ever she likes to stay. My dear, you really cannot tell what a difficulty we experience in getting servants who are not 'uppish,' and who are trustworthy and do not mind working, and if you can find us one in those pretty villages round you, we shall be so much obliged," etc.

The fact that a servant from the country is supposed, in the nature of things, to be honest and willing, hardworking, strong, and healthy, and almost everything else, speaks well for the general character of the girls brought up in agricultural cottages. It is, however, quite a mistake to suppose the supply to be limitless; it is just the reverse; the really good servants from any particular district are quickly exhausted, and then, if the friends in town will insist upon a girl from the country, they cannot complain if they do not get precisely what they want. The migration, indeed, of servants from the villages to the towns has, for the time being, rather overdone itself. The best of those who responded to the first demand were picked out some time since; many of those now to be had are not of the first class, and the young are not yet grown up. After a while, as education progresses—bringing with it better manners—there may be a fresh supply; meantime, really good country girls are difficult to obtain. But the demand is as great as ever. From the squire's lady down to the wife of the small tenant-farmer, one and all receive the same requests from friends in town. The character of the true country servant stands as high as ever.

Let us hope that the polish of progress may not too much overlay the solid if humble virtues which procured that character for her class. Some efforts are being made here and there to direct the course of young girls after leaving the village schools—to put them in the right way and give them the benefit of example. As yet such efforts are confined to individuals. The object is certainly worth the formation of local organisations, for, too often, on quitting the school, the young village girl comes in contact with anything but elevating influences, and, unfortunately, her own mother is not always the best guide. The position of a servant in town is well known, the antecedents of a girl before she reaches town perhaps not so thoroughly, while the lives of those who remain in the villages drop out of sight of the great world.

As a child, the cottage girl "roughs" it in the road and in the fields. In winter she learns to slide, and to endure the cold and rain, till she often becomes what, to any one accustomed to a more delicate life, seems positively impervious to weather. The servants in old-fashioned farmhouses really did not seem to know what it was to feel cold. Even now-a-days, a servant fresh from an outlying hamlet, where her parents probably could procure but little fuel beyond what was necessary for cooking, at first cares not an atom whether there be a fire in the kitchen or not. Such girls are as hardy as the men of their native place. After a time, hot rooms and a profusion of meat and good living generally saps and undermines this natural strength. Then they shiver like town-bred people.

The cottage child is often locked out by her parents, who go to work and leave her in charge of her still smaller brothers and sisters. They play about the hedges and ditches, and very rarely come to any harm. In autumn their little fingers are employed picking up the acorns fallen from the oaks, for which the farmers pay so much per bushel. In spring is their happiest time. The joy of life—the warm sunshine and pleasant breeze of spring—is not wholly lost upon them, despite their hard fare, and the not very affectionate treatment they receive at home. Such a girl may then be seen sitting under a willow beside the brook, with her charges around her—the little brother that can just toddle, the baby that can but crawl and crow in the green fresh grass. Between them lies a whole pile of flowers—dandelion stems made into rings, and the rings joined together so as to form a chain, rushes plaited, blue-bells, cowslips tied up in balls, and cowslips loose, their yellow petals scattered over the sward.

The brook flows murmuring by, with an occasional splash, as a water-rat dives from the bank or a fish rises to an insect. The children weave their flowers and chant some old doggrel rhymes with little or no meaning. Long afterwards that girl will retain an unconscious memory of the scene, when, wheeling her employer's children out on some suburban road, she seeks a green meadow and makes a cowslip ball for the delighted infants. In summer they go down to the hay-field, but dare not meddle with the hay, which the bailiff does not like to see disturbed; they remain under the shadow of the hedge. In autumn they search for the berries, like the birds, nibbling the hips and haws, tasting crabs and sloes, or feasting on the fruit of a hazel-bush.

Be it spring or summer, autumn or winter, wherever the child may be, her eyes are ever on the watch to find a dead stick or a broken branch, too heavy to lift, but which may be dragged behind, in order to feed the cottage fire at night. That is her first duty as a child; if she remains in the hamlet that will be her duty through life, and to the last, as an aged woman. So in London, round the purlieus of buildings in the course of erection—even in the central thoroughfares, in busy Fleet Street—children hang about the temporary hoardings, and pick up the chips and splinters of deal. But the latter have not the pleasure of the blue-bells and cowslips, nor even of the hips and haws, nor does the fresh pure breeze play upon their foreheads.

Rough though it be, the childhood of the cottage girl is not without its recompenses, the most valuable of which is sturdy health. Now that good schools are open to every village, so soon as the children are old enough to walk the distance, often considerable, they are sent off every morning. At all events, if it does nothing else, it causes the mothers to give them a daily tidying up, which is in itself an advantage. They travel under the charge of the girl; often two or three such small parties join company, coming from as many cottages. In the warmer months, the lanes and fields they cross form a long playground for them, and picking flowers and searching for birds'-nests pass away the time. In winter they have to face the mire and rain.

When the girl leaves school she is hardly old enough to enter service, and too often in the year or so that elapses before she "goes out" much mischief is done. She is then at an age when the mind is peculiarly receptive, and the ways of the young labourers with whom she is thrown into contact are not very refined. Her first essay at "service" is often as day-nursemaid at some adjacent farmhouse, taking care of the younger children in the day, and returning home to sleep. She then wanders with the children about the same fields she visited long before. This system used to be common enough, but latterly it has not worked well, because the parents expect the girl to progress so rapidly. She must be a woman and receive a woman's wages almost before she has ceased to be a girl. If she does not disdain to enter a farmhouse as kitchen-maid her wages will probably be about six pounds a year at first. Of course the exact sum varies very much in different localities and in different cases. It is but a small sum of money, yet it is often all she is worth.

The cottage is a poor preparation even for the humblest middle-class home. Those ladies in towns who have engaged country servants are well aware of the amount of teaching they require before they can go through the simplest duties in a satisfactory manner. But most of these girls have already been out several times before reaching town. What a difficulty, then, the first farmer's wife must have had in drilling the rudiments of civilised life into them! Indeed, the vexations and annoyances connected with servants are no light weight upon the patience of the tenant-farmer. His wife is perpetually preparing servant girls for the service of other people.

She is a kind of unpaid teacher, for ever shaping the rough material which, so soon as it is worth higher wages than a tenant-farmer can usually pay, is off, and the business has to be begun over again. No one who had not seen it would believe how clumsy and unthinking such girls are on first "going out." It is, too, the flightiest and giddiest period of their existence—before the girl sobers down into the woman. In the houses of the majority of tenant-farmers the mistress herself has to be a good deal in the kitchen, and therefore comes into close personal contact with the servants, and feels these things acutely. Except in the case of gentlemen-farmers it may, perhaps, be said that almost all the wives of farmers have had experience of this kind.

The girls are not nearly so tractable as formerly—they are fully aware of their own value and put it extremely high; a word is sufficient, and if not pleased they leave immediately. Wages rise yearly to about the limit of twelve pounds. In mentioning that sum it is not set down as an exact figure, for circumstances of course vary in every case. But it is seldom that servants in farmhouses of the middle class receive more than that. Until recently few obtained so much. Most of them that are worth anything never rest till they reach the towns, and take service in the villas of the wealthy suburban residents. Some few, however, remain in the country from preference, feeling a strong affection for their native place, for their parents and friends. Notwithstanding the general tendency to roam, this love of home is by no means extinct, but shows itself very decidedly in some of the village girls.

The fogger, or milker, who comes to the farmhouse door in the morning, may not present a very attractive appearance in the eyes of those accustomed to see well-dressed people; but it may be quite different with the young girl whose early associations have made her oblivious of dirt. She does not notice the bits of hay clinging to the smockfrock, the greasy hat, and begrimed face, or the clumsy boots thickly coated with mud. A kiss may be quite as sweet, despite these mere outside accidents. In her way she is full of imagination and fancy—what her mistress would call "giddy." Within doors an eye may be on her, so she slips out to the wood-stack in the yard, ostensibly to fetch a log for the fire, and indulges in a few moments of flirtation behind the shelter of the faggots. In the summer she works doubly hard in the morning, and gets everything forward, so that she may go out to the field haymaking in the afternoon, when she may meet her particular friend, and also, perhaps, his rival.

On Sundays she gladly walks two or more miles across the fields to church, knowing full well that some one will be lounging about a certain stile, or lying on the sward by a gate waiting for her. The practice of coquetry is as delightful in the country lane as in the saloons of wealth, though the ways in which it exhibits itself may be rude in comparison. So that love is sometimes the detaining force which keeps the girl in the country. Some of the young labourers are almost heirs to property in their eyes. One is perhaps the son of the carrier;

who owns a couple of cottages let out to tenants; or the son of the blacksmith, at whom several caps are set, and about whom no little jealousy rages. On the whole, servants in the country, at least at farmhouses, have much more liberty than they could possibly get in town.

The work is hard in the morning, but generally much less for the rest of the day; in the evening there is often scarcely anything to do. So that the farmhouse servant has much time to herself, and is not too strictly confined indoors when not at work. There is a good deal of "company," too; men coming to the door, men in the rick-yards and cattle-yards, men in the barn, labourers passing to their work, and so on. It is not so dull a life as might appear. Indeed, a farmhouse servant probably sees twice as many of her own class in the course of a week as a servant in town.

Vanity, of course, is not to be shut out even from so simple an existence: the girl must have a "fashionable" bonnet, and a pair of thin tight boots, let the lanes be never so dirty or the fields never so wet. In point of education they have much improved of late, and most can now read and write. But when they write home the letter is often read to the mother by some friend; the girl's parents being nearly or quite illiterate. Tenant-farmers' wives are often asked to act as notaries in such cases by cottage women on the receipt of letters from their children.

When such a girl marries in the village, she usually finds the work of the cottage harder than that of the farmhouse. It is more continuous, and when children arrive the trouble of nursing has to be added to the other duties, and to occasional work in the fields. The agricultural labourer's wife, indeed, has a harder lot than her husband. His toil is for the most part over when he leaves the field, but the woman's is never finished. When the man reaches home he does not care, or will not turn his hand to anything, except, perhaps, to fetch a pail of water, and he is not well pleased if asked to do that. The want of conveniences like an accessible water supply is severely felt by the women in many villages and hamlets; whilst in others there is a quantity running to waste. Many of the men obtain a more than liberal amount of beer, while the women scarcely get any at all. While working in the field they are allowed a small quantity by some farmers; at home they have none.

Very few cottage women are inclined to drink, and they are

seldom seen at "public" or intoxicated. On Saturdays most of them walk into the nearest town, perhaps five or more miles distant, in order to buy household stuff. Often a whole bevy of neighbours then meet and return home together, and that is about the only time when they call at the roadside inn. Laden with heavy parcels, with a long walk yet before them, and after a hard week's work, it is not surprising that they should want some refreshment, but the quantity of ale then purchased is very small. When there are a number of young children, and the parents endeavour to keep them decent, the woman works very hard indeed. Many farmers' wives take much interest in such families, where there is an evident endeavour to go straight, and assist the women in various ways, as with cast-off clothing for the children. A basketful of apples even from the farmer's orchard is a treat to the children, for, though better fed than formerly, their diet is necessarily monotonous, and such fruit as may be grown in the cottage garden is, of course, sold.

With the exception of vegetables the cottager now buys almost everything and produces nothing for home use; no home-spun clothing—not even a home-baked loaf. Instances have been observed where cottagers have gone to much expense (for them) to build ovens, and after baking a few batches abandoned the project. Besides the cheap outfitters in the towns, the pack-drapers come round visiting every cottage. Such drapers have no shop-window, and make no display, but employ several men carrying packs, who work through the villages on foot and range over a wide stretch of country.

Agricultural women, other than those belonging to the families of tenant-farmers, may be summed up as employed in the following manner. Bailiffs' wives and daughters: these are not supposed, on extensive farms, to work in the field. The wife frequently has charge of the small home dairy, and the daughter assists at the house. Sometimes they also attend to the poultry, now occasionally kept in large numbers. A bailiff's daughter sometimes becomes housekeeper to a farmer. Dairymaids of the ordinary class—not competent to make special cheese—are becoming rarer, on account of the demand for their services decreasing—the milk trade and cheap foreign cheese having rendered common sorts of cheese unprofitable. They are usually cottagers. Of the married labouring women and the indoor servants something has already been said. In most villages a seamstress or two may be found, and has plenty of work to do for the farmers' families. The better class of housekeepers, and those professional dairymaids who superintend the making of superior cheese, are generally more or less nearly related to the families of tenant-farmers.

CHAPTER XXIII

THE LOW "PUBLIC"—IDLERS

THE wise old saw that good wine needs no bush does not hold true in the case of the labourer; it would require a very large bush indeed to attract him to the best of beer offered for sale under legitimate conditions. In fact, he cares not a rap about good beer—that is, intrinsically good, a genuine product of malt and hops. He would rather grumble at it, unless, perchance, it was a gift; and even then would criticise it behind the donor's back, holding the quart cup aslant so as to see the bottom in one place, and get a better view of the liquor. The great breweries whose names are household words in cities, and whose interest it is to maintain a high standard of quality for the delectation of their million consumers, do not exalt their garish painted advertisements in gilded letters as tall as Tom Thumb over the doors of village alehouses. You might call for Bass at Cairo, Bombay, Sydney, or San Francisco, and Bass would be forthcoming. But if you knocked the trestle-table with the bottom of a tankard (the correct way) in a rural public, as a signal to the cellar you might call for Bass in vain.

When the agricultural labourer drops in on his way home from his work of a winter evening—heralding his approach by casting down a couple of logs or bundle of wood which he has been carrying with a thud outside the door—he does not demand liquor of that character. When in harvest time, after sundown, when the shadows forbid further cutting with the fagging hook at the tall wheat—he sits on the form without, under the elm tree, and feels a whole pocketful of silver, flush of money like a gold digger at a fortunate rush, he does not indulge in Allsopp or Guinness. He hoarsely orders a "pot" of some local brewer's manufacture—a man who knows exactly what he likes, and arranges to meet the hardy digestion of the mower and the reaper. He prefers a rather dark beer with a certain twang faintly suggestive of liquorice and tobacco, with a sense of "body," a thickness in it, and which is no sooner swallowed than a clammy palate demands a second gulp to wash away the relics of the first. Ugh! The second requires a third swig, and still a fourth, and appetite increasing with that it feeds on, the stream rushes down the brazen throat that burns for more.

Like the Northern demi-god who drank unwittingly at the ocean from a horn and could not empty it, but nevertheless caused the ebb of the sea, so our toper, if he cannot contain the cask, will bring it down to the third hoop if time and credit will but serve. It would require a gauger's staff to measure his capacity—in fact, the limit of the labourer's liquor-power, especially in summer, has never yet been reached. A man will lie on his back in the harvest field, under a hedge sweet with the June roses that smile upon the hay, and never move or take his lips away till a gallon has entered into his being, for it can hardly be said to be swallowed. Two gallons a day is not an uncommon consumption with men who swing the scythe or reaping-hook.

This of course is small beer; but the stuff called for at the low public in the village, or by the road just outside, though indescribably nauseous to a non-vitiated palate, is not "small." It is a heady liquid, which if any one drinks, not being accustomed to it, will leave its effects upon him for hours afterwards. But this is what the labourer likes. He prefers something that he can feel; something that, if sufficiently indulged in, will make even his thick head spin and his temples ache next morning. Then he has had the value of his money. So that really good ale would require a very large bush indeed before it attracted his custom.

It is a marked feature of labouring life that the respectable inn of the village at which the travelling farmer, or even persons higher in rank, occasionally call, which has a decent stable, and whose liquors are of a genuine character, is almost deserted by the men who seek the reeking tap of the ill-favoured public which forms the clubhouse of all the vice of the village. While the farmer or passing stranger, calling at the decent house really for refreshment, drinks but a glass or two and departs, the frequenters of the low place never quit their seats till the law compels them, so that for sixpence spent in the one by men with cheque-books in their pockets, five shillings are spent in the other by men who have not got a loaf of bread at home for their half-starving children and pinched wife. To an unprincipled landlord clearly this sort of custom is decidedly preferable, and thus it is that these places are a real hardship to the licensed victualler whose effort it is to keep an orderly house.

The influence of the low public upon the agricultural labourer's life is incalculable—it is his club, almost his home. There he becomes brutalised; there he spends his all; and if he awakes to the wretched state of his own family at last, instead of remembering that it is his own act, he turns round, accuses the farmer of starvation wages, shouts for what is really Communism, and perhaps even in his sullen rage descends to crime. Let us go with him into such a rural den.

Beware that you do not knock your head against the smoke-blackened beams of the low ceiling, and do not put your elbow carelessly on the deal table, stained with spilled ale, left uncleaned from last night, together with little heaps of ashes, tapped out from pipes, and spots of grease from the tallow candles. The old-fashioned settles which gave so cosy an air in the olden time to the inn room, and which still linger in some of the houses, are not here—merely forms and cheap chairs. A great pot hangs over the fire, for the family cooking is done in the public apartment; but do not ask to join in the meal, for though the food may be more savoury than is dreamed of in your philosophy, the two-grained forks have not been cleaned these many a day. Neither is the butcher's wooden skewer, just extracted from the meat, an elegant toothpick if you are fastidious.

But these things are trifles when the dish is a plump pheasant, jugged hare, brown partridges, or trout—perhaps not exactly in season—as the chance may be; or a couple of boiled fowls, or a turkey, or some similar toothsome morsel. Perhaps it is the gamey taste thus induced that enables them to enjoy joints from the butcher which are downright tainted, for it is characteristic of the place and people on the one hand to dine on the very best, as above, and yet to higgle over a halfpenny a pound at the shop. Nowhere else in all the parish, from the polished mahogany at the squire's mansion to the ancient solid oaken table at the substantial old-fashioned farmer's, can there be found such a constant supply of food usually considered as almost the privilege of the rich. Bacon, it is true, they eat of the coarsest kind; but with it eggs new laid and delicious. In brief, it is the strangest hodgepodge of pheasant and bread and cheese, asparagus and cabbage. But somehow, whatever is good, whatever is held in estimation, makes its appearance in that grimy little back room on that ragged, dirty table-cloth.

Who pays for these things? Are they paid for at all? There is no licensed dealer in game in the village nor within many miles, and it seems passing strange. But there are other things almost as curious. The wood pile in the back yard is ever high and bulky; let the fire burn never so clear in the frosty days there is always a regular supply of firewood. It is the same with coal. Yet there is no copse attached to the place, nor is the landlord ever seen chopping for himself, nor are the farmers in the habit of receiving large orders for logs and faggots. By the power of some magic spell all things drift hitherward. A magnet which will draw logs of timber and faggots half across the parish, which will pull pheasants off their perch, extract trout from the deep, and stay the swift hare in midst of her career, is a power indeed to be envied. Had any enchanter of mediæval days so potent a charm?

Perhaps it is the engaging and attractive character of the landlord himself. He is a tall, lanky man, usually seen in slippers, and trousers too short for his limbs; he "sloppets" about in his waistcoat and shirt-sleeves, hands in pockets, and shoulders forward almost in a hump. He hangs about the place, now bringing in a log, now carrying a bucket, now spinning a mop, now slouching down the garden to feed the numerous fowls that scratch around the stumps of cabbages. Anything, in short, but work. Sometimes, however, he takes the trap and horse, and is supposed to be gone on a dealing expedition. Sometimes it is only to carry a jar of beer up to the men in the field, and to mouch a good armful of fresh-cut clover for provender from the swathe. He sips gin the livelong day—weak gin always—every hour from morn till a cruel Legislature compels the closing of the shutters. He is never intoxicated—it is simply a habit, a sort of fuel to feed the low cunning in which his soul delights. So far from intoxication is he, that there is a fable of some hard knocks and ill usage, and even of a thick head being beaten against the harder stones of the courtyard behind, when the said thick head was helpless from much ale. Such matters are hushed up in the dark places of the earth. So far from intoxication is he, that he has the keenest eye to business.

There is a lone rick-yard up in the fields yonder to which the carters come from the farm far away to fetch hay, and straw, and so forth. They halt at the public, and are noticed to enjoy good living there, nor are they asked for their score. A few trusses of hay, or bundles of straw, a bushel of corn, or some such trifle is left behind merely out of good fellowship. Waggons come up laden with tons of coal for the farms miles above, far from a railway station; three or four teams, perhaps, one after the other. Just a knob or two can scarcely be missed, and a little of the small in a sack-bag. The bundles of wood thrown down at the door by the labourers as they enter are rarely picked up again; they disappear, and the hearth at home is cold. The foxes are blamed for the geese and the chickens, and the hunt execrated for not killing enough cubs, but Reynard is not always guilty. Eggs and poultry vanish. The shepherds have ample opportunities for disposing of a few spare lambs to a general dealer whose trap is handy. Certainly, continuous gin does not chill the faculties.

If a can of ale is left in the outhouse at the back and happens to be found by a few choice spirits at the hour when the vicar is just commencing his sermon in church on Sunday, it is by the purest accident. The turnip and swede greens left at the door, picked wholesale from the farmers' fields; the potatoes produced from coat pockets by fingers which have been sorting heaps at the farmstead; the apples which would have been crushed under foot if the labourers had not considerately picked them up—all these and scores of other matters scarce worth naming find their way over that threshold. Perhaps the man is genial, his manners enticing, his stories amusing, his jokes witty. Not at all. He is a silent fellow, scarce opening his mouth except to curse the poor scrub of a maid servant, or to abuse a man who has not paid his score. He slinks in and lights his pipe, smokes it silently, and slinks out again. He is the octopus of the hamlet, fastening on the cottage homes and sucking the life-blood from them. He misses nothing, and nothing comes amiss to him.

His wife, perhaps, then, may be the centre of attraction? She is a short, stout woman, whose cheeks as she walks wobble with fat, whose face is ever dirty, and dress (at home) slatternly. But mayhap her heart is in the right place, and when Hodge is missed from his accustomed seat by the fire of an evening, when it is bruited abroad that he is down with illness, hurriedly slips on her bonnet, and says nothing, carries a basket of good things to cheer the inner man? Or, when his wife is confined, perhaps she brings some little delicacies, a breast of pheasant, a bottle of port wine, and strengthens her with motherly counsel in the hour of her travail. Is this so? Hodge's wife could tell you that the cottage door hàs never been darkened by her presence: that she indeed would not acknowledge her if passed by chance on the road. For the landlady sails forth to the adjacent town in all the glory of those fine feathers that proverbially make the fine bird.

It is a goodly spectacle to see her in rustling ample silk, in costly sealskin, in a bonnet "loud" but rich, shading a countenance that glows ruddy red as a furnace. A gold chain encircles her portly neck, with a gold watch thereto attached; gold rings upon her fingers, in one of which sparkles a brilliant diamond; gold earrings, gold brooch, kid gloves bursting from the fatness of the fingers they encase. The dingy trap and limping rawboned hack which carry her to the outskirts of the town scarcely harmonise with so much glory. But at the outskirts she alights, and enters the street in full dignity. By some potent alchemy the sweat of Hodge's brow has become condensed into that sparkling diamond, which is disclosed when the glove is drawn off in the shops, to the admiration of all beholders.

Or, if not the wife, perhaps it may be the daughter who is the magnet that draws the very timber across the parish? She is not ill-looking, and might pass muster in her best dress were it not for a squareness of build, like the set of a man rather than the full curves associated with woman. She is rarely seen in the house at all, and neither talks to the men nor the women who enter. She sallies forth at night, and her friends are the scampish among the sons of the lower class of tenant-farmers.

This is the family. How strange and yet how undeniable is it that such a house should attract the men whose self-interest, one would imagine, would lead them to shun it, and if they must spend their hard-won earnings, at least to get a good article for their money! It proves that an appeal to reason is not always the way to manage the working man. Such a low house is always a nest of agitation: there the idle, drunken, and ill-conditioned have their rendezvous, there evil is hatched, and from there men take their first step on the road that leads to the gaol. The place is often crowded at night—there is scarcely room to sit or stand, the atmosphere is thick with smoke, and a hoarse roar of jarring voices fills it, above which rises the stave of a song shouted in one unvarying key from some corner. Money pours in apace—the draughts are deep, and long, and frequent, the mugs are large, the thirst insatiate. The takings, compared with the size and situation of the house, must be high, and yet, with all this custom and profit, the landlord and his family still grovel. And grovel they will in dirt, vice, low cunning, and iniquity —as the serpent went on his belly in the dust—to the end of their days.

Why do these places exist? Because in England justice is ever tempered with mercy; sometimes with too much mercy. The resident squire and magistrate knows the extent of the evil only too well. He sees it with his own eyes in the village; he sees it brought before him on the bench; the clergyman tells him of it, so do the gamekeeper and the policeman. His tenants complain of it. He is perpetually reminded of it, and of what it may ultimately mean as these places become the centres of communistic propagandas. But though perfectly aware of the evil, to suppress it is quite another matter.

First, you must find the power, and then, having the power, the question arises, is it wise to exercise it? Though the men who frequent such dens are often of the lowest type, or on their way to that condition, they are not all of that character. Men of a hard-working and honest stamp go there as well. All have their rights alike—rights and liberties which must be held sacred even at some disadvantage. In short, the reprobate nature of the place may be established, but while it is the chosen resort of the people, or of a section of them, unless some great and manifest harm arises it cannot be touched. The magistrate will willingly control it as far as lies in his province, but unless directly instructed by the Legislature he cannot go farther. The truth is, it lies with the labourer himself. He is not obliged to visit there. A respectable inn may be found in every village if he desires that wholesome conviviality which, when it does not overstep certain bounds, forms a bond between man and man. Were such low houses suddenly put down, what an outcry would be raised of favouritism, tyranny, and so on! When the labourer turns against them himself, he will speedily find powerful friends to assist in attaining the object.

If ever a man deserved a good glass of beer it is the agricultural labourer upon the conclusion of his day's work, exposed as he is to the wear and tear of the elements. After following the slow plough along the furrows through the mist; after tending the sheep on the hills where the rain beats with furious energy; after grubbing up the tough roots of trees, and splitting them with axe and wedge and mallet, a man may naturally ask for refreshment. And it is equally natural that he should desire to take it in the society of his fellows, with whom he can associate freely and speak his mind unchecked. The glass of ale would not hurt him; it is the insidious temptation proffered in certain quarters to do evil for an extra quart. Nothing forms so strong a temptation as the knowledge that a safe receiver is near at hand.

He must not be harshly judged because of the mere quantity he can take, for a quart of ale to him is really no more than a glass of wine to the "City" gentleman who lives delicately. He is to be pitied rather than condemned, and aided out of the blunder rather than chastised. Punishment, indeed, waits upon him only too doggedly, and overtakes him too quickly in the shape of sorrows and privations at home. The evil lies not in the ale, but in the character of the man that sold him the ale, and who is, at the same time, the worst enemy of the legitimately-trading innkeeper. No one, indeed, has better cause than the labourer to exclaim, "Save me from my friends!" To do the bulk of the labourers bare justice it must be stated that there is a certain bluff honesty and frankness among them, a rude candour, which entitles them to considerable respect as a body. There are also men here and there whose strength of character would certainly have obtained favourable acknowledgment had their lot been cast in a higher rank of life. But, at the same time, the labourer is not always so innocent and free from guile—so lamblike as it suits the purpose of some to proclaim, in order that his rural simplicity may secure sympathy. There are very queer black sheep in the flock, and it rather unfortunately happens that these, in more ways than one, force themselves, sometimes most unpleasantly, upon the notice of the tenant-farmer and the landlord.

A specimen or two may easily be selected from that circle of choice manhood whose head-quarters are at the low "public." A tall, well-built man stands forward, and at the first glance a stranger might take him for a favourable example. He holds himself more upright than most of his class, he is not ill-looking, and a marked air of deference towards those who address him conveys rather a pleasing impression. He can read fairly well and sign his name. This man, who is still young, began life as carter's lad, in which occupation he had not been long engaged before the horse-hair carefully accumulated as a perquisite disappeared. Whipcord and similar small articles next vanished, and finally a handsome new whip. This last, not being so easily disposed of, was traced to his possession and procured him a sound thrashing. Some short time afterwards a carthorse was found in the fields stabbed in several places, though, fortunately, not severely. Having already the bad name that hangs the dog, he was strongly suspected of this dastardly act in revenge for the thrashing from the carter, and threat of dismissal from the employer. No evidence, however, could be procured, and though he was sent about his business he escaped punishment. As he grew older he fell in with a tribe of semi-gipsies, and wandered in their company for a year or two, learning their petty pilfering tricks. He then returned to agricultural labour, and, notwithstanding the ill-flavour that clung about his doings, found no difficulty in obtaining employment.

It is rare in agriculture for a man to be asked much about his character, unless he is to be put into a position of some trust. In trades and factories—on railways, too—an applicant for employment is not only questioned, but has to produce evidence as to his immediate antecedents at least. But the custom in farming prescribes no such checks; if the farmer requires a man, the applicant is put on to work at once, if he looks at all likely. This is especially the case in times of pressure, as when there is a great deal of hoeing to be done, in harvest, and when extra hands are wanted to assist in feeding the threshing machine. Then the first that comes along the road is received, and scarcely a question asked. The custom operates well enough in one way, since a man is nearly sure of procuring employment, and encounters no obstacles; on the other hand, there is less encouragement to preserve a good character. So the fellow mentioned quickly got work when he applied for it, and went on pretty steadily for a period. He then married, and speedily discovered the true use of women—*i.e.*, to work for idle men. The moment he learnt that he could subsist upon her labour he ceased to make any effort, and passed his time lounging about.

The wife, though neither handsome nor clever, was a hard-working person, and supported herself and idle husband by taking in washing. Indignation has often been expressed at the moral code of savages, which permits the man to lie in his hammock while the woman cultivates the maize; but, excepting the difference in the colour of the skin, the substitution of dirty white for coppery redness, there is really no distinction. Probably washing is of the two harder work than hoeing maize. The fellow "hung about," and doubtless occasionally put in practice the tricks he had acquired from his nomad friends.

The only time he worked was in the height of the harvest, when high wages are paid. But then his money went in drink, and drink often caused him to neglect the labour he had undertaken, at an important juncture when time was of consequence. On one such occasion the employer lost his temper and gave him a piece of his mind, ending by a threat of proceedings for breach of contract. A night or two afterwards the farmer's rickyard was ablaze, and a few months later the incendiary found himself commencing a term of penal servitude. There he was obliged to work, began to walk upright, and acquired that peculiarly marked air of deference which at first contrasts rather pleasantly with the somewhat gruff address of most labourers. During his absence the wife almost prospered, having plenty of employment and many kind friends. He signalised his return by administering a thrashing —just to re-assert his authority—which, however, the poor woman received with equanimity, remarking that it was only his way. He recommenced his lounging life, working occasionally when money was to be easily earned—for the convict stain does not prevent a man getting agricultural employment —and spending the money in liquor. When tolerably sober he is, in a sense, harmless; if intoxicated, his companions give him the road to himself.

Now there is nothing exceptionally characteristic of the agricultural labourer in the career of such a man. Members of other classes of the working community are often sent to penal servitude, and sometimes men of education and social position. But it is characteristic of agricultural life that a man with the stigma of penal servitude can return and encounter no overpowering prejudice against him. There are work and wages for him if he likes to take them. No one throws his former guilt in his face. He may not be offered a place of confidence, nor be trusted with money, as the upper labourers—carters for instance—sometimes are. But the means of subsistence are open to him, and he will not be driven by the memory of one crime to commit another.

There is no school of crime in the country. Children are not brought up from the earliest age to beg and steal, to utter loquacious falsehood, or entrap the benevolent with sham suffering. Hoary thieves do not keep academies for the instruction of little fingers in the art of theft. The science of burglary is unstudied. Though farmhouses are often situate in the most lonely places a case of burglary rarely occurs, and if it does, is still more rarely traced to a local resident. In such houses there is sometimes a good deal of old silver plate, accumulated in the course of generations—a fact that must be perfectly well known to the labouring class, through the women indoor-servants. Yet such attempts are quite exceptional. So, too, are robberies from the person with violence. Serious crime is, indeed, comparatively scarce. The cases that come before the Petty Sessions are, for the most part, drunkenness, quarrelling, neglect or absenteeism from work, affiliation, petty theft, and so on.

The fact speaks well for the rural population; it speaks very badly for such characters as the one that has been described. If he will not turn into the path of honest labour, that is his own fault. The injury he does is this, that he encourages others to be idle. Labouring men quit the field under the influence of temporary thirst, or that desire for a few minutes' change which is not in itself blameworthy. They enter the low "public," call for their quart, and intend to leave again immediately. But the lazy fellow in the corner opens conversation, is asked to drink, more is called for, there is a toss-up to decide who shall pay, in which the idle adept, of course, escapes, and so the thing goes on. Such a man becomes a cause of idleness, and a nuisance to the farmers.

Another individual is a huge, raw-boned, double-jointed giant of a man, whose muscular strength must be enormous, but whose weakness is beer. He is a good workman, and of a civil, obligin; disposition. He will commence, for instance, making drains for a farmer with the greatest energy, and in the best of tempers. A drain requires some little skill. The farmer visits the work day by day, and notes with approval that it is being done well. But about the third or fourth day the clever workman, whose immense strength makes the employment mere child's play to him, civilly asks for a small advance of money. Now the farmer has no objection to that, but hands it to him with some misgiving. Next morning no labourer is to be seen. The day passes, and the next. Then a lad brings the intelligence that his parent is just recovering from a heavy drinking bout and will be back soon. There is the history of forty years!

The same incident is repeated once or twice a month all the year round. Now it is a drain, now hedge-cutting, now hoeing, now haymaking, and now reaping. Three or four days' work excellently performed; then a bed in a ditch and empty pockets. The man's really vast strength carries him through the prostration, and the knocks and bangs and tumbles received in a helpless state. But what a life! The worst of it is the man is not a reprobate—not a hang-dog, lounging rascal, but perfectly honest, willing to oblige, harmless and inoffensive even when intoxicated, and skilful at his labour. What is to be done with him? What is the farmer to do who has only such men to rely on—perhaps in many cases without this fellow's honesty and good temper—qualities which constantly give him a lift? It is simply an epitome of the difficulties too commonly met with in the field—bright sunshine, good weather, ripe crops, and men half unconscious, or quite, snoring under a hedge! There is no encouragement to the tenant to pay high wages in experiences like this.

A third example is a rakish-looking lad just rising into manhood. Such young men are very much in demand, and he would not have the slightest difficulty in obtaining employment yet he is constantly out of work. When a boy he began by summoning the carter where he was engaged for cuffing him, charging the man with an assault. It turned out to be a trumpery case, and the Bench advised his parents to make him return and fulfil his contract. His parents thought differently of it. They had become imbued with an inordinate sense of their own importance. They had a high idea of the rights of labour; Jack, in short, was a good deal better than his master, and must be treated with distinguished respect. The doctrines of the Union countenanced the deduction; so the boy did not return. Another place was found for him.

In the course of a few months he came again before the Bench. The complaint was now one of wrongful dismissal, and a claim for a one pound bonus, which by the agreement was to have been paid at the end of the year if his conduct proved satisfactory. It was shown that his conduct had been the reverse of satisfactory; that he refused to obey orders, that he "cheeked" the carters, that he ran away home for a day or two, and was encouraged in these goings on by the father. The magistrates, always on the side of peace, endeavoured to procure a reconciliation, the farmer even paid down the bonus, but it was of no use. The lad did not return.

With little variations the same game has continued ever since. Now it is he that complains, now it is his new master; but any way there is always a summons, and his face is as familiar in the court as that of the chairman. His case is typical. What is a farmer to do who has to deal with a rising generation full of this spirit?

Then there are the regular workhouse families, who are perpetually applying for parochial relief. From the eldest down to the youngest member they seem to have no stamina; they fall ill when all others are well, as if afflicted with a species of paralysis that affects body, mind, and moral sense at once. If the phrase may be used without irreverence, there is no health in them. The slightest difficulty is sufficient to send an apparently strong, hale man whining to the workhouse. He localises his complaint in his foot, or his arm, or his shoulder; but, in truth, he does not know himself what is the matter with him. The real illness is weakness of calibre—a looseness of fibre. Many a labourer has an aching limb from rheumatism, and goes to plough all the same; many a poor cottage woman suffers from that prevalent agony, and bravely gets through her task, and keeps her cottage tidy. But these people cannot do it—they positively cannot. The summer brings them pain, the winter brings pain, their whole life is one long appeal *ad misericordiam*.

The disease seems to spread with the multiplication of the family: the sons have it, and the sons' sons after them, so much so that even to bear the name is sufficient to stamp the owner as a miserable helpless being. All human wretchedness is, of course, to be deeply commiserated, and yet it is exasperating to see one man still doing his best under real trouble, and another eating contentedly the bread of idleness when there seems nothing wrong except a total lack of energy. The old men go to the workhouse, the young men go, the women and the children; if they are out one month the next sees their return. These again are but broken reeds to rely upon. The golden harvest might rot upon the ground for all their gathering, the grass wither and die as it stands, without the touch of the scythe, the very waggons and carts fall to pieces in the sheds. There is no work to be got out of them.

The village, too, has its rookery, though not quite in the same sense as the city. Traced to its beginning, it is generally found to have originated upon a waste piece of ground, where some squatters settled and built their cabins. These, by the growth of better houses around, and the rise of property, have now become of some value, not so much for the materials as the site. To the original hovels additions have been made by degrees, and fresh huts squeezed in till every inch of space is as closely occupied as in a back court of the metropolis. Within the cottages are low pitched, dirty, narrow, and contracted, without proper conveniences, or even a yard or court.

The social condition of the inhabitants is unpleasant to contemplate. The young men, as they grow up, arrive at an exaggerated idea of the value of their parents' property—the cottage of three rooms—and bitter animosities arise between them. One is accused of having had his share out in money, another has got into trouble and had his fine paid for him; the eldest was probably born before wedlock; so there are plenty of materials for recrimination. Then one, or even two of them bring home a wife, or at least a woman, and three families live beneath a single roof—with results it is easy to imagine, both as regards bickering and immorality. They have no wish to quit the place and enter cottages with better accommodation: they might rent others of the farmers, but they prefer to be independent, and, besides, will not move lest they should lose their rights. Very likely a few lodgers are taken in to add to the confusion. As regularly as clockwork cross summonses are taken out before the Bench, and then the women on either side reveal an unequalled power of abuse and loquacity, leaving a decided impression that it is six to one and half-a-dozen to the other.

These rookeries do not furnish forth burglars and accomplished pickpockets, like those of cities, but they do send out a gang of lazy, scamping fellows and coarse women, who are almost useless. If their employer does not please them—if he points out that a waste of time has taken place, or that something has been neglected—off they go, for, having a hole to creep into, they do not care an atom whether they lose a job or not. The available hands, therefore, upon whom the farmers can count are always very much below the sum total of the able-bodied population. There must be deducted the idle men and women, the drunkards, the never satisfied, as the lad who sued every master; the workhouse families, the rookery families, and those who every harvest leave the place, and wander a great distance in search of exceptionally high wages. When all these are subtracted, the residue remaining is often insufficient to do the work of the farms in a proper manner. It is got through somehow by scratch-packs, so to say—men picked up from the roads, aged men who cannot do much, but whose energy puts the younger fellows to shame, lads paid far beyond the value of the work they actually accomplish.

Work done in this way is, of course, incomplete and unsatisfactory, and the fact supplies one of the reasons why farmers seem disinclined to pay high wages. It is not because they object to pay well for hard work, but because they cannot get the hard work. There is consequently a growing reliance upon floating labour—upon the men and women who tramp round every season—rather than on the resident population. Even in the absence of any outward agitation—of a strike or open movement in that direction—the farmer has considerable difficulties to contend with in procuring labour. He has still further difficulties in managing it when he has got it. Most labourers have their own peculiar way of finishing a job; and however much that style of doing it may run counter to the farmer's idea of the matter in hand, he has to let the man proceed after his own fashion. If he corrected, or showed the man what he wanted, he would run the risk of not getting it done at all. There is no one so thoroughly obstinate as an ignorant labourer full of his own consequence. Giving, then, full credit to those men whose honest endeavours to fulfil their duty have already been acknowledged, it is a complete delusion to suppose that all are equally manly.

CHAPTER XXIV

THE COTTAGE CHARTER—
FOUR-ACRE FARMERS

THE songs sung by the labourer at the alehouse or the harvest home are not of his own composing. The tunes whistled by the ploughboy as he goes down the road to his work in the dawn were not written for him. Green meads and rolling lands of wheat—true fields of the cloth of gold—have never yet inspired those who dwell upon them with songs uprising from the soil. The solitude of the hills over whose tops the summer sun seems to linger so long has not filled the shepherd's heart with a wistful yearning that must be expressed in verse or music. Neither he nor the ploughman in the vale have heard or seen aught that stirs them in Nature. The shepherd has never surprised an Immortal reclining on the thyme under the shade of a hawthorn bush at sunny noontide; nor has the ploughman seen the shadowy outline of a divine huntress through the mist that clings to the wood across the field.

These people have no myths; no heroes. They look back on no Heroic Age, no Achilles, no Agamemnon, and no Homer. The past is vacant. They have not even a "Wacht am Rhein" or "Marseillaise" to chaunt in chorus with quickened step and flashing eye. No; nor even a ballad of the hearth, handed down from father to son, to be sung at home festivals, as a treasured silver tankard is brought out to drink the health of an honoured guest. Ballads there are in old books—ballads of days when the yew bow was in every man's hands, and war and the chase gave life a colour; but they are dead. A cart comes slowly down the road, and the labourer with it sings as he jogs along; but. if you listen, it tells you nothing of wheat, or hay, or flocks and herds, nothing of the old gods and heroes. It is a street ditty such as you may hear the gutter arabs yelling in London, and coming from a music hall.

So, too, in material things—in the affairs of life, in politics, and social hopes—the labourer has no well-defined creed of race. He has no genuine programme of the future; that which is put forward in his name is not from him. Some years ago, talking with an aged labourer in a district where at that time no "agitation" had taken place, I endeavoured to get from him something like a definition of the wants of his class. He had lived many years, and worked all the while in the field; what was his experience of their secret wishes? what was the Cottage Charter? It took some time to get him to understand what was required; he had been ready enough previously to grumble about this or that detail, but when it came to principles he was vague. The grumbles, the complaints, and so forth, had never been codified. However, by degrees I got at it, and very simple it was:—Point 1, Better wages; (2) more cottages; (3) good-sized gardens; (4) "larning" for the children. That was the sum of the cottager's creed—his own genuine aspirations.

Since then every one of these points has been obtained, or substantial progress made towards it. Though wages are perhaps slightly lower or rather stationary at the present moment, yet they are much higher than used to be the case. At the same time vast importations of foreign food keep the necessaries of life at a lower figure. The number of cottages available has been greatly increased—hardly a landlord but could produce accounts of sums of money spent in this direction. To almost all of these large gardens are now attached. Learning for the children is provided by the schools erected in every single parish, for the most part by the exertions of the owners and occupiers of land.

Practically, therefore, the four points of the real Cottage Charter have been attained, or as nearly as is possible. Why, then, is it that dissatisfaction is still expressed? The reply is, because a new programme has been introduced to the labourer from without. It originated in no labourer's mind, it is not the outcome of a genuine feeling widespread among the masses, nor is it the heartbroken call for deliverance issuing from the lips of the poet-leader of a downtrodden people. It is totally foreign to the cottage proper—something new, strange, and as yet scarcely understood in its full meaning by those who nominally support it.

The points of the new Cottage Charter are—(1) The confiscation of large estates; (2) the subdivision of land; (3) the abolition of the laws of settlement of land; (4) the administration of the land by the authorities of State; (5) the confiscation of glebe lands for division and distribution; (6) the abolition of Church tithes; (7) extension of the county franchise; (8) education gratis, free of fees, or payment of any kind;

(9) high wages, winter and summer alike, irrespective of season, prosperity, or adversity. No. 6 is thrown in chiefly for the purpose of an appearance of identity of interest between the labourer and the tenant against the Church. Of late it has rather been the cue of the leaders of the agitation to promote, or seem to promote, a coalition between the labourer and the dissatisfied tenant, thereby giving the movement a more colourable pretence in the eyes of the public. Few tenants, however dissatisfied, have been deceived by the shallow device.

This programme emanated from no carter or shepherd, ploughman or fogger. It was not thought out under the hedge when the June roses decked the bushes; nor painfully written down on the deal table in the cottage while the winter rain pattered against the window, and, coming down the wide chimney, hissed upon the embers. It was brought to the cottage door from a distance; it has been iterated and reiterated till at last some begin to think they really do want all these things. But with the majority even now the propaganda falls flat. They do not enter into the spirit of it. No. 9 they do understand; that appeals direct, and men may be excused if, with a view which as yet extends so short a space around, they have not grasped the fact that wages cannot by any artificial combination whatever be kept at a high level. The idea of high wages brings a mass of labourers together; they vote for what they are instructed to vote, and are thus nominally pledged to the other eight points of the new charter. Such a conception as the confiscation and subdivision of estates never occurred to the genuine labourers.

An aged man was listening to a graphic account of what the new state of things would be like. There would be no squire, no parson, no woods or preserves—all grubbed for cabbage gardens—no parks, no farmers. "No farmers," said the old fellow, "then who's to pay I my wages?" There he hit the blot, no doubt. If the first four points of the new charter were carried into effect, agricultural wages would no longer exist. But if such a consummation depends upon the action of the cottager it will be a long time coming. The idea did not originate with him—he cares nothing for it—and can only be got to support it under the guise of an agitation for wages. Except by persistent stirring from without he cannot be got to move even then. The labourer, in fact, is not by any means such a fool as his own leaders endeavour to make him out. He is perfectly well aware that the farmer, or any person who stands in the position of the farmer, cannot pay the same money in winter as in summer.

Two new cottages of a very superior character were erected in the corner of an arable field, abutting on the highway. As left by the builders a more uninviting spot could scarcely be imagined. The cottages themselves were well designed and well built, but the surroundings were like a wilderness. Heaps of rubbish here, broken bricks there, the ground trampled hard as the road itself. No partition from the ploughed field behind beyond a mere shallow trench enclosing what was supposed to be the garden. Everything bleak, unpromising, cold, and unpleasant. Two families went into these cottages, the men working on the adjoining farm. The aspect of the place immediately began to change. The rubbish was removed, the best of it going to improve the paths and approaches; a quickset hedge was planted round the enclosure. Evening after evening, be the weather what it might, these two men were in that garden at work—after a long day in the fields. In the dinner hour even they sometimes snatched a few minutes to trim something. Their spades turned over the whole of the soil, and planting commenced. Plots were laid out for cabbage, plots for potatoes, onions, parsnips.

Then having provided necessaries for the immediate future they set about preparing for extras. Fruit trees—apple, plum, and damson—were planted; also some roses. Next beehives appeared and were elevated on stands and duly protected from the rain. The last work was the building of pigsties—rude indeed and made of a few slabs—but sufficient to answer the purpose. Flowers in pots appeared in the windows, flowers appeared beside the garden paths. The change was so complete and so quickly effected I could hardly realise that so short a time since there had been nothing there but a blank open space. Persons travelling along the road could not choose but look on and admire the transformation.

I had often been struck with the flourishing appearance of cottage gardens, but then those gardens were of old date and had reached that perfection in course of years. But here the thing seemed to grow up under one's eyes. All was effected by sheer energy. Instead of spending their evenings wastefully at "public," these men went out into their gardens and made what was a desert literally bloom. Nor did they seem conscious of doing anything extraordinary, but worked away in the most matter-of-fact manner, calling no one's attention to their progress. It would be hard to say which garden of the two showed the better result. Their wives are tidy, their children clean, their cottages grow more cosy and homelike day by day; yet they work in the fields that come up to their very doors, and receive nothing but the ordinary agricultural wages of the district.

This proves what can be done when the agricultural labourer really wants to do it. And in a very large number of cases it must further be admitted that he does want to do it, and succeeds. If any one when passing through a rural district will look closely at the cottages and gardens he will frequently find evidence of similar energy, and not unfrequently of something approaching very nearly to taste. For why does the labourer train honeysuckle up his porch, and the out-of-door grape up the southern end of his house? Why does he let the houseleek remain on the roof; why trim and encourage the thick growth of ivy that clothes the chimney? Certainly not for utility, nor pecuniary profit. It is because he has some amount of appreciation of the beauty of flowers, of vine leaf, and green ivy. Men like these are the real backbone of our peasantry. They are not the agitators; it is the idle hangdogs who form the disturbing element in the village.

The settled agricultural labourer, of all others, has the least inducement to strike or leave his work. The longer he can stay in one place the better for him in many ways. His fruit-trees, which he planted years ago, are coming to perfection, and bear sufficient fruit in favourable years not only to give him some variety of diet, but to bring in a sum in hard cash with which to purchase extras. The soil of the garden, long manured and dug, is twice as fertile as when he first disturbed the earth. The hedges have grown high, and keep off the bitter winds. In short, the place is home, and he sits under his own vine and fig-tree. It is not to his advantage to leave this and go miles away. It is different with the mechanic who lives in a back court devoid of sunshine, hardly visited by the fresh breeze, without a tree, without a yard of earth to which to become attached. The factory closes, the bell is silent, the hands are discharged; provided he can get fresh employment it matters little. He leaves the back court without regret, and enters another in a distant town. But an agricultural labourer who has planted his own place feels an affection for it. The young men wander and are restless; the middle-aged men who

266

have once anchored do not like to quit. They have got the four points of their own genuine charter; those who would infuse further vague hopes are not doing them any other service than to divert them from the substance to the shadow.

Past those two new cottages which have been mentioned there runs a road which is a main thoroughfare. Along this road during the year this change was worked there walked a mournful procession—men and women on tramp. Some of these were doubtless rogues and vagabonds by nature and choice; but many, very many, were poor fellows who had really lost employment, and were gradually becoming degraded to the company of the professional beggar. The closing of collieries, mines, workshops, iron furnaces, etc., had thrown hundreds on the mercy of chance charity, and compelled them to wander to and fro. How men like these on tramp must have envied the comfortable cottages, the well-stocked gardens, the pigsties, the beehives, and the roses of the labourers!

If the labourer has never gone up on the floodtide of prosperity to the champagne wages of the miner, neither has he descended to the woe which fell on South Wales when children searched the dust-heaps for food, nor to that suffering which forces those whose instinct is independence to the soup-kitchen. He has had, and still has, steady employment at a rate of wages sufficient, as is shown by the appearance of his cottage itself, to maintain him in comparative comfort. The furnace may be blown out, and strong men may ask themselves, What shall we do next? But still the plough turns up the earth morning after morning. The colliery may close, but still the corn ripens, and extra wages are paid to the harvest men.

This continuous employment without even a fear of cessation is an advantage, the value of which it is difficult to estimate. His wages are not only sufficient to maintain him, he can even save a little. The benefit clubs in so many villages are a proof of it—each member subscribes so much. Whether conducted on a "sound financial basis" or not, the fact of the subscriptions cannot be denied, nor that assistance is derived from them. The Union itself is supported in the same way; proving that the wages, however complained of, are sufficient, at any rate, to permit of subscriptions.

It is held out to the labourer, as an inducement to agitate briskly, that, in time, a state of things will be brought about when every man will have a small farm of four or five acres

267

upon which to live comfortably, independent of a master. Occasional instances, however, of labourers endeavouring to exist upon a few acres have already been observed, and illustrate the practical working of the scheme. In one case a labourer occupied a piece of ground, about three acres in extent, at a low rental paid to the lord of the manor, the spot having originally been waste, though the soil was fairly good. He started under favourable conditions, because he possessed a cottage and garden and a pair of horses with which he did a considerable amount of hauling.

He now set up as a farmer, ploughed and sowed, dug and weeded, kept his own hours, and went into the market and walked about as independent as any one. After a while the three acres began to absorb nearly all his time, so that the hauling, which was the really profitable part of the business, had to be neglected. Then, the ready money not coming in so fast, the horses had to go without corn, and pick up what they could along the roadside, on the sward, and out of the hedges. They had, of course, to be looked after while thus feeding, which occupied two of the children, so that these could neither go to school nor earn anything by working on the adjacent farms. The horses meantime grew poor in condition; the winter tried them greatly from want of proper fodder; and when called upon to do hauling they were not equal to the task. In the country, at a distance from towns, there is not always a good market for vegetables, even when grown. The residents mostly supply themselves, and what is raised for export has to be sold at wholesale prices.

The produce of the three acres consequently did not come up to the tenant's expectation, particularly as potatoes, on account of the disease, could not be relied on. Meantime he had no weekly money coming in regularly, and his wife and family had often to assist him, diminishing their own earnings at the same time; while he was in the dilemma that if he did hauling he must employ and pay a man to work on the "farm," and if he worked himself he could not go out with his team. In harvest time, when the smaller farmers would have hired his horses, waggon, and himself and family to assist them, he had to get in his own harvest, and so lost the hard cash.

He now discovered that there was one thing he had omitted, and which was doubtless the cause why he did not flourish as he should have done according to his calculations. All the agriculturists around kept live stock—he had none. Here was the grand secret—it was stock that paid: he must have a cow. So he set to work industriously enough, and put up a shed. Then, partly by his own small savings, partly by the assistance of the members of the sect to which he belonged, he purchased the desired animal and sold her milk. In summer this really answered fairly well while there was green food for nothing in plenty by the side of little-frequented roads, whither the cow was daily led. But so soon as the winter approached the same difficulty as with the horses arose—*i.e.*, scarcity of fodder. The cow soon got miserably poor, while the horses fell off yet further, if that were possible. The calf that arrived died; next, one of the horses. The "hat" was sent round again, and a fresh horse bought; the spring came on, and there seemed another chance. What with milking and attending to the cow, and working on the "farm," scarcely an hour remained in which to earn money with the horses. No provision could be laid by for the winter. The live stock—the cow and horses—devoured part of the produce of the three acres, so that there was less to sell.

Another winter finished it. The cow had to be sold, but a third time the "hat" was sent round and saved the horses. Grown wiser now, the "farmer" stuck to his hauling, and only worked his plot at odd times. In this way, by hauling and letting out his team in harvest, and working himself and family at the same time for wages, he earned a good deal of money, and kept afloat very comfortably. He made no further attempt to live out of the "farm," which was now sown with one or two crops only in the same rotation as a field, and no longer cultivated on the garden system. Had it not been for the subscriptions he must have given it up entirely long before. Bitter experience demonstrated how false the calculations had been which seemed to show—on the basis of the produce of a small allotment—that a man might live on three or four acres.

He is not the only example of an extravagant estimate being put upon the possible product of land: it is a fallacy that has been fondly believed in by more logical minds than the poor cottager. That more may be got out of the soil than is the case at present is perfectly true; the mistake lies in the proposed method of doing it.

There was a piece of land between thirty and forty acres in extent, chiefly arable, which chanced to come into the possession of a gentleman, who made no pretence to a knowledge of agriculture, but was naturally desirous of receiving the highest rental. Up to that time it had been occupied by a farmer at thirty shillings per acre, which was thought the full value. He did not particularly want it, as it lay separated from the farm proper, and gave it up with the greatest alacrity when asked to do so in favour of a new tenant. This man turned out to be a villager—a blustering, ignorant fellow—who had, however, saved a small sum by hauling, which had been increased by the receipt of a little legacy. He was confident that he could show the farmers how to do it—he had worked at plough, had reaped, and tended cattle, and had horses of his own, and was quite sure that farming was a profitable business, and that the tenants had their land dirt cheap. He "knowed" all about it.

He offered three pounds an acre for the piece at once, which was accepted, notwithstanding a warning conveyed to the owner that his new tenant had scarcely sufficient money to pay a year's rent at that rate. But so rapid a rise in the value of his land quite dazzled the proprietor, and the labourer—for he was really nothing better, though fortunate enough to have a little money—entered on his farm. When this was known, it was triumphantly remarked that if a man could actually pay double the former rent, what an enormous profit the tenant-farmers must have been making! Yet they wanted to reduce the poor man's wages. On the other hand, there were not wanting hints that the man's secret idea was to exhaust the land and then leave it. But this was not the case—he was honestly in earnest, only he had got an exaggerated notion of the profits of farming. It is scarcely necessary to say that the rent for the third half year was not forthcoming, and the poor fellow lost his all. The land then went begging at the old price, for it had become so dirty—full of weeds from want of proper cleaning—that it was some time before any one would take it.

In a third case the attempt of a labouring man to live upon a small plot of land was successful—at least for some time. But it happened in this way. The land he occupied, about six acres, was situated on the outskirts of a populous town. It was moderately rented and of fairly good quality. His method of procedure was to cultivate a small portion—as much as he could conveniently manage without having to pay too much for assistance—as a market garden. Being close to his

customers, and with a steady demand at good prices all the
season, this paid very well indeed. The remainder was
ploughed and cropped precisely the same as the fields of
larger farms. For these crops he could always get a decent
price. The wealthy owners of the villas scattered about, some
keeping as many horses as a gentleman with a country seat,
were glad to obtain fresh fodder for their stables, and often
bought the crops standing, which to him was especially
profitable, because he could not well afford the cost of the
labour he must employ to harvest them.

In addition, he kept several pigs, which were also profitable,
because the larger part of their food cost him nothing but
the trouble of fetching it. The occupants of the houses in the
town were glad to get rid of the refuse vegetables, etc.; of
these he had a constant supply. The pigs, too, helped him
with manure. Next he emptied ash-pits in the town, and
sifted the cinders; the better part went on his own fire, the
other on his land. As he understood gardening, he undertook
the care of several small gardens, which brought in a little
money. All the rubbish, leaves, trimmings, etc., which he
swept from the gardens he burnt, and spread the ashes
abroad to fertilise his miniature farm.

In spring he beat carpets, and so made more shillings; he
had also a small shed, or workshop, and did rough carpentering. His horse did his own work, and occasionally that of
others; so that in half-a-dozen different ways he made money
independent of the produce of his land. That produce, too,
paid well, because of the adjacent town, and he was able to
engage assistance now and then. Yet, even with all these
things, it was hard work, and required economical management to eke it out. Still it was done, and under the same
conditions doubtless might be done by others. But then everything lies in those conditions. The town at hand, the knowledge of gardening, carpentering, and so on, made just all
the difference.

If the land were subdivided in the manner the labourer is
instructed would be so advantageous, comparatively few of
the plots would be near towns. Some of the new "farmers"
would find themselves in the centre of Salisbury Plain, with
the stern trilithons of Stonehenge looking down upon their
efforts. The occupier of a plot of four acres in such a position
—many miles from the nearest town—would experience a
hard lot indeed if he attempted to live by it. If he grew vege-

tables for sale, the cost of carriage would diminish their value; if for food, he could scarcely subsist upon cabbage and onions all the year round. To thoroughly work four acres would occupy his whole time, nor would the farmers care for the assistance of a man who could only come now and then in an irregular manner. There would be no villa gardens to attend to, no ash-pits to empty, no tubs of refuse for the pig, no carpets to beat, no one who wanted rough carpentering done. He could not pay any one to assist him in the cultivation of the plot.

And then, how about his clothes, boots and shoes, and so forth? Suppose him with a family, where would their boots and shoes come from? Without any wages—that is, hard cash received weekly—it would be next to impossible to purchase these things. A man could hardly be condemned to a more miserable existence. In the case of the tenant of a few acres who made a fair living near a large town, it must be remembered that he understood two trades, gardening and carpentering, and found constant employment at these, which in all probability would indeed have maintained him without any land at all. But it is not every man who possesses technical knowledge of this kind, or who can turn his hand to several things. Imagine a town surrounded by two or three thousand such small occupiers, let them be never so clever; where would the extra employment come from; where would be the ash-pits to empty? Where one could do well, a dozen could do nothing. If the argument be carried still further, and we imagine the whole country so cut up and settled, the difficulty only increases, because every man living (or starving) on his own plot would be totally unable to pay another to help him, or to get employment himself. No better method could be contrived to cause a fall in the value of labour.

The examples of France and China are continually quoted in support of subdivision. In the case of France, let us ask whether any of our stalwart labourers would for a single week consent to live as the French peasant does? Would they forego their white, wheaten bread, and eat rye bread in its place? Would they take kindly to bread which contained a large proportion of meal ground from the edible chestnut? Would they feel merry over vegetable soups? Verily the nature of the man must change first; and we have read something about the leopard and his spots. You cannot raise beef and mutton upon four acres and feed yourself at the same time; if you raise bacon you must sell it in order to buy clothes.

The French peasant saves by stinting, and puts aside a franc by pinching both belly and back. He works extremely hard, and for long hours. Our labourers can work as hard as he, but it must be in a different way; they must have plenty to eat and drink, and they do not understand little economies.

China, we are told, however, supports the largest population in the world in this manner. Not a particle is wasted, not a square foot of land but bears something edible. The sewage of towns is utilised, and causes crops to spring forth; every scrap of refuse manures a garden. The Chinese have attained that ideal agriculture which puts the greatest amount into the soil, takes the greatest amount out of it, and absolutely wastes nothing. The picture is certainly charming.

There are, however, a few considerations on the other side. The question arises whether our labourers would enjoy a plump rat for supper? The question also arises why the Six Companies are engaged in transhipping Chinese labour from China to America? In California the Chinese work at a rate of wages absolutely impossible to the white man—hence the Chinese difficulty there. In Queensland a similar thing is going on. Crowds of Chinese enter, or have entered, the country eager for work. If the agriculture of China is so perfect; if the sewage is utilised; if every man has his plot; if the population cannot possibly become too great, why on earth are the Chinese labourers so anxious to get to America or Australia, and to take the white man's wages? And is that system of agriculture so perfect? It is not long since the Chinese Ambassador formally conveyed the thanks of his countrymen for the generous assistance forwarded from England during the late fearful famine in China. The starvation of multitudes of wretched human beings is a ghastly comment upon this ideal agriculture. The Chinese yellow spectre has even threatened England; hints have been heard of importing Chinese into this country to take that silver and gold which our own men disdained. Those who desire to destroy our land system should look round them for a more palatable illustration than is afforded by the great Chinese problem.

The truth in the matter seems to be this. A labourer does very well with a garden; he can do very well, too, if he has an allotment in addition, provided it be not too far from home.

Up to a quarter of an acre—in some cases half an acre—it answers, because he can cultivate it at odd times, and so receive his weekly wages without interruption. But when the plot exceeds what he can cultivate in this way—when he has to give whole weeks to it—then, of course, he forfeits the cash every Saturday night, and soon begins to lose ground. The original garden of moderate size yielded very highly in proportion to its extent, because of the amount of labour expended on it, and because it was well manured. But three or four acres, to yield in like degree, require an amount of manure which it is quite out of a labourer's power to purchase; and he cannot keep live stock to produce it. Neither can he pay men to work for him; consequently, instead of being more highly cultivated than the large farms, such plots would not be kept so clean and free from weeds, or be so well manured and deeply ploughed as the fields of the regular agriculturist.

CHAPTER XXV

LANDLORDS' DIFFICULTIES —THE LABOURER AS A POWER —MODERN CLERGY

THE altered tone of the labouring population has caused the position of the landlord, especially if resident, to be one of considerable difficulty. Something like diplomatic tact is necessary in dealing with the social and political problems which now press themselves upon the country gentleman. Forces are at work which are constantly endeavouring to upset the village equilibrium, and it is quite in vain to ignore their existence. However honestly he may desire peace and goodwill to reign, it is impossible for a man to escape the influence of his own wealth and property. These compel him to be a sort of centre around which everything revolves. His duties extend far beyond the set, formal lines—the easy groove of old times—and are concerned with matters which were once thought the exclusive domain of the statesman or the philosopher.

The growth of a public opinion among the rural population

274

is a great fact which cannot be overlooked. Some analogy may be traced between the awaking of a large class, hitherto almost silent, and the strange new developments which occur in the freshly-settled territories of the United States. There, all kinds of social experiments are pushed to the extreme characteristic of American energy. A Salt Lake City and civilised polygamy, and a variety of small communities endeavouring to work out new theories of property and government, attest a frame of mind escaped from the control of tradition, and groping its way to the future. Nothing so extravagant, of course, distinguishes the movement among the agricultural labourers of this country. There have been strikes; indignation meetings held expressly for the purpose of exciting public opinion; an attempt to experimentalise by a kind of joint-stock farming, labourers holding shares; and a preaching of doctrines which savour much of Communism. There have been marches to London, and annual gatherings on hill tops. These are all within the pale of law, and outrage no social customs. But they proclaim a state of mind restless and unsatisfied, striving for something new, and not exactly knowing what.

Without a vote for the most part, without an all-embracing organisation—for the Union is somewhat limited in extent—with few newspapers expressing their views, with still fewer champions in the upper ranks, the agricultural labourers have become in a sense a power in the land. It is a power that is felt rather individually than collectively—it affects isolated places, but these in the aggregate reach importance. This power presses on the landlord—the resident country gentleman—upon one side; upon the other, the dissatisfied tenant-farmers present a rugged front.

As a body the tenant-farmers are loyal to their landlords—in some cases enthusiastically loyal. It cannot, however, be denied that this is not universal. There are men who, though unable to put forth a substantial grievance, are ceaselessly agitating. The landlord, in view of unfavourable seasons, remits a percentage of rent. He relaxes certain clauses in leases, he reduces the ground game, he shows a disposition to meet reasonable, and even unreasonable, demands. It is useless. There exists a class of tenant-farmers who are not to be satisfied with the removal of grievances in detail. They are animated by a principle—something far beyond such trifles. Unconsciously, no doubt, in many cases that principle

275

approximates very nearly to the doctrine proclaimed in so many words by the communistic circles of cities. It amounts to a total abolition of the present system of land tenure. The dissatisfied tenant does not go so far as minute subdivisions of land into plots of a few acres. He pauses at the moderate and middle way which would make the tenant of three or four hundred acres the owner of the soil. In short he would step into the landlord's place.

Of course, many do not go so far as this; still there is a class of farmers who are for ever writing to the papers, making speeches, protesting, and so on, till the landlord feels that, do what he may, he will be severely criticised. Even if personally insulted he must betray no irritation, or desire to part with the tenant, lest he be accused of stifling opinion. Probably no man in England is so systematically browbeaten all round as the country gentleman. Here are two main divisions—one on each side—ever pressing upon him, and, besides these, there are other forces at work. A village, in fact, at the present day, is often a perfect battle-ground of struggling parties.

When the smouldering labour difficulty comes to a point in any particular district the representatives of the labourers lose no time in illustrating the cottager's case by contrast with the landlord's position. He owns so many thousand acres, producing an income of so many thousand pounds. Hodge, who has just received notice of a reduction of a shilling per week, survives on bacon and cabbage. Most mansions have a small home farm attached, where, of course, some few men are employed in the direct service of the landlord. This home farm becomes the bone of contention. Here, they say, is a man with many thousands a year, who, in the midst of bitter wintry weather, has struck a shilling a week off the wages of his poor labourers. But the fact is that the landlord's representative—his steward—has been forced to this step by the action and opinion of the tenant-farmers.

The argument is very cogent and clear. They say, "We pay a rent which is almost as much as the land will bear; we suffer by foreign competition, bad seasons and so on, the market is falling, and we are compelled to reduce our labour expenditure. But then our workmen say that at the home farm the wages paid are a shilling or two higher, and therefore they will not accept a reduction. Now you must reduce your wages or your tenants must suffer." It is like a tradesman with a large independent income giving his workmen high wages out of that independent income, whilst other tradesmen, who have only their business to rely on, are compelled by this example to pay more than they can afford. This is obviously an unjust and even cruel thing. Consequently though a landlord may possess an income of many thousands, he cannot without downright injustice to his tenants, pay his immediate *employés* more than those tenants find it possible to pay.

Such is the simple explanation of what has been described as a piece of terrible tyranny. The very reduction of rent made by the landlord to the tenant is seized as a proof by the labourer that the farmer, having less now to pay, can afford to give him more money. Thus the last move of the labour party has been to urge the tenant-farmer to endeavour to become his own landlord. On the one hand, certain dissatisfied tenants have made use of the labour agitation to bring pressure upon the landlord to reduce rent, and grant this and that privilege. They have done their best, and in great part succeeded, in getting up a cry that rent must come down, that the landlord's position must be altered, and so forth. On the other hand, the labour party try to use the dissatisfied tenant as a fulcrum by means of which to bring their lever to bear upon the landlord. Both together, by every possible method, endeavour to enlist popular sympathy against him.

There exists a party in cities who are animated by the most extraordinary rancour against landlords without exception—good, bad, and indifferent—just because they are landlords. This party welcomes the agitating labourer and the discontented tenant with open arms, and the chorus swells still louder. Now the landlords, as a body, are quite aware of the difficulties under which farming has been conducted of late, and exhibit a decided inclination to meet and assist the tenant. But it by no means suits the agitator to admit this; he would of the two rather the landlord showed an impracticable disposition, in order that there might be grounds for violent declamation.

Fortunately there is a solid substratum of tenants whose sound common sense prevents them from listening to the rather enchanting cry, "Every man his own landlord." They may desire and obtain a reduction of rent, but they treat it as a purely business transaction, and there lies all the difference. They do not make the shilling an acre less the groundwork of a revolution; because ten per cent. is remitted at the audit they do not cry for confiscation. But it is characteristic of common sense to remain silent, as it is of extravagance to make a noise. Thus the opinion of the majority of tenants is not heard; but the restless minority write and speak; the agitating labourer, through his agent, writes and speaks, and the anti-landlord party in cities write and speak. A pleasant position for the landlord this! Anxious to meet reasonable wishes, he is confronted with unreasonable demands, and abused all round.

Besides the labour difficulty, which has been so blazed abroad as to obscure the rest, there are really many other questions agitating the village. The school erected under the Education Act, whilst it is doing good work, is at the same time in many cases a scene of conflict. The landlord can hardly remain aloof, try how he will, because his larger tenants are so closely interested. He has probably given the land and subscribed heavily—a school board has been avoided; but, of course, there is a committee of management, which is composed of members of every party and religious denomination. That is fair enough, and the actual work accomplished is really very good. But, if outwardly peace, it is inwardly contention. First, the agitating labourer is strongly of opinion that, besides giving the land and subscribing, and paying a large voluntary rate, the landlord ought to defray the annual expenses and save him the weekly pence. The sectarian bodies, though neutralised by their own divisions, are ill-affected behind their mask, and would throw it off if they got the opportunity. The one thing, and the one thing only, that keeps them quiet is the question of expense. Suppose by a united effort—and probably on a poll of the parish the chapel-goers in mere numbers would exceed the church people—they shake off the landlord and his party, and proceed to a school board as provided by the Act? Well, then they must find the annual expenses, and these must be raised by a rate.

Now at present the cottager loudly grumbles because he is asked to contribute a few coppers; but suppose he were called upon to pay a heavy rate? Possibly he might in such a case turn round against his present leaders, and throw them overboard in disgust. Seeing this possibility all too clearly, the sectarian bodies remain quiescent. They have no real grievance, because their prejudices are carefully respected; but it is not the nature of men to prefer being governed, even to their good, to governing. Consequently, though no battle royal takes place, it is a mistake to suppose that because "education" is now tolerably quiet there is universal satisfaction. Just the reverse is true, and under the surface there is a constant undermining process proceeding. Without any downright collision there is a distinct division into opposing ranks.

Another matter which looms larger as time goes on arises out of the gradual—in some cases the rapid—filling up of the village churchyards. It is melancholy to think that so solemn a subject should threaten to become a ground for bitter controversy; but that much animosity of feeling has already appeared is well known. Already many village graveyards are overcrowded, and it is becoming difficult to arrange for the future. From a practical point of view there is really but little difficulty, because the landlords in almost every instance are willing to give the necessary ground. The contention arises in another form, which it would be out of place to enter upon here. It will be sufficient to recall the fact that such a question is approaching.

Rural sanitation, again, comes to the front day by day. The prevention of overcrowding in cottages, the disposal of sewage, the supply of water—these and similar matters press upon the attention of the authorities. Out of consideration for the pockets of the ratepayers—many of whom are of the poorest class—these things are perhaps rather shelved than pushed forward; but it is impossible to avoid them altogether. Every now and then something has to be done. Whatever takes place, of course the landlord, as the central person, comes in for the chief share of the burden. If the rates increase, on the one hand, the labourers complain that their wages are not sufficient to pay them; and, on the other, the tenants state that the pressure on the agriculturist is already as much as he can sustain. The labourer expects the landlord to relieve him; the tenant grumbles if he also is not relieved. Outside and beyond the landlord's power as the owner of the soil, as magistrate and *ex-officio* guardian, and so on, he cannot divest himself of a personal—a family—influence, which at once gives him a leading position, and causes everything to be expected of him. He must arbitrate here, persuade there, compel yonder, conciliate everybody, and subscribe all round.

This was, perhaps, easy enough years ago, but it is now a very different matter. No little diplomatic skill is needful to balance parties, and preserve at least an outward peace in the parish. He has to note the variations of public opinion, and avoid giving offence. In his official capacity as magistrate the same difficulty arises. One of the most delicate tasks that the magistracy have had set them of recent years has been arbitrating between tenant and man—between, in effect, capital and labour. That is not, of course, the legal, but it is the true, definition. It is a most invidious position, and it speaks highly for the scrupulous justice with which the law has been administered that a watchful and jealous—a bitterly inimical party—ever ready, above all things, to attempt a sensation—have not been able to detect a magistrate giving a partial decision.

In cases which involve a question of wages or non-fulfilment of contract it has often happened that a purely personal element has been introduced. The labourer asserts that he has been unfairly treated, that implied promises have been broken, perquisites withheld, and abuse lavished upon him. On the opposite side, the master alleges that he has been made a convenience—the man staying with him in winter, when his services were of little use, and leaving in summer; that his neglect has caused injury to accrue to cattle; that he has used bad language. Here is a conflict of class against class—feeling against feeling. The point in dispute has, of course, to be decided by evidence, but whichever way evidence leads the magistrates to pronounce their verdict, it is distasteful. If the labourer is victorious, he and his friends "crow" over the farmers; and the farmer himself grumbles that the landlords are afraid of the men, and will never pronounce against them. If the reverse, the labourers cry out upon the partiality of the magistrates, who favour each other's tenants. In both cases the decision has been given according to law. But the knowledge that this kind of feeling exists—that he is in reality arbitrating between capital and labour—renders the resident landlord doubly careful what steps he takes at home in his private capacity. He hardly knows which way to turn when a question crops up, desiring, above all things, to preserve peace.

It has been said that of late there has come into existence in the political world "a power behind Parliament." Somewhat in the same sense it may be said that the labourer has become a power behind the apparent authorities of the rural community. Whether directly, or through the discontented tenant, or by aid of the circles in cities who hold advanced views, the labourer brings a pressure to bear upon almost every aspect of country life. That pressure is not sufficient to break in pieces the existing order of things; but it is sufficient to cause an unpleasant tension. Should it increase, much of the peculiar attraction of country life will be destroyed. Even hunting, which it would have been thought every individual son of the soil would stand up for, is not allowed to continue unchallenged. Displays of a most disagreeable spirit must be fresh in the memories of all; and such instances have shown a disposition to multiply. Besides the more public difficulties, there are also social ones which beset the landowner. It is true that all of these do not originate with the labourer, or even concern him, but he is dragged into them to suit the convenience of others. "Coquetting with a vote" is an art tolerably well understood in these days; the labourer has not got a nominal vote, yet he is the "power behind," and may be utilised.

There is another feature of modern rural life too marked to be ignored, and that is the increased activity of the resident clergy. This energy is exhibited by all alike, irrespective of opinion upon ecclesiastical questions, and it concerns an inquiry into the position of the labourer, because for the most part it is directed towards practical objects. It shows itself in matters that have no direct bearing upon the Church, but are connected with the every-day life of the people. It finds work to do outside the precincts of the Church—beyond the walls of the building. This work is of a nature that continually increases, and as it extends becomes more laborious.

The parsonage is often an almost ideal presentment of peace and repose. Trees cluster about it that in summer cast a pleasant shade, and in winter the thick evergreen shrubberies shut out the noisy winds. Upon the one side the green meadows go down to the brook, upon the other the cornfields stretch away to the hills. Footpaths lead out into the wheat and beside the hedge, where the wild flowers bloom— flowers to be lovingly studied, food for many a day-dream. The village is out of sight in the hollow—all is quiet and still, save for the song of the lark that drops from the sky. The house is old, very old; the tiles dull coloured, the walls grey, the calm dignity of age clings to it.

A place surely this for reverie—the abode of thought. But the man within is busy—full of action. The edge of the great questions of the day has reached the village and he must be up and doing. He does not, indeed, lift the latch of the cottage or the farmhouse door indiscreetly—not unless aware that his presence will not be resented. He is anxious to avoid

281

irritating individual susceptibilities. But wherever people are gathered together, be it for sport or be it in earnest, wherever a man may go in open day, thither he goes, and with a set purpose beforehand makes it felt that he is there. He does not remain a passive spectator in the background, but comes as prominently to the front as is compatible with due courtesy.

When the cloth is cleared at the ordinary in the market town, and the farmers proceed to the business of their club, or chamber, he appears in the doorway, and quietly takes a seat not far from the chair. If the discussion be purely technical he says nothing; if it touch, as it frequently does, upon social topics, such as those that arise out of education, of the labour question, of the position of the farmer apart from the mere ploughing and sowing, then he delivers his opinion. When the local agricultural exhibition is proceeding and the annual dinner is held he sits at the social board, and presently makes his speech. The village benefit club holds its *fête*—he is there too, perhaps presiding at the dinner, and addresses the assembled men. He takes part in the organisation of the cottage flower show; exerts himself earnestly about the allotments and the winter coal club, and endeavours to provide the younger people with amusements that do not lead to evil—supporting cricket and such games as may be played apart from gambling and liquor.

This is but the barest catalogue of his work; there is nothing that arises, no part of the life of the village and the country side, to which he does not set his hand. All this is apart from abstract theology. Religion, of course, is in his heart; but he does not carry a list of dogmas in his hand, rather keeping his own peculiar office in the background, knowing that many of those with whom he mingles are members of various sects. He is simply preaching the practical Christianity of brotherhood and good will. It is a work that can never be finished, and that is ever extending. His leading idea is not to check the inevitable motion of the age, but to tone it.

He is not permitted to pursue this course unmolested; there are parties in the village that silently oppose his every footstep. If the battle were open it would be easier to win it, but it is concealed. The Church is not often denounced from the housetop, but it is certainly denounced under the roof. The poor and ignorant are instructed that the Church is their greatest enemy, the upholder of tyranny, the instrument of their subjection, synonymous with lowered wages and privation, more iniquitous than the landowner. The clergyman is a Protestant Jesuit—a man of deepest guile. The coal club, the cricket, the flower show, the allotments, the village *fête*, everything in which he has a hand is simply an effort to win the good will of the populace, to keep them quiet, lest they arise and overthrow the property of the Church. The poor man has but a few shillings a week, and the clergyman is the friend of the farmer, who reduces his wages—the Church owns millions and millions sterling. How self-evident, therefore, that the Church is the cottager's enemy!

See, too, how he is beautifying that church, restoring it, making it light and pleasant to those who resort to it; see how he causes sweeter music and singing, and puts new life into the service. This is a lesson learnt from the City of the Seven Hills—this is the mark of the Beast. But the ultimate aim may be traced to the same base motive—the preservation of that enormous property.

Another party is for pure secularism. This is not so numerously represented, but has increased of recent years. From political motives both of these silently oppose him. Nor are the poor and ignorant alone among the ranks of his foes. There are some tenant-farmers among them, but their attitude is not so coarsely antagonistic. They take no action against, but they do not assist, him. So that, although, as he goes about the parish, he is not greeted with hisses, the clergyman is full well aware that his activity is a thorn in the side of many. They once reproached him with a too prolonged reverie in the seclusion of the parsonage; now they would gladly thrust him back again.

It may be urged, too, that all his efforts have not produced much visible effect. The pews are no more crowded than formerly; in some cases the absence of visible effect is said to be extremely disheartening. But the fact is that it is yet early to expect much; neither must it be expected in that direction. It is almost the first principle of science that reaction is equal to action; it may be safely assumed, then, that after a while these labours will bear fruit. The tone of the rising generation must perforce be softened and modified by them.

There exists at the present day a class that is morally apathetic. In every village, in every hamlet, every detached group of cottages, there are numbers of labouring men who are simply indifferent to church and to chapel alike. They neither deny nor affirm the primary truths taught in all places of worship; they are simply indifferent. Sunday comes and sees them lounging about the cottage door. They do not drink to excess, they are not more given to swearing than others, they are equally honest, and are not of ill-repute. But the moral sense seems extinct—the very idea of anything beyond gross earthly advantages never occurs to them. The days go past, the wages are paid, the food is eaten, and there is all.

Looking at it from the purely philosophic point of view there is something sad in this dull apathy. The most pronounced materialist has a faith in some form of beauty— matter itself is capable of ideal shapes in his conception. These people know no ideal. It seems impossible to reach them, because there is no chord that will respond to the most skilful touch. This class is very numerous now—a disheartening fact. Yet perhaps the activity and energy of the clergyman may be ultimately destined to find its reaction, to produce its effect among these very people. They may slowly learn to appreciate tangible, practical work, though utterly insensible to direct moral teaching and the finest eloquence of the pulpit. Finding by degrees that he is really endeavouring to improve their material existence, they may in time awake to a sense of something higher.

What is wanted is a perception of the truth that progress and civilisation ought not to end with mere material— mechanical—comfort or wealth. A cottager ought to learn that when the highest wages of the best paid artisan are reached it is *not* the greatest privilege of the man to throw mutton chops to dogs and make piles of empty champagne bottles. It might almost be said that one cause of the former extravagance and the recent distress and turbulence of the working classes is the absence of an ideal from their minds.

Besides this moral apathy, the cottager too often assumes an attitude distinctly antagonistic to every species of authority, and particularly to that *prestige* hitherto attached to property. Each man is a law to himself, and does that which seems good in his own eyes. He does not pause to ask himself, What will my neighbour think of this? He simply thinks of no one but himself, takes counsel of no one, and cares not what the result may be. It is the same in little things as great. Respect for authority is extinct. The modern progressive cottager is perfectly certain that he knows as much as his immediate employer, the squire, and the parson put together with the experience of the world at their back. He is now the judge—the infallible authority himself. He is wiser far than all the learned and the thoughtful, wiser than the prophets themselves. Priest, politician, and philosopher must bow their heads and listen to the dictum of the ploughman.

This feeling shows itself most strikingly in the disregard of property. There used to be a certain tacit agreement among all men that those who possessed capital, rank, or reputation should be treated with courtesy. That courtesy did not imply that the landowner, the capitalist, or the minister of religion, was necessarily in himself superior. But it did imply that those who administered property really represented the general order in which all were interested. So in a court of justice, all who enter remove their hats, not out of servile adulation of the person in authority, but from respect for the majesty of the law, which it is every individual's interest to uphold. But now, metaphorically speaking, the labourer removes his hat for no man. Whether in the case of a manufacturer or of a tenant of a thousand-acre farm the thing is the same. The cottager can scarcely nod his employer a common greeting in the morning. Courtesy is no longer practised. The idea in the man's mind appears to be to express contempt for his employer's property. It is an unpleasant symptom.

At present it is not, however, an active, but a passive force; a moral *vis inertiae*. Here again the clergyman meets with a cold rebuff. No eloquence, persuasion, personal influence even, can produce more than a passing impression. But here again, perhaps, his practical activity may bring about its reaction. In time the cottager will be compelled to admit that, at least, coal club, benefit society, cricket, allotment, etc., have done him no harm. In time he may even see that property and authority are not always entirely selfish—that they may do good, and be worthy, at all events, of courteous acknowledgment.

These two characteristics, moral apathy and contempt of property—*i.e.*, of social order—are probably exercising considerable influence in shaping the labourer's future. Free of mental restraint, his own will must work its way for good or evil. It is true that the rise or fall of wages may check or hasten the development of that future. In either case it is not, however, probable that he will return to the old grooves; indeed, the grooves themselves are gone, and the logic of events must force him to move onwards. That motion, in its turn, must affect the rest of the community. Let the mind's eye glance for a moment over the country at large. The villages among the hills, the villages on the plains, in the valleys, and beside the streams represent in the aggregate an enormous power. Separately such hamlets seem small and feeble— unable to impress their will upon the world. But together they contain a vast crowd, which, united, may shoulder itself an irresistible course, pushing aside all obstacles by mere physical weight.

The effect of education has been, and seems likely to be, to supply a certain unity of thought, if not of action, among these people. The solid common sense—the law-abiding character of the majority—is sufficient security against any violent movement. But how important it becomes that that common sense should be strengthened against the assaults of an insidious Socialism! A man's education does not come to an end when he leaves school. He then just begins to form his opinions, and in nine cases out of ten thinks what he hears and what he reads. Here, in the agricultural labourer class, are many hundred thousand young men exactly in this stage, educating themselves in moral, social, and political opinion.

In short, the future literature of the labourer becomes a serious question. He will think what he reads; and what he reads at the present moment is of anything but an elevating character.. He will think, too, what he hears; and he hears much of an enticing but subversive political creed, and little of any other. There are busy tongues earnestly teaching him to despise property and social order, to suggest the overthrow of existing institutions; there is scarcely any one to instruct him in the true lesson of history. Who calls together an audience of agricultural labourers to explain to and interest them in the story of their own country? There are many who are only too anxious to use the agricultural labourer as the means to effect ends which he scarcely understands. But there are few, indeed, who are anxious to instruct him in science or literature for his own sake.

CHAPTER XXVI

A WHEAT COUNTRY

THE aspect of a corn-growing district in the colder months is perhaps more dreary than that of any other country scene. It is winter made visible. The very houses at the edge of the village stand out harsh and angular, especially if modern and slated, for the old thatched cottages are not without a curve in the line of the eaves. No trees or bushes shelter them from the bitter wind that rushes across the plain, and, because of the absence of trees round the outskirts, the village may be seen from a great distance.

The wayfarer, as he approaches along the interminable road, that now rises over a hill and now descends into a valley, observes it from afar, his view uninterrupted by wood, but the vastness of the plain seems to shorten his step, so that he barely gains on the receding roofs. The hedges by the road are cropped—cut down mercilessly—and do not afford the slightest protection against wind, or rain, or sleet. If he would pause awhile to rest his weary limbs no friendly bush keeps off the chilling blast. Yonder, half a mile in front, a waggon creeps up the hill, always just so much ahead, never overtaken, or seeming to alter its position, whether he walks slow or fast. The only apparent inhabitants of the solitude are the larks that every now and then cross the road in small flocks. Above, the sky is dull and gloomy; beneath, the earth, except where some snow lingers, is of a still darker tint. On the northern side the low mounds are white with snow here and there. Mile after mile the open level fields extend on either hand; now brown from the late passage of the plough, now a pale yellow where the short stubble yet remains, divided by black lines; the low-cropped hedges bare of leaves. A few small fir copses are scattered about, the only relief to the eye; all else is level, dull, monotonous.

When the village is reached at last it is found to be of considerable size. The population is much greater than might have been anticipated from the desert-like solitude surrounding the place. In actual numbers, of course, it will not bear comparison with manufacturing districts, but for its situation, it is quite a little town. Compared with the villages situate in the midst of great pastures—where grass is the all-important crop—it is really populous. Almost all the inhabitants find employment in the fields around, helping to produce wheat and barley, oats and roots. It is a little city of the staff of life—a metropolis of the plough.

Every single house, from that of the landowner, through the rent; that of the clergyman, through the tithe—down to the humblest cottage, is directly interested in the crop of corn. The very children playing about the gaps in the hedges are interested in it, for can they not go gleaning? If the heralds had given the place a coat of arms it should bear a sheaf of wheat. And the reason of its comparative populousness is to be found in the wheat also. For the stubborn earth will not yield its riches without severe and sustained labour. Instead of tickling it with a hoe, and watching the golden harvest leap forth; scarifier and plough, harrow and drill in almost ceaseless succession, compel the clods by sheer force of iron to deliver up their treasure. In another form it is almost like the quartz-crushing at the gold mines—the ore ground out from the solid rock. And here, in addition, the ore has to be put into the rock first in the shape of manure.

All this labour requires hands to do it, and so—the supply for some time, at all events, answering the demand—the village teemed with men. In the autumn comes the ploughing, the couch-picking and burning, often second ploughing, the sowing by drill or hand, the threshing, etc. In the spring will come more ploughing, sowing, harrowing, hoeing. Modern agriculture has increased the labour done in the fields. Crops are arranged to succeed crops, and each of these necessitates labour, and labour a second and a third time. The work on arable land is never finished. A slackness there is in the dead of winter; but even then there is still something doing—some draining, some trimming of hedges, carting manure for open field work. But beyond this there are the sheep in the pens to be attended to as the important time of lambing approaches, and there are the horned cattle in the stalls still fattening, and leaving, as they reach maturity, for the butcher.

The arable agriculturist, indeed, has a double weight upon his mind. He has money invested in the soil itself, seed lying awaiting the genial warm rain that shall cause it to germinate, capital in every furrow traced by the plough. He has money, on the other hand, in his stock, sheep, and cattle. A double anxiety is his; first that his crops may prosper, next that his stock may flourish. He requires men to labour in the field, men

288

to attend to the sheep, men to feed the bullocks; a crowd of labourers are supported by him, with their wives and families. In addition to these he needs other labour—the inanimate assistance of the steam-engine, and the semi-intelligent co-operation of the horse. These, again, must be directed by men. Thus it is that the corn village has become populous.

The original idea was that the introduction of machinery would reduce all this labour. In point of fact, it has, if anything, increased it. The steam-plough will not work itself; each of the two engines requires two men to attend to it; one, and often two, ride on the plough itself; another goes with the watercart to feed the boiler; others with the waggon for coal. The drill must have men—and experienced men—with it, besides horses to draw it, and these again want men. The threshing-machine employs quite a little troop to feed it; and, turning to the stock in the stalls, roots will not pulp or slice themselves, nor will water pump itself up into the troughs, nor chaff cut itself. The chaff-cutter and pump, and so on, all depend on human hands to keep them going. Such is but a very brief outline of the innumerable ways in which arable agriculture gives employment. So the labourer and the labourer's family flourish exceedingly in the corn village. Wages rise; he waxes fat and strong and masterful, thinking that he holds the farmer and the golden grain in the hollow of his hand.

But now a cloud arises and casts its shadow over the cottage. If the farmer depends upon his men, so do the men in equal degree depend upon the farmer. This they overlooked, but are now learning again. The farmer, too, is not independent and self-sustained, but is at the mercy of many masters. The weather and the seasons are one master; the foreign producer is another; the markets which are further influenced by the condition of trade at large, form a third master. He is, indeed, very much more in the position of a servant than his labourer. Of late almost all these masters have combined against the corn-growing farmer. Wheat is not only low but seems likely to remain so. Foreign meat also competes with the dearly-made meat of the stalls. The markets are dull and trade depressed everywhere. Finally a fresh master starts up in the shape of the labourer himself, and demands higher wages.

For some length of time the corn-grower puts a courageous face on the difficulties which beset him, and struggles on, hoping for better days. After awhile, however, seeing that his capital is diminishing, because he has been, as it were, eating it, seeing that there is no prospect of immediate relief, whatever may happen in the future, he is driven to one of two courses. He must quit the occupation, or he must reduce his expenditure. He must not only ask the labourer to accept a reduction, but he must, wherever practicable, avoid employing labour at all.

Now comes the pressure on the corn village. Much but not all of that pressure the inhabitants have brought upon themselves through endeavouring to squeeze the farmer too closely. If there had been no labour organisation whatever, when the arable agriculturist began to suffer, as he undoubtedly has been suffering, the labourer must have felt it in his turn. He has himself to blame if he has made the pain more acute. He finds it in this way. Throughout the corn-producing district there has been proceeding a gradual shrinkage, as it were, of speculative investment. Where an agriculturist would have ploughed deeper, and placed extra quantities of manure in the soil, with a view to an extra crop, he has, instead, only just ploughed and cleaned and manured enough to keep things going. Where he would have enlarged his flock of sheep, or added to the cattle in the stalls, and carried as much stock as he possibly could, he has barely filled the stalls, and bought but just enough cake and foods. Just enough, indeed, of late has been his watchword all through, just enough labour and no more.

This cutting down, stinting, and economy everywhere has told upon the population of the village. The difference in the expenditure upon a solitary farm may be but a trifle—a few pounds; but when some score or more farms are taken, in the aggregate the decrease in the cash transferred from the pocket of the agriculturist to that of the labourer becomes something considerable. The same percentage on a hundred farms would amount to a large sum. In this manner the fact of the corn-producing farmer being out of spirits with his profession reacts upon the corn village. There is no positive distress, but there is just a sense that there are more hands about than necessary. Yet at the same moment there are not hands enough; a paradox which may be explained in a measure by the introduction of machinery.

As already stated, machinery in the field does not reduce the number of men employed. But they are employed in a different way. The work all comes now in rushes. By the aid of the reaping machine acres are levelled in a day, and the cut corn demands the services of a crowd of men and women all at once, to tie it up in sheaves. Should the self-binders come into general use, and tie the wheat with wire or string at the moment of cutting it, the matter of labour will be left much in the same stage. A crowd of workpeople will be required all at once to pick up the sheaves, or to cart them to the rick; and the difference will lie in this, that while now the crowd are employed, say twelve hours, then they will be employed only nine. Just the same number—perhaps more—but for less time. Under the old system, a dozen men worked all the winter through, hammering away with their flails in the barns. Now the threshing machine arrives, and the ricks are threshed in a few days. As many men are wanted (and at double the wages) to feed the machine, to tend the "elevator" carrying up the straw to make the straw rick, to fetch water and coal for the engine, to drive it, etc. But instead of working for so many months, this rush lasts as many days.

Much the same thing happens all throughout arable agriculture—from the hoeing to the threshing—a troop are wanted one day, scarcely anybody the next. There is, of course, a steady undercurrent of continuous work for a certain fixed number of hands; but over and above this are the periodical calls for extra labour, which of recent years, from the high wages paid, have been so profitable to the labourers. But when the agriculturist draws in his investments, when he retrenches his expenditure, and endeavours, as far as practicable, to confine it to his regular men, then the intermittent character of the extra work puts a strain upon the rest. They do not find so much to do, the pay is insensibly decreasing, and they obtain less casual employment meantime.

In the olden times a succession of bad harvests caused sufferings throughout the whole of England. Somewhat in like manner, though in a greatly modified degree, the difficulties of the arable agriculturist at the present day press upon the corn villages. In a time when the inhabitants saw the farmers, as they believed, flourishing and even treading on the heels of the squire, the corn villagers, thinking that the farmer was absolutely dependent upon them, led the van of the agitation for high wages. Now, when the force of circumstances has compressed wages again, they are loth to submit. But discovering by slow degrees that no organisation can compel, or create a demand for labour at any price, there are now signs on the one hand of acquiescence, and on the other of partial emigration.

Thus the comparative density of the population in arable districts is at once a blessing and a trouble. It is not the "pranks" of the farmers that have caused emigration, or threats of it. The farmer is unable to pay high wages, the men will not accept a moderate reduction, and the idle crowd, in effect, tread on each other's heels. Pressure of that kind, and to that extent, is limited to a few localities only. The majority have sufficient common sense to see their error. But it is in arable districts that agitation takes its extreme form. The very number of the population gives any movement a vigour and emphasis that is wanting where there may be as much discontent but fewer to exhibit it. That populousness has been in the past of the greatest assistance to the agriculturist, and there is no reason why it should not be so in the future, for it does not by any means follow that because agriculture is at present depressed it will always be so.

Let the months roll by and then approach the same village along the same road under the summer sun. The hedges, though low, are green, and bear the beautiful flowers of the wild convolvulus. Trees that were scarcely observed before, because bare of leaves, now appear, and crowds of birds, finches and sparrows, fly up from the corn. The black swifts wheel overhead, and the white-breasted swallows float in the azure. Over the broad plain extends a still broader roof of the purest blue—the landscape is so open that the sky seems as broad again as in the enclosed countries—wide, limitless, very much as it does at sea. On the rising ground pause a moment and look round. Wheat and barley and oats stretch mile after mile on either hand. Here the red wheat tinges the view; there the whiter barley; but the prevailing hue is a light gold. Yonder green is the swede, or turnip, or mangold; but frequent as are the fields of roots, the golden tint overpowers the green. A golden sun looks down upon the golden wheat —the winds are still and the heat broods over the corn. It is pleasant to get under the scanty shadow of the stunted ash. Think what wealth all that glorious beauty represents. Wealth to the rich man, wealth to the poor.

Come again in a few weeks' time and look down upon it. The swarthy reapers are at work. They bend to their labour till the tall corn overtops their heads. Every now and then they rise up, and stand breast high among the wheat. Every field is full of them, men and women, young lads and girls, busy as they may be. Yonder the reaping machine, with its strange-looking arms revolving like the vast claws of an unearthly monster beating down the grain, goes rapidly round and round in an ever-narrowing circle till the last ears fall. A crowd has pounced upon the cut corn. Behind them—behind the reapers—everywhere abroad on the great plain rises an army, regiment behind regiment, the sheaves stacked in regular ranks down the fields. Yet a little while, and over that immense expanse not one single, solitary straw will be left standing. Then the green roots show more strongly, and tint the landscape. Next come the waggons, and after that the children searching for stray ears of wheat, for not one must be left behind. After that, in the ploughing time, while yet the sun shines warm, it is a sight to watch the teams from under the same ash tree, returning from their labour in the after-noon. Six horses here, eight horses there, twelve yonder, four far away; all in single file, slowly walking home, and needing no order or touch of whip to direct their steps to the well-known stables.

If any wish to see the work of farming in its full flush and vigour, let them visit a corn district at the harvest time. Down in the village there scarcely any one is left at home; every man, woman, and child is out in the field. It is the day of prosperity, of continuous work for all, of high wages. It is, then, easy to understand why corn villages are populous. One cannot but feel the strongest sympathy with these men. The scene altogether seems so thoroughly, so intensely English. The spirit of it enters into the spectator, and he feels that he, too, must try his hand at the reaping, and then slake his thirst from the same cup with these bronzed sons of toil.

Yet what a difficult problem lies underneath all this! While the reaper yonder slashes at the straw, huge ships are on the ocean rushing through the foam to bring grain to the great cities to whom—and to all—cheap bread is so inestimable a blessing. Very likely, when he pauses in his work, and takes his luncheon, the crust he eats is made of flour ground out of grain that grew in far distant Minnesota, or some vast Western State. Perhaps at the same moment the farmer himself sits at his desk and adds up figure after figure, calculating the cost of production, the expenditure on labour, the price of manure put into the soil, the capital invested in the steam-plough, and the cost of feeding the bullocks that are already intended for the next Christmas. Against these he places the market price of that wheat he can see being reaped from his window, and the price he receives for his fattened bullock. Then a vision rises before him of green meads and broad pastures slowly supplanting the corn; the plough put away, and the scythe brought out and sharpened. If so, where then will be the crowd of men and women yonder working in the wheat? Is not this a great problem, one to be pondered over and not hastily dismissed?

Logical conclusions do not always come to pass in practice; even yet there is plenty of time for a change which shall retain these stalwart reapers amongst us, the strength and pride of the land. But if so, it is certain that it must be preceded by some earnest on their part of a desire to remove that last straw from the farmer's back—the last straw of extravagant labour demands—which have slowly been dragging him down. They have been doing their very best to bring about the substitution of grass for corn. And the farmer, too, perhaps, must look at home, and be content to live in simpler fashion. To do so will certainly require no little moral courage, for a prevalent social custom, like that of living fully up to the income (not solely characteristic of farmers), is with difficulty faced and overcome.

CHAPTER XXVII
GRASS COUNTRIES

On the ground beside the bramble bushes that project into the field the grass is white with hoar frost at noonday, when the rest of the meadow has resumed its dull green winter tint. Behind the copse, too, there is a broad belt of white—every place, indeed, that would be in the shadow were the sun to shine forth is of that colour.

The eager hunter frowns with impatience, knowing that though the eaves of the house may drip in the middle of the day, yet, while those white patches show in the shelter of the bramble bushes the earth will be hard and unyielding. His horse may clear the hedge, but how about the landing on that iron-like surface? Every old hoof-mark in the sward, cut out sharp and clear as if with a steel die, is so firm that the heaviest roller would not produce the smallest effect upon it. At the gateways where the passage of cattle has trodden away the turf, the mud, once almost impassable, is now hardened, and every cloven hoof that pressed it has left its mark as if cast in metal. Along the furrows the ice has fallen in, and lies on the slope white and broken, the shallow water having dried away beneath it. Dark hedges, dark trees—in the distance they look almost black—nearer at hand the smallest branches devoid of leaves are clearly defined against the sky.

As the northerly wind drifts the clouds before it the sun shines down, and the dead, dry grass and the innumerable tufts of the "leaze" which the cattle have not eaten, take a dull grey hue. Sheltered from the blast behind the thick, high hawthorn hedge and double mound, which is like a rampart reared against Boreas, it is pleasant even now to stroll to and fro in the sunshine. The long-tailed titmice come along in parties of six or eight, calling to each other as in turn they visit every tree. Turning from watching these—see, a redbreast has perched on a branch barely two yards distant, for, wherever you may be, there the robin comes and watches you. Whether looking in summer at the roses in the garden, or waiting in winter for the pheasant to break cover or the fox to steal forth, go where you will, in a minute or two, a red-breast appears intent on your proceedings.

Now comes a discordant squeaking of iron axles that have not been greased, and the jolting sound of wheels passing over ruts whose edges are hard and frost-bound. From the lane two manure carts enter the meadow in slow procession, and, stopping at regular intervals, the men in charge take long poles with hooks at the end and drag down a certain quantity of the fertilising material. The sharp frost is so far an advantage to the tenant of meadow land that he can cart manure without cutting and poaching the turf, and even without changing the ordinary for the extra set of broad-wheels on the cart. In the next meadow the hedge-cutters are busy, their hands fenced with thick gloves to turn aside the thorns.

Near by are the hay-ricks and cow-pen where a metallic rattling sound rises every now and then—the bull in the shed moving his neck and dragging his chain through the ring. More than one of the hay-ricks have been already half cut away, for the severe winter makes the cows hungry, and if their yield of milk is to be kept up they must be well fed, so that the foggers have plenty to do. If the dairy, as is most probably the case, sends the milk to London, they have still more, because then a regular supply has to be maintained, and for that a certain proportion of other food has to be prepared in addition to the old-fashioned hay. The new system, indeed, has led to the employment of more labour out-of-doors, if less within. An extra fogger has to be put on, not only because of the food, but because the milking has to be done in less time—with a despatch, indeed, that would have seemed unnatural to the old folk. Besides which the milk carts to and fro the railway station require drivers, whose time—as they have to go some miles twice a day—is pretty nearly occupied with their horses and milk tins. So much is this the case that even in summer they can scarcely be spared to do a few hours' haymaking.

The new system, therefore, of selling the milk instead of making butter and cheese is advantageous to the labourer by affording more employment in grass districts. It is steady work, too, lasting the entire year round, and well paid. The stock of cows in such cases is kept up to the very highest that the land will carry, which, again, gives more work. Although the closing of the cheese lofts and the superannuation of the churn has reduced the number of female servants in the house, yet that is more than balanced by the extra work without. The cottage families, it is true, lose the buttermilk which some farmers used to allow them; but wages are certainly better.

There has been, in fact, a general stir and movement in dairy districts since the milk selling commenced, which has been favourable to labour. A renewed life and energy has been visible on farms where for generations things had gone on in the same sleepy manner. Efforts have been made to extend the area available for feeding by grubbing hedges and cultivating pieces of ground hitherto given over to thistles, rushes, and rough grasses. Drains have been put in so that the stagnant water in the soil might not cause the growth of those grasses which cattle will not touch. Fresh seed has been sown, and "rattles" and similar plants destructive to the hay crop have been carefully eradicated. New gates, new carts, and traps, all exhibit the same movement.

The cowyards in many districts were formerly in a very dilapidated condition. The thatch of the sheds was all worn away, mossgrown, and bored by the sparrows. Those in which the cows were placed at calving time were mere dark holes. The floor of the yard was often soft, so that the hoofs of the cattle trod deep into it—a perfect slough in wet weather. The cows themselves were of a poor character, and in truth as poorly treated, for the hay was made badly—carelessly harvested and the grass itself not of good quality—nor were the men always very humane, thinking little of knocking the animals about.

Quite a change has come over all this. The cows now kept are much too valuable to be treated roughly, being selected from shorthorn strains that yield large quantities of milk. No farmer now would allow any such knocking about. The hay itself is better, because the grass has been improved, and it is also harvested carefully. Rickcloths prevent rain from spoiling the rising rick, mowing machines, haymaking machines, and horse rakes enable a spell of good weather to be taken advantage of, and the hay got in quickly, instead of lying about till the rain returns. As for the manure, it is recognised to be gold in another shape, and instead of being trodden under foot by the cattle and washed away by the rain, it is utilised. The yard is drained and stoned so as to be dry—a change that effects a saving in litter, the value of which has greatly risen. Sheds have been new thatched, and generally renovated, and even new roads laid down across the farms, and properly macadamised, in order that the milk carts might reach the highway without the straining and difficulty consequent upon wheels sinking half up to the axles in winter.

In short, dairy farms have been swept and garnished, and even something like science introduced upon them. The thermometer in summer is in constant use to determine if the milk is sufficiently cooled to proceed upon its journey. That cooling of the milk alone is a process that requires more labour to carry it out. Artificial manures are spread abroad on the pastures. The dairy farmer has to a considerable extent awakened to the times, and, like the arable agriculturist, is endeavouring to bring modern appliances to bear upon his business. To those who recollect the old style of dairy farmer the change seems marvellous indeed. Nowhere was the farmer more backward, more rude and primitive, than on the small dairy farms. He was barely to be distinguished from the labourers, amongst whom he worked shoulder to shoulder; he spoke with their broad accent, and his ideas and theirs were nearly identical.

In ten years' time—just a short ten years only—what an alteration has taken place! It is needless to say that this could not go on without the spending of money, and the spending of money means the benefit of the labouring class. New cottages have been erected, of course on modern plans, so that many of the men are much better lodged than they were, and live nearer to their work—a great consideration where cows are the main object of attention. The men have to be on the farm very early in the morning, and if they have a long walk it is a heavy drag upon them. Perhaps the constant inter-course with the towns and stations resulting from the double daily visit of the milk carts has quickened the minds of the labourers thus employed. Whatever may be the cause, it is certain that they do exhibit an improvement, and are much "smarter" than they used to be. It would be untrue to say that no troubles with the labourers have arisen in meadow districts. There has been some friction about wages, but not nearly approaching the agitation elsewhere. And when a recent reduction of wages commenced, many of the men themselves admitted that it was inevitable. But the average earnings throughout the year still continue, and are likely to continue far above the old rate of payment. Where special kinds of cheese are made the position of the labourer has also improved.

Coming to the same district in summer time, the meadows have a beauty all their own. The hedges are populous with birds, the trees lovely, the brook green with flags, the luxuri-antly-growing grass decked with flowers. Nor has haymaking lost all its ancient charm. Though the old-fashioned sound of the mower sharpening his scythe is less often heard, being superseded by the continuous rattle of the mowing machine, yet the hay smells as sweetly as ever. While the mowing machine, the haymaking machine, and horse rake give the farmer the power of using the sunshine, when it comes, to the best purpose, they are not without an effect upon the labouring population.

Just as in corn districts, machinery has not reduced the actual number of hands employed, but has made the work come in spells or rushes; so in the meadows the haymaking is shortened. The farmer waits till good weather is assured for a few days. Then on goes his mowing machine and levels the crop of an entire field in no time. Immediately a whole crowd of labourers are required for making the hay and getting it when ready on the waggons. Under the old system the mowers usually got drunk about the third day of sunshine, and the work came to a standstill. When it began to rain they recovered themselves, and slashed away vigorously—when it was not wanted. The effect of machinery has been much the same as on corn lands, with the addition that fewer women are now employed in haymaking. Those that are employed are much better paid.

The hamlets of grass districts are not, as a rule, at all populous. There really are fewer people, and at the same time the impression is increased by the scattered position of the dwellings. Instead of a great central village there are three or four small hamlets a mile or two apart, and solitary groups of cottages near farmhouses. One result of this is, that allotment gardens are not so common, for the sufficient reason that, if a field were set apart for the purpose, the tenants of the plots would have to walk so far to the place that it would scarcely pay them. Gardens are consequently attached to most cottages, and answer the same purpose; some have small orchards as well.

The cottagers have also more firewood than is the case in some arable districts on account of the immense quantity of wood annually cut in copses and double-mound hedges. The rougher part becomes the labourers' perquisite, and they can also purchase wood at a nominal rate from their employers. This more than compensates for the absence of gleaning. In addition, quantities of wood are collected from hedges and ditches and under the trees—dead boughs that have fallen or been broken off by a gale.

The aspect of a grazing district presents a general resemblance to that of a dairy one, with the difference that in the grazing everything seems on a larger scale. Instead of small meadows shut in with hedges and trees, the grazing farms often comprise fields of immense extent; sometimes a single pasture is as large as a small dairy farm. The herds of cattle are also more numerous; of course they are of a different class, but, in mere numbers, a grazier often has three times as many bullocks as a dairy farmer has cows. The mounds are quite as thickly timbered as in dairy districts, but as they are much farther apart, the landscape appears more open.

To a spectator looking down upon mile after mile of such pasture land in summer from an elevation it resembles a park of illimitable extent. Great fields after great fields roll away to the horizon—groups of trees and small copses dot the slopes—roan and black cattle stand in the sheltering shadows.

299

A dreamy haze hangs over the distant woods—all is large, open, noble. It suggests a life of freedom—the gun and the saddle—and, indeed, it is here that hunting is enjoyed in its full perfection. The labourer falls almost out of sight in these vast pastures. The population is sparse and scattered, the hamlets are few and far apart; even many of the farmhouses being only occupied by bailiffs. In comparison with a dairy farm there is little work to do. Cows have to be milked as well as foddered, and the milk when obtained gives employment to many hands in the various processes it goes through. Here the bullocks have simply to be fed and watched, the sheep in like manner have to be tended. Except in the haymaking season, therefore, there is scarcely ever a press for labour. Those who are employed have steady, continuous work the year through, and are for the most part men of experience in attending upon cattle, as indeed they need be, seeing the value of the herds under their charge.

Although little direct agitation has taken place in pasture countries, yet wages have equally risen. Pasture districts almost drop out of the labour dispute. On the one hand the men are few, on the other the rise of a shilling or so scarcely affects the farmer (so far as his grassland is concerned, if he has much corn as well it is different), because of the small number of labourers he wants.

The great utility of pasture is, of course, the comparatively cheap production of meat, which goes to feed the population in cities. Numbers of bullocks are fattened on corn land in stalls, but of late it has been stated that the cost of feeding under such conditions is so high that scarcely any profit can be obtained. The pasture farmer has by no means escaped without encountering difficulties; but still, with tolerably favourable seasons, he can produce meat much more cheaply than the arable agriculturist. Yet it is one of the avowed objects of the labour organisation to prevent the increase of pasture land, to stop the laying down of grass, and even to plough up some of the old pastures. The reason given is that corn land supports so many more agricultural labourers, which is so far true; but if corn farming cannot be carried on profitably without great reduction of the labour expenses the argument is not worth much, while the narrowness of the view is at once evident. The proportion of pasture to arable land must settle itself, and be governed entirely by the same conditions that affect other trades—i.e., profit and loss.

It has already been pointed out that the labourer finds it possible to support the Union with small payments, and also to subscribe to benefit-clubs. The fact suggests the idea that, if facilities were afforded, the labourer would become a considerable depositor of pennies. The Post-office Savings Banks have done much good, the drawback is that the offices are often too distant from the labourer. There is an office in the village, but not half the population live in the village. There are far-away hamlets and tithings, besides lonely groups of three or four farmhouses, to which a collective name can hardly be given, but which employ a number of men. A rural parish is "all abroad"—the people are scattered. To go into the Post-office in the village may involve a walk of several miles, and it is closed, too, on Saturday night when the men are flush of money.

The great difficulty with penny banks on the other hand is the receiver—who is to be responsible for the money? The clergyman would be only too glad, but many will have nothing to do with anything under his influence simply because he is the clergyman. The estrangement that has been promoted between the labourer and the tenant farmer effectually shuts the latter out. The landlord's agent cannot reside in fifty places at once. The sums are too small to pay for a bank agent to reside in the village and go round. There remain the men themselves; and why should not they be trusted with the money? Men of their own class collect the Union subscriptions, and faithfully pay them in.

Take the case of a little hamlet two, three, perhaps more miles from a Post-office Savings Bank, where some thirty labourers work on the farms. Why should not these thirty elect one of their own number to receive their savings every Saturday—to be paid in by him at the Post-office? There are men among them who might be safely trusted with ten times the money, and if the Post-office cannot be opened on Saturday evenings for him to deposit it, it is quite certain that his employer would permit of his absence, on one day, sufficiently long to go to the office and back. If the men wish to be absolutely independent in the matter, all they have to do is to work an extra hour for their agent's employer, and so compensate for his temporary absence. If the men had it in their own hands like this they would enter into it with far greater interest, and it would take root among them. All that is required is the consent of the Post-office to receive moneys so deposited, and some one to broach the idea to the men in the various localities. The great recommendation of the Post-office is that the labouring classes everywhere have come to feel implicit faith in the safety of deposits made in it. They have a confidence in it that can never be attained by a private enterprise, however benevolent, and it should therefore be utilised to the utmost.

To gentlemen accustomed to receive a regular income, a small lump sum like ten or twenty pounds appears a totally inadequate provision against old age. They institute elaborate calculations by professed accountants, to discover whether by any mode of investment a small subscription proportionate to the labourer's wages can be made to provide him with an annuity. The result is scarcely satisfactory. But, in fact, though an annuity would be, of course, preferable, even so small a sum as ten or twenty pounds is of the very highest value to an aged agricultural labourer, especially when he has a cottage, if not his own property, yet in which he has a right to reside. The neighbouring farmers, who have known him from their own boyhood, are always ready to give him light jobs whenever practicable. So that in tolerable weather he still earns something. His own children do a little for him. In the dead of the winter come a few weeks when he can do nothing, and feels the lack of small comforts. It is just then that a couple of sovereigns out of a hoard of twenty pounds will tide him over the interval.

It is difficult to convey an idea of the value of these two extra sovereigns to a man of such frugal habits and in that position. None but those who have mixed with the agricultural poor can understand it. Now the wages that will hardly, by the most careful management, allow of the gradual purchase of an annuity, will readily permit such savings as these. It is simply a question of the money-box. When the child's money-box is at hand the penny is dropped in, and the amount accumulates; if there is no box handy it is spent in sweets. The same holds true of young and old alike. If, then, the annuity cannot be arranged, let the money-box, at all events, be brought nearer. And the money-box in which the poor man all over the country has the most faith is the Post-office.

CHAPTER XXVIII

HODGE'S LAST MASTERS—
CONCLUSION

AFTER all the ploughing and the sowing, the hoeing and the harvest, comes the miserable end. Strong as the labourer may be, thick-set and capable of immense endurance; by slow degrees that strength must wear away. The limbs totter, the back is bowed, the dimmed sight can no longer guide the plough in a straight furrow, nor the weak hands wield the reaping-hook. Hodge, who, Atlas-like, supported upon his shoulders the agricultural world, comes in his old age under the dominion of his last masters at the workhouse. There, indeed, he finds almost the whole array of his rulers assembled. Tenant farmers sit as the guardians of the poor for their respective parishes; the clergyman and the squire by virtue of their office as magistrates; and the tradesman as guardian for the market town. Here are representatives of almost all his masters, and it may seem to him a little strange that it should require so many to govern such feeble folk.

The board-room at the workhouse is a large and apparently comfortable apartment. The fire is piled with glowing coals, the red light from which gleams on the polished fender. A vast table occupies the centre, and around it are arranged seats for each of the guardians. The chairman is, perhaps, a clergyman (and magistrate), who for years has maintained something like peace between discordant elements. For the board-room is often a battle-field where political or sectarian animosities exhibit themselves in a rugged way. The clergyman, by force of character, has at all events succeeded in moderating the personal asperity of the contending parties. Many of the stout, elderly farmers who sit round the table have been elected year after year, no one disputing with them that tedious and thankless office. The clerk, always a solicitor, is also present, and his opinion is continually required. Knotty points of law are for ever arising over what seems so simple a matter as the grant of a dole of bread.

The business, indeed, of relieving the agricultural poor is no light one—a dozen or fifteen gentlemen often sit here the

whole day. The routine of examining the relieving officers'
books and receiving their reports takes up at least two hours.
Agricultural unions often include a wide space of country,
and getting from one village to another consumes as much
time as would be needed for the actual relief of a much
denser population. As a consequence, more relieving officers
are employed than would seem at first glance necessary.
Each of these has his records to present, and his accounts to
be practically audited, a process naturally interspersed with
inquiries respecting cottagers known to the guardians present.

Personal applications for out-door relief are then heard.
A group of intending applicants has been waiting in the porch
for admission for some time. Women come for their
daughters; daughters for their mothers; some want assistance
during an approaching confinement, others ask for a small
loan, to be repaid by instalments, with which to tide over their
difficulties. One cottage woman is occasionally deputed by
several of her neighbours as their representative. The labourer
or his wife stands before the Board and makes a statement,
supplemented by explanation from the relieving officer of the
district. Another hour thus passes. Incidentally there arise
cases of "settlement" in distant parishes, when persons have
become chargeable whose place of residence was recently,
perhaps, half across the country. They have no parochial
rights here and must be returned thither, after due inquiries
made by the clerk and the exchange of considerable correspondence.

The master of the workhouse is now called in and delivers
his weekly report of the conduct of the inmates, and any
events that have happened. One inmate, an ancient labourer,
died that morning in the infirmary, not many hours before
the meeting of the Board. The announcement is received with
regretful exclamations, and there is a cessation of business
for a few minutes. Some of the old farmers who knew the
deceased recount their connection with him, how he worked
for them, and how his family has lived in the parish as
cottagers from time immemorial. A reminiscence of a grim
joke that fell out forty years before, and of which the deceased
was the butt, causes a grave smile, and then to business again.
The master possibly asks permission to punish a refractory
inmate; punishment is now very sparingly given in the house.
A good many cases, however, come up from the Board to
the magisterial Bench—charges of tearing up clothing, fight-

ing, damaging property, or of neglecting to maintain, or to repay relief advanced on loan. These cases are, of course, conducted by the clerk.

There is sometimes a report to be read by one of the doctors who receive salaries from the Board and attend to the various districts, and occasionally some nuisance to be considered and order taken for its compulsory removal on sanitary grounds. The question of sanitation is becoming rather a difficult one in agricultural unions.

After this the various committees of the Board have to give in the result of their deliberations, and the representative of the ladies' boarding-out committee presents a record of the work accomplished. These various committees at times are burdened with the most onerous labours, for upon them falls the duty of verifying all the petty details of management. Every pound of soap, or candles, scrubbing-brushes, and similar domestic items, pass under their inspection, not only the payments for them, but the actual articles, or samples of them, being examined. Tenders for grocery, bread, wines and spirits for cases of illness, meat, coals, and so forth are opened and compared; vouchers, bills, receipts, invoices, and so forth checked and audited.

The amount of detail thus attended to is something immense, and the accuracy required occupies hour after hour. There are whole libraries of account-books, ledgers, red-bound relief-books, stowed away, pile upon pile, in the house; archives going back to the opening of the establishment, and from which any trifling relief given or expenditure incurred years ago can be extracted. Such another carefully-administered institution it would be hard to find; nor is any proposed innovation or change adopted without the fullest discussion— it may be the suggested erection of additional premises, or the introduction of some fresh feature of the system, or some novel instructions sent down by the Local Government Board.

When such matters or principles are to be discussed there is certain to be a full gathering of the guardians and a trial of strength between the parties. Those who habitually neglect to attend, leaving the hard labour of administration to be borne by their colleagues, now appear in numbers, and the board-room is crowded, many squires otherwise seldom seen coming in to give their votes. It is as much as the chairman can do to assuage the storm and to maintain an approach to personal politeness. Quiet as the country appears to the casual observer, there are, nevertheless, strong feelings under the surface, and at such gatherings the long-cherished animosities burst forth.

Nothing at all events is done in a corner; everything is openly discussed and investigated. Every week the visiting committee go round the house, and enter every ward and store-room. They taste and test the provisions, and the least shortcoming is certain to be severely brought home to those who are fulfilling the contracts. They pass through the dormitories, and see that everything is clean; woe betide those responsible if a spot of dirt be visible! There is the further check of casual and unexpected visits from the guardians or magistrates. It is probable that not one crumb of bread consumed is otherwise than good, and that not one single crumb is wasted. The waste is in the system—and a gigantic waste it is, whether inevitable as some contend, or capable of being superseded by a different plan.

Of every hundred pounds paid by the ratepayers how much is absorbed in the maintenance of the institution and its ramifications, and how very little reaches poor deserving Hodge! The undeserving and mean-spirited, of whom there are plenty in every village, who endeavour to live upon the parish, receive relief thrice as long and to thrice the amount as the hard-working, honest labourer, who keeps out to the very last moment. It is not the fault of the guardians, but of the rigidity of the law. Surely a larger amount of discretionary power might be vested in them with advantage! Some exceptional consideration is the just due of men who have worked from the morn to the very eve of life.

The labourer whose decease was reported to the Board upon their assembling was born some seventy-eight or seventy-nine years ago. The exact date is uncertain; many of the old men can only fix their age by events that happened when they were growing from boys into manhood. That it must have been nearer eighty than seventy years since is known, however, to the elderly farmers, who recollect him as a man with a family when they were young. The thatched cottage stood beside the road at one end of a long narrow garden, enclosed from the highway by a hedge of elder. At the back there was a ditch and mound with elm-trees, and green meadows beyond. A few poles used to lean against the thatch, their tops rising above the ridge, and close by was a stack of thorn faggots. In the garden three or four aged and mossgrown apple-trees stood among the little plots of potatoes, and as many plum-trees in the elder hedge. One tall pear-tree with scored bark grew near the end of the cottage; it bore a large crop of pears, which were often admired by the people who came along the road, but were really hard and woody. As a child he played in the ditch and hedge, or crept through into the meadow and searched in the spring for violets to offer to the passers-by; or he swung on the gate in the lane and held it open for the farmers in their gigs, in hope of a half-penny.

As a lad he went forth with his father to work in the fields, and came home to the cabbage boiled for the evening meal. It was not a very roomy or commodious home to return to after so many hours in the field, exposed to rain and wind, to snow, or summer sun. The stones of the floor were uneven, and did not fit at the edges. There was a beam across the low ceiling, to avoid which, as he grew older, he had to bow his head when crossing the apartment. A wooden ladder, or steps, not a staircase proper, behind the white-washed partition, led to the bed-room. The steps were worm-eaten and worn. In the sitting-room the narrow panes of the small window were so overgrown with woodbine as to admit but little light. But in summer the door was wide open, and the light and the soft air came in. The thick walls and thatch kept it warm and cosy in winter, when they gathered round the fire. Every day in his manhood he went out to the field; every item, as it were, of life centred in that little cottage. In time he came to occupy it with his own wife, and his children in their turn crept through the hedge, or swung upon the gate. They grew up, and one by one went away, till at last he was left alone.

He had not taken much conscious note of the changing aspect of the scene around him. The violets flowered year after year; still he went to plough. The May bloomed and scented the hedges; still he went to his work. The green summer foliage became brown and the acorns fell from the oaks; still he laboured on, and saw the ice and snow, and heard the wind roar in the old familiar trees without much thought of it. But those old familiar trees, the particular hedges he had worked among so many years, the very turf of the meadows over which he had walked so many times, the view down the road from the garden gate, the distant sign-post and the red-bricked farmhouse—all these things had become part of his

307

life. There was no hope nor joy left to him, but he wanted to stay on among them to the end. He liked to ridge up his little plot of potatoes; he liked to creep up his ladder and mend the thatch of his cottage; he liked to cut himself a cabbage, and to gather the one small basketful of apples. There was a kind of dull pleasure in cropping the elder hedge, and even in collecting the dead branches scattered under the trees. To be about the hedges, in the meadows, and along the brooks was necessary to him, and he liked to be at work.

Three score and ten did not seem the limit of his working days; he still could and would hoe—a bowed back is no impediment, but perhaps rather an advantage, at that occupation. He could use a prong in the haymaking; he could reap a little, and do good service tying up the cut corn. There were many little jobs on the farm that required experience, combined with the plodding patience of age, and these he could do better than a stronger man. The years went round again, and yet he worked. Indeed, the farther back a man's birth dates in the beginning of the present century the more he seems determined to labour. He worked on till every member of his family had gone, most to their last home, and still went out at times when the weather was not too severe. He worked on, and pottered round the garden, and watched the young green plums swelling on his trees, and did a bit of gleaning, and thought the wheat would weigh bad when it was threshed out.

Presently people began to bestir themselves, and to ask whether there was no one to take care of the old man, who might die from age and none near. Where were his own friends and relations? One strong son had enlisted and gone to India, and though his time had expired long ago, nothing had ever been heard of him. Another son had emigrated to Australia, and once sent back a present of money, and a message, written for him by a friend, that he was doing well. But of late he, too, had dropped out of sight. Of three daughters who grew up, two were known to be dead, and the third was believed to be in New Zealand. The old man was quite alone. He had no hope and no joy, yet he was almost happy in a slow unfeeling way wandering about the garden and the cottage. But in the winter his half-frozen blood refused to circulate, his sinews would not move his willing limbs, and he could not work.

His case came before the Board of Guardians. Those who knew all about him wished to give him substantial relief in his own cottage, and to appoint some aged woman as nurse— a thing that is occasionally done, and most humanely. But there were technical difficulties in the way; the cottage was either his own or partly his own, and relief could not be given to any one possessed of "property." Just then, too, there was a great movement against out-door relief: official circulars came round warning Boards to curtail it, and much fuss was made. In the result the old man was driven into the work-house; muttering and grumbling, he had to be bodily carried to the trap, and thus by physical force was dragged from his home. In the workhouse there is of necessity a dead level of monotony—there are many persons but no individuals. The dining-hall is crossed with forms and narrow tables, some-what resembling those formerly used in schools. On these at dinner-time are placed a tin mug and a tin soup-plate for each person: every mug and every plate exactly alike. When the unfortunates have taken their places, the master pro-nounces grace from an elevated desk at the end of the hall.

Plain as is the fare, it was better than the old man had existed on for years; but though better it was not his dinner. He was not sitting in his old chair, at his own old table, round which his children had once gathered. He had not planted the cabbage, and tended it while it grew, and cut it himself. So it was, all through the workhouse life. The dormitories were clean, but the ward was not his old bedroom up the worm-eaten steps, with the slanting ceiling, where as he woke in the morning he could hear the sparrows chirping, the chaffinch calling, and the lark singing aloft. There was a garden attached to the workhouse, where he could do a little if he liked, but it was not his garden. He missed his plum-trees and apples, and the tall pear, and the lowly elder hedge. He looked round raising his head with difficulty, and he could not see the sign-post, nor the familiar red-bricked farmhouse. He knew all the rain that had fallen must have come through the thatch of the old cottage in at least one place, and he would have liked to have gone and re-thatched it with trembling hand. At home he could lift the latch of the garden gate and go down the road when he wished. Here he could not go outside the boundary—it was against the regulations. Everything to appearance had been monotonous in the cottage —but there he did not feel it monotonous.

At the workhouse the monotony weighed upon him. He used to think as he lay awake in bed that when the spring came nothing should keep him in this place. He would take his discharge and go out, and borrow a hoe from somebody, and go and do a bit of work again, and be about in the fields. That was his one hope all through his first winter. Nothing else enlivened it except an occasional little present of tobacco from the guardians who knew him. The spring came, but the rain was ceaseless. No work of the kind he could do was possible in such weather. Still there was the summer, but the summer was no improvement; in the autumn he felt weak, and was not able to walk far. The chance for which he had waited had gone. Again the winter came, and he now rapidly grew more feeble.

When once an aged man gives up, it seems strange at first that he should be so utterly helpless. In the infirmary the real benefit of the workhouse reached him. The food, the little luxuries, the attention were far superior to anything he could possibly have had at home. But still it was not home. The windows did not permit him from his bed to see the leafless trees or the dark woods and distant hills. Left to himself, it is certain that of choice he would have crawled under a rick, or into a hedge, if he could not have reached his cottage.

The end came very slowly; he ceased to exist by imperceptible degrees, like an oak-tree. He remained for days in a semi-conscious state, neither moving nor speaking. It happened at last. In the grey of the winter dawn, as the stars paled and the whitened grass was stiff with hoar frost, and the rime coated every branch of the tall elms, as the milker came from the pen and the young ploughboy whistled down the road to his work, the spirit of the aged man departed.

What amount of production did that old man's life of labour represent? What value must be put upon the service of the son that fought in India; of the son that worked in Australia; of the daughter in New Zealand, whose children will help to build up a new nation? These things surely have their value. Hodge died, and the very grave-digger grumbled as he delved through the earth hard-bound in the iron frost, for it jarred his hand and might break his spade. The low mound will soon be level, and the place of his burial shall not be known.